The Serpents of Paradise

A John Macrae Book

HENRY HOLT AND COMPANY
NEW YORK

The Serpents of Paradise

A READER

Edward Abbey

EDITED BY JOHN MACRAE

Henry Holt and Company, Inc.
Publishers since 1866
115 West 18th Street
New York, New York 10011

Henry Holt® is a registered trademark of Henry Holt and Company, Inc.

Published in Canada by Fitzhenry & Whiteside Ltd.,
195 Allstate Parkway, Markham, Ontario L3R 4T8.

Library of Congress Cataloging-in-Publication Data
Abbey, Edward, 1927–1989.
The serpents of paradise: a reader / by Edward Abbey;
edited by John Macrae.—1st ed.
p.   cm.
"A John Macrae book."
Includes bibliographical references.
1. Man—Influence on nature—Literary collections.
2. Wilderness areas—Literary collections.
3. West (U.S.)—Literary collections.
I. Macrae, John. II. Title.
PS3551.B2A6   1995   94-44065
813'.54—dc20   CIP

ISBN 0-8050-3132-4

Henry Holt books are available for special promotions
and premiums. For details contact: Director, Special Markets.

First Edition—1995

Designed by Kate Nichols

Printed in the United States of America
All first editions are printed on acid-free paper. ∞

1   3   5   7   9   10   8   6   4   2

Contents

Editor's Note   xi

I. Ned: The Early Years   1

1927–37: Stump Creek, West Virginia   3
Hallelujah on the Bum   22
How It Was   31
Drunk in the Afternoon   44
Journal IV: November 10, 1951—Edinburgh, Scotland   50

II. Ed: The Early Years   57

From *The Fool's Progress*   59
From *The Brave Cowboy*   72
Manhattan Twilight, Hoboken Night   85
Author's Introduction to *Desert Solitaire*   95
The First Morning   98
The Serpents of Paradise   104
Polemic: Industrial Tourism and the National Parks   110
Tukuhnikivats, the Island in the Desert   128
Appalachian Pictures   141
Appalachia, Good-bye   150
My Life as a P.I.G., or The True Adventures of Smokey
  the Cop   153

III. Ed Moves On   163

From *Black Sun*   166
1971–77: Henry in Love—An Interlude   175
The Wooden Shoe Conspiracy   219
The Raid at Comb Wash   233

Death Valley Junk   255
Meeting the Bear   260
Aravaipa Canyon   264

IV. Postlude   269

A Colorado River Journal   272
From *Good News*   287
Desert Images   298
The Damnation of a Canyon   311
Gather at the River   318
River Solitaire: A Daybook   348
Free Speech: The Cowboy and His Cow   358
Theory of Anarchy   366
Eco-Defense   370
Immigration and Liberal Taboos   373
A Writer's Credo   377
Postlude to *The Fool's Progress*   390

"A Few Words in Memory of Edward Abbey" by Wendell Berry   395
A Selected Bibliography of Works by Edward Abbey   397
Acknowledgments   399

If certain ideas and emotions are expressed in these pages with what seems an extreme intransigence, it is not merely because I love an argument and wish to provoke (though I do), but because I am—really am—an extremist, one who lives and loves by choice far out on the very verge of things, on the edge of the abyss, where this world falls off into the depths of another. That's the way I like it.

—E.A.

(From the Introduction to *The Journey Home*)

Editor's Note

THIS BOOK is different from any other Edward Abbey book. It includes essays, travel pieces and fictions to reveal Ed's life directly, in his own words.

The selections gathered here are arranged chronologically by incident, not by date of publication, to offer Edward Abbey's life from the time he was the boy called Ned in Home, Pennsylvania, until his death in Tucson at age 62. A short note introduces each of the four parts of the book and attempts to identify what's happening in the author's life at the time. When relevant, some details of publishing history are provided.

"Abbey was an autobiographer: whether writing fact or fiction, he remains Edward Abbey," declares the farmer-poet Wendell Berry, "speaking as and for himself, fighting, literally, for dear life. He understands that to defend and conserve oneself as a human being in the fullest, truest sense, one must defend and conserve many others and much else." Berry believes that Abbey "is fighting for the survival not only of nature, but of *human* nature, of culture, as only our heritage of works and hopes can define it."

One of Abbey's friends, the poet Richard Shelton, has worried publicly that when the *underground* (read *subversive*) tag is applied to Abbey's work, his enemies, especially the boomers and the serpents—those bent on destroying the remnant paradise—are given leave to dismiss it. Shelton writes:

"Abbey's very specific suggestions are aimed at conserving, not destroying. And if, when he makes them, his tone at times is somewhat strident and abrasive, beneath it I always hear the voice of a lover trying desperately to protect the thing he loves."° Fact is Abbey knew what he was writing about: the details checked out. To confound his vehemence with inaccuracy is a mistake.

Because the writing represented here covers every style and period of the artist's life, the collection serves as an Edward Abbey retrospective. The author's character connects the pieces to each other and to literature, offering what Larry McMurtry has called Abbey's "fine particularity," the authority of "a writer who feels a lot and then manages to transcend his own notions of himself."

J.M.
New York City
August 2, 1994

° *Resist Much, Obey Little: Some Notes on Edward Abbey.* Edited by James Hepworth and Gregory McNamee. Tucson, Ariz.: Harbinger House, 1989.

The Serpents of Paradise

I.

Ned: The Early Years

HE WAS BORN on a farm in the Allegheny Mountains. Mother Mildred was kind, loving, religious. Paul Revere Abbey, her agnostic husband, put what faith he had in his own brand of socialism. Unlike their five spirited children, both parents were lifelong teetotalers.

Nancy, Bill, Howard (you'll meet him as Will in Abbey's novel *The Fool's Progress*—Ed scrambled the names and ages), and John (Johnny to Ed) were Ed's siblings. Ned, as he was then called, was the firstborn; he didn't become Ed until he was inducted into the U.S. Army in 1945. Ed served a year as an MP in occupied Italy (good duty), made corporal, but was busted six months before he was discharged, honorably, in 1947.

Abbey's first trip west was in 1944—the summer after his high school graduation. His father contributed $20 and a few words of advice. Ed traveled the old-fashioned way: by foot, thumb, bus and boxcar (Abbey offers the details in two pieces, "Hallelujah on the Bum" and "How It Was," pp. 22–43).

The G.I. Bill allowed Ed's love of the Southwest to blossom. At the University of New Mexico he studied philosophy and girls, he said; in his senior year, August 1950, he married a student named Jean. The following year Abbey won a Fulbright Fellowship, which sent the young couple to Scotland's Edinburgh University, where two hundred years earlier nominalist David Hume had argued that passions based on human experience, not faith or ideology, are what count. Abbey agreed, but Jean, troubled by his profligate passions, returned to the United States to file for divorce after only three months abroad. (Student Abbey's interests, as well as his early prose style, are revealed in a section from his 1951 journal, p. 50.)

Though Ed preferred the desert above all other landscapes—as you'll see in many of the pages that follow—his love of the mountains also lasted a lifetime. But before we join him in the Appalachian highlands, let's first repair to the green grass of his memory and childhood in the misty hills of Home, Pennsylvania, as revealed in the novel *The Fool's Progress*.

1927–37 :
Stump Creek, West Virginia

L ORRAINE MY MOTHER lay in bed in the antique gothic farmhouse, in the little bedroom on the second floor where the child was conceived. She was breathing the fumes from an ether-soaked bandana held under her nose by Joe Lightcap her husband, while bald wrinkled Doc Wynkoop pulled the baby gently, fairly easily, from the exit of the womb.

According to the father, a minute before actual birth the baby's head had emerged from the natal aperture, opened its eyes, took one quick look around—saw the light of the kerosene lamp glimmering on the floral wallpaper, saw Joe's dark anxious aboriginal face, the red face and bloodshot eyes of the doctor, the ancestral portraits of old Lightcaps, Shawnees, Gatlins and Holyoaks hung on the walls, saw the double-barreled twelve-gauge, loaded, which stood in the corner near the head of the bed, saw the Bible on the night table, Mother's cedar chest, the wardrobe closet, the lace curtains, etc.—took everything in and then retreated, withdrew, slid right back into the dark radiant chamber of conception.

No thanks. Thanks but no thanks.

At that point Doc Wynkoop grasped the baby firmly by the ears and head, rotating the body forty-five degrees, and drew it forth. *Drew me forth,*

From *The Fool's Progress: An Honest Novel* (1988)

protesting mightily—no need here for a whack on the rump—and tied off the cord, knotting the umbilicus in a knot that's held to this very day. He swabbed away the silvery caul, that shining suit of lights, like the garb of a traveler from outer space, smeared the tender parts with unguent oil, and laid the child on his mother's breast. She took him to suck at once, silencing for a time the howls of indignation. She named the boy Henry.

The doctor passed the afterbirth to Joe, who probably fed it to the hogs. Grandmother Gatlin arrived soon afterward, a little late. Joe passed a five-dollar bill to the doctor and the promise to deliver, within a week, five bushel of potatoes and a home-cured ham.

Doc Wynkoop climbed into his black Model A Ford and drove down the rutted red-dog road through night and falling curtains of snow toward the highway and the town of Shawnee, ten miles south. We had no doctor in Stump Creek. Not since the death of Doctor Jim fifty years before—and Doctor Jim was an Indian, a shaman Shawnee medicine man, not an M.D.

Henry Holyoak Lightcap was the second child. My brother William, about two years older, complained loudly from his crib in the adjoining room, beneath the sloping ceiling of the east roof, under the impression that he'd been temporarily forgotten. Correct.

Winter nights. In frozen February the child lay snug in his mother's arms. Outside, beyond frost-covered windows, the ice-shagged pines stood under the Appalachian moon, mute with suffering. Frost glittered on crusty waves of snow that covered the pasture, the frozen brook, the stubble of the corn-fields. The moonlight tinted the snow with the pale blue tones of skim milk. Through the stillness came the sound of an old oak cracking in the woods, branch split by freezing sap. Then came the wail of the iron locomotive on the C&O line, burning coal as it chugged up grade toward Trimble's crossing a mile away, pulling fifty-five gondola cars of bituminous coal to the coke ovens of Morgantown and Wheeling and Pittsburgh.

Desolation of the iron cry—Song of the Old 97—loneliness of the silent hills, silvered furl of black smoke and white steam rising toward the moon.

The moon shone down on rigid ice floes in Crooked Creek, on Stump Creek, Rocky Glen and Cherry Run, on the nameless streamlet that drained the wooded hillsides of Lightcap Hollow. The moonlight glanced and glinted on the ice-filled ruts of the road, lay on the granite and sandstone monuments of the Jefferson Church graveyard where tiny American flags hung stiff in the gelid air above brass stars bearing the initials GAR—Grand Army of the Re-public. The winter moon was so bright, so clear, you could read the names on the stone, the names of our buried neighbors: Ginter, Gatlin, Hinton,

Hankerson, Fetterman, Finley, Rayne, Risheberger, Holyoak, Mears, Light-cap, Clymer, Trumbull, Trimble, Stuart, Stewart, Stitler, Prothrow, Groft, Bennett, Duncan, Dalton . . . to name but the oldtimers, kinsmen and neigh-bors, enemies and strangers.

Economists would have called it a "depressed area." A land of marginal and submarginal farms, small coal-mine operations, third-growth timber cut-ting, crossroad market towns like Shawnee, seat of Shawnee County. Haunted country—haunted by the ghosts of the Indians who gave the place its title, who left little but their name when they were driven out late in the eighteenth century by a Colonel George Rogers Clark who burned their vil-lages, torched their cornfields and ruined the survivors with smallpox, alcohol and tuberculosis.

INCONSOLABLE MEMORIES:

Pump and pump handle sheathed in ice on winter mornings; my first chore of the day, recalled Henry, was taking a hot kettle from the kitchen stove to thaw and prime that pump and fill the kitchen water buckets.

Herding in the milk cows on frosty mornings, I'd stand where the cows had lain to keep my bare feet warm.

With a green willow stick, whipping a crab apple halfway across the val-ley, I aimed at my big brother, Will, or at little brother, Paul, or at our baby sister, Marcie.

The smell of the flowering dogwood in April.

Summer: heat lightning. Thunder above the hayfield. Fireflies and light-ning bugs. The June bug game. The leap from crossbeam into haymow twenty feet above the floor, high in the dusty air of the barn.

Dumping wooden ashes into the two-hole privy below the house—an-other of my childhood chores. Will had graduated to harnessing our team of horses to the plow, the spring-tooth harrow, the manure spreader, the seed drill, the cultivator, the mower, the wagon. But Will was a precocious boy, big for his age; he always worked hard. He liked it.

Splitting kindling wood for the kitchen stove, after I'd pumped two buck-ets of water. Hewer of wood and drawer of water—that was my role for years, until Paul grew big enough to do it in his turn.

Our half-Shawnee grandmother—Milly Cornflower Lightcap—was the daughter of a medicine man known to the whites as Doctor Jim (a conde-scending honorific) because of his healing arts and herbal lore. Doctor Jim never revealed his secret tribal name, not to any kin of ours; there was dangerous power in the name, easily lost. He lived alone in a one-room cabin in the woods, last of the Shawnee full bloods, and survived for eighty years by trapping, hunting, poaching, by odd jobs, charity and scavenging, and by his medical skills, much in demand locally. When he died he died alone, chanting (we presume) his personal death song, and lamenting the destruction and exile of his people. Never did go to Oklahoma. Never did join the cash nexus. Never did get baptized.

Grandmother Cornflower was half white by ancestry, *her* mother an indentured servant named Tillie Ostrander who'd run away from a family of Pennsylvania Dutch (Germans) in Lancaster County, Pennsylvania. Tillie crossed over the mountains and allowed herself to become the third or fourth wife (he outlived them all) of Doctor Jim. It was tolerable then for a white man to take an Indian girl as wife—not honorable but tolerable—but for an all-white girl to bed down with an Indian, a buck savage, a male aborigine, a witch doctor, and to love him, stay with him, refuse to leave him even when her brothers came looking for her all the way from beyond the Allegheny Mountains—that was a shameful thing. A thing to be spoken of in whispers. A disgrace near as low—not quite—as Negro blood.

There was talk in Shawnee of lynching Doctor Jim, or at least running him out of the territory, packing him off to Oklahoma with the rest of his drunken, trashy, idle, defeated tribe—those shattered remnants from the Trail of Tears.

Nothing came of it. Doctor Jim defied his enemies, making it clear he would die fighting before he'd leave his homeland. The runaway girl stood with him, beside him, bore him a girl-child and died in the process. My grandfather Jacob Lightcap married the shaman's daughter, the half-breed girl Cornflower. She was dark-skinned, with rich thick hair of mahogany brown. Her eyes were a bright gray-green, strange to see in the broad face with its high Mongolian cheekbones.

Grandmother Lightcap: Cornflower: I remember you from childhood: short, heavy-bodied, mother of six, your face wrinkled as a dried apple, your easy smile and the dazzling white false teeth you were so proud of, the round little granny glasses you wore about forty years before they became a brief fashion. Grandmaw, I remember your sweet and gentle voice, that voice so soft we had to *really listen* when you talked or we'd miss the tail on the fable, the moral pinned to the hinder end of your thousand and one stories. How the rabbit got his cottontail. How the toad got his warts. How the bear got his claws and the loon his necklace and the panther his scream and the owl his huge eyes . . .

She showed us, me and brother Will, her oaken chest full of treasures. The cream-colored doeskin dress, fringed and beaded, with high-top moccasins to match. The bearskin robe old Doctor Jim had dressed and cured and worn for thirty years. Her father's calumet or ceremonial pipe, the bowl made of clay, the stem of wild cane. The shaman's deerskin medicine pouch in which he carried his important herbal powders and such sacred objects as a set of bear claws, an eagle feather, a mountain lion's tooth, the corn pollen, the native tobacco, a witch's toe, three tiny copper bells and a copper medallion inlaid with turquoise and garnet—objects which had come from central Mexico centuries before, passed and bartered on from hand to hand, tribe to tribe, until finally reaching some Shawnee ancestor in the Appalachian hills, long ago.

Grandmaw gave the pouch to Will, since he was the older of us, obviously the more responsible. To be guarded with his life, she said, and passed on. I was seven years old when she died and so remember her only dimly but sweetly, an ancient gray-haired woman with the sweetest most beguiling voice, the most rich delightful laugh of any woman, any human, I've ever known.

She died; our father buried her beside her father, Doctor Jim, on the hillside at the edge of the red oaks near the spring and sunken ruins of the old man's cabin. Cornflower was a Baptist Christian but only formally. Not spiritually. Like Doctor Jim she was buried where she wanted to be, in a corner of the earth that had sustained her woodland people for maybe—who knows?— one thousand, ten thousand, twenty thousand years.

Our father too always said he wanted to be planted there, among those moldering Indian bones, with a red oak for his monument. Unlike other members of the Lightcap clan he claimed pride, honor, glory in his redskin genesis. Even boasted of it sometimes, even in public, which embarrassed our aunts and uncles. They preferred to stress the Saxon side—that antique strain of hillbillies, bowmen, thieves, peasants, woodcutters and deer poachers stretching back into the murk and misery of medieval England. Those merry times of overlord and gibbet, of peasant and serfdom, of the rack and the wheel which followed the massacre of the English forests. When the trees were gone freedom disappeared. Soon after the time of the death of Robin Hood, betrayed—like Che Guevara—by a nun.

We come from lowly lineage, us Lightcaps, from the worst of a bad lot, escaped bondsmen and indenture-jumping servants, the scum of Europe, the riffraff and ruffians of the Old World. But we have learned to live with our heritage. "Your criticism is greatly appreciated," says my Uncle Jack's business card, "but fuck you all the same." He deals in fertilizer.

Our mother was a Presbyterian. She'd be buried, if she ever consented to die, among her Holyoaks and Gatlins in the official compost pile, the rich good consecrated ground, of Jefferson Church. Her church. Hers—who else kept it going as much as she? Who else played the organ, supervised the children's Sunday school and conducted the cracked old voices of her geriatric choir week after week, year after year? "You sound good," I told her once, after she'd apologized for a performance, "you sound downright angelic." "Well we should," she said, "we're all pretty near halfway to Heaven already."

ON CLOUDY OCTOBER AFTERNOONS the boys followed their father down the furrows of the potato patch. Joe turned up the spuds with a plow hitched to a single bay mare, the old nag we called Bessie. Our father sang as he tramped over the clods, gripping the plow handles, the reins (seldom used) draped over his neck. He guided the horse mainly by cluck and call. "Haw!" for a turn to the left, "Gee!" for the right. And "Whoa . . . whoa there . . ." as he paused near the end of the row to look back at Will and Henry and Little Paul.

The boys stooped low above the sandy loam, dragging gunnysacks, resurrecting the potatoes—les pommes de terre, apples of the earth—rich brown solid nuggets of pleasure and nutrition, raw, fried, boiled or baked.

"Don't miss any, boys," says Joe, "dig down there. Get 'em out. That means you too, Henry. Mind now, every one you miss costs you a nickel." The father watches for a minute, dark gaunt face half amused, half serious, then turns back to his plow, clucks at the horse. She steps ahead on ponderous shaggy feet, iron shoes crushing the weeds at field's edge, turning right— Gee!—as Joe Lightcap turns the plow on its side to ease it around for the return row. The horse clomps into the dried-out drab-green potato plants straggling over the ground. Joe sets the plow, the share digs in, the moldboard rolls the damp earth elegantly up and aside. The buried tubers reveal themselves, ready to be gathered, stored, cooked, eaten.

The boys are well paid for their work, by 1930s values: ten cents a bushel. Every Saturday night, payday, after supper, by the light of a kerosene lamp hanging over the dining room table, Joe will teach his boys the finer points of poker—stud, draw, lowball, anaconda, Montana Gouge—and win back most of the wages that he's paid them. Not all; he's a kindly, generous man.

Our mother did not approve of this weekly ceremony. Darning socks, she watched with scornful eyes as Joe raked in another pot. The washtub simmered on the cookstove: almost time for the boys' weekly bath. She was eager to break up the game before Henry, the most careless player, lost everything he'd earned. Sunday school tomorrow morning. The game continued for another half hour before Lorraine interrupted. Joe had reduced Will's earnings for the week to two dollars, Henry's to fifty cents, Paul's to one dollar.

"Joe," says Lorraine much later, as they nestled together in bed, "you shouldn't do that to the boys."

"Why not?" he says, grinning in the dark. "Them boys got to learn to hang on to their pay. Besides, they love the game."

"Poor little Henry. You took all his wages but fifty cents. That was mean."

"He's got to learn. Got to learn to stop trying to bluff too much, stop trying to fill inside straights, learn when to raise and when to fold. Anyhow he'd waste the money on soda pop and Little Big Books."

"They worked hard for that money."

"Will did. Will worked hard." Joe listened to the sound of the old hemlock tree thrashing in the night wind, brushing against the clapboard siding under the eaves. "Henry don't. Henry never worked hard in his life. That limb is still worryin' the corner. Got to cut that thing off."

Lorraine turned a little away from Joe. "In his life? Henry is ten years old. He's a bright boy. Mrs. Lingenfelter says Henry's I.Q. is one hundred ten. She says Henry's the brightest pupil she's ever had."

"You mean he ain't dumb enough to be a farmer, Lorrie? Is that what you're saying?" No answer. "I don't believe in that I.Q. business anyway. I.Q.—what the hell does that mean? I quit? I'm queer? I think it's a lot of happy horseshit, that I.Q. business."

"Joe, don't talk like that." But now *she* was smiling in the dark. "If he studies hard and does well in high school, Mrs. Lingenfelter says Henry might go on to State Teachers' College in Shawnee."

"He's so smart why can't he play poker?"

"Joe, Joe . . . he's still a little boy. He's only a child."

"Yeah? Well Will's only twelve and he can do the work of a grown man." The limb of the hemlock, seized by the wind, thumped against the outside wall. "Maybe I ought to saw down that whole tree before it comes through the attic roof some night."

"They're both good boys. But they're different."

"You mean Will's a Lightcap and Henry's a Holyoak. Ain't that what you mean?"

"They're both good boys. And yes, you're right—Will is more like your family. And please don't cut down our old tree. That tree is . . . part of the family. That tree looks like I feel, sometimes."

"It's old, Lorrie. Bark's full of beetles. It's fallin' apart. It's a danger. One of them widow-makers falls on a kid someday, then you'll be sorry. Ain't I right? What's more there's near as much brains in my side of the family as ever there was in yours. Just because we hain't throwed off any bank clerks or schoolteachers yet don't mean the Lightcaps ain't as smart as anybody. Smarter'n most. Like my Daddy used to say, one man's as good as the next—if not a damn sight better."

"All right, Joe, all right. They're both good boys. All I meant was Henry is—quicker."

"You mean smarter. Maybe he is. But Will is doggeder. I mean that Will is a dogged son of a gun. I like that in a boy, that doggone doggedness. He lends a hand, grabs a root and hangs on. Like a badger. I sure do like that in a boy."

"All right, Joe, you're right. They're both ours."

"You mean shut up and go to sleep."

"That's not what I meant."

"Goddamnit, Lorrie—" Joe felt his black temper rise, instantly. He choked it off, changed the subject. "Should cut that tree down." The autumn wind brushed the shoulders of the farmhouse, prying at the clapboards, lifting at the eaves, trying the asphalt shingling on the roof; the wind pushed the big limb of the hemlock back and forth, bumping on the outer wall.

"I love that tree," she said. "I love the sound of it touching the house. Please don't cut it down."

"Okay, honey. Just that big limb. I'll leave the tree stand." His huge rough hand caressed her bare shoulder. "Just for you, Lorrie."

"Joe, please . . ." For he was turning upon her now, his powerful arms pinning her down, one hard thigh sprawled across her legs. "I'm not ready . . . " she said.

"We never was," he said.

I CAN SEE HER, my five-foot four-inch one-hundred-pound mother, walking up the road under the autumn arcade of flaming sugar maple trees. She walks fast, briskly, with big strides for so small a body, head high and eyes up as she watches the blaze of October colors. She carries a light willow stick and swings it like a boy. She wears an old sweater, darned and patched, a man's sweater that comes below her hips, an ankle-length homemade dress, a red bandana tied around her head.

She was a beautiful woman despite four babies and two miscarriages in the space of ten years (those ravished years of her youth); she had fine flaxen hair that fell to the small of her back when she let it down; we loved to watch as she washed her hair. She had bright hazel eyes, widely spaced—sign of intelligence—a thin fragile-looking little hen's beak of a nose and a narrow but expressive mouth trembling most of the time on the verge of laughter. Or of grief.

She was about thirty years old then, a young woman. Fierce with energy, forever busy, always working at something, cleaning up, nursing a child, feeding chickens and gathering eggs, chopping at weeds in her garden with abrupt, harsh, angry strokes of the hoe. Each Monday she did the family wash (down in the cellar in winter, outside under the walkway in summer) with the sputtering gasoline-powered Maytag that the old man had found for her, somewhere, years before. One by one she guided each soaked garment through the hard rubber rollers of the wringer into the rinsing tub and back again into a basket. Paul and I would help her hang the damp things on the line.

In the evening after dark after she'd tucked us all in bed, our father out in the barn seeing to the stock one last time or down in the cellar fixing harness, sharpening tools, whittling another stretch board for the pelts of fox, muskrat, skunk, then—why then and then only—our mother, free at last for a little while to live a private life, would sit at her piano and play. Lying in our double-decker bunks under the sloping ceiling, half asleep but listening, trying to stay awake, we heard the soothing, lyric sound of nocturnes and sonatas by Chopin and Debussy, or perhaps a few tunes from the hymnbook, something not too rousing, appropriate for bedtime—What a Friend We Have in Jesus, The Old Rugged Cross, He Walked with Me, Take My Life and Let It Be, Amazing Grace, or Leaning on the Everlasting Arms . . .

Striding through the October wind. Women don't stride, not small skinny frail-looking overworked overworried Appalachian farm women like Lorraine Holyoak-Lightcap. But our mother did. She strode over the reddish dirt of the road, the burned slag from the coke ovens of Deerlick, Blacklick, the coal-mining towns. She walked rapidly in the windwashed afternoon, switching her stick. She gazed at the red-gold leaves of oak, beech, elm, maple and poplar and hickory—chlorophyll withdrawn for the freezing times ahead, leaving behind in each veined leaf the flame-colored chemistry of fall—and stared up at the streamlined clouds in the silver blue of the sky.

What she longed for, I suppose, was something far away from the ramshackle farmhouse, the unpainted barn, the pigpen chickencoop outhouse toolshed springhouse wagonshed of Lightcap Hollow. Lorraine was the daughter of a professional schoolteacher; her brother was a cashier in a bank; her sisters lived in town in houses with hardwood floors, electricity, hot and cold running water, centralized heating, even refrigerators.

INCONSOLABLE MEMORIES. Appalachian autumn. Rustle of wind through the dry corn, rattle of dead leaves beneath our feet, the frosty breath of morning, the sleepy stasis of Indian summer.

Mornings and at night we walked our trapline with flashlight and .22 rifle. Hoping for fox, silver fox (wealth!), but catching mostly only skunk and muskrat. Sometimes in early dawn we'd find a muskrat dead in our trap, half frozen into the ice. Or now and then, not often, one small furry foot with chewed-off stump clutched in the steel jaws. A cruel business, our mother kept reminding us. Will shrugged, I was embarrassed, the old man scoffed.

"Look, Lorrie," Paw would growl, "they don't hurt much. The trap grabs and holds 'em, that's all. Those poor critters are gonna die anyhow, out there in the cold and dark. We're just harvestin' the surplus."

"You don't *harvest* living creatures," Mother said. "What a disgusting word. You're killing them for personal profit."

"All right, all right. But we need the money and you know it."

One evening Paw brought one of our Victor single-spring varmint traps up from the cellar. He was going to settle the cruelty argument with Mother once and for all. Carefully, while Mother watched, knitting, our old man squeezed the spring and spread the trap flat on the dinner table. He latched the bait pan to the release trigger and drew back. The trap was ready. "Okay, Lorrie, now watch this." Paw clenched his big right hand into a fist and smashed it down on the pan. The trap sprang shut. Grinning, he held up his caught right hand and the trap, its tether chain dangling. "See?" he said. "See that, goddamnit? I told you, Lorrie, it hardly hurts a-tall. I hardly feel it. See?" Triumphantly he looked at me, at Will, at Paul. "Ain't this what I been telling you boys all along?"

Impressed, we looked at Mother to see what she would say. Smiling her ironic smile, needles clicking in her fingers, she said, "You're not finished, Joe."

"What's that mean?"

She paused. "Now we want to see you gnaw your hand off."

THE FIELD CORN RIPENED, the silk at the tip of each ear turned rusty brown. We picked the dried silk and rolled it with pages from the Monkey Ward mail-order catalog into enormous, evil, sickening stogies. We sat high in the shadowy barn, on the square ax-hewn crossbeams above the granary, lit up and smoked ourselves sick. We were hiding from the old man in a bad place to hide: if he ever caught us smoking in the barn there'd be trouble. We heard him too, hollering for Will and me.

"Will!" he hollered. "Henry! You rascals in there?"

We grinned at each other, holding our breath. Quietly, Will crushed out his cornsilk stogie with his thumb and forefinger.

"Will!" Paw bellowed again. "We got corn to cut."

Choking back laughter, we froze in silence as he stomped across the planking of the barn floor, heard him swear as he whacked a heavy blade into a post. The corn knife, like a sword, like a machete, swished through the air when he swung it. We heard Paw go out through the hinged door set in the sliding main door and from there down the earthen ramp to the workshop. Then came the rumble of the grindstone gaining speed as he treadled it with one foot, the screech of steel against stone. Sparks would be flying under the drip of water from the cooling can.

Will stirred uneasily, unable to relax while near a man working. Such a sober serious conscientious fellow, he felt what I seldom felt—the urge to help out. To lend a hand. To grab ahold. "Guess we better go." He made no move to relight his cigar. "Guess we better go, Henry."

"You go, I'm a-stayin' right here."

Will made a threatening gesture, I shrank back, he laughed, stood up and nonchalantly walked the twelve-inch beam to the corner post, dropped down the pegged ladderway to the floor, disappeared. Uncomfortably I watched him leave. I knew I'd be in trouble if I didn't follow. Not that Will would ever tell on me, any more than he'd tell on anybody. But the old man would growl at him, badger him. Anyhow I needed the wages. Another tough poker game coming up Saturday night.

They were halfway to the cornfield when I ran to catch up. Paw carried the twelve-gauge and two fresh-sharpened corncutters—one for me. The beagle hounds ranged ahead, quartering left and right, reading the ground. The sun was noon high but low in the south, obscured by a gray scud of overcast. A raw wind blew in from the northwest. I turned down the earflaps on my brand-new corduroy hunting cap. Proud of that cap. The field corn was ripe but the leaves and stalks appeared a rusty green; that's why we were cutting and stacking it now, husking later.

The old man wore his usual autumn outfit: the billed cap, the tan canvas hunting coat with last year's hunting license in celluloid case pinned between the shoulders. Under the coat he wore bib overalls, felt boots buckled tight around the pantlegs.

We attacked the standing corn. Paw took the outside row next to the rail fence, Will the next, me the third. When we each had an armful Paw took our loads in his big hands, holding the bundle vertical, and mashed it down onto the sharp stubble. The bundle stood upright on its own to become the center of a shock, a tepee, a wigwam of corn.

Paw set a hard pace. Will kept up with him but I had trouble. My back seemed to hurt; I lacked motivation. Will was big, strong for his age and enjoyed the work—actually thought it important.

We reached the end of the field, or they did, where the big woods comes down the hill from Frank Gatlin's place. Paw and Will started their return, passing me going in the opposite direction. My corncutter clashed against Will's—a flash of sparks—and for a moment we struggled hand to hand, sword against sword, like Errol Flynn and Basil Rathbone in *Captain Blood*.

"Cut that out," growls the old man, "afore one of you gets hurt."

The beagles burst into yelps of discovery, off and running. They'd jumped a rabbit. Paw set his machete down carefully, didn't want to nick that fine-honed edge, and picked up the shotgun. He broke it open, loaded two shells into the breech, snapped it shut. Thumb on the safety, he watched the dogs.

They were coursing up the slope of the field by the edge of the woods. Fifty feet before them ran the rabbit, white tail bobbing through the weeds, the auburn grass, the copper-colored blackberry vines. The rabbit veered to the right, traversing the brown hayfield above the corn. The circle was beginning. None of us moved a step. Soon the rabbit would turn right again and come bounding through the corn toward us, followed by the eager hounds. Would be a tough shot, though, in the standing corn, unless the rabbit was stupid enough to cross the wide swath of six-inch stubble before us.

"Lemme get it, Paw," begged Will quietly.

Joe hesitated, then said, "Come here."

Will stepped beside him. Joe placed the heavy, double-barreled gun in Will's hands. Will hefted it to ready position, leaning way back.

"Hey," I whined, "when's it my turn? Will—"

"Shush!" growled the old man. "Don't scare that bunny. He's a-coming." To Will he said, "Push the safety." The beagles were racing down the hill, baying as they crashed through the corn. The rabbit was somewhere close in front of them, running silently for its life. Will raised the shotgun to his shoulder, legs spread wide, leaning back from the waist under the weight.

"Push hard against your shoulder," Paw whispered. "It'll buck. Don't forget the second trigger." He stared into the corn toward the cry of the hounds. "Here it comes. Lead him by a foot."

Will peered down the sightline between the barrels, cheek pressed against the stock. The rabbit leaped from the thicket of corn fifty feet away and raced across the lane of stubble. Will fired—a violent blast—and seemed to miss.

"Shoot again."

Barrels swinging as he led the rabbit, Will pulled the second trigger. The cottontail somersaulted through the air, thumped backside first against the bottom rail of the fence and came to rest.

"Good shot," says the old man.

"Lucky shot," I said. "You missed the first time."

"Maybe," Paw said. "Maybe he missed and then again maybe that rabbit was runnin' so fast he couldn't stop even though he was already dead. Stop at that speed he'd be wearin' his asshole for a collar."

The beagles began to worry the dead rabbit. "Git!" shouted Paw and they backed off, whimpering, eyes shifting uneasily from Joe to the rabbit and back. "All right Will, you shot your rabbit now clean it. Got your knife?"

Will nodded, pulled the jackknife from its pocket on the side of his high-top leather boot, flipped the blade out, picked the rabbit up by the ears and opened it with one quick slit from sternum to anus. He pulled out the steaming guts—entrails, stomach, liver and lungs—and tossed them to the dogs. He wiped his knifeblade on the soft fur of his kill and handed the rabbit to Paw. Paw stuffed it into the game pocket inside the back of his coat. "Okay boys, we got our meat, now let's get this goddamn corn patch cut and shocked."

He kept us going into twilight. The old man was doubling on me now, doing two rows to every one of mine—even Will could hardly keep up with him. I longed for the sound of Mother rapping on the bell by the kitchen door: for suppertime.

The full moon of November—following close upon the setting sun—is the longest moon of the year: the harvest moon, the hunter's moon. We saw it rising round as a banjo through the mists above the eastern hills when finally we heard the bell.

"Suppertime!" I cried, dropping my machete in the dirt. My back ached, my hands ached. I jammed my armful of corn into the final shock and bolted for the house.

"Henry!" yelled the old man. "You come back here. Pick up your corn-cutter, don't leave it on the ground to get all rusty from the dew, Jesus jumping blue Christ."

Okay, I thought, *okay*. Minutes later I was in the kitchen. The warm and comforting kitchen: red coals glowed through cracks in the cast-iron cook-stove. My mother stood by the stove under the amber glow of a lamp bracketed to the wall. She was stirring a pot of stew. She looked tired. The two kids and the baby sat at the oilcloth-covered table, rosy faces smeared with food. I smelled potato soup, stew meat, gravy. I started to wash my hands in the tin basin of soapy water on the stand beside the door.

"Henry," says Mother, "where's Will and your father?"

"They're a-comin'. Got one more row to cut."

"Bring us a pail of water before you wash up?"

I took the bucket from the nail on the wall, stepped outside to the pump. There was a coffee can on the planks, full of water and drowned insects. I hung the bucket on the lip of the spout, primed the pump and cranked the handle, long as a baseball bat, up and down. The pump gasped and croaked, leather suckers four years old. A column of water rose by imperfect suction to the spout and gushed into my bucket.

One shoulder sagging, I lugged the water into the kitchen and hoisted it to the washstand.

Paw and Will came in. Will displayed the dead rabbit to Mother and the kids. They seemed impressed. Will hung the rabbit outside in the cold air, under the porch roof, out of reach of the dogs.

Sitting at the table finally, we watched as Mother bowed her head and clasped hands together prayerwise. "Dear God . . . bless this house and all who dwell in it. Bless this food we are about to receive, for which we thank thee. For thy many gifts we are humbly grateful, Lord. Amen."

Grace would normally be said by the head of the household. But our father would not pray to anybody.

Mother raised her head and little Paul, age six, blurted out, "Pass the taters, pass the meat, thank our Lord and let's eat."

Mother looked at him. Paul blushed and lowered his face. Paw smiled. After a brief silence, Mother dished out thick potato soup, filling first Paw's bowl, then Will's, then mine and her own. The children had already eaten. Paw sliced four chunks from the round loaf of homemade bread in the middle of the table. We ate fast, Will and me.

"Take your time, boys," Mother said. "Elbows off the table, please."

"Goin' to Houser's," I said between gulps. We played basketball in Ernie's barn; he lived in Stump Creek and had electric lights in the barn. Four miles by bicycle.

Paw looked at Will. "You too?"

"I figured on it. You settin' out more traps tonight?"

Paw pulled the watch from the bib pocket of his overalls, studied it. "Coal train's comin' up the grade in about fifty-five minutes."

"Joe," Mother said, "you're not going down there tonight? Not with the boys. Please."

Paw buttered another hunk of bread. "We need the coal, Lorrie. It's gonna be a long winter."

"We could buy it for once."

"How?" said our father.

She was silent for a moment. "You could dig some more out of the old mine on the hill. Like you used to."

"You looked in that hole lately? Props are rotten. Roof's gonna cave in most anytime."

"Then you should seal it."

"I been meanin' to do that for a year." He scooped more stew onto his plate. "But tonight we got to get coal. Full moon's up, it's a good night for it."

"The brakemen will see you."

"You think they care? Good Christ, Lorrie—" Mother hated swearing, especially at table. "God, Lorrie, there's ten million men out of work these days. Why do you think Roosevelt's fixin' to get us into another war?" Angrily he broke his bread. "Ten million!"

"Joe, promise me this," Mother said. "Don't let Will climb on the train."

"Oh, Maw," Will said. "I can do that easy."

"Promise me," she repeated.

"Sure," Paw muttered.

WE WALKED down the road under the maple trees. Paw wore his miner's helmet with the carbide lamp attached to the front. We each carried a bundle of sooty burlap sacks. The moon sailed high; silver light lay on the dirt road before our feet.

"But why not, Paw?"

"Not this time, Will, I promised her."

"You could load twice as much."

"I know it, son. Don't I know it? Next time."

Will stopped complaining. He knew when it was useless to argue with our old man. We heard a screech owl in the pine trees. A fox barked far up the hill, followed by the howls of our beagles behind us, brokenhearted, tied up under the front porch.

We came to the railway trestle. We climbed the concrete abutment and walked two hundred yards down the tracks—I walked on a rail—to where the grade began. We could hear the steam locomotive a mile away, whistle wailing as it approached Groft's crossing. I felt vibrations in the steel rail. Paw strode ahead between the tracks, big boots treading on every other crosstie, his shadow hard-edged in the moonlight.

We waited near the start of the mile-long hill. Paw took our sacks and draped them over his shoulder. He carried a bundle of short tie strings—binder twine—in his pocket, ends dangling. He repeated the usual instructions:

"I'll load and tie and drop the sacks off along the tracks. You boys drag the coal to the bottom. I'll be with you soon as I can. If either one of you tries to climb aboard this train I'll tan your hide good."

The beam of a headlamp swung across the trees; the engine appeared around the bend, rocking slightly from side to side, belching smoke and sparks from the stack. We backed into the elderberry bushes. The locomotive roared past in thunder, making a race for the grade. We saw the engineer with a pipe in his teeth leaning out his window, studying the tracks ahead, old hogger's steady hand on the throttle lever. A red glow lit up the interior of the cab as the fireman opened the firebox hatch and shoveled in coal. Then they were gone, followed by the tender with its steel sentry box for a brakeman, followed by the chain of iron gondola cars heaped with blue-black bituminous coal.

Paw stepped onto the shoulder of the roadbed. The train was slowing. He winked at me and Will, grinned, trotted along beside a gondola, caught the ladder, swung aboard and climbed to the top. As he moved away we saw him pull a sack from his shoulder and commence to stuffing it with coal. He faded into the moonlight.

The train was moving slower and slower. Will and I looked at each other. "Dare you," I said. I knew if he did I could. He knew it too. Paw was out of sight. We heard a faint thump ahead as the first sack of coal fell to the cinderbank.

Will hesitated for about two seconds. "Okay," he said. "Watch me close. Run with the train. Don't forget to lean forward when you jump off. Land a-runnin'." He glanced both ways. The train kept rattling around the curve, car after car. "We'll get off as soon as we cross the bridge."

He turned and jogged, grasped a steel rung and lifted himself from the ground, standing with one foot on the bottom step. I reached for the ladder of the next car, grabbed and hung on. The train jerked me forward but I got my feet on the ladder. I watched Will holding on with one hand, showing off, leaning far out to see ahead to the trestle crossing.

The train rumbled slowly on. Will's gondola crossed the bridge; he jumped off and ran forward a few steps, easily keeping his balance. Paw's first sack of coal, neatly tied, lay on the cinders beside the track. Many more beyond. Will looked up at me as I glided past. "Okay, Henry, jump off." I grinned and clung to the ladder. "Henry!" he shouted, "you get off there." I thumbed my nose at him and rode on.

I was enjoying the ride. Just a little bit farther, I thought, then I'll jump. Looking back I saw Will drag a sack of coal to the edge of the embankment and roll it down toward the wagon lane in the woods. That reminded me how angry Paw would get if he found out I hadn't helped.

I'll ride to the top of the grade, I thought, then jump off, sneak around the old man and rejoin Will at the lower end. I looked ahead but could not see the engine; it was already in the big cut at the top of the hill.

A man walked toward me down the shoulder of the railway. It was Paw. I shrank against the dark side of the gondola, trying to make myself invisible. He stooped over a loaded sack, checking the tie and pushing it off the bank. He never noticed me.

Now, I thought, better get off this here train before I get in trouble. I looked down at the cinders and crossties beneath my feet. They were passing faster than before. I braced my nerves to let go, make the jump. But hesitated.

You got to jump, I told myself. But it was too late; I sensed it in the rattle of the wheels over the joints in the rails, the scream of the whistle, the locomotive highballing down the far grade. An icy wind streamed past my ears. Wait for the next hill, I thought. I crawled into the space under the sloping bulkhead of the car and found protection from the wind. Not much. I pulled down the earflaps of my cap, buttoned the collar of my coat, sat tight and waited.

The scattered lamps of Stump Creek flashed by. I was already four miles by road from home. We raced through the village of Pine Run—five miles. The next little town would be Sawmill—seven. Close to Sawmill the train slowed suddenly, air brakes hissing. I cracked my frozen limbs into action, found the ladder and jumped to the cinders before the train stopped. Men with lanterns hurried toward me. They seemed to be yelling my name. Railroad bulls, I said to myself. They're gonna put me in jail. I stumbled across a ditch, climbed a fence and ran into the dark.

A long train ride but it was a longer walk home. Took me half the night. I followed the highway as far as Stump Creek, dodging into the bushes whenever I saw the lights of a car approaching. This side of the village I took the shortcut over the hill. The moon was low and the Big Dipper heeled over on its handle when I limped up Lightcap Hollow under the tunnel of trees. Two lamps glowed in the windows at our house. I was hoping to sneak in through the cellar door and crawl in bed before anyone knew I was home, but the hounds started yapping. When they recognized my scent it was too late.

Mother was glad to see me. She cried as she hugged me. Paw looked solemn. He must have caught hell from Mother and that meant I was in trouble with him. Will wasn't around: in hiding, maybe, or maybe in bed. He would be looking for me too, come morning.

Paw led me out to the barn, where Mother wouldn't hear, and gave me ten whops across the rear with his belt. Not too hard. It didn't hurt much. I had a copy of the *West Virginia Farmer* folded inside my pants. The old man said he'd given Will twelve licks because Will was two years older and should've known better than to let me climb on that train.

Will got me on the way to school next morning, down by the macadam road where we waited for the bus. Little Paul watched and tried to pull Will off my back but that was a waste of time. When the bus finally came Will let me up. I picked the gravel out of my face, staunched my bleeding nose with my bandana and climbed aboard after Will and Paul. Duane Bishop, the driver, looked at my face but didn't say a word. He knew better than to question Will.

But I didn't care. I was a hero for nearly a week.

What's more we got in the coal the next night, all of it, by team and wagon in the moonlight. Thirty bushels of good lump coal—about a ton and a half, Paw said. Enough to keep our house warm for the next four months, along with a few cords of oak and beech from the woodlot. The wood was free. Like the coal.

One night in bed, after my train ride, our mother said to her husband, "He hung on to that train all the way to Sawmill. Seven miles in freezing cold. Then got off and walked home. At night. A ten-year-old boy. Who would you say is dogged now, Joe?"

Joe Lightcap stared through the moonlit gloom at the ceiling and thought about it. After a while he said, "Lorrie, there's dogged and there's stupid. Will is dogged."

"I see."

Joe lay back and thought some more. "Henry ain't stupid though. That's what worries me. He's in for a life of lots of complicated complications."

My mother smiled to herself. "At least it won't be a dull life."

A pause. "Just what do you mean by that, Lorrie?"

Another pause. "Only what I said."

Hallelujah on the Bum

IN THE SUMMER of 1944, the year before the year I fell in love, I hitchhiked from Pennsylvania to Seattle by way of Chicago and Yellowstone National Park; from Seattle down the coast to San Francisco; and from there by way of Barstow and Needles via boxcar, thumb and bus through the Southwest back home to the old farm, three months later. I started out with twenty dollars in my pocket and a piece of advice, cryptic I'd say, from my old man: "Don't let anybody take you for a punk." I didn't know what he meant. I was seventeen: wise, brown, ugly, shy, poetical; a bold, stupid, sun-dazzled kid, out to see the country before giving his life in the war against Japan. A kind of hero, by God! Terrified but willing.

Chicago. A good truck driver took me through the core of the city, right through the Loop, and even in the summer it seemed to me the bleakest, hardest, coldest town I'd ever seen; I've never been back. In Minnesota I was picked up by a kindly middle-aged shoe salesman who tried to seduce me; I didn't understand what he wanted and resisted his timid advances. I was so innocent, so ignorant, I had never even heard of homosexuality. Maybe that is what saved me. Meantime I was scribbling, scribbling, keeping a log all the way, suffering already the first pangs of the making of books.

From *The Journey Home: Some Words in Defense of the American West* (1977)

South Dakota. Broke. I stacked wheat for ten days under the summer sun, huge sheaves heavy with dew, and got sick drinking the hard artesian water. In a little town named Pierre I stopped in a drugstore near the capitol for a thin wartime vanilla milkshake. A group of giant plainsmen in gabardine suits and big hats sat near me drinking coffee, talking politics. One introduced himself to me, said he was the governor of South Dakota. I believed him. He was.

Through the Badlands. Another milkshake at Wall's. On to Wyoming, where near Greybull I saw for the first time something I had dreamed of seeing for ten years. There on the western horizon, under a hot, clear sky, sixty miles away, crowned with snow (in July), was a magical vision, a legend come true: the front range of the Rocky Mountains. An impossible beauty, like a boy's first sight of an undressed girl, the image of those mountains struck a fundamental chord in my imagination that has sounded ever since.

Among the forests, bears, paint pots, boiling pools and gushing geysers of Yellowstone. Traffic was getting mighty scarce. Picked up and then left at a side road in the Idaho Panhandle, I walked all afternoon, all evening, all through the night, along the deserted highway, through a dark forest in the high country, and heard a cougar scream. I stopped once and slept for a while in a deep, dry, grassy ditch until the cold drove me up and onward.

In the morning a rancher picked me up, took me along for another fifty miles. He offered me a job for the summer, said he'd teach me to be a cowboy. My God, but I was tempted; yet the westering urge was too strong in me. I thought I couldn't wait to see the Pacific Ocean and declined his offer. A mistake.

Seattle was just another big city. All cities tend to look pretty much alike from the hitchhiker's point of view. I didn't even see the ocean. Going south to Portland, I got a ride with a long, lean fellow from Oklahoma, who said his name was Fern. He was a hard, tough, rambling hombre, and he looked like Gary Cooper; I liked him at once, especially when he stopped in the woods and let me fire his revolver at some whiskey bottles. He said he was a wounded veteran, not a draft dodger. He showed me his tattoos: on his left arm a mermaid, on his right the motto Semper Fidelis.

He had no money; I bought the food and was also privileged to stand guard at night while Fern, with his rubber hose (Okie credit card), siphoned gas from cars parked on dark streets in small Oregon towns.

One evening I sat alone in the car for half an hour, on a side street, while Fern went off with his gun to see a friend, he said. He came back in a hurry, breathing heavily, giggling, and we roared into the night, out of that town.

Driving south, he pulled a bottle from a brown paper sack, opened it, drank, offered me a swig. My first taste of hard liquor. After another drink, grinning, he showed me a wad of greenbacks. I was scared, but impressed. He said he was going to get him a big fat woman that night. And he did. . . .

Next day we drove into northern California, to Sacramento. We stopped at a gas station, where I went to the toilet; when I came back outside, Fern and his car were gone. With him went my coat, my hat, my satchel containing everything else I possessed except the shirt, pants and shoes I was wearing. My wallet and some twenty dollars were also gone, since Fern had advised me to keep my money and papers locked in the glove compartment of the car. Safer, he'd explained.

I had ten cents in my pocket and a jackknife. I was hungry. The first thing I did was put to good use one of the few useful things Fern had taught me: how to make a meal from a cup of coffee. Entering a drugstore and taking a counter stool, I ordered one cup of coffee and pulled the cream pitcher and the sugar bowl close. As I slowly drank the coffee, I kept adding as much sugar and cream as the mug would hold, making a thick, sweet sludge, highly nourishing, which I scooped up with the spoon. Fortified, I walked out. And I still had a nickel in my pocket.

The following day I was knocking pecans out of a tree for pay. There was this pecan tree and a tarp spread out on the ground beneath it and a wooden mallet in my hands. Every time I whacked the trunk a shower of pecans, leaves, dust, twigs, bugs, caterpillars and birds' nests fell out of the tree and into my hair and down inside my shirt. After one afternoon of pecan knocking, I took my pay and thumbed a ride to Stockton, where I'd been told they needed hands for the peach canneries.

For two weeks I worked in the cannery, slopping around over the juicy floors, the squashed and quartered peaches. The air, hot and steamy, reeked with the sweet stink of rotten fruit. I carried crates of peaches off the loading dock and up to the women on the line, whose work was to skin and slice the peaches. Since they were paid by the crate, they preferred large peaches— less work, same money—and whenever I brought one of these ladies a crate of small peaches she would scream at me in language I shudder to remember and sometimes fling a few hard green ones at me as I retreated fast, ducking down behind the stacks of empties. They were all sick, those women, sick with fury and insult, overwork and boredom, abandoned by their menfolk, fighting one another, penned up all day in that foul shed. They worked with sharp little knives; one day I saw a woman running down the aisle with her hands over her face, blood streaming between her fingers.

Taking my pay, I left them there, those poor women in their outrage and misery, and took off afoot for Yosemite Valley. I wanted to see the big trees, the high waterfalls and the granite face of El Capitan. Made it too, by God, after a couple of days' trudging through the golden hills, past the manzanita and Emory oaks, along the narrow asphalt road that led into John Muir's range of light.

Later. . . . Back into the flat and sweltering Central Valley, south through Fresno—where I saw Saroyan's home—to Bakersfield, up over the Tehachapi Pass and into the desert. At once I felt as if I had left California behind and was mighty glad of it. A long, windy night on the back of a flatbed truck, under the new moon, brought me at dawn to the town of Needles and my first view of the Colorado River.

Needles in August must be one of the two or three hottest inhabited places on earth. A fearful, scalding heat that makes you hurry from shade to shade. With forty dollars in my shoe and hope in my heart, I stood all day on the eastern edge of town, thumb out, begging for a lift. Nobody stopped. Across the river waited a land that filled me with strange excitement: crags and pinnacles of naked rock, the dark cores of ancient volcanoes, a vast and silent emptiness smoldering with heat, color and indecipherable significance, above which floated a small number of pure, clear, hard-edged clouds. For the first time I felt I was getting close to the West of my deepest imaginings— the place where the tangible and the mythical become the same.

All day long I waited at the side of the highway, sheltering in the scant shade of a mesquite tree, cocking my thumb at the few cars and trucks that approached. They were very few; this was wartime and not many people had business in the backlands of Arizona. I would have walked, but had sense enough to perceive that the desert sun could make walking not merely un-pleasant but hazardous—even suicidal. I did not have sense enough, how-ever, to understand that most southwesterners, in those years before the advent of air-conditioning, stayed passive and shaded up during the summer days and did their driving at night. And nobody in Needles cared to take the enormous trouble of telling me about it. Nearby, across the broken glass, the weeds, the junkyard, the ditch, ran the tracks of the Atchison, Topeka and Santa Fe ("Holy Faith") Railroad. Now and then I could see a freight train forming up in the yards, brakemen hanging one-handed to the ladders, some old hog in bib overalls, blue-striped cap and necktie peering out of the engine cab. I waved; they waved back like all good railroaders.

At evening time, drinking my third quart of milk that day, still stranded, I became aware of a black man standing in the brush between me and the tracks. He was watching me with care. There's something in my face that never fails to catch the eye of panhandlers. I've never been missed by a bum yet. And so, when the white-haired old black man came close and mumbled a few words at my ear, I had to go into the café across the highway and buy a couple of hamburgers and another quart of milk and bring them back to him. He tried to explain why he didn't want to go into the café himself, but at the time I couldn't quite figure it out.

We had supper together under the mesquite tree at the edge of the quiet highway. Exchanged intelligence. His name I no longer recollect, but his destination was Chicago. Mine was Home—Home, Pennsylvania. He offered to show me how to get there.

After sundown, in the lavender loveliness of the desert twilight, we crept through the junk and creosote bushes toward the railway and squatted down in a comfortable ditch within spitting distance of the rails. From the division yards to the west came the clash and shock of coupling iron, the screech of hot metal, the rumble of switch engines. We waited, smoking my companion's hand-rolled Bull Durham cigarettes.

We heard two sharp whistles—the highball signal. Presently the train came slowly through the gloom, three big diesels pulling a string of boxcars so long we couldn't see the caboose. Ponderously the cars rolled by, slowly picking up speed; I could see the wooden ties sinking under the wheels, rising between them. Sealed boxcars passed us bearing brands from all over the nation: Southern Pacific, Great Northern, New York Central, Denver and Rio Grande, Union Pacific, Baltimore and Ohio, Pennsy, Santa Fe, Wabash, Lackawanna, Eastern Seaboard (Route of Phoebe Snow). . . . The first empty appeared, doors open; we stood up, stepped into the cinders and gravel of the roadbed, began to trot along beside the train. As the empty came abreast of us, my new friend threw his bundle in, grabbed hold of the edge of the doorway, pulled himself up and half into the car. He turned to give me assistance as I ran along. I was clutching at the edge of the sliding door with one hand, holding my pack and bedroll with the other, reluctant to toss them inside because now I wasn't certain I could get aboard. The floor of the boxcar was chest high and the train was gaining speed. As I hesitated, the old black man grappled me at the wrist with both his big paws and hauled me halfway in; I danced along the ties on tiptoe at twenty miles per hour. "Come on, boy," he hollered, "pitch your roll up and get in here." I made it.

We rattled half the night up and out of the valley of the Colorado, up into the highlands of western Arizona. We sat in the corner of the boxcar, forward out of the wind, on piles of moldy straw, jounced and jolted by the iron wheels, the hard boards, the shaking, swaying car. Nevertheless, I slept. Missed the moonlight on the mesas. Awoke as the train slowed down outside Kingman, pulling into the division. We decided to stay aboard, though it meant chancing capture by the yard bulls. The train stopped in the center of the yards, surrounded by floodlights, other trains, the cyclone fences. An express roared through in a blast of iron, whistle blaring away and off into the distance. We huddled in the darkest corner of our boxcar, waiting, and heard the brakemen pass swinging their lanterns and talking. Nobody looked in. Our train backed off the siding, detached or attached a few more cars, lurched forward onto the mainline. Again we were rolling eastward, climbing in wide arcs toward the summit of the Colorado Plateau, into the yellow pine forests of the high country. Though it was still August, the night became very cold; the old bum and I squeezed together for warmth.

At Flagstaff I got caught. Not by the railroad men, but by the city cops. We'd jumped off the train as it was pulling into the yard and taken a detour around the station, intending to catch another freight on the east side of town. Half frozen, we also needed something hot to eat and drink. While my buddy skulked in the shadows, I walked toward the center of town to find a café that might still be open. It must've been after midnight. The cops picked me up. I still had forty dollars in my left shoe, but I wasn't going to tell them about it. They drove me to City Hall, booked me for vagrancy and threw me into the drunk tank for the rest of the night.

Cold steel, cold cement, a rabble of coughing, drunken, sick bums sprawled on the floor, curled up in the corners. The smell of vomit and urine, the fumes of sweet wine, the peculiar stale and bitter odor of old sweat-soaked rags. There were no benches, no bunks, no tables, nothing but this tank of steel and concrete and in the center of the ceiling, protected by mesh wire, one yellow light bulb.

Ah, one other thing, most weird and marvelous, like something out of a dream. Did I really see it? Perhaps it was a dream. As I write these words a quarter of a century later, I am no longer certain what was real, what was unreal.

There was a cage within the cage. Yes. And the bars of this inner cage were painted yellow. And inside the inner cage—alone—was one giant, gleaming, half-naked Negro, mad as the moon, who howled and bellowed and sang and jabbered all night long.

In the morning the guards marched us into a courtroom. The judge kept us waiting half an hour, to teach us respect for the law, then came shuffling in, black gown and all. The guards made us stand up. The judge sat down. We sat

down. Justice moved swiftly. The drunks pleaded guilty—most of them Indians—and received their sentences on the spot. Which they had already
served. When my turn came, I pleaded not guilty, creating a small sensation
behind the bench. The judge and the clerk held a consultation; then the judge
informed me that my trial was scheduled for December 10, about three and
a half months hence, and that I would be confined in the city jail until that
time unless I was prepared to post bond in the amount of fifty dollars. I said I
didn't have fifty dollars. He asked me how much I had. After a moment's
hesitation I said a dollar and forty cents, which was the amount the police had
confiscated, along with my pocketknife, pack and bedroll, when they locked
me up. The judge asked me if I was a draft dodger. I said no. He asked to see
my draft card. I told him I was only seventeen and therefore not registered.
He reduced the bail to one dollar and told me to get the hell out of Flagstaff
and never come back.

The cops gave me back my possessions, including the balance of my apparent funds, the forty cents. One of them took me into a restaurant and
bought me a good lunch and returned my dollar and then drove me to the
eastern edge of town and dropped me by the highway. He warned me to stay
off the trains because some of them carried military equipment and armed
guards who were dying for an opportunity to shoot a potential saboteur. This
seemed like good advice; during the day before, at Needles, I had noticed the
tanks, trucks and artillery pieces chained to the flatbeds, although I had not
seen any guards on the trains. I spent the remainder of the day hitchhiking,
but got exactly nowhere. After sundown and supper I slunk into the forest,
spread my sleeping bag under the pines and shivered through a second bitter
night. Early in the morning I caught an eastbound freight, alone this time,
pulling myself into another empty boxcar just as the train was beginning to
roll out of the yards.

A magnificent day—warm, clear, brilliant with sunshine. All through the
morning we rumbled, rattled and roared across the great plateau of northern
Arizona, stopping now and then to let more important trains pass, but making
good time all the same. Through the wide-open door of my side-door Pullman
I saw for the first time in my life the high rangelands of the Navajos, the fringes
of the Painted Desert, the faraway buttes and mesas of Hopi country. Sometimes I would catch a glimpse of a hogan under a scrap of sandstone, a team
and wagon hitched by the door, a couple of Indians sprawled in the shade of
a juniper tree. It all looked good to me. And then we came to New Mexico.

Brightest New Mexico. The sharp, red cliffs of Gallup. Mesas and mountains in the distance. Lava beds baking under the sun. Old volcanoes. Indian villages, cornfields, antique adobe churches, children splashing in a stream, an enchanted mesa. And over all a golden light, a golden stillness, a sweet but awesome loneliness—one old white horse browsing on a slope miles away from any sign of man; no fences; one solitary windmill standing by a grove of junipers, cowpaths radiating toward the horizon; a single cottonwood tree, green as life, in the hot red sand of a dry riverbed.

Proud of my freedom and hobohood I stood in the doorway of the boxcar, rocking with the motion of the train, ears full of the rushing wind and the clattering wheels, and stared and stared and stared, like a starving man, at the burnt, barren, bold, bright landscape passing before my eyes. Telegraph poles flashed by close to the tracks, the shining wires dipped and rose, dipped and rose; but beyond the line and the road and the nearby ridges, the queer foreign shapes of mesa and butte seemed barely to move at all; they revolved slowly at an immense distance, strange right-angled promontories of rose-colored rock that remained in view, from my slowly altering perspective, for an hour, for two hours, at a time. And all of it there, simply *there*, neither hostile nor friendly, but full of a powerful, mysterious promise.

In the evening we came to a town of 35,000 souls that lay in a shallow valley in the desert between volcanoes on the west and—on the east—a mountain range pink as the heart of a watermelon.

Albuquerque. Through the middle of this small dusty city ran a wide but shallow river the color of mud, shining like polished brass under the cloud-reflected light of sunset.

The train slowed, approaching the yards, I jumped off and rolled in the cinders, tumbleweeds and broken wine bottles of the ditch. Dragging my gear I crawled to my feet and limped along the street toward the heart of town. Great golden spokes of light streamed across the sky. Blue herons croaked in the willows by the water. Three rough-looking toughs in blue jeans and straw cowboy hats followed me up the road, laughing, welcoming me to New Mexico. "*Chinga tu madre, cabrón.*" Sons of Pancho Villa. I said nothing. They lost interest in me and turned away. I entered the city, up First Street into Albuquerque's skid row. It looked familiar.

After three months of wandering I was homesick. I longed for the warm green hills of Pennsylvania, for the little wooden baseball towns, the sulfurous creeks and covered bridges, the smoky evenings rich with fireflies; I thought of the winding red-dog road that led under oak and maple trees toward the creaking old farmhouse that was our home, where the dogs waited on the front porch, where my sister and my brothers played in the twilight under the giant sugar maple, where my father and mother sat inside in the amber light of kerosene lamps, listening to their battery-powered Zenith radio, waiting for me. I was sick for home.

Safe in the Greyhound bus depot, I took off my shoe and bought a ticket straight through to Pennsylvania.

How It Was

THE FIRST TIME I had a glimpse of the canyon country was in the summer of 1944. I was a punk kid then, scared and skinny, hitchhiking around the United States. At Needles, California, bound home for Pennsylvania, I stood all day by the side of the highway, thumb out. Nobody stopped. In fact, what with the war and gasoline rationing, almost nobody drove by. Squatting in the shade of a tree, I stared across the river at the porphyritic peaks of Arizona, crazy ruins of volcanic rock floating on heat waves. Purple crags, lavender cliffs, long blue slopes of cholla and agave—I had never before even dreamed of such things.

In the evening an old black man with white whiskers crept out of the brush and bummed enough money from me for his supper. Then he showed me how to climb aboard an open boxcar when a long freight train pulled slowly out of the yards, rumbling through the twilight, eastward bound. For half the night we climbed the long grade into Arizona. At Flagstaff, half frozen, I crawled off the train and into town looking for warmth and hospitality. I was locked up for vagrancy, kicked out of jail the next morning and ordered to stay away from the Santa Fe Railway. And no hitchhiking, neither. And don't never come back.

From *Slickrock: The Canyon Country of Southeast Utah* (1971)

Humbly I walked to the city limits and a step or two beyond, held out my thumb and waited. Nobody came. A little after lunch I hopped another freight, all by myself this time, and made myself at home in a big comfortable empty side-door Pullman, with the doors open on the north. I found myself on a friendly train, in no hurry for anywhere, which stopped at every yard along the line to let more important trains roar past. At Holbrook the brakemen showed me where to fill my canteen and gave me time to buy a couple of sandwiches before we moved on.

From Flag to Winslow to Holbrook; and then through strange, sad, desolate little places called Adamana and Navajo and Chambers and Sanders and Houck and Lupton—all the way to Albuquerque, which we reached at sundown. I left that train when two rough-looking customers came aboard my boxcar; one of them began paring his fingernails with a switchblade knife while the other stared at me with somber interest. I had forty dollars hidden in my shoe. Not to mention other treasures. I slipped out of there quick. Suddenly homesick I went the rest of the way by bus, nonstop, about twenty-five hundred miles, the ideal ordeal of travel, second only to a seasick troopship.

But I had seen the southern fringe of the canyon country. And did not forget it. For the next two years, through all the misery and tedium, humiliation, brutality and ugliness of my share of the war and the military, I kept bright in my remembrance, as the very picture of things that are free, decent, sane, clean and true, what I had seen and felt—yes, and even smelled—on that one blazing afternoon on a freight train rolling across the Southwest.

I mean the hot dry wind. The odor of sagebrush and juniper, of sand and black baking lava rock. I mean I remembered the sight of a Navajo hogan under a bluff, red dust, a lonesome horse browsing far away down an empty wash, a windmill and water tank at the hub of cattle trails radiating toward a dozen different points on the horizon, and the sweet green of willow, tamarisk and cottonwood trees in a stony canyon. There was a glimpse of the Painted Desert. For what seemed like hours I could see the Hopi Buttes, far on the north, turning slowly on the horizon as my train progressed across the vast plateau. There were holy mountains in the far distance. I saw gleaming meanders of the Little Colorado and the red sandstone cliffs of Manuelito. Too much. And hard-edged cumulus clouds drifting in fleets through the dark blue sea of the sky. And most of all, the radiance of that high desert sunlight, which first stuns then exhilarates your senses, your mind, your soul.

But this was only, as I said, the fringe. In 1947 I returned to the Southwest and began to make my first timid, tentative explorations toward the center of

that beautiful blank space on the maps. From my base at the University of
New Mexico, where I would be trying, more or less, for the next ten years, off
and on, to win a degree, I drove my old Chevy through mud and snow, brush
and sand, to such places as Cabezon on the Rio Puerco and from there south
to Highway 66. They said there was no road. They were right. But we did it
anyhow, me and a lad named Alan Odendahl (a brilliant economist since de-
voured by the insurance industry), freezing at night in our kapok sleeping
bags and eating tinned tuna for breakfast, lunch and supper. Tire chains and
skinned knuckles; shovels and blisters; chopping brush to fill in a boghole, I
missed once and left the bite of the ax blade in the toe of my brand-new Red
Wing engineer boots. (In those days philosophy students wore boots; now—
more true to the trade—they wear sandals, as Diogenes advised, or go bare-
foot like Socrates.) Next we made it to Chaco Canyon, where we looked
amazed at Pueblo Bonito in January. And then to the south rim of Canyon de
Chelly—getting closer—and down the foot trail to White House Ruin. An
idyllic place, it seemed then; remote as Alice Springs and far more beautiful.

On one long holiday weekend another friend and I drove my old piece of
iron with its leaky gas tank and leaky radiator northwest around the Four
Corners to Blanding, Utah, and the very end of the pavement. From there we
went by dusty washboard road to Bluff on the San Juan and thought we were
getting pretty near the end of the known world. Following a narrow wagon
road through more or less ordinary desert we climbed a notch in Comb Ridge
and looked down and out from there into something else. Out *over* something else. A landscape that I had not only never seen before but that did not
resemble anything I had seen before.

I hesitate, even now, to call that scene beautiful. To most Americans, to
most Europeans, natural beauty means the sylvan—pastoral and green,
something productive and pleasant and fruitful—pastures with tame cows, a
flowing stream with trout, a cottage or cabin, a field of corn, a bit of forest, in
the background a nice snow-capped mountain range. At a comfortable distance. But from Comb Ridge you don't see anything like that. What you see
from Comb Ridge is mostly red rock, warped and folded and corroded and
eroded in various ways, all eccentric, with a number of maroon buttes, purple
mesas, blue plateaus and gray dome-shaped mountains in the far-off west.
Except for the thin track of the road, switchbacking down into the wash a
thousand feet below our lookout point, and from there climbing up the other
side and disappearing over a huge red blister on the earth's surface, we could
see no sign of human life. Nor any sign of any kind of life, except a few acid-
green cottonwoods in the canyon below. In the silence and the heat and the

glare we gazed upon a seared wasteland, a sinister and savage desolation. And found it infinitely fascinating.

We stared for a long time at the primitive little road tapering off into the nothingness of the southwest, toward fabled names on the map—Mexican Hat, Monument Valley, Navajo Mountain—and longed to follow. But we didn't. We told ourselves that we couldn't: that the old Chev would never make it, that we didn't have enough water or food or spare parts, that the radiator would rupture, the gas tank split, the retreads unravel, the water pump fail, the wheels sink in the sand—fifty good reasons—long before we ever reached civilization on the other side. Which at that time would have been about Cameron, maybe, on U.S. 89. So we turned around and slunk back to Albuquerque the way we'd come, via the pavement through Monticello, Cortez and Farmington, like common tourists.

Later, though, I acquired a pickup truck—first of a series—and became much bolder. Almost every weekend or whenever there was enough money for gas we took off, all over New Mexico, over into Arizona, up into Colorado and eventually, inevitably, back toward the Four Corners and beyond—toward whatever lay back of that beyond.

The words seem too romantic now, now that I have seen what men and heavy equipment can do to even the most angular and singular of earthly landscapes. But they suited our mood of that time. We were desert mystics, my few friends and I, the kind who read maps as others read their holy books. I once sat on the rim of a mesa above the Rio Grande for three days and nights, trying to have a vision. I got hungry and saw God in the form of a beef pie. There were other rewards. Anything small and insignificant on the map drew us with irresistible magnetism. Especially if it had a name like Dead Horse Point or Wolf Hole or Recapture Canyon or Black Box or Old Paria (abandoned) or Hole-in-the-Rock or Paradox or Cahone (pinto bean capital of the world) or Mollie's Nipple or Dirty Devil or Pucker Pass or Pete's Mesa. Or Dandy Crossing.

Why Dandy Crossing? Obvious: because it was a dandy place to cross the river. So, one day in July 1953 we loaded the tow chain and the spare spare, the water cans and gas cans, the bedrolls and bacon and beans and boots into the back of the truck and bolted off. For the unknown. Well, unknown to us.

Discovered that, also unbeknownst to us, the pavement had been surreptitiously extended from Monticello down to Blanding while we weren't looking, some twenty miles of irrelevant tar and gravel. A trifling matter? Perhaps. But I felt even then (thirty years ago) a shudder of alarm. Something alien was moving in, something queer and out of place in the desert.

At Blanding we left the pavement and turned west on a dirt track into the sweet wilderness. Wilderness? It seemed like wilderness to us. Till we reached the town of Green River 180 miles beyond, we would not see another telephone pole. Behind us now was the last drugstore, the final power line, the ultimate policeman, the end of all asphalt, the very tip of the monster's tentacle.

We drove through several miles of pygmy forest—pinyon pine and juniper—and down into Cottonwood Wash, past Zeke's Hole and onward to the crest of Comb Ridge. Again we stopped to survey the scene. But no turning back this time. While two of my friends walked down the steep and twisting road to remove rocks and fill in holes, I followed with the pickup in compound low, riding the brake pedal. Cliff on one side, the usual thousand-foot drop on the other. I held the wheel firmly in both hands and stared out the window at my side, admiring the scenery. My girl friend watched the road.

The valley of Comb Wash looked like a form of paradise to me. There was a little stream running through the bright sand, a grove of cottonwoods, patches of grass, the color-banded cliffs on either side, the woods above—and not a house in sight, not even a cow or horse. Eden at the dawn of creation. What joy it was to know that such places still existed, waiting for us when the need arose.

We ate lunch by the stream, under the cottonwood trees, attended by a few buzzing flies and the songs of canyon wren and pinyon jay. Midsummer: the cattle were presumably all up in the mountains now, fattening on larkspur and lupine and purple penstemon. God bless them—the flowers, I mean. The wine passed back and forth among the four of us, the birds called now and then, the thin clear stream gurgled over the pebbles, bound for the San Juan River (which it would not reach, of course; sand and evaporation would see to that). Above our heads an umbrella of living, lucent green sheltered us from the July sun. We enjoyed the shade as much as the wine, the birds and flies and one another.

For another twenty miles we drove through the pinyon-juniper woods, across the high mesa south of the Abajo Mountains. The road was rough, full of ruts and rocks and potholes, and we had to stop a few times, get out the shovel and do a little roadwork, but this was more a pleasure than otherwise. Each such stop gave all hands a chance to stretch, breathe deep, ramble, look—and see. Why hurry? It made no difference to us where nightfall might catch us. We were ready and willing to make camp anywhere. And in this splendid country, still untouched by development and industrialism, almost any spot would have made a good campsite.

Storm clouds overhead? Good. What's July in the desert without a cloud-
burst? My old truck creaked and rattled on. Bouncing too fast down into a
deep wash I hit a pointed rock embedded in the road and punched a hole
through one of the tires. We installed one of the spares and rumbled on.

Late in the afternoon we reached Natural Bridges. We drove down a
steep, narrow, winding dirt lane among the pinyon pines—fragrant with oozing gum—and into the little campground. One other car was already there. In
other words, the place was badly overcrowded, but we stayed. We spent the
next day in a leisurely triangular walk among the three great bridges—Owachomo, Sipapu and Kachina—and a second night at the little Park Service campground. It was the kind of campground known as "primitive," meaning no
asphalt driveways, no flush toilets, no electric lights, no numbered campsites,
no cement tables, no police patrol, no fire alarms, no traffic controls, no movies, slide shows or press-a-button automatic tape-recorded natural history
lectures. A terrible, grim, deprived kind of campground, some might think.
Nothing but stillness, stasis and stars all night long.

In the morning we went on, deeper into the back country, back of beyond. The "improved" road ended at Natural Bridges; from there to the river,
forty-five miles, and from there to Hanksville, about another forty, it would
be "unimproved." Good. The more unimproved the better, that's what we
thought. We assumed, in those innocent days, that anything good would be
allowed to remain that way.

Our little road wound off to the west, following a big bench, with the
sheer cliffs of a plateau on the south and the deep, complicated drainages of
White Canyon on the north. Beyond White Canyon were Woodenshoe Butte,
the Bear's Ears, Elk Ridge and more fine blank areas on the maps. Nearby
were tawny grass and buff-colored cliffs, dark-green junipers and sandstone
scarps.

As we descended toward the river, the country opened up, wide and wild,
with nowhere any sign of man but the dirt trail road before us. We liked that.
Why? (*Why* is always a good question.) Why not? (Always a good answer.)
But why? One must attempt to answer the question—someone always raises
it, accusing us of "disliking people."

Well then, it's not from simple misanthropy. Speaking generally, for myself, I like people. Speaking particularly, I like some people, dislike others.
Like everyone else who hasn't been reduced to moronism by our commercial
Boy Scout ethic, I like my friends, dislike my enemies and regard strangers
with a tolerant indifference. But why, the questioner insists, why do people
like you pretend to love uninhabited country so much? Why this cult of wil-

derness? Why the surly hatred of progress and development, the churlish resistance to all popular improvements?

Very well, a fair question, but it's been asked and answered a thousand times already; enough books to drive a man stark naked mad have dealt in detail with the question. There are many answers, all good, each sufficient. Peace is often mentioned; beauty; spiritual refreshment, whatever that means; re-creation for the soul, whatever that is; escape; novelty, the delight of something different; truth and understanding and wisdom—commendable virtues in any man, anytime; ecology and all that, meaning the salvation of variety, diversity, possibility and potentiality, the preservation of the genetic reservoir, the answers to questions that we have not yet even learned to ask, a connection to the origin of things, an opening into the future, a source of sanity for the present—all true, all wonderful, all more than enough to answer such a dumb dead degrading question as "Why wilderness?"

To which, nevertheless, I shall append one further answer anyway: *because we like the taste of freedom; because we like the smell of danger.*

Descending toward the river the junipers become scarce, give way to scrubby, bristling little vegetables like black brush, snakeweed and prickly pear. The bunch grass fades away, the cliff rose and yucca fall behind. We topped out on a small rise and there ahead lay the red wasteland again—red dust, red sand, the dark smoldering purple reds of ancient rocks, Chinle, Shinarump and Moenkopi, the old Triassic formations full of radium, dinosaurs, petrified wood, arsenic and selenium, fatal evil monstrous things, beautiful, beautiful. Miles of it, leagues of it, glittering under the radiant light, swimming beneath waves of heat, a great vast aching vacancy of pure space, waiting. Waiting for what? Why, waiting for us.

Beyond the red desert was the shadowy crevasse where the river ran, the living heart of the canyonlands, the red Colorado. Note my use of the past tense here. That crevasse was Glen Canyon. On either side of the canyon we saw the humps and hummocks of Navajo sandstone, pale yellow, and beyond that, vivid in the morning light, rich in detail and blue in profile, the Henry Mountains, last-discovered (or at least the last-named) mountain range within the coterminous United States. These mountains were identified, as one might expect, by Major John Wesley Powell, and named in honor of his contemporary, Joseph Henry, secretary of the Smithsonian Institution. Beyond the mountains we could see the high Thousand Lake and Aquarius plateaus, some fifty miles away by line of sight. In those days before the potash mills, cement plants, uranium mills and power plants, fifty miles of clear air was nothing—to see mountains one hundred miles away was considered commonplace, a standard of vision.

We dropped down into that red desert. In low gear. Moved cautiously across a little wooden bridge that looked as if it might have been built by old Cass Hite himself, or even Padre Escalante, centuries before. Old yellow-pine beams full of cracks and scorpions, coated with the auburn dust. Beneath the bridge ran a slit in the sandstone, a slit about ten feet wide and one hundred feet deep, so dark down in there we could hardly make out the bottom. We paused for a while to drop rocks. The sunlight was dazzling, the heat terrific, the arid air exhilarating.

I added water to the radiator, which leaked a little, as all my radiators did in my student days, and pumped up one of the tires, which had a slow leak, also to be expected, and checked the gas tank, which was a new one and did not leak, yet, although I could see dents where some rocks had got to it. We climbed aboard and went on. Mighty cumuli-nimbi massed overhead—battleships of vapor, loaded with lightning. They didn't trouble us.

We jounced along in my overloaded pickup, picking our way at two miles an hour in and out of the little ditches—deadly axle busters—that ran across, not beside the road, heading the side canyons, climbing the benches, bulling our way through the sand of the washes. We were down in the land of standing rock, the world of sculptured sandstone, crazy country, a bad dream to any dirt farmer—except for the canyon bottoms not a tree in sight.

We came to the crossing of White Canyon, where I gunned the motor hard, geared down into second and charged through the deep sand. Old cottonwoods with elephantine trunks and sweet green trembling leaves caught my eye. Lovely things, I thought, as we crashed over a drop-off into a stream. Glimpsed sandpipers or killdeer scampering out of the way as a splash of muddy water drenched the windshield. "Hang on," I said. Heard a yelp as my friend's girl friend fell off the back of the truck. Couldn't be helped. The truck lurched up the farther bank, streaming with water, and came to a halt on the level road above, more or less by its own volition.

We got out to investigate. Nobody hurt. We ate our lunch beneath the shade of the trees. In the desert, under the summer sun, a shade tree makes the difference between intolerable heat and a pleasant coolness. The temperature drops thirty degrees inside the shadow line when there is free ventilation. If homes and public buildings in the Southwest were properly designed, built for human pleasure instead of private profit, there would be no need for air conditioning. The humblest Papago peasant or Navajo sheepherder knows more about efficient hot-country architecture than a whole skyscraper full of Del Webbs.

After the siesta, in midafternoon, we drove up from the ford and around a bench of naked rock several miles long and through a notch or dugway in a red wall. Below us lay Hite, Dandy Crossing, the river.

We descended, passed a spring and more cottonwoods, and came to the combination store, gas station and post office, which was not only the business center but almost the whole of Hite. At that time I believe there were no more than three families living in the place, which must have been one of the most remote and isolated settlements in the forty-eight states. There were also a few miscellaneous individuals—prospectors, exiles, remittance men—hanging about. The total population fluctuated from year to year with the fortunes of the uranium industry. Eventually the dam was built, the river backed up and everybody flooded out.

We stopped to buy gas—fifty cents a gallon, cheap at the price—and a round of beer. I met Mr. Woody Edgell, proprietor, who was already unhappy about the future prospects of Glen Canyon. He took a dim view both of the dam and of the Utah State Highway Department's proposed bridge-building schemes for the vicinity. Not because they would put him out of the business—they wouldn't; he could relocate—but because he liked Hite and Glen Canyon the way they were, neolithic.

Not everybody felt that way. I talked with a miner's wife, and she said that she hated the place, claimed that her husband did too, and said that only lack of money kept them there. She looked forward with gratitude to the flooding of Hite—a hundred feet under water was not deep enough, she thought. She'd be glad to be forced to leave.

There was a middle-aged fellow sitting outside the store, on a bench in the shade, drinking beer. He had about a month's growth of whiskers on what passed for a face. I bought him another can of Coors and tried to draw him into conversation. He was taciturn. Would not reveal his name. When I asked him what he did around there he looked up at the clouds and over at the river and down at the ground between his boots, thinking hard, and finally said: "Nothing."

A good and sufficient answer. Taking the hint, I went away from there, leaving him in peace. My own ambition, my deepest and truest ambition, is to find within myself someday, somehow, the ability to do likewise, to do nothing—and find it enough.

Somewhat later, half waterlogged with watery beer, we went for a swim in an eddy of the river, naked, and spouted silty water at the sky. The river tugged at our bodies with a gentle but insistent urge:

Come with me, the river said, *close your eyes and quiet your limbs and float with me into the wonder and mystery of the canyons, see the unknown and the little known, look upon the stone gods face to face, see Medusa, drink my waters, hear my song, feel my power, come along and drift with me toward the distant, ultimate and legendary sea. . . .*

Sweet and subtle song. Perhaps I should have surrendered. I almost did. But didn't. We piled ourselves wet and cooled back into the truck and drove down the shore to the ferry crossing, a mile beyond the store. There was a dirt-covered rock landing built out from shore, not far, and a pair of heavy cables strung across the river to the western bank. The ferry itself was on the far side where Art Chaffin, the ferryman, lived in a big house concealed by cottonwoods. We rang the bell, as instructed by a signboard. Nothing happened. We rang it again. After a while a man appeared among the trees on the opposite shore, stepped aboard his ferry and started the engine, engaged the winch. The strange craft moved across the river's flow toward us, pulling itself along the sagging cable. It was not a boat. It appeared to be a homemade barge, a handmade contraption of wood and steel and baling wire—gasoline engine, passenger platform, vehicle ramp and railings mounted on a steel pontoon. Whatever it was, it worked, came snug against the landing. I drove my pickup aboard, we shook hands with Art Chaffin and off we went, across the golden Colorado toward that undiscovered West on the other side.

The Hite Ferry had a history, short but rich. Following old Indian trails, Cass Hite came to and named Dandy Crossing in 1883. It was one of the very few possible fords of the river in the 240 miles between Moab and Lee's Ferry. That is, it could be negotiated by team and wagon during low water (late summer, winter). But it did not become a motor vehicle crossing until 1946, when Chaffin built his ferry. The first ferry sank in 1947; Chaffin built a second, which he sold in 1956 to a man named Reed Maxfield. In 1957 Reed Maxfield had an accident and drowned in the river. His widow kept the ferry in operation until a storm in November of 1957 tore the barge loose from its mooring and sank it. By this time the ferry had become well known and its service was in some demand; the Utah State Highway Department was obliged to rebuild it. Mrs. Maxfield was hired to continue running it, which she did until Woody Edgell took over in 1959. He was the last ferryman, being finally flooded out by the impounded waters of Glen Canyon Dam in June 1964. To replace the ferry the Utah Highway Department had to build not one but three bridges: one over the mouth of the Dirty Devil, one over the

Colorado at Narrow Canyon and the third over White Canyon. Because of the character of the terrain in there—hard to believe unless you see it for yourself—there is no other feasible way to get automobiles across the canyons. Thus, three big bridges, built at the cost of many million dollars, were required to perform the same service that Art Chaffin's home-designed ferry had provided adequately for eighteen years.

Back to 1953: As we were leaving the river, Mr. Chaffin, glancing at the clouded sky, advised me to watch for flash floods in North Wash.

"North Wash?" I said. "Where's that?"

"Where you're going," he said. "The only road out of here."

We followed the right bank of the river for a couple of miles upstream, rough red cliffs shutting off the view of the mountains and high country beyond. The sky was dark. The willows on the banks were lashing back and forth under a brisk wind, and a few raindrops exploded against the windshield.

Somebody suggested camping for the night beside the river, waiting out the storm. A good idea. But there was one idiot in our party who was actually *hoping* to see a flash flood. And he prevailed. In the late afternoon, under a turbulent sky, we turned away from the river and drove into a deep, narrow canyon leading west and north, where the road (you might call it that) wound up and out, toward the open country twenty miles above. According to my road map. Which also said, quote, *Make local inquiry before attempting travel in this area.*

A good canyon. A little creek came down it, meandering between vertical walls. The road crossed that stream about ten times per mile, out of necessity. I tested the brakes occasionally. Wet drums. No brakes. But it hardly mattered, since we were ascending. The sprinkling of rain had stopped, and everyone admired the towering canyon walls, the alcoves and grottoes, the mighty boulders strewn about on the canyon floor. The air was cool and sweet, the tamarisk and redbud and box elders shivered in the breeze on their alluvial benches. Flowers bloomed, as I recall. Birds chirruped now and then, humble and discreet.

I became aware of a deflating tire and stopped the pickup in the middle of the wash, spanning the rivulet of clear water. It was the only level place immediately available.

Our girl friends walked ahead up the road while my buddy and I jacked up the truck and pulled the wheel. We checked the tire and found that we'd picked up a nail, probably by the Hite store.

We were standing there bemused and barefooted, in the stream, when we heard the women begin to holler from somewhere out of sight up the canyon. Against the noise of the wind, and something like a distant waterfall, it was hard to make out their words.

Mud? Blood? Flood?

As we stood there discussing the matter I felt a sudden surge in the flow of water between my ankles. Looking down, I saw that the clear water had turned into a thick, reddish liquid, like tomato soup.

Our spare tire was packed away beneath a load of duffle, pots and pans and grub boxes. So we jammed the flat tire back on and lugged it down quick with a couple of nuts. My friend picked up the hub cap before it floated away with the rest of the wheel nuts, and stared up the canyon. We couldn't see anything yet but we could hear it—a freight train rolling full speed down North Wash. Where there never was a railway.

We jumped in the truck, I started the motor and tried to drive away. The engine roared but nothing moved. One wheel still jacked off the ground. No positive traction in that pickup. We had to get out again; we pushed the truck forward, off the jack, and discovered that it was in gear. The truck humped ahead and stalled. The main body of the flood appeared around the bend up canyon. We got back in the truck and lurched and yawed, flat tire flopping, out of the bottom of the wash and onto the safety of higher ground. The flood roared past below.

The girls joined us. There was no rain where we stood, and the ground was dry. But we could feel it tremble. From within the flood, under the rolling red waters, we heard the grating of rocks as they clashed on one another, a sound like the grinding of molars in leviathan jaws.

Our road was cut off ahead and behind. We camped on the bench that evening, made supper in the violet twilight of the canyon while thousands of cubic tons of semiliquid sand, silt, mud, rock, uprooted junipers, logs, a dead cow, rumbled by twenty feet away.

The juniper fire smelled good. The food was even better. A few clear stars switched on in that narrow slot of sky between the canyon walls overhead. We built up the fire and sang. My girl friend was beautiful. My friend's girl friend was beautiful. My old pickup truck was beautiful, and life itself seemed like a pretty good deal.

Sometime during the night the flood dropped off and melted away, almost as abruptly as it had come. We awoke in the morning to the music of canyon wrens and a trickling stream, and found that our road was still in the canyon, though kind of folded over and tucked in and rolled up in corners here and there. It took us considerable roadwork and all day long to get out of North Wash. And it was worth every minute of it. Never had such interesting work again till the day I tried to take a Hertz rental Super-Sport past Squaw Spring and up Elephant Hill in The Needles. Or the time another friend and I carried his VW Beetle down through Pucker Pass off Dead Horse Point after a good rain.

At North Wash we had a midday rest at Hog Spring, halfway out. We met a prospector in a jeep coming in. He said we'd never make it. Hogwash. We said he'd never make it. He looked as pleased as we were, and went on.

Today the old North Wash trail road is partly submerged by the reservoir, the rest obliterated. The state has ripped and blasted and laid an asphalt highway through and around the area to link the new tin bridges with the outside world. The river is gone, the ferry is gone, Dandy Crossing is gone. Most of the formerly primitive road from Blanding west has been improved beyond recognition. All of this, the engineers and politicians and bankers will tell you, makes the region easily accessible to everyone, no matter how fat, feeble or flaccid. That is a lie.

It is a lie. For those who go there now, smooth, comfortable, quick and easy, sliding through as slick as grease, will never be able to see what we saw. They will never feel what we felt. They will never know what we knew, or understand what we cannot forget.

Drunk in the Afternoon

I'VE ALWAYS WANTED to write a story about getting drunk in the afternoon. Getting drunk in the afternoon was something I once did on a regular, weekly basis for many years. Me and my friends, such as they were. I say "were" because most of them are now dead, have disappeared or—making a transitive verb of it as in carefree colorful romantic Latin America—have *been* disappeared.

Alan was one. Fred made two, Bob the third.

These are fictitious names. The originals might have wives, children, family still living. Of course they do.

Friday was our favorite day of the operation, since none of us had classes on Saturday. We were students at the University of New Mexico when neither that university nor that state were much known outside of little circles in Carmel, Santa Monica, Cambridge, Greenwich Village, North Beach or Palma de Mallorca.

I'm talking about 1946–50. The three of us were World War II vets, G.I. Joes loafing through school on something called the G.I. Bill. Government issue: everything in the American world had somehow become Government issue. And we didn't object one bit. We were anarchists. The Govern-

From *Northwest: The Sunday Oregonian,* July 30, 1989

ment had only recently tried to kill us, tried hard and seriously, shipping us overseas to Italy where people we had never met or even heard of, perfect strangers, did their best to shoot us dead with Mauser rifles, Luger pistols, burp guns, mortar fire, screaming Mimi's, the Anzio Express.

We met for lunch at Okie Joe's, an all-male beer joint right off campus. We began with a pitcher of beer. Then hamburgers to help absorb the second pitcher. When the third pitcher was empty, we swaggered outside into the blaze of the New Mexico sun. I mean a desert sun, unmitigated by clouds, unmediated by humidity. We were a mile above sea level and the sun only about one mile higher. You could feel the flames.

Appearance is reality, said Lucretius, taking a tip from Epicurus and Democritus, and I thought he had it about right.

I was a philosophy major. Second lieutenant anyhow. Alan was crazy for economics, Fred for math, Bob for political science—politics. And we had plans. I mean plans for reshaping things a little nearer to the natural desires of the human heart.

WE CLIMBED into Alan's car, a black Lincoln convertible about twelve years old. Beaten but functional. The doors worked but we climbed in, over the doors. Why not? Why the hell not? The top was down. I mean the top was always down, and why not? It never rained in New Mexico anyway, and if it did we'd simply drive faster, that's all, speed forward beneath the rain. Let it rain.

Fred pulled a pint of bourbon from his inside jacket pocket, unscrewed the cap, breaking the seal, and threw the cap away. Overboard. Into the abyss of eternity. My concept, his bottle cap, Alan's terminology, Bob's perception.

We headed north along the Rio Grande River on a street called—I forget what it was called. I'm not sure I knew even then. Probably it was called Rio Grande Street. Gone now, anyhow, superseded by eight lanes of stinking asphalt, the Interstate, or by something like Calle de Valle Oro or some such land-developer's poesy.

And we always called the river the Rio Grande River. Any objections? We were veterans. Me and my friends had pushed the Germans all the way from Salerno to the Alps. With 40 million Italians trying to help out.

The wind roared over our heads. The sun roared down—yes, you could hear it bellowing. Like a crown fire in a forest. Like a blast furnace with the hatch open. Bellowing, screaming, howling, the cry of the hydrogen inferno.

We heard and felt it and we raced north at eighty miles an hour in that black open speedboat of a car.

Passing the pint around. Shouting at each other. Rosy mountains on the east, the black warts of old volcanoes on the west, the brown desert and the skinny river in between.

We discussed my new model for the moral universe. Romantic naturalism, I called it. All values grounded upon the new. Only change, I argued, makes life possible, therefore all that is good is necessarily derived from—novelty.

The flaw in my scheme was that word "novelty." Somehow it lacked the weight and dignity of, say, "Sein" or "Neant" or "Process" or "Reality" or even "Frijoles." Think of refried frijoles. The intractable density of matter. Think of nausea.

THE PINT was near empty. We stopped at the next village, Alameda, for refueling. The bar was called La Cantina Contenta. A number of locals sat on a bench in the shade by the open door, watching us climb from the car. Bob fell down but rose quickly, brushed his pants and led the way. Nobody laughed. The sunlight, bouncing off whitewashed adobe walls, burned our eyes. The locals muttered to each other in Spanish, avoiding stares. Fred and Bob were large fellows, bulky, and carried knives strapped to their belts.

Inside it was so dark we stumbled into each other, feeling our way toward the bar. Alan ordered four long-necked bottles of Lone Star, a fair regional beer from Dallas, Texas. Fred bought another bottle of bourbon, a full quart this time. Old Crow. He checked the seal. We all had money in our pockets. This was early in the month; our G.I. checks had arrived only two days before.

Bob found the jukebox and played our cantina theme, an old ranchero song: *Adios, muchachos, compañeros de mi vida.* A Zapatista song, but applicable to World War II. We liked it. We loved it. It was a big hit that year. I pulled out some greenbacks and ordered drinks for every fatherless biped in the house. A safe gesture; there seemed to be only four or five campesinos lounging about in the darkness. I could afford it. As soon as the bartender started pouring, however, the men outside heard the news and hurried in.

But I could afford it. I had sixty dollars in my pocket. Saludas! we greeted one another, all ten or eleven of them, the four of us. Everybody, everybody, joined the chorus. Good-bye boys, buddies of my life. Comrades. Pals. Brothers. Mates. Hadn't Mexico also declared war on the Axis? Yes, I think it did.

Maybe it didn't, but Mexico, New Mexico, Anglo and Chicano, we were all in this cool dark stinking little barroom together, if only for the moment.

Outside, early afternoon, the white light poured down with pure, divine intensity, forced the green leaves of the cottonwoods to shake and rustle, made the street's pale dust shimmer like a carpet of crystals, gave every shadow a hard edge and a deep absolute obscurity. Alan's black car, outlined in auras of reflected heat, floated six inches above the ground. We could see it through the open doorway, baking in the sun. We could see the two little boys on the far side of the car, removing a hubcap with a big screwdriver. The bartender ran out and drove them off, waving his arms, shouting. He set the hubcap, open side up, like a plate, on the bar before us.

Fred explained his theory of irrational numbers, binary electives and organic equations. Would lead, he argued, when he found the key connection, to a kind of cybernetic thinking machine that could digest numerical data in such quantity and at such velocity that science itself would make a quantum leap into whole new dimensions of power over nature.

Got too much power already, Bob argued, following Alan out into the blaze of light. We blinked, we staggered, we crawled up over the gunwales of the open boat and flopped inside. Four of us in the front seat, nobody in the rear except a case of beer that Alan had acquired somehow, as we left. Elbows and impacted ribs, shoulders jammed, we shuffled the bottle left and right as somebody, Alan perhaps, piloted the car northward under the spangled light of the trees, up the dusty street scattering chickens, pursued by yapping curs, the final passionate farewells of our new friends at La Cantina Contenta still resounding in our ears, minds, blood, corazones. *Mi corazon es su corazon, compadre.* Remember that.

Power is our destiny, Fred argued in return. We are bound for Andromeda and beyond. The Earth is but a footstool to the stars. God is our goal, God is our fate, and by God if God doesn't exist we shall create the S.O.B.

The wind howled, the sun screamed, the motor sang.

Red-tail hawks squinted at us from the telephone poles, one hawk per mile, regular as command posts along the Manfred Line. One black buzzard soared above, waiting. The red needle crept to seventy, eighty, eighty-five.

I never saw so blue a sky. A sky so bloody blue, so deeply transparent you could see infinity through it, the fine-grained blackness of outer space, the stellar clouds of the Horsehead Nebula.

We stopped at Algodones, next town up the road, for brief refreshment. Bob's turn to stand us all a round, and he knew it. Alan performed a four-wheel drift on the plaza dust. Nice old mission church there, two wooden bell towers mounted on adobe walls four feet thick. Black crosses. Golden light. Magpies screeching in the cornfields. The bar did not have a name and didn't need one. Like the other it was black as a pit inside, cool, roomy, not crowded yet, stinking of stale beer and male sweat and dried urine, the way we liked it.

We ordered tequila, salt, limes. The management had no limes. Nor lemons neither. *Si, no tenemos lemones.*

Who needs fruit, explained Bob.

We poured salt on our wrists, tipped off a shot of tequila, licked the salt, drank a second, chased it with beer, licked salt, felt good, shoved one another around a bit and rambled out into the heat and the light.

WHO'S DRIVING this car? Alan? Who's that under the wheel? Nobody's driving. We're all driving. Who's in charge here? We're all in charge. This here's America, my friends, this here's democracy, and if somebody doesn't step a little harder on the gas we'll never get to Santa Fe.

Pit stop! yelled Fred.

Brake drums screamed. The car lurched from the pavement, fishtailed through a hedge of rabbit brush, bounded down the embankment of the roadway into a ravine.

Hang on! I shouted or somebody shouted. Or maybe we only thought it.

The Lincoln leaped from a four-foot cutbank and crashed onto a crust of red sand. A cloud of dust engulfed us.

Don't stop! Fred shouted. Keep going.

Alan, Bob, me, whoever was driving, kept the wheels spinning as we sashayed across the sand toward the mud bank on the opposite side, a thicket of chamisa, a grove of cottonwoods. We pulled into the shade, rammed a tree trunk, halted. The engine died. We piled out, clutching beer bottles by the neck.

We stared at the sky. Our little auburn-colored dust cloud floated past. Far above, black against blue, redheaded against the infinite darkness of the universe, the solitary vulture cruised in lazy spirals, contemplating life, contemplating us. Where there's life, the vulture reasons, there is also death. And where there's death there's hope.

Bob knelt in the grass and weeds, vomiting. Terrible sounds, terrible, the death rattle of a dying soldier. But he'd feel better when he was finished.

Hot water streamed from the mashed radiator of the car.

Fred opened another beer, handed it to me, opened another for himself and another for Alan. My friends, he said, my good comrades, buddies, pals, compañeros de mi vida, let me tell you something. I want to tell you guys something you will always remember, never forget. I want you to remember this glorious moment, this radiant damn hour, this splendid shining immortal day, for the rest of our miserable lives.

We got home that night, some way. We graduated from that New Mexico cow college a month later. We wandered off in various directions. For a few years we exchanged letters, then postcards, then Christmas cards, then nothing. That was thirty-seven years ago. I don't know anything about any of them now.

Journal IV

November 10, 1951—Edinburgh, Scotland

O H ! F O R L O V E , for the painfully nourished, tenderly cherished, sweet frenzied illusion, the known-illusion within the globule of sentimental cynicism. For romantic love, then, I sacrifice honor, decency, human kindness, charity, honesty, friendship and the future—all, (ah!) for love! Let this simple valediction be my benediction, and this nonsense my good sense in this, the latest and God help me the last, of my sordid adventures in humanity . . .

The grim grimy grisly details can be of little interest; look them up in my official biography. What matters is the heart of the affair, the whistling spirit behind the facade of surface data; guilt, the sense of guilt, and who am I to sacrifice not only my own but perhaps another's happiness upon the bloody stinking altar of romantic love?

Yes indeed, but here we go despite all. All for love? Again, yes again! Yes.

> *The harlot's cry from street to street*
> *Shall weave old England's winding sheet.*

From *Confessions of a Barbarian: Selections from the Journals of Edward Abbey, 1951–1989* (1994)

Edinburgh. A soft gray loveliness, fog-shrouded, gray-green, gray-blue, gray-gray, mauve, melting, misting over, grave. And old, with the stench of ages old, built up on packed and repacked mounds of human charnel: excrement, dead bones, blood-woven earth soaked in saltwater urine and piled over high the heaped-up bodies of the dead and dying.

Medieval, yes; dark-aged, grim ecclesiastical spire-populated, spire-pointed, steeple-spired, gothic-inspired, a clawing toothy saber-toothy jag-ragged sky-scratching skyline, spear-clutching sky-bound city; soul fleeing earth. The slimy streets, the smeary streets, the slime-smear-shining streets: dung, piss, spit, snot and ever-present wetness, water, fish blood, foggy sky, smoky, pressed down by its own weight upon the city's streets.

Dark.

Grave.

A dusky graveyard of the lithe lissome spirit, possibly—I'll make no verdicts there. Smoke-fog everywhere, a heavy foggy smoggy sky pushed damply down upon the city under its own foul-filthy fatness, dump-lidded bosom-sky.

Scruff from an itching scalp.

A shod horse on a cobbled street is a whistling echo from the dimmest past, a fifty-years = fifty-thousand light-years ago past. Lost voices wind-borne from the ghostly past. The ghostly ghastly past, aghast against the past.

> *Prometheus Bounded Up and Down*
> *From a Crag in the Caucasus*

NO MORE OF THIS NONSENSE, ABBEY!

THREE TRAMPS: A novel vindicating the philosophy of adventure & disorder, soaked in the democratic popular culture of contemporary U.S.A. (A modern *Huckleberry Finn*?) Three grown men, one a Negro, wander from California to Texas and Louisiana and back (maybe), singing, guitar-playing, whoring, stealing, talking, a paean to irresponsibility. The climax might be an attempted lynching in the South.

Philosophical Correlative = the values of the earthbound sensuous life (value in adventure, too) against a background of cosmic melancholia: freight trains, used cars, bad jobs, blues and hillbillies, out on the desert, mountain cabin, ghost town. Mexico, New Orleans, fine drunks (*Tortilla Flat* stuff?); rain on the roof, fire in the stove, venison hanging from the rafters, a case of beer on the floor; Pure Sentimentality, emphasizing equality, liberty, good living, brotherhood; change and adventure and uncertainty made both real and ideal.

Everything. I'll throw everything in. Whole hog. Hog wild. A great big fat beautiful obscene book, the most hilarious, tear-jerking, side-splitting, throat-choking, belly-busting, heartbreaking book ever written. Don't forget the book *in* the book. (The proper place for parody.)

Throw everything in? Maybe you'd better throw in the towel.

[MANUEL] DE FALLA'S Harpsichord Concerto; *Greensleeves*—another of the farawaymysticalstrangelyhauntinghearttroubling melodies.

Imagine the thrill of the composer, hearing a smudgefaced child in the street singing a tune of his; hearing, by the sea—the great curve of sand, leaning trees, clouds, gulls, crags, the wind-whistle, the waves larrup, the screebirds' cry, the vaulting distance echo—a personal music.

There is a music in me, too, not much yet but growing. I'll have to soon put in a stretch at some conservatory, getting the means to release this musical pressure. Nothing in the literary or ideational can fully express it. Two or three symphonies, a handful of songs, things for flutes, piano, guitar, timpani, harp, Indian drums, Indian themes, the Indian desert world.

THE WALKING WONDER, the PENTARACHNID, the rolling pictographic crypto-man, all legs, arms, backwardlooking head, all feet and hands, quintesticled. [Abbey's sketches of this five-limbed anthropomorphic tumbleweed figure appear scores of times throughout the early journals.]

EVERYTHING IN THE UNIVERSE converges upon me.

I radiate light upon everything in the universe.

I am an egocentric predicament (and love it!).

I find arrows shooting, rockets streaming spaceward, most fascinating—no doubt because I am a sex maniac.

NEEDED: "A General Theory of Anarchism" outlining aims, methods, metaphysical justification and teleological value (Principle of Evolutionary Differentiation). Try H. Read [Sir Herbert], Bakunin, Geronimo, Proudhon, Kropotkin, Tolstoy.

SOCIETY AND SOLITUDE—another significant polarity. What influence does or can a certain landscape have over a person? Should the great desert (for example) provoke moods, feelings and finally permanent traits of expansive openness, broadness, universality, oneness with the natural world, a cosmic (subspecies *eternitatis*) outlook? Or would it result in an analogous aridity, sterility, death-dealing and stalking? The mountain ... the great space ... what happens there to the human spirit?

The human world of artifice and imagination can never equal the richness and variety and wonder of the real natural nonhuman world. But man belongs to the world; he is no more enemy or alien than the saguaro, the jaguar or the spinning spider.

Science can tell us *what* is happening, and *how*, but surely not *why*. And even then, scientific explanations are always hypothetical, of limited certitude and subject to change without notice.

In other words, there is no good reason to assume that the world was constructed, or constructs itself, to fit an *a priori* mathematical scheme. Rather, we construct mathematical schemes to fit the world. (This looks like an unabashed nominalism.) An important question following this, then, is: What limitations does this place upon science and upon our knowledge in general?

If the world is irrational, we can never know it (either it or its irrationality)?

THE ABBEY CURSE: In my opinion all Abbeys suffer from a family blood curse, invoked somewhere in the dim past by unknown Enemies and as malignant and powerful in its operations today as ever it might have been in the past. Its prevailing effects are (1) miserable loneliness (2) constant disunity and friction, disintegration (3) heartbreaking aspirations (4) social failure and trouble.

THE PROMETHEAN GESTURE:

> *"This is the glory of earthborn men and women*
> *not to cringe, never to yield, but standing,*
> *take defeat implacable and defiant*
> *die unsubmitting."*

NOT BABY-KILLERS, these latter-day Papists, but mother-killers. (What a monstrous "morality" it is that would let good mothers die for the sake of one more digit in the number of souls in Heaven! "Let the known and loved personality die; we *must* baptize that embryo!") The spiritual life.

ABOUT TIME, my friend, about time to think about the book, the first spasmodic effort of the reluctant soul harrowing itself for something to say; do I have something to say? Your goddamned ass I have something to say!
What?
You call me, sir, a rank materialist—sir, I accept the appellation and I accept with pride, sir, and glory. Never shall this flower of the spirit reject the good earth from which it grows—never shall I live in an alabaster spirit-city, separated from my mother by concrete or gold, by white robes, ineffables, or multicolored sewage and communication systems, not this nigger, no sir!
I celebrate the Earth, my home, my mother, my grave, and as long as men are Man they must, if they would preserve the integrated being, do the same—[and preserve] with it the body—this rank casual hungry smelly sweaty lusting transitory body, my oozy pulpy liquid-bag-swollen body, bones, blood, hair, glands, my bejeweled sex; I love and celebrate it all. Never to let men forget that they are animals as much as gods—that is one thing I shall say.
From the above, certain theorems naturally derive: If the earth and the animal are valuable, then every earthborn man and woman, every animal, has an inherent right to a portion of this earth, to its produce, to its free air, its seas, sands, mountains, deserts and sunrises—this means some kind of socialism, social justice, economic democracy, decentralized, voluntary, cooperative; and a spacious commonwealth, with lots of room for all (birth control) in the Green Utopia. Here is something to fight for that will never desert me in my lifetime.
The free man I sing, the anti-authoritarian, the libertine; material for several volumes in this theme.
The common man, too, the everyday ordinary hardworking family man—someone someday must write a book about him. Mine, perhaps, the small southwestern rancher with his starved cows, pickup, kids, windmill.
PASSION: passion-light must be brought back into Literature. If no one else can or will do it, I must.

FOR THE TRAVEL BOOK on Europe (*Rolled Over on Europe?*):

France. France is that country which must be traversed by any traveler going from Britain to Germany, Switzerland, Italy or Spain, or by any traveler going from one of those countries to Britain. (If you can afford it, take an airplane.)

Paris. Paris is the capital of France.

England. After a few months in England, one finds that one likes the Scotch very much.

I'VE DECIDED to be a regional writer. My region will be the U.S.A., Mexico. Guatemala, Easter Island, Spain, Isle of Skye, Persia, Kenya, South Africa, Australia, New Zealand and Tasmania. Area posted. Squatters are warned. Prosecution. Fine.

Art of the Novel: Maximizing order in maximum chaos—complex symmetry as opposed to simple symmetry—simultaneity—counterpoint and contrary motion—the novel should appeal primarily to the intellect; for the emotions there is music, for the senses, color and form.

SIBELIUS, the First [symphony]—the lean prelude and then the lightning's flash, the thunder's roll, the strike and strike again! Then later, quiet interludes, tho always present the sense of tension, of something coming, something straining to be free, to . . . how the distant music plays upon, pulls at, turns over and echoes thru the listening heart—the incredible wistful dim dreaming distant impossible promise—how sure and certain that here, for once, the music speaks of something more than itself, of something beyond itself, not a place, not an idea, not a story, but something, some kind of deep aesthetic intuition—a memory? An anticipation? A vision? A symbol of emotion?

But what kind of sentimental gush is all this? Am I taking a cue from the music and drifting down into pretty fantasy? Possibly—oh, but why should I not? There is too much simple loveliness here to be scorned, too much meaning and truth to be ignored. I'll not be the one to try to back down the old man—let him stand. Love him. And listen. Listen. Awake, sleepers, dogmatic slumberers . . . listen here to the voice of innocence, the song. . . .

II

Ed: The Early Years

IN DECEMBER of 1952 Ed married Rita Deanin, the mother of his first two sons, Joshua and Aaron. Within a year they were in New Haven in search of Ed's doctorate in philosophy at Yale (Rita waited tables at a Howard Johnson). They lasted exactly thirteen days.

During the balance of the fifties, Abbey worked at a variety of jobs, earned an M.A., published *Jonathan Troy* (1954), a less than satisfactory novel about an inconstant and inauthentic writer-anarchist who is an early stand-in for the fictional Abbey; in 1956 he published *The Brave Cowboy*, in which Ed introduced a more substantial (and longer-lived) anarchist named Jack Burns. Kirk Douglas, who played the Burns character in the movie version, *Lonely Are the Brave*, considered the maverick antihero Burns, who fights rich and powerful ranchers and government toads, his best movie role. Though Jack Burns is apparently killed escaping the police (he's run over by a truck carrying plumbing supplies), he returns to star in two later Abbey novels: *Good News* (1982) and *Hayduke Lives!* (1990).

Ed's tumultuous, on-again/off-again marriage to Rita, an artist who became an art historian, took him to Hoboken and New York City ("Manhattan Twilight, Hoboken Night," p. 85), with longer stops in Utah and Nevada, New Mexico and Arizona. He worked as a park ranger, fire lookout, garbage collector, welfare caseworker and school-bus driver (after Rita split). *Desert*

Solitaire recounts Abbey's passionate impressions of life and beauty (and decay) during three seasons at Arches National Monument (now Arches National Park). Written while Ed lived in New Mexico, Hoboken and between runs driving schoolkids in Ash Meadow, Nevada, the book reveals the full-blooded passions of a voice exploring the connections and contradictions, as Abbey put it, "between wildness, wilderness and human community."

Abbey's twenty years (almost) as a part-time employee of the feds, as park and forest ranger, could be seen as a continuation of his role as an MP. Smokey the Bear is today an enforcer who packs a .38; Ed's essay "My Life as a P.I.G., or The True Adventures of Smokey the Cop," p. 153, explains his statement "I've never known a serious policeman who had much respect for the law."

Ed was also railing against the lawlessness of special-interest government. Freedom and wilderness (two necessary parts of the democratic equation) were disappearing. Control of the Republic, he despaired, had moved into the hands of fix-and-favor lobbyists, businessmen and politicians: fat cats—whether in Washington, Wall Street, Aspen or high in the saddle—had turned over government-owned land for private gain at taxpayers' expense, especially in the eleven western states. Even the good guys, the brothers Udall (Moe and Stew), for example, couldn't be trusted. Look at the Central Arizona Project, at what happened to the Colorado River, the drowning of Glen Canyon. Abbey's only answer, *the* only answer, he would say, quietly and politely, time and time again, is to spread chaos, to follow old Henry David down the road of civil disobedience, *vigorously*. Wasn't private property, despite the propaganda about competition and market economics, little more than theft? And what about special-interest socialism, the private uses of public land for timber or cattle barons? Ed's beliefs were outside "the system," any system, even his own, and the words were delivered in a voice as personal and distinctive as Emerson's.

                                                                      J.M.

From The Fool's Progress

Y OU WHAT? Got a new job. What do you mean you got a new job? I
mean I got a new job. What about the old job—the assistantship?
Sank it; I quit. What do you mean you quit? I mean I got fired. Fired—what
do you mean? I flunked the orals. You flunked the orals? Yep. You've
got to be kidding. Nope. Henry, your whole career depends on getting that
M.A. this semester. Not now it don't. What do you mean—and stop talking
like a peasant. I mean I got a new career. What do you *mean* you've
got a new career? I mean a new career. Like what? State Highway Department. What? New Mexico State Highway Department; we're paving the
road from here to Albuquerque. We? Yep, we, me and the boys. And that's
your new job? Yes'm. You're going to shovel asphalt out of a truck? No, I'm
gonna inspect asphalt. You'll what? I'll be workin' for the state, not the contractor; we inspect the stuff, keep them up to standards. So you're going to
inspect asphalt? my husband is going to be an inspector of asphalt? Well,
someday; right now I'm only an asphalt inspector trainee. Henry, I don't believe this. Sorry, Myra. I can't believe it. I know, honey, but goddamnit you
should've seen those smug bastards sitting there in that office staring at me.
But you've ruined your life. I know. Don't you care? I suppose. Do you
really want to be an asphalt inspector? Not really. And what about our
married life—suppose I'm pregnant? What kind of a life can we give

our baby? I don't know. I thought you knew everything. I know. I hate
know-it-alls. I know it.

HE ALSO FILED job applications with the U.S. Forest Service and the
National Park Service. What he really wanted, perhaps, was to ride a horse
through the primeval forest while composing poetry—a verse in the wilderness!—or guide timid but willing young lady tourists up mountain trails toward the giddy summit of their mutual desires. He knew or had heard that
such pleasant work was available on a seasonal basis from time to time, at
one place or another, and that his college diploma (B.A., thirty-third per-
centile) made him eligible and his not dishonorable discharge from the wartime Army of the United States gave him a five-point veteran's preference
over other applicants. He mailed off the official forms, with covering letter,
to three different national parks and forgot about them. Meanwhile he inspected the asphalt.

Eight hours a day five days a week Henry dug circular core samples from
hot asphalt paving before the steamrollers reached it, lugged his samples into
the NM Hwy Dept's mobile housetrailer laboratory and subjected them to a
series of tests and analyses. The procedures were simple and routine, the
mathematical formulas cut, dried and preestablished, the quality standards
highly adaptable, depending on the mood of the supervisor, the amount of
the payoff, the political influence of the contractor.

Every day he saw the chief inspector and the construction company fore-
man engaged in private discussion at the far end of the trailer lab. The thundering and continual boom of the asphalt plant twenty yards up the road
drowned out their words. Black smoke billowed over the trailer, infiltrated
the ventilation system. He worked in a world of pitch, tar, gravel, sand, smoke,
oil, bombinating uproar, blatant corruption and the rich gentlemanly smell of
bitumen. He drove his pickup home in the evening with face and hands and
neck blackened as a coal miner's. He might as well have been back in West
Virginia.

Henry built up the fire in the kitchen stove and carried in six buckets of
water, half filling the galvanized tub. When the water became hot he climbed
in and scrubbed himself, using a rough brush and a cake of gray gritty Lava
soap. Splashing soapy water everywhere, stove lids sizzling.

Myra stood in the doorway in her paint-smeared artist's smock, a spatter
of paint on her nose and eyebrows. (Highly arched, distinguished brows, he
thought, above intelligent and mocking eyes.) She watched him, her man her

husband (good God!) wiping the dried sweat and smeared soot from his face upon a clean rag and said, Happy now? Satisfied?

It's okay. You're okay. I'm okay. He got out of the tub, swabbed himself vigorously with a big towel. It's them other folks are in bad shape.

Stop talking like a fool. You threw away four years of graduate school to become an asphalt inspector.

Trainee. It's only temporary. He pulled on his jeans. No underwear.

Trainee. And now look at you. How am I supposed to explain this to my family? How can I explain it to myself?

Henry smiled, putting on a clean shirt. Remember what your father said. "Sleep over with him, liff around with him but for the luff of Gott *marry* him? Him for a husband you twist the knife in my heart."

He never said any such thing.

That's what you told me.

And don't you make fun of my poor old father either. He's dying, you know.

Everybody dies. He's almost sixty years old. He makes too much fuss about it.

Her eyes grew narrow. You cruel bastard. You cruel heartless pig. He's a better man than you'll ever be. He worked all his life. He provided for his family. He never cheated on his wife. He's a good man, a good kind honest man. . . . The tears welled up in her eyes.

Henry stopped buttoning the shirt. Sorry, Myra. I'm sorry I said that. He reached for her, tried to embrace her. She struck his arms away, turned her back to him. Honest, honey, I'm sorry. That was a stupid thing to say.

How would you feel if you had to go through heart surgery over and over?

I don't know. But he thought: Men who know how to live know how to die.

Maybe you wouldn't be so brave either.

I know. Although . . . The devil whispered in his ear. I guess I wouldn't have to clip my toenails anymore.

What a bastard you are. How can you *be* such a rotten, cheap bastard.

It's hard. He embraced her from behind, spoke softly in her ear. I'm sorry. He'll be all right. They'll fix him up, it happens all the time. People live with it. They go on.

She stood sobbing in his arms, her back against him. He bent and kissed the delicate skin of her neck, the tender flesh below the ears, and murmured in her hair. Please, honey, let's not talk about it. Think about Sunday. He unbuttoned his jeans, letting them fall to his shanks.

What about Sunday?

The party, beautiful, the party. Our grand opening. Roast goat. *Cabrito*. Champagne punch, wine, Ritz crackers, four different kinds of surplus commodity cheese. (What a friend we have in cheeses.) The housewarming, honey. All your friends are gonna be here. We have forty people pledged to show up. *The* social event of the season. We might even, who knows, sell a couple of—paintings? He lifted her big globed breasts in his hands. Hey? Whatta you say? He nudged her against the kitchen table, bending her forward over the edge. He lifted the stiff smock and tugged down on her baggy dungarees.

No, she said, not now. She rolled from beneath him and stalked out of the room, hoisting her pants high around her waist.

Her husband gaped after her with outspread pleading arms—useless. Hobbled by the copper-riveted jeans around his ankles, he made no attempt to pursue. With breaking heart, his rejected aching hard-on twitching high in the air, he whined like a sick hound, Myra . . . my Myra . . . my only Myra. . . .

The sound of one door slamming.

Pause.

He looked at his good right hand. Still couldn't see, after all these years, any hairs growing out of the palm. Nor was he any crazier than before. Masturbation is a lonely art, he reflected, but there's this to be said in its favor: you do build a good relationship with yourself.

UNDISMAYED and undeterred, Henry Lightcap made his preparations. Saturday morning he bought a young he-goat from a neighbor, one Cipriano Peralta Santiago Morales; after forty-five minutes of friendly haggling he got the price down from $20 to $6.50 with a lead rope thrown in for free. He led the frisky little fella home and tethered him to a dead tree in the orchard. The goat began at once to graze on the dry stubble, the tumbleweed, the old yellowed newspapers and the bark of the tree. It was not a fat goat but big for its age; the little horns were twice the size of Henry's thumbs.

Taking his spade, Henry dug a knee-deep pit in the soft dirt of what had once been a garden. The goat watched through the slotted pupils of its eyes, perturbed by some image from its racial unconscious, then returned to feeding. Henry lined his pit with stones and filled it with well-cured applewood, stacked log-cabin style to form a well-drawing pyre. He cut and piled more dead applewood nearby. Almost noon by the sun. Henry pulled a whetstone from its sheath and began to sharpen his knife.

The goat heard, looked and bolted, breaking off the rope at the base of the tree. Henry ran, trapped it between a corner of the house and the barbed-wire fence and caught it with a diving tackle. Should hang him up first by the hind feet, he thought, alive, then slit the throat. But that wouldn't be easy now. Sitting on the goat's back, he drew his pocketknife and flipped it open, yanked the hard head up and backward—the calm yellow-green eyes stared into his. O Death, thou comest when I had thee least in mind. Henry could feel the violent beating of the animal's heart, the surging lift and fall of lungs and rib case beneath his own 180 pounds of human weight, human power, human domination, human greed. Good God, he thought, I can't do it. I can't do it. Cursing, he sliced the keen edge of the blade across the goat's throat and did it.

There was no further struggle; the beast died quietly. Henry hung it by the pasterns to a tree near the fire pit.

Feeling sick and hollow, he let the goat complete its bleeding, catching the blood in a pail, then gutted it—dropping the steaming viscera on spread-out newspapers—and skinned the animal clean. Flayed, the young goat looked pale as a dead baby. A few flies gathered but not many; the air was chill, silent clouds floating across the face of the sun. Henry lit his fire, pausing to watch the flames rise and dance.

Myra stepped out on the back porch of the store to drop rags and papers into the trash barrel. She stopped and stared. Her husband, with blood-smeared hands, forearms, face, knelt at the side of a blazing pit. Behind him, a naked child hung upside-down from a dead tree.

Henry. Good God.

He stared back, grinned: *Cabrito,* Myra. Goat. We got to feed our guests. Got to get things ready.

She stared at him, the goat, the fire. Disgusting, she muttered, but he thought he saw a sneaking admiration in her eyes. Hell, she was a carnivore too; hadn't Henry felt her sharp teeth often enough? Disgusting, she repeated, returning to her studio.

He wrapped the unwanted organs and guts in several layers of newspaper—setting aside heart, liver, kidneys—and stashed them for the time being on the roof of the tool shed, shady side, beyond reach of the village dogs. He weighted the package down with rocks. Later he'd bury it in the pit in the garden; would make good fertilizer. He stretched the hide on the same roof, tacking it down flesh-side up toward the winter sun, and scraped off the remaining tallow. Goatskin gloves, men. Handbags, ladies.

He took down the goat and laid it in a tub filled with his secret marinade: six bottles of beer plus honey, garlic, red chili and oregano. He soaked it

through the afternoon and into the night, meanwhile keeping a fire going in
the pit. Near midnight, Myra sleeping, Henry wrapped the goat in marinated
cheesecloth and layers of wet burlap and carried it into the dark backyard.

The fire had died to a shimmering bed of red-hot coals. He shoveled most
of the coals from the pit, exposing the glowing stones. He lowered his bundle
into the opening, covered it with wet alfalfa, replaced the hot coals, covered
the coals with dirt and tamped the dirt firm with the back of the shovel. He
put his hand on the bare dirt and felt no warmth. The heat stayed buried
below, doing its work.

Meantime, during the afternoon, Henry had engaged the village band
for Sunday. The band consisted of old man Apodaca, accordionist; old man
Vigil, guitarist; and old man Peralta, fiddler. None were under sixty-five; the
young men of El Culito, busy melting down the springs of their Chevies,
played only radios.

After hiring the band, five dollars per player, he drove his truck to La
Cantina Contenta, Eddie Vigil, Prop., and bought the essential ingredients
for a proper art-salon soiree: ten gallons of Gallo Brothers Dago Red, a keg of
beer, a magnum of La Corona Superlativa champagne (*hecho en Mexico*),
universally acknowledged to be the world's worst but cheapest champagne.
Myra had insisted on champagne punch for her gallery opening. He also
bought a gallon of Gallo's fine Oakland Bay Chablis to fill out the champagne.

On the way home Henry paused at Mama Vigil's little one-stop general
store for a dollar's worth of gasoline—empty the hose, por favor—and a large
economy bottle of Alka-Seltzer tablets.

This party was costing him a pretty peso, a full week's pay to be precise,
and Myra, when she figured it out, would throw a conniption fit. But really,
what else is money good for? And would there be enough to drink? Naturally
he'd invited everyone in the village to come, as well as his gringo friends to the
north, and if only a tenth of the locals showed up the beer and wine might
drain away fast. But Henry's friends, the wiser heads among them, would
bring booze of their own.

He looked forward with confidence to the consummation of his plans and
hopes.

WILLEM VAN HOSS, that enormous excessive fellow, arrives in the
early afternoon, driving up in clouds of dust and a cold blue wind from the
north. Great belly sagging over his bull rider's buckle, red beard draped over

his chest, black hat clamped on his balding head, he stomps in boots across
the planking of the veranda and bursts into La Galerie, shouting—

"Chinga los cosmos!" He seizes Myra in his arms and crushes her to his
broad frame, kissing her sloppily on mouth and eyes. "You sullen sexy little
slut, what's a girl like you doing in this slum? Let me take you away, away
forever, into the romance and the wonder of Albuquerque." She submits
briefly, helpless but smiling, then slips from his grasp as van Hoss spots Henry
stirring the champagne punch. "Hah, there he is, the lean skulking hillbilly
himself." He strides to Henry and lifts him off his feet with a bear hug, then
drops him, takes the ladle from Henry's fingers and samples the punch. He
makes a face.

"I know," says Henry. "Flat, ain't it." Glancing toward Myra, he sees her
going to the door to greet van Hoss's latest girlfriend, still outside in the car
repainting her face with the aid of a rearview mirror. Henry opens the bottle
of Alka-Seltzer tablets and empties the entire contents into the punch. A ju-
bilant fizzing begins at once in the murky depths of the bowl. He adds a chunk
of dry ice. Billows of vapor rise whirling in the air.

"Lightcap, my friend, my very best friend, you're a scoundrel." Van Hoss
draws a pint of bourbon from his pocket, offers the bottle. "Drink this, Henry,
and let's have a look at this *palacio* of yours."

Henry drinks, returns the bottle, wiping his mouth on back of hand. "First
I want to meet your new lady there."

The girl approaches the table, staring with exaggerated awe at Myra's
huge paintings hung on the walls, then at the red-hot stove in the center of the
gallery, then at the paintings again. She wears a fur coat, black cocktail dress,
high heels; a mane of golden hair spills across her shoulders. She stares boldly
at Henry and he remembers her instantly, a painful twinge of recognition.
The yellow-haired chickadee. . . .

"You like Camus?" he says.

"I love him." Her eyes glow. "How did you know that?"

"We must talk."

"How did you know?"

Henry smiles wisely. "I'm a philosopher too."

Myra butts in, bringing new arrivals to the punch bowl: art students, mod-
els, dancers, a couple of young art-history professors—*her* crowd. Politely
they taste the champagne, toast her new studio, before moving on to the warm
red wine displayed on the table, the keg of beer in the corner.

And now more guests come crowding in as the winter sun goes down, bringing with them the smell of fresh cold air and windblown dust. Dodging his primary responsibilities as host, Henry takes van Hoss on a tour of the property, out the back door and into the garden.

You said her name is Melissa? That's right. And she lives in Papaya Hall? I didn't say, Henry, but that's a good guess; who'd you bury here? *El cabrito.* They kneel to touch the raw mound. Slightly warm, a little heat seeping through, the goat should be ready. She's only a sophomore, Henry, much too young and innocent for the likes of a dog like you; and besides, you're a married man. I'm married but I ain't dead. Henry, Henry, you shock me; you disappoint me; you're in for a life of trouble, young man. I like trouble. Yes you do, Henry, and you'll get it; but in the meantime—. Yeah? Willy's big paw squeezes his shoulder—You'll have to wait your turn.

They take shelter from the wind in the doorway of the farthest room, drawing out the bottle again. Van Hoss throws the cap away. They watch the yellow grit of El Culito swirl in moaning minitornados through the dead trees. Kill it. You kill it. Okay. Henry kills it, tossing the bottle away, and leads his guest back to the studio-gallery by way of the boarded-up, dungeonlike rooms of the north wing, stumbling over loose boards, old bottles, bound stacks of antique magazines—*Woman's Home Companion, Arizona Highways, Ladies' Home Journal, The New Mexico Stockman.*

They go on through floating dust into the master bedroom, where a fire smolders in the big fireplace. The high winds outside are creating a downdraft; wisps of smoke lick over the mantel. Henry adds wood to the flames and as he does so something heavy rattles down the chimney, ricocheting from side to side, and crashes into the ashes. Another fragment of brick. They stoop and attempt to peer up inside the flue but can see only soot, the turbulent smoke. Should check out that chimney, Henry. First thing in the morning, Henry says.

From beyond the door leading to the gallery comes the sound of the El Culito string band and a labored wheezing of accordion—Vigil, Peralta and Apodaca at work.

You should buy this place, Henry, it's a ruin but you should buy it. Why?—I'm the caretaker. How many acres go with it? Fifteen, I think. What's the asking price? Twelve thousand dollars. And how far from town? Twenty miles. Buy it, Henry; ten years from now this place will be worth a cool million; in twenty years three million. Who cares? Albuquerque's growing, my friend, this will become a ritzy suburb; that old mission church across the plaza will make this place a big draw someday—you'll have millionaire trustfunder R. C. Bohemes from Boston, Chicago, New York genuflecting to your dog for a chance to live here. Ain't got a dog, ain't got the twelve thousand dollars, and anyhow I'm a fucking anti-reductionist natural empiric pancreatic philosopher not a fucking real estate developer. What's the difference, Henry? Outlook and insight, that's the difference. Insight maybe, but not much foresight; if you don't buy it I will. You're kidding, Henry says.

They rejoin the party. The dancing has begun. Myra and her friends are waltzing around the room to the creaky but jaunty strains of "La Varsuviana":

> *Put your little foot*
> *Put your little foot*
> *Put your little foot right out . . .*

Straight from the sixteenth-century ballrooms of Old Castile. The existential blonde, aloof and amused, stands alone by the table, so beautiful she intimidates the boys. Van Hoss and Henry bear down upon her but van Hoss gets there first and sweeps her into the ragged quadrille. Henry and old friends Morton Bildad and Jack Roggoway go into the backyard to dig up the goat: time to eat.

Another party, offshoot of the first, is under way outside. Somebody has set fire to Henry's shithouse by dropping a cigarette into the bumhole. A circle of drunken savages, encouraged by bongo drums, prances around the pillar of flames. The blazing shack subsides into its fiery cavity. The dancers leap through the flames, howling with joy. Chaos and old night descend on El Culito.

By the glare of the fire Henry and friends excavate the scapegoat, knock off the hot earth and bear the offering, too hot to touch, on a platter into the hall. They set it on the table among the half-empty wine jugs, the near-empty but still fizzing punch bowl.

Proudly, licking his burned fingers, Henry peels off the singed burlap, then the smoking cheesecloth, to unveil the sacrifice. The hard little head with its horns and blank broasted eyeballs stares at the guests. A woman screams. Only the gourmets of tongue and brain find the head appealing but elsewhere, below the neck, the flesh is a tasty light brown, like breast of turkey, and falls easily from the bones. Bildad, a vegetarian, turns away, chanting his mantra in horror.

Lacking enough flatware, Henry serves the meat buffet-style on paper picnic plates. A few of the women hesitate at first (Good God Henry did you have to leave the head on?) but not for long. He manages to get fair portions to the members of the orchestra and to some of his shyer, soberer village neighbors before the goat is reduced to skull and bones, a rack of ribs, tibia, femur, vertebrae and feet—the mute cloven lightfoot hooves of Pan.

Success. The orchestra, fed and lubricated, resumes its music, the fire rumbles in the stove, the wind fumbles and mumbles under the eaves outside, through the loft, into and out of the attic; sheet metal rattles on the roof. One of the dancers peels down to a black leotard; another leaps onto the table and strips off her dress, revealing her artist-model's figure clothed in nothing but blue and yellow body paint. Inspired, Willem van Hoss advances to the table, bellowing like a bull, unbuttons his fly and lays his great rubicund cock, semierect, upon the boards. He challenges any female in the hall to have a crack at that. Myra picks up a carving knife, van Hoss retreats. Some of the neighbors depart, crossing themselves. Henry delivers his set speech on the joys of voluntary poverty. The dance goes on, the party rages forward, upward, outward, in all directions. Everything that rises must diverge—like a fountain, like the universe, like the branches of the tree of life itself.

HE DREAMED, a downward dream. He dreamed of Hell. He smelled the odor of burning brains, heard the sound of falling iron. Something like a ball peen hammer kept rapping, gently tapping, on his skull. He sensed deep trouble in his entrails, smelled death on his breath.

Henry opened leaden eyelids in the gray miasma of his bedroom. A bare-shouldered woman lay across his right arm, her nose in his armpit, snoring through open mouth. Not his wife. Not Myra. Nor was it the girl with the bell of golden hair. This was a stranger, a complete stranger, someone he could swear he'd never seen before, a sad worn-out woman with bad breath, bad teeth, skinny wrinkled neck and a little purple pouch of flesh under each eye. He felt sorry for her, his heart went out to her, but he knew at once that more than anything else in the world he wanted to get out of that bed without waking her up. Had to. But how? He thought of a fox in a steel trap, patiently at work on itself: yes, he would gnaw his arm off.

Meanwhile the rapping on and in his head continued unrelenting, increasing in tempo, accompanied by what seemed to be the clapperclaw of crows. He turned to the window. The blanket had fallen. Two desperate nuns in black, with spectacles, were scratching on the broken glass, screaming at him through the fog of his bleared vision, the cataracts on his intelligence. Screaming what? He couldn't make out the words. Something like—fway-go? fway-ho? They pointed upward straight at Heaven with extended forefingers. Way to go? Yes, ma'am, the Way. The One Way.

He nodded. Yes, sister, I understand. I understand. He crossed himself, turning his sick head away, and saw a brown stain on the ceiling directly over the bed, a stain that grew and spread and darkened even as he watched. A busy noise, like a hurlyburly of rats, rustled through the attic. The stain broke open and fragments of plaster and burning wood dropped to the floor. Orange flames, bright as sprites, flickered around the edge of the opening.

Fuego.

Henry leaped up naked, pulled the woman off the bed—the nuns fled— and draped the double sleeping bag around her nudity. Groggily awake, she stared in panic at the burning hole in the ceiling. Henry grabbed his pants, shirt, boots. A section of the roof caved in, blocking their escape through the front door.

This way. . . . He clutched her wrist and led her through the south door into the gallery, Myra's studio, the barnlike interior of the old store. Things fell, streaming with flame. Two bodies lay on the floor under the trestle table. Henry kicked them awake. They stumbled up and followed him and the woman through smoke and fire out the back door and into the clean breathable air of the yard. Some neighbors had gathered to watch. Blue woolly smoke with happy flames gushed from the roof. The whole house from end to end, throughout the attic, appeared to be on fire.

It's all right, adobe can't burn, the woman said.

Right, said Henry, yanking on his pants, his boots. He looked wildly around for assistance, saw a bucket hanging to the spout of the pump. He ran to it but the bucket was empty. Someone had kicked over the can of priming water. He jerked the pump handle up and down. Nothing came forth but the croak of dry air. He tied his bandana across nose and mouth and ran back into the studio. The smoke was so dense he could barely see.

Myra! he shouted, Myra!

No answer. Her easel stood in a corner near the empty and overturned beer keg, her latest and half-completed painting resting on its crossarm. Embers fell on his hair, his shirtless shoulders. He seized a painting from the wall, snatched up the easel and its canvas and blundered out the narrow doorway in back, stumbling with his awkward load.

Where's Myra? he hollered. Anybody see Myra?

His friend Roggoway, the shivering girl in the body paint, the woman wrapped in the sleeping bags stared at him in wonder. Six stunned and fearstruck eyes. She left last night, the girl said. Went back to town with the others. God but it's cold. She huddled in the arms of Roggoway, seeking warmth. Bildad, like van Hoss, was nowhere to be seen.

Put her in your car, Henry said. She's naked as a snake, take her home.

Can't, Roggoway said. He pointed to his Chevy convertible crouching nose-down in the weeds, both its front wheels stolen. The ragtop smoked with fire.

Yeah . . . well. . . . Henry checked his pickup truck. It too seemed incomplete. Both rear wheels were gone. They got us, he thought. *La Raza* strikes again. He unzipped the twin sleeping bags, gave one to the painted girl. There seemed nothing more to do. He and his friends backed off a piece and sat down to enjoy the fire.

Church bells rang for early mass.

The Los Lunas Fire Department arrived sometime after sunrise— around eleven o'clock—and hosed the contents of their pumper unit over the flaming store, the smoking wreckage of the house. The local population watched with interest. The water created dazzling clouds of steam but did little to discourage the fire. When their 250-gallon tank ran dry the crew turned the truck around and raced back to the Rio Grande, five miles off at the nearest access point, to refill.

There were no fire hydrants in El Culito de San Pedro Mártir. There was no public water system. The fire continued as the peaked roof and attic of the building, supporting beams burned through, collapsed with a spectacular turmoil, like a sinking ship, into the inferno within the adobe walls. A sigh of satisfaction mingled with awe and pleasure rose en masse from the spectators.

The fire department—*el cuerpo de los bomberos*—returned and again plied the conflagration with jets of water, futile but earnest, dampening but scarcely slowing the consummation of Henry Lightcap's new home. Grinning happily, the men returned the shouts of the crowd.

An insurance adjuster, investigating a claim from the Mather Realty Company, arrived at 2:00 P.M. He found Henry and Roggoway trying to mount the two remaining wheels from the Chevy convertible onto the rear of Henry's pickup.

What's your name again, young man? Henry H. Lightcap, sir. And what were you doing here? I'm the caretaker of this property; Mrs. Mather hired me herself. I see, I see—you didn't quite do the job, did you, Lightcap? I did my best, sir. Your best is none too good. Well sir, it won't happen again. No it won't—the building is a total loss, Lightcap, as any fool can plainly see. Well you see it plainer than I do, mister. I *beg* your pardon? Them walls are solid adobe brick, mister, two feet thick—they'll last for five hundred years.

But Henry was wrong about that too. With the lintels burned out above every window and doorway, ridgepole, frames, sills, rafters and crossbeams gone, no roof for shelter, the massive walls began to crumble like cookies. Within a year, vulnerable to frost and snow, wind and rain, they would be no more than eroded remnants of their former selves, silent and dwindling monuments to the vanity of human aspiration.

Henry Lightcap revised and refined his old plans, made new plans. He conceded nothing to fate.

From The Brave Cowboy

. . . THE GREAT CLIFFS leaned up against the flowing sky, falling
through space as the earth revolved, turning amber as whisky in the long-
reaching lakes of light from the evening sun. But the light had no power to
soften the jagged edges and rough-spalled planes of the granite; in that clear
air each angle and crack cast a shadow as harsh, clean, sharp, real, as the rock
itself—so that though they had endured as they were for ten million years, the
cliffs held the illusion of a terrible violence suddenly arrested, paralyzed in
time, latent with power.

At the foot of the cliffs were the little stony hills, the incidental rubble
that had fallen and merged as the earth split open and shoved one edge above
the other. Around the hills were litters of boulders, the remains of the ancient
pulverized landscape, and a complicated but systematic pattern of ditches,
gullies, ravines and canyons that conducted whatever water might fall toward
the valley and the river below.

Near one of these hills, beside a sandy wash, in the shadow of the cliffs, a
man had once built a house, using the materials that destruction and catastrophe had spawned—stone, mud, wood. The house remained, though the
man was gone: now the windows were blank and empty like the cavities of a
skull, long since stripped of glass, if they had ever held glass, and the doorway,
leaning in a curious way to the east—for the house had shifted without mov-

ing from its foundation—was without a door; the rain had undercut the slanting walls, and the flat roof, sagging on rotten beams, half open to the sky, functioned now only as a home for finches and spiders and centipedes and for one stray buckhorn cactus that had somehow taken root in the sand and decayed pine above the front doorway.

To the rear of this ruin was the arroyo, sandy and dust-dry except for a thread of water trickling from a tiny seep-like spring near the front of a rock ledge. Three cottonwoods, great towering plants in this arid zone of cactus and greasewood, were huddled together like gossiping old women around the miniature spring, their buried mouths sucking moisture up from the sand and the aquiferous limestone below. The modest overflow from the spring dripped over the lip of the rock and spread along the base of the ledge, soaking through rather than flowing over the sand; for a stretch of about ten yards there was enough water to support a little grass, some watercress and cattails, a few stunted willows. Beyond this patch of green was a delta of damp sand, thoroughly chopped up by the hooves of deer and cattle, where the last of the water disappeared, its long journey from near the mountain's rim five thousand feet above, beginning under a pocket of snow in some pine grove, falling from there down through ravines and gorges to the canyon, from one climate and world to a greatly different one, ending here in silent evaporation and a vague dispersal underground.

The leaves of the cottonwoods, dry and fragile and lemon-yellow, stirred briefly, rattled and rustled together, and several drifted to the ground. A tufted bluejay flew darkly from one tree to the next, lit on a slender branch and shook more of the dead leaves free.

Below the trees, near the red-stemmed willows, a picketed horse grazed industriously on the strip of grass, switching its tail now and then at a few idle, indifferent flies.

The cowboy was not far away. He lay in the sun near a boulder on the far side of the arroyo, away from the abandoned house; his head was propped against his saddle, and the floppy black hat covered most of his face, revealing only the bearded chin and the mouth, the latter relaxed, partly open, emitting at regular intervals the deep prolonged sighs of sleep. His property was close at hand—the saddlebags, the rifle in its scabbard, the bedroll, all still attached to the saddle itself; while the guitar and the bridle hung from handy stubs on a nearby juniper.

A raven circled above the arroyo and the spring, descended and landed with a cumbersome flapping of wings in the top of the highest cottonwood, shattering a few leaves and sending a wave of tremors through all the others.

It spread its black wings, wobbling somewhat on its perch, and bent its head to search for lice. The bluejay in the adjoining tree squawked, chattered and then flew away. After that, except for the routine murmur of a few insects near the spring, the arroyo was allowed to resume its original and fundamental silence.

Burns slept on, his hands across his belly, his legs apart and fully extended over the ground.

Ten miles away and a thousand feet below, the gleaming river wound through the valley and through the dark ragged crawl of the city and beyond the city into the far haze of the south. The city steamed and glimmered faintly, smoky and alive and obscure, while a few airplanes droned in circles above it like flies over a poisonous dump. West of the river the volcanoes, black as obsidian against the light, cast long tapering shadows over the tawny skin of the plain, and to the southwest, more than sixty miles away, the jagged peaks of Thieves' Mountain burned into the southern sky with a strange vaporish flaming purple, as if illuminated from within by furnaces of radiant energy.

The raven launched itself awkwardly, like a vivified scarecrow, out of the cottonwood tree and flapped up into the static yawning vacancy of the canyon beyond the arroyo and the ruined house.

The silence flowed back in the wake of whispering echoes.

A lizard scurried down the face of the big rock near Burns, stopped for a moment to watch him, pushing itself up and down on its forelegs like an exercising athlete, and then hurried jerkily on and disappeared under the edge of the rock.

The long evening shadows crept over the sleeping man, darkening his boots, his knees, his lean overalled thighs . . .

Something woke him: partly the change in temperature, partly the sensation of time elapsed and lost, partly fear—he heard something which was not a normal element in the auditory character of the arroyo—the birdcries, the leaves, the insects, the movements and feeding of his horse, the sound of his own breathing. He opened his eyes and reached cautiously for his rifle at the same time; however, he did not immediately pull the rifle from its case— when his groping fingers contacted the cool metal and smooth walnut of butt and stock he was satisfied and let his hand rest there. Rolling over on one side but not getting up, he concentrated his energies on an intensive inspection of the visible and audible world around him.

Three Virginia deer stood at the head of the arroyo. At first he did not see them; uncertain as to where the sound had come from, he looked west, down the arroyo and toward the dirt road that ran north and south, paralleling the mountains; then swung his gaze around in a slow half-circle—southwest, across the arroyo and toward the city, south, past the old ruin and along the base of the foothills, southeast, where the great looming wall of the canyon blocked his vision at once, and at last up the slope, eastward, up into the arroyo past the cottonwoods and the spring and the tiers of eroded rock to the little saddle in the ridge that separated the arroyo from the main canyon. And there, among the junipers and cactus and boulders, he spotted the three motionless deer.

Three does, less than fifty yards away, looking as insubstantial and ephemeral as shadows, suggesting even in their alert stillness the grace and silence of flight;—Burns stared at them and suddenly realized that they had not seen him—they were watching the horse below the spring. He tightened his grip on the butt of the rifle and slowly, with patience and extreme care, drew it from the scabbard and passed it under his chest and into the crook of his left arm. Now he had to lever a cartridge from the magazine into the firing chamber, an operation that could not be performed without a minimal clicking and mesh of metal parts. Of course the deer heard the noise: their ears stiffened and their heads swung slightly, in perfect unison, toward the man. But Burns was already in position, taking a bead on the foremost of the three, aiming at a certain vital point on the withers, just under the skin, where the spinal column became part of the neck. A difficult target, even at that range: if he hit too low he would destroy good meat and perhaps only cripple the animal; if he fired an inch too high he would miss. Therefore he did not hurry but waited for a perfect alignment of notched read sight, beaded front sight, and the invisible nexus of nerves on the crest of the doe. When it came he settled into it, holding his breath easily, and began very slowly to squeeze the trigger.

The crash never came; before he could fire he heard a shake and whinny from the mare, and the deer were gone, vanishing instantly, fading like ghosts into the golden jumble of boulders and the gold-tinged olivedrab of the chaparral.

Burns let the hammer down with his thumb; he looked reproachfully down into the arroyo at the mare. "Whisky, old girl," he murmured, "where's your hoss sense? You sure let me down this time, you know that?" The mare stared at him, snorted and shook her mane again. "Don't try to bushwah me," Burns said. "I heard you." He looked sadly up the arroyo toward the saddle over which the deer had disappeared. He decided that he might as well go up there and have a look, however; the deer might not have been badly frightened—besides they were apparently in search of water, which meant that they would not run far. And he needed meat; if he did not get it now he would have to get it tomorrow.

He got to his feet, brushed the sand and ants from his shirt and looked around again. He saw nothing which should have frightened the deer, and concluded that they must have been startled by Whisky giving a sudden jerk on the picket rope. He pushed his saddle and the gear fastened to it hard up against the overhanging wall of the boulder, then went down into the arroyo to check the stake and rope. He drove the stake in a little farther with his bootheel, had himself a quick drink at the spring and started up the arroyo with the carbine cradled in his left arm. Pulling himself up over the ledges and shelves of rock that made the arroyo something like a stairway for giants, he was annoyed by the scraping and clashing of his spurs and knelt down to take them off. He left them there on the bare rock, in a place which he felt sure he could find again, and went on up.

After climbing over a stratum of compressed shale near the head and at one side of the arroyo, he found himself among the runty trees where he had seen the deer. Now he proceeded more slowly and carefully, and as he approached the crest of the saddle went down on his hands and knees and crawled the last few feet to the top. There he halted. Below him was the mouth of the canyon, to his right the canyon itself going steeply up, shelf after shelf, toward the main bulk of the mountain, and across from him on the opposite slope, moving slowly upward among the rock and brush, were the three deer. As he had expected, they had not gone far. But they were well out of range, and moving away. He decided to follow and stalk them.

He tested the wind, such as it was, and found it favoring neither him nor his quarry but drifting up the canyon between them. He advanced over the saddle, crouching under the limbs of juniper and pin oak, and moved down onto the slope below, where the growth was denser, this being the northern snow-holding side of the ridge. He did not go very far down but stayed on the slope, moving quietly but swiftly among the small grubby trees in a direction paralleling the progress of the deer.

A near-silent world: he heard nothing but his own breathing, the faint scrape of his boots on stone and gravel, the whispering boughs of the juniper, the rattle of the oak, the vague, distant and intermittent whistle, like a bad flute, of a mourning dove. Over everything, stone and plant and animal, over the canyon wall, over the face of the mountain far above, the sun radiated its patina of warm, rye-golden, evening light.

Burns felt eager, hungry, intensely aware of every shade, sound, smell and movement in his environment; a keen convergence of his powers and intentions made each step seem vital, made the actions of his limbs consensual with the purpose in his mind. For the first time in nearly two days and nights he felt himself to be a whole and living creature, a man again and not a derelict stumbling through a mechanical world he could not understand.

Something burst into action above him, on his right; he glanced up and saw the blurred gray rump of a jackrabbit bounding over a log to crash and disappear into the snapping brush beyond.

He moved on, crouching a little as he advanced from tree to tree, circling around open areas where the cover was too meagre, making good time on occasional stretches of almost level ground where piñon trees had forced out the juniper and scrub oak. He had gained rapidly on the deer, though they were still out of range, perhaps three hundred yards away. So long as they continued to move he could not hope to get much closer without attracting their attention; only when they stopped would he have time for the slow, painstaking stealth of a stalking approach.

The ground tilted more steeply under his feet as the slope began to merge with the nearly perpendicular wall of the canyon. He had to angle downwards now, toward the rock ledges and sand floor of the canyon. As he worked his way down, going slow and carefully, he watched the deer: they had a similar choice to make—climbing back and up over the crest of the ridge or descending into the canyon. They chose to go down—and Burns smiled gratefully.

But he had another worry: light and time. He knew by the amber richness of the light that the sun was low in its arc; he looked back once to the west and saw the sun was low in its arc; he looked back once to the west and saw the sun about to fall into the crater of a volcano, separated from the black horizon by only a sliver of yellow sky. The river and the city—what he could see of its northern extension—were already caught in a shadow that was now sweeping on a broad front across the mesa, toward him and the shining mountain. While he watched the sun dropped lower, suddenly, like the twitching of the hour hand on a big clock, and the silhouette of the volcano cut a chunk from its blinding gold disc.

He turned and continued his diagonal descent, going forward across the face of the slope as much as the terrain permitted. He saw the deer still going down, headed apparently for a thicket of willows and bear grass that darkened a pocket in the floor of the canyon. Probably another spring or seep of water there, he noted, and good cover for the deer as well. But the place might also be a trap: the pocket of green ended at the base of a twenty foot water-slide of smooth bare polished stone.

He went more slowly than ever now, though the light passed far above his head and the shadow of the horizon surrounded him. He saw the three deer spring onto the sand of the canyon floor and merge, not quite totally disappearing, with the thicket of willows and high grass. He advanced another hundred yards or so on his feet, taking advantage of every bit of cover, and then, being within three hundred yards of his prey, he went down on his hands and knees and crawled forward, taking the most extreme pains to avoid being seen or heard, stopping often to listen and to study the arrangement of the rocks and cactus and trees ahead. He was now well down on the slope of the canyon, not far from the floor, and as he was anxiously aware, upwind from the deer: at any moment they might catch his scent, leave off their grazing and drinking and go leaping upward across the far slope and over the ridge and not stop until the smell of man was left miles behind. But there was nothing Burns could do about it now; hours would be required in climbing up the slope, going around behind the canyon wall and coming down again from above and farther up the canyon. Already the twilight was spreading over the canyon; thousands of feet above, the rim reflected the final rays of the sun. He had to get closer to the deer as quickly as it was strategically possible and when he was close enough, shoot accurately—there would be little chance for a second shot.

He crept ahead over the stony slope, over dead limbs of piñon, under the low boughs of junipers and around the cholla and yucca near the canyon floor. There he sank down flat on his belly and inched his way forward, keeping his head and butt down, pulling the rifle along by his side, until he was within a hundred yards of the deer.

Only then did he estimate that he was close enough for a decent shot—considering the now-treacherous quality of the light. He peered around the righthand corner of a rock and stared into the clump of willows until he could make out clearly and with certainty the outline of two deer—the third was hidden, probably lying down in the grass. Very gently he pulled back the hammer of the rifle, pressing the breech against his chest to muffle the click of the gunlock. Even then one of the does seemed to hear it; she lifted her head quickly and faced toward him. He was not yet ready to aim and fire, the carbine on its side and partly underneath his body; he waited for the doe to forget the sound and lower its head again. He had to wait about five minutes before that happened; then he was able to slide the rifle forward a little more, get the butt into his shoulder and the stock under his cheek. He aimed.

Both deer raised their heads, alert and sniffing, and took a few steps toward the far slope. The third deer sprang up out of the grass and then all three began to move, not fast yet but with the tense electric grace of creatures about to break into sudden motion. Burns cursed in silent despair, unable in that gloom to follow his target over the sights; he rose to his knees, swearing quietly, and just as the deer were about to break and run, he shivered the silence of the canyon with a sharp whistle. Instantly they stopped, all three of them, and stared at him in mild surprise. He aimed at the nearest, at a point just behind its shoulder, and fired. The crash of the discharge rang through the air, shocking in its violence; at the same moment the doe leaped forward with spasmodic energy, going from sight behind a boulder, while the two others danced up the slope and vanished in seconds. Echoes of the shot were falling from every direction as Burns ran forward, rifle in his hands, ejecting the empty shell and reloading as he ran. He crossed the canyon floor near the thicket, panting a little, his boots crunching into the damp sand, and scrambled up among the rocks and cane cactus on the other side.

Behind the big rock, sprawled on its side and quite still, he found the doe—a small tan faded heap of hide and flesh and bone dropped carelessly on the ground. He uncocked the carbine and set it down, pulled the jackknife from his pocket, opened it and stepped close to the deer. Although certain it was dead, he approached it from above, away from the sharp little hooves. He knelt and raised the doe's head with its big glazed bewildered eyes and pressed the point of his blade into the warmth and softness of its throat. There he held it for a moment, not yet pushing through the skin.

"Sleep long, little sister," he said softly, holding the warm head on his lap. "Don't be mad at me—I'm gonna make real good use of you. Yes sir . . ." He forced the blade through the skin and cut straight across the throat; the warm bright blood came gushing out with alacrity, as though meant to spill on that barren ground. Burns placed his hand under the cut and caught a palmful of the blood and drank it; then he lowered the head and raised the hindquarters, speeding the drain.

When the flow of blood began to lessen he rolled the doe on its back and gutted it, making a straight incision from the ribs down to the pelvic bone, taking care not to puncture any of the internal organs. He laid the knife down, spread the cut hide apart and carefully and tenderly removed the paunch— severing and setting aside the liver—and handling the slippery mass gingerly, like a paper bag bloated with water, he dragged it some distance away and covered it with brush. He went back to the carcass, squatted down, wiped some of the blood and slime from his hands onto the hide and ate part of the raw, hot, smoking liver. When he had had enough he threw the rest up the hill and looked around for a tree to hang the carcass from. There was nothing around him now but boulders and cactus; he saw that he would have to pack the doe back across the canyon floor and up to one of the piñons on the other slope.

He got up and walked a few steps away and urinated, rubbing the back of his neck with his free hand and listening to the crickets down in the willows. The twilight had deepened into evening; a solution of dense violet light, like an intangible rain, filled the canyon from wall to wall.

Burns went back to the deer, lifted it over his shoulders, picked up his rifle and stumbled down the slope, across the sand and up the other side to the tallest of the nearby piñons. He opened his knife again and cut a stake about two feet long, sharpening each end, then spread apart the doe's hind legs and braced them with the stake, piercing the shanks with the pointed tips. Now he could have used a piece of rope; since he had none he broke a branch from the limb he had chosen and hung the carcass to the stub. The limb bent slightly under the weight and the doe's forehooves, swinging a little, grazed the black carpet of needles on the ground.

The cowboy built a small fire next, his mind on supper—he had eaten just enough of the liver to really rouse his appetite. He brushed off a level spot among the rocks, pulled up some dry bunch grass and crushed it into a ball, sprinkled with pine needles and shreds of bark and a handful of broken twigs and added a flaming match. When the tinder caught fire, crackling brightly and sending up a thin gray fuse of smoke, he got up and prowled around for a while gathering fuel—dead juniper, a few skeletal stalks of cane cactus. He broke these into short lengths, set several on the flames and in a few minutes had a comfortable little squaw fire blazing away.

He was thirsty; for the first time in over an hour he discovered himself with nothing immediate and urgent to do, so he went down to the willow thicket and through it to the rock face. He found water dripping from fissures in the rock, filling a natural stone basin on the first ledge. He put one hand on the rock, still faintly warm from the sunlight, and bent down and drank, sparingly, and then went back to his fire and the deer, brushing drops of water out of his whiskers. As he approached, something black and awkward, like a ragged mop, rose out of the piñon tree and paddled slowly away down the canyon, each ponderous stroke of its wings accompanied by a swish of air. Burns cursed himself—tentatively—and hurried forward to examine the interior of the carcass. He was relieved to find no sign of the scavenger anywhere on the meat; he had returned in time to save the deer, not from much actual pillage, of course, but from what he considered a particularly odious kind of defilement.

The fire had burned down to a hot, incandescent heap of charcoal; Burns reached into the abdominal cavity of the deer with both hands and cut away a long tender roll of the loins and laid it on the fiery coals. While the meat seared and crackled, gracing the air with its fragrance, he went back to the carcass, cut out the heart, the lungs and the diaphragm, threw the latter two organs away and set the heart down on the edge of the fire, intending to roast it. He cut a chunk from the half-raw half-burnt sirloin and ate it while considering what to do next.

The evening thickened about him, a lavender fog of gloom; he began to think that there was not much time or light left for moving camp—that is, for loading his gear on the mare and leading her up the canyon. It would be quite dark by the time he could climb back down to the spring and the cottonwoods where he had left her; coming back up with only a few stars for light would be a difficult and exhausting task. On the other hand, to carry the deer down there was out of the question; he had no intention of jerking all that meat in a place where the smoke could be seen from miles away in several directions.

He ate some of the sirloin, leaving most of it still on the coals, got up off his heels and staggered down to the canyon floor. Working fast, he cut and broke off a big solid armful of greasewood, scrambled back up the steep slope to the piñon and packed his rough materials into the deer's gaping bellycase, making it a firm, thorny, bristling mass that only a fly could penetrate. That done, he went back to the fire, squatted down and ate the rest of the seared meat, feeding himself steadily and seriously but not fast; he took his time.

The fire was low, a flicker and shimmer of red, blue, violet embers; he shoved the tough heart into the center of the fire and with a stick heaped coals over it. He added a few knots of juniper, then lay back on the ground, half-gorged, immensely satisfied and sleepy. There was only one thing more that he desired: he searched through his pockets for tobacco, found the pipe and tobacco that Jerry had given him and filled the pipe. He sat up again, leaned toward the fire, picked up a burning coal and dropped it on top of the bowl of the pipe. He puffed slowly, tasting the unfamiliar, highly aromatic tobacco with caution; he decided that he liked it, stretched out on the ground again and smoked freely.

Looking up at the strip of sky between the canyon walls, he saw a faint blinking formation of stars that looked like the Seven Sisters—the Pleiades—and this reminded him that the night was coming on. He belched, lying on his back, and considered the possibility of not going down after the mare and his equipment. He would miss his sleepingbag a little, if he did not go down, but then it would not be the first time he had slept on the ground and covered himself with nothing but his shirt and his own back. But there were two serious disadvantages in leaving things as they were: first, the possibility that his horse or gear might be discovered by some Ranger or prowling police officer; second, the certainty that if he waited till dawn to get his outfit he would find the deer riddled with blowflies when he came back up the canyon.

Burns puffed again on the pipe, watching the gray smoke drift toward the stars, picked some fragments of meat out of his teeth, and then sat up, grunting. He straightened the hat on his head, picked up his Winchester and hauled himself heavily to his feet; he started down the canyon, weaving a little in the uncertain light, belching again and wiping his greasy mouth on his shirtsleeve. A locust, dry and brittle as glass, rattled out of the brush and struck him on the chest; he slapped at it in surprise, broke it and brushed it off, then shuffled on over the firm sand, following the narrow winding floor of the canyon. He came to the first big rock ledge and climbed, slid and jumped down the face of it, landing in greasewood and sand again; he marched past a stand of pampas grass, silvery and graceful, and around a bend in the canyon, and suddenly, unexpectedly, the view opened wide and the whole western world lay before him: the canyon dropping down step by step like an imperial stairway for gods, the gaunt purple foothills, the mesa rolling out for miles, the faint gleam of the river, the vast undulant spread of the city ten miles away, transformed by the evening dusk into something fantastic and grand and lovely, a rich constellation of jewels glimmering like the embers of a fire—and beyond the city and west mesa and the five volcanoes another spectacle, a garish and far more immense display of clouds and color and dust and light against a bottomless, velvet sky. Burns stopped for a moment to stare and admire, belched gently and continued his descent.

Half an hour later he entered the deep gloom under the cottonwoods. He felt better: the city was now hidden from him by the banks of the arroyo, the great flare in the west had faded and died, his supper was partly digested—or at least well shaken down—and he could smell and hear his horse. Whisky greeted him with a complaining whinny. He walked close to her and patted her neck, while she nuzzled him in the chest. "Glad to see me, old girl?" he said; "You think I forgot you? No sirree; you just take it easy now." She snorted and tried to lick his face. "Easy, girl, easy; I'll feed you right off." He climbed out of the arroyo toward the slab of rock that sheltered his saddle and other belongings. He put the rifle in the scabbard, slung the guitar on his back, lifted the saddle to his shoulder and went back down to the mare. He filled his hat with a mixture of bran and barley from one of the saddlebags, about a peck, and set it in the sand before the mare. While she fed he threw on the saddlepad and the saddle and cinched the latigo down tight. He checked off his equipment: bedroll, saddlebags, canteen, rifle, rope—only the bridle was missing. He thought of the twenty-five pounds of jerked venison he was going to add to that burden in about three days and reminded himself that he would never get far toward Sonora without a packhorse. Tomorrow night, perhaps, he would go look for one; tonight he was going to get some sleep. He went back to the boulder above the arroyo and looked for the bridle; he could not find it and did not remember where he had left it until he took a second look at the scrubby juniper near the rock.

He was sliding down the loose bank of the arroyo when he heard a noise that stopped him in his tracks: the slam of a car door. He stood frozen, listening, while his muscles tensed with the instinct to flee. He could hear nothing more, nothing but the whine of cicada and from somewhere down the wash the occasional zoom and groan of a striking bullbat. Quickly but carefully he stepped over the stretch of sand that separated him from the mare, put one hand over her nostrils to prevent a possible nicker and with the other, letting the bridle fall, reached up over the saddle and slid the rifle out of its smooth worn case. He laid the barrel across the saddlebow, leaving the action uncocked, and waited.

For what seemed like a long time, perhaps five minutes, he heard nothing unusual. He could see very little, with the high bank of the arroyo directly in front of him, and the night closing in. Although his cover was good there in the darkness under the trees and between the walls of the arroyo, he was also painfully aware that if he should be discovered he would be pretty well boxed in, with escape possible only by a run down the wash toward the mesa. And he had not even had a chance to bridle the mare. Balancing the rifle with his forearm, he started to untie the rope around Whisky's neck that tethered her to the picket.

Then he saw and almost *felt* a beam of light that swung quickly through the air over his head, danced over the leaves of the cottonwoods and disappeared. A few seconds later he heard the crunch and scrape of gravel under heavy, slow feet. He heard no voices, however, and gratefully assumed that he probably had only one man to deal with. The footsteps approached the bank of the arroyo—while Burns stopped breathing, his thumb set firm on the hammer—and then halted, not coming to the edge. Burns listened; he watched the top of the bank but could see only the dark sky and the tall slender black silhouette of a yucca. From down the arroyo he heard the roar of a bullbat again.

Presently, after a minute or so, he heard the author of the footsteps tramping off, this time apparently in the direction of the old house. Listening

intently, he heard the steps grow fainter, then the short crash of a dislodged
rock, the rattle of a loose board. He lifted the carbine up from its rest on the
saddlebow and wedged it between the cantle and the bedroll, and bent down
and felt around on the sand for the bridle. He found it without trouble, disentangled the reins from the headstall, forced the bit into the mare's mouth,
slipped the stall over her ears and buckled the throatlatch. He was ready now;
he reached for the carbine again and waited and listened, breathing, slowly
and quietly.

He heard nothing, nothing human, for another five minutes; then came
the second slam of an automobile door and he breathed more freely. When
he heard an engine starting he left the mare and struggled up the bank of the
arroyo, and saw the car at once, a dull lustre of enamel and chrome backing
and turning on the old wagon road below the ruin. He watched the car get
turned around, start forward and go bouncing down the rutted, twisted road,
rocks clanging on its fenders, brakelights flicking on and off, the headlights
sweeping over a forlorn landscape of boulders and cactus and crouching juniper.

When the car was well on its way back to the city, Burns returned to the
mare, replaced the rifle in the scabbard, coiled his rope and tied it to the swell,
stowed the picket in the bedroll, had one more drink at the spring and
climbed at last into the saddle, a very considerable pleasure which he had
been anticipating for the last two or three hours; he forbore to think of the
canyon ahead, where he would have to walk and lead over at least half the
distance.

"Hup, girl," he said, and touched the mare with his heels. Fresh and eager, she started off as though bent on a free run through woods and green
fields, and he had to rein her in at once to keep her to a walk. He rode up and
around the ledge behind the spring, recovered his spurs, rode on up to the
head of the arroyo and up the bank there, and over the saddle of the hill and
into the canyon. Above him leaned the canyon walls, and above them the
mountain with its granite cliffs; far above and beyond the mountain the stars
began to appear, one by one, the chill blue glittering stars of the autumn.

Burns felt tired, very tired, and cold.

Manhattan Twilight,
Hoboken Night

HOBOKEN, NEW JERSEY, is not one of the five boroughs of New York City. But it should be, for it's closer and quicker to the center of Manhattan from Hoboken than from any point in Brooklyn, the Bronx, Queens or Staten Island. Fifteen minutes by bus, via the Lincoln Tunnel, takes you from Washington Street in Hoboken to the Port Authority Bus Terminal on Forty-first Street; ten minutes by train via the Hudson Tubes takes you from the Erie-Lackawanna Terminal to Ninth Street and Sixth Avenue—the Village. A dash under the river, a roar of iron, and you're there: in Glitter Gulch, U.S.A.—Times Square, the Big Midway, the hanging gardens of electricity. Or down yonder in Green Witch Village. What more could you want? And if New York is not Manhattan, it is nothing. A little worse than nothing. Meanwhile the insane, medieval burgs of New Jersey—Union City, West New York, Jersey City—lie divorced from Hoboken by a wall older than the Great Wall of China. I mean the Palisades, that sill of diabase left over from the Triassic period.

I make this effort to incorporate Hoboken into New York City (where it belongs) rather than allowing it to remain in New Jersey (for which it is much too sweet, pure, romantic) because it is from the Hoboken point of view, the

From *The Journey Home: Some Words in Defense of the American West* (1977)

Hoboken mystique, the Hoboken metaphysic, that I must describe what I remember and what I know of New York. Meaning Manhattan. Of the rest I know nothing. The other four boroughs are as remote to my imagination as the Malebolges of the Eighth Circle of Hell. Perhaps only Dante could tell us the truth about them. Perhaps only Dante—and Dostoevski—could tell us the truth about New York.

For two years I lived in Hoboken, far from my natural habitat. The bitter bread of exile. Two years in the gray light and the sulfur dioxide and the smell of burning coffee beans from the Maxwell House plant at the end of Hudson Street. In a dark, dank, decaying apartment house where the cockroaches— shell-backed, glossy, insolent *Blatella germanica*—festered and spawned under the linoleum on the sagging floors, behind the rippled wallpaper on the sweating walls, among the teacups in the cupboard. Everywhere. While the rats raced in ferocious packs, like wolves, inside the walls and up and down the cobblestone alleyways that always glistened, night and day, in any kind of weather, with a thin chill greasy patina of poisonous dew. The fly ash everywhere, falling softly and perpetually from the pregnant sky. We watched the seasons come and go in a small rectangle of walled-in space we called our yard: in spring and summer the black grass; in fall and winter the black snow. Overhead and in our hearts a black sun.

Down in the cellar and up in the attic of that fantastic house—four stories high, brownstone, a stoop, wide, polished banisters, brass fittings on the street entrance, a half-sunken apartment for the superintendent, high ceilings, high windows and a grand stairway on the main floor, all quite decently middle class and in the better part of town, near the parks, near the Stevens Institute of Technology—hung draperies of dust and cobweb that had not been seen in the light of day or touched by the hand of man since the time of the assassination of President William McKinley.

In the sunless attic the spiders had long since given up, for all their prey had turned to dust; but the rats roamed freely. Down in the basement, built like a dungeon with ceiling too low to permit a man of normal stature to stand erect, there were more rats, of course—they loved the heat of the furnace in winter—and dampish stains on the wall and floor where the great waterbugs, like cockroaches out of Kafka, crawled sluggishly from darkness into darkness. One might notice here, at times, the odor of sewer gas.

The infinite richness. The ecology, the natural history of it all. An excellent workshop for the philosopher, for who would venture out into that gray miasma of perpetual smoke and fog that filled the streets if he might remain walled up with books, sipping black coffee, smoking black Russian cigarettes, thinking long, black, inky thoughts? To be sure. But there were the streets. The call of the streets.

We lived one block from the waterfront. The same waterfront where Marlon Brando once played Marlon Brando, where rust-covered tramp steamers, black freighters, derelict Dutchmen, death ships, came to call under Liberian flags to unload their bananas, baled hemp, teakwood, sacks of coffee beans, cowhides, Argentine beef, to take on kegs of nails, jeep trucks, Cadillacs and crated machine guns. Abandoned by the Holland-American Line in '65, at least for passenger service, the Hoboken docks—like Hoboken bars and Hoboken tenements—were sinking into an ever deepening state of decay. The longshoremen were lucky to get two days' work a week. Some of the great warehouses had been empty for years; the kids played Mafia in them.

The moment I stepped out the front door I was faced again with Manhattan. There it was, oh splendid ship of concrete and steel, aluminum, glass and electricity, forging forever up the dark river. (The Hudson—like a river of oil, filthy and rich, gleaming with silver lights.) Manhattan at twilight: floating gardens of tender neon, the lavender towers where each window glittered at sundown with reflected incandescence, where each crosstown street became at evening a gash of golden fire, and the endless flow of the endless traffic on the West Side Highway resembled a luminous necklace strung round the island's shoulders.

Who would believe the city could be so beautiful? On winter evenings when the sun went down early and all the office lights stayed lit, the giant glass buildings across the river glowed like blocks of radium with a cool soft Venusian radiance, magnetic and fatal. And above them all stood the Vampire State Building with its twin beams stroking through the mist and the red spider eyes on the radio mast blinking slowly off and on, off and on, all through the New York night. While deep-sea liners bayed in the roadstead, coming up the Narrows, and tugboats shaped like old shoes and croaking like alligators glided by in the opposite direction, towing freight trains or barges filled with traprock. Once I saw a large dark ship, no visible running lights at all, pass between me and the clustered constellations of the city—a black form moving across a field of stars.

One night Manhattan itself became that dark ship. Under moonlight the city appeared to be deserted, abandoned, empty as a graveyard except for the dim beams of automobiles groping through the blacked-out canyons, fumbling for the way home. From where I stood in Hoboken, on a hill above the waterfront, I could hear not the faintest sound of life, not a heartbeat, from New York. The silence was impressive. But by the next night the power was back and the city shining like a many-colored vision of wealth and glory. From the little park in Weehawken where Aaron Burr shot Alexander Hamilton (good shot!) you could look right down the center line of Forty-second Street. With glasses powerful enough, you could watch the sports and pastimes of the folk who dwell in the City of Dreadful Night.

If the Lower East Side is now the East Village, Hoboken was (still is, if urban renewal has not yet destroyed it all) the West Village. Down on River Street just past the gothic gables of the Christian Seamen's Home began our own little Bohemia, where the otherwise omnipresent odor of sewer gas, burning coffee beans and the Hudson River was sweetened by the smell of marijuana and smoking joss sticks. Under the vacant eyes of condemned tenements lived the Peace People, the Flower Children, in happy polygamous squalor. Woven god's-eyes dangled from the ceilings; on once blank and dusty storefront windows appeared the American flag, handpainted, with five, six or seven stripes and anywhere from a dozen to twenty stars, asymmetrical as nebulae. The men wore bands on their heads, beards on their jaws, and their old ladies were as slender, sweet and comely as their tresses were long. My friend Henry the painter was painting nothing but gas stations that year. Esso gas stations. And Rini the sculptor was busy welding and reworking junked auto parts into surreal hobgoblins of iron.

"Look here, Rini," I said to her, "instead of dragging the goddamn junkyard into the art galleries, why don't you throw the goddamn art galleries into the junkyard?"

"That's exactly what we're doing," she replied.

They had a coffeehouse—the Baby Bull—and nocturnal police raids and finally even a murder of their very own. Anything Haight-Ashbury had we had too.

Hoboken may be the only city in America where some of the police were actually caught red-handed in the act of tampering with the voting machines: there was a resolution on the ballot in the election that year that if approved would have authorized a substantial pay increase for the fuzz and the firemen.

Which suggests the role of *power* again: When I lived in Hoboken it was the most densely populated square-mile city in the United States, inhabited largely by babies; you could not walk down the main drag, Washington Street, at any time during daylight hours without threading your way through traffic jams of loaded baby carriages, many of them containing twins, some triplets, each carriage powered by a pregnant mother with two or three toddlers dragging at her skirts. And who ruled this fecund mass?

The character of the population was mixed, a typical American polyglot boiling pot of Italians, Irish, Puerto Ricans, Poles, Jews, Germans and Blacks. But there could be little doubt which *ethnos* dominated the structure of authority when you read in the local paper of the latest gathering of dignitaries at the Union Club: "Present were *Mayor Grogan, Councilman Hogan, Bishops Malarkey* and *Moone, Commissioners Hoyle* and *Coyle* and *Boyle.*"

Who were those others we sometimes glimpsed on rare occasions, those heavy short swarthy men with Homburg hats, velvet-collared overcoats, fat cigars, who rode far back in the rear corners of black limousines rolling swiftly, quietly (no sound but the hiss of rubber on asphalt) down the evening streets? Who were the two Mongolian wrestlers in front dressed like FBI operatives, one driving, one scanning the sidewalks with stonefish eyes?

Hoboken. Weehawken. Hohokus. Secaucus. Paramus. Manhattan. And the five boroughs of New York. True, we were separated by a river from the center of the city. But are not the others also cut off by water? The Harlem River. The East River. What is the Brooklyn Bridge for? What is the function of the Staten Island Ferry? New York is a city of waters and islands, like Venice, floating on sewer lagoons, under a sea of fog and smoke and drizzling acid mists. You have to be tough to live there—even the clams on the offshore shelf are full of polluted pride. The chickadees, starlings, sparrows and alley cats of Hoboken were a hardier meaner breed than you find elsewhere. The old trees in the little parks along Boulevard East and Hudson Street seemed lifeless as statuary most of the year; yet in April there came an astonishing outburst of delicate green along the length of those blackened limbs. As if leaves should grow upon gun barrels and—but why not?—bright, fuzzy flowers spring up from the mouths of cannon.

Perhaps I liked best the sunflowers along the railroad tracks, and the little purple asters that rose between the ties, out of the cinders. Or the cattails in the ditches and the rank nameless weeds that flourished by the iron wheels of rotting boxcars—*Erie-Lackawanna—The Great White Way—Route of Phoebe Snow*—forgotten on sidings. Or the feral hollyhocks tall as corn along the walls of the gate tender's shack at the railway crossing, transpiring through July. There was a bitter, forlorn yet stubborn beauty everywhere you looked in Hoboken. Even the smog of heavy summer evenings played a helpful part, enhancing the quality of light and shadow on old brick walls, lending to things only a block away the semblance of magic and mystery.

When I was there I thought New York was dying. Maybe it really is. I know I was dying to get out. But if it's dying then it's going to be a prolonged, strange, infinitely complex process, a death of terror and grandeur. Imagine a carcinoma three hundred miles long, a mile thick, embracing 50 million souls.

Whatever else (I tell myself) you may think about New York now, looking back at it from this desert perspective, you've got to admit that Wolf Hole, Arizona, can never have so rich a death.

There are three ways to get from Hoboken to Manhattan. There were four. You can take the Number 6 bus, dive into the Lincoln Tunnel (holding your breath), roar through that tube of tile and light, where the tunnel cops pace forever up and down their cement walkways or stand in glass boxes built into the walls (we used to discuss the question, which is the world's worst job: subway motorman? city bus driver? slaughterhouse worker? switchboard operator? or tunnel cop?), to emerge suddenly into the blue air of the Port Authority Bus Terminal. Or you can take the Hudson Tubes under the river, ride the trains through the sweating tunnels, where little green lights blink dimly beside the rails, and come out in the Village or stay on the train and ride it uptown as far as Macy's, Gimbel's, Herald Square. The third way, if you have a car, is to drive it yourself through either the Lincoln Tunnel or the Holland Tunnel and drive it back through the other way when you realize finally that there is almost no place on all of God's Manhattan where you can park your machine.

The fourth way was to take the Lackawanna Ferry and although the slowest this was by far the best. (A fifth way will be to walk on the water when the Hudson finally coagulates.) Getting to the ferry slips at the railway terminal was part of the pleasure: For whether you went by Washington Street, Hudson Street or River Street, you passed not only such places as the hippie communes and the Christian Seamen's Home but also the most shabby dingy rundown smelly half-lighted dangerous and downright picturesque little Mom-and-Pop bars in North America.

It was said, on good authority, that Hoboken had more taverns per square block than any other city in the world except Anchorage, Alaska. I believe it. I never did get into all of them, though for two years I tried. Some I remember: the Old Empire, the Seven Seas, Allie and Jopie's, Anna Lee's, Portview, El Jim's, the Dutch Mill, the Elysian Fields Bar and Grill, the River Street, the Cherokee, the Old Holland House, McSharry's Irish House, the Continental, the Little Dipsy Doodle, the Grand, the Inn, the Idle Hours (how true), Pat's, Pete's, Lou's, Joe's and Mom's. And the Silver Trail, Hoboken's only genuine western bar, with live western music and authentic cowboy stomp dancing every Saturday night; and Nelson's Marine Bar and Grill, my favorite, where the bartender, Herman Nelson, sole owner and proprietor, is or was the man who *almost* became world welterweight champ in 1931; and the stand-up bar of the Clam Broth House, men only (then), free clam broth, Löwenbrau on tap, the crackle of clamshells underfoot.

Anyway, if you made it past all the bars and the three Chinese laundries—Sam Toy's, Harry Lew's, Gong Lee's—and past the hash peddlers, cops, hippies, Christian seamen, bohemes, bums, panhandlers, whores, winos, shoeshine boys, muggers, rapists and shiv artists, you arrived at the Erie-Lackawanna building. End of the line. Mouth of the tubes. Home of the ferryboats. The E-L building (is it still there?) looked like a square fruitcake coated with green mold. It was enormous, its cavernous interior capacious enough for a dozen trains plus shops and offices and waiting rooms. Paying our fare at the turnstiles, we stormed up the ramp onto the "Next Boat."

All on board, gangplanks winched up with a rattle of chains, the ferry surged out of the slip and bore east-southeast across the Hudson toward the Barclay Street docks on the far side. Moving partly with the current and partly across it, the ferry left a curving wake as it churned from shore to shore. In winter we glided among drifting ice floes the color of urine; in summer through trails of garbage bobbing in the wake of ships, seagulls screaming as they wheeled and dove for supper. I liked to stand on the open forward deck facing the wind and the solemn monuments of lower Manhattan. For a few minutes at least we were all free, commuters, drifters and students alike, liberated from the confines of lubberly life and at home—so we thought—with sailors and seabirds, the allure of the open sea. It seemed to me I could read on the faces of even the most resigned commuters an emotion the same as mine: exultance.

It was strange, that approach to Manhattan over the open water. No sound but the slap of waves, the wind, the gulls, the distant signals of other boats. The city itself swung slowly toward us silent as a dream. No sign of life but puffs of steam from skyscraper chimneys, the motion of the traffic. The mighty towers stood like tombstones in a graveyard, leaning against the sky and waiting for—for what? Someday we'll know.

And then as we came close we began to hear the murmur of the city's life, the growing and compelling roar, the sound of madness. Newspapers were folded, overcoats buttoned, hat brims tugged—those gray near-brimless little felt hats that all the men wore and which had the peculiar virtue of rendering the wearer invisible. Everyone crowded toward the front of the boat. You could see the tension stealing over each face as two hundred full-grown men prepared themselves for the stampede to taxis, buses, the subway trains.

But those were the mornings. Mornings were always absurd and desperate in New York. In the evening, going to the city, the mood was different, only a few of us on the boat, going the wrong way—the right way—against the mainstream of human traffic. In the evening the great glittering ship of Manhattan seemed to promise the fulfillment of every desire, every wish; one sailed toward it through the purple twilight with a heart full of hope. Hope for what? Hard to say—hope for those things a young man desires so much he hesitates to name them: for love; for adventure; for revelation; for triumph. All of it waiting there in that golden city of electric glory. All of it almost within reach.

That was the view from the water, the fantasy of the river crossing. Close to, the scene came into a different focus; we found ourselves back in the profane world of people with problems, embittered cab drivers, Sam Schwartz and his roasted chestnuts, the quiet tragedy of human relationships. No amount of weed or booze or sex or heavy art could permanently alter any of that.

I was a walker. I usually walked from Barclay Street up to the Village, preferring the grim and empty downtown streets to the infernal racket and doomed faces of the subway. Pausing at the White Horse for a drink to the memory of Dylan—the one from Cardigan Bay—the real Dylan, and thence to Dillon's where I *might* meet somebody I knew, and from there to the Cedars, international intersection of all Volkswagen Bohemia where I *always* met somebody I knew, where anybody meets somebody, we threw a few back while deciding whose opening, whose screening, whose party to crash on this wild, full-of-wonder, high-blossoming night.

After a quick trip to the john to read the writing on the wall—Socrates Loves Alcibiades; Joy Shipmates Joy!; Here I Sit Anonymous as Hieronymus Bosch; Caligula Come Back; Mene Mene Tekel—it was out on the jam-packed streets again, through the multitudes, and up a tunnel of stairways into somebody's loft—THIS FLOOR WILL SAFELY SUSTAIN A LOAD OF 70 LB PER SQUARE FOOT—and into The Party.

The Party was permanent, like the revolution, always in swing somewhere, with the same conglutinate crowd, the same faces, the same wilted potato chips, the same red wine, the same dense atmosphere of smoke and heat and intellection, the same blonde lovely girls down from Boston for the weekend, the same paintings of Esso gas stations on the walls, the same raccoon-eyed lank-haired crepe-clad pale-faced vampire lass hesitating in the doorway, to whom some catty chick would say, "Well do creep in." Somebody like Norman Mailer was always there, a drink in each hand, and Dwight Mac-Donald, and Joel Oppenheimer, and Joseph Heller, and the man who invented Happenings, I forget his name. Everyone was there but the host, who usually could not be found.

There were other parts of the town I got to know, a little. For a while I had a girl friend who lived on Fourteenth Street, near Union Square; I worked briefly as a technical writer for General Electric in an office building on Lower Broadway, editing training manuals for DEW Line soldiers on how to dispose of sewage in permafrost; we all had to wear white shirts—that was mandatory—and I was fired at the end of two weeks for spending too much time staring out the window. I was invited a few times to publishers' offices in the midtown region, to an agent's office in Rockefeller Center, to lunches at Sardi's. My wife had an M.D. with an office in the East Sixties. Once I went to Wilt Chamberlain's nightclub in Harlem. And I worked for a time as a welfare caseworker in the Atlantic Avenue district of Brooklyn—but that is another story, that was another world, that was lower Mississippi we were dealing with there; let us now praise famous men. But I lived in Hoboken.

The Party is over, for me. In the gray light of dawn with the Sunday *Times,* world's most preposterous newspaper—all those dead trees!—rolled under my arm, I navigated the deserted streets. Bleak and God-forsaken Sunday. Down into the subway entrance, down into the dim calamitous light of the tubes. Into an empty car. The placards on the walls implored me: GIVE: multiple sclerosis; muscular dystrophy; heart disease; lung cancer; mental illness; cystic-fibrosis; nephritis; hepatitis; cerebral palsy; VD; TB; acute leukemia. Buy Bonds: Keep Freedom in Your *Future!* Good God. The train jolted forward, began to move; the dripping steam pipes, the little blue lights, the sweating walls slide greasily by. Just a happy little journey through hell. The train paused at the Christopher Street station. Before it moved on again I had time to contemplate a pair of rubber gloves lying in a pool of oil beside the tracks.

We plunged beneath the river. I slept all day. At evening I walked once more along the waterfront and gazed across the river at the somber forms of Manhattan, the great towers largely dark, for on Sunday no one is at work over there but the janitors. I don't know how New York can survive.

I believe the city is doomed. The air is poisonous, not so much with filth and disease as with something deadlier—human hatred. Yes, there's hatred in Arizona, too, but here it is easily dissipated into the nothingness of space: walk one-half mile away from the town, away from the road, and you find yourself absolutely alone, under the sun, under the moon, under the stars, within the sweet aching loneliness of the desert.

That loneliness is not enough. We must save the city. It is essence and substance of us all—we cannot lose it without diminishing our stature as a nation, without a fatal wound.

My words therefore are dedicated to that city we love, that visionary city of the prophecies, humane and generous, that city of liberty and beauty and joy which will come to be, someday, on American earth, on the shore of the sea.

Author's Introduction to

Desert Solitaire

ABOUT TEN YEARS AGO I took a job as a seasonal park ranger in a place called Arches National Monument near the little town of Moab in southeast Utah. Why I went there no longer matters; what I found there is the subject of this book.

My job began on the first of April and ended on the last day of September. I liked the work and the canyon country and returned the following year for a second season. I would have returned the third year too and each year thereafter but unfortunately for me the Arches, a primitive place when I first went there, was developed and improved so well that I had to leave. But after a number of years I returned anyway, traveling full circle, and stayed for a third season. In this way I was better able to appreciate the changes which had been made during my absence.

Those were all good times, especially the first two seasons when the tourist business was poor and the time passed extremely slowly, as time should pass, with the days lingering and long, spacious and free as the summers of childhood. There was time enough for once to do nothing, or next to nothing, and most of the substance of this book is drawn, sometimes direct and unchanged, from the pages of the journals I kept and filled through the undi-

From *Desert Solitaire: A Season in the Wilderness* (1968)

vided, seamless days of those marvelous summers. The remainder of the book consists of digressions and excursions into ideas and places that border in varied ways upon that central season in the canyonlands.

This is not primarily a book about the desert. In recording my impressions of the natural scene I have striven above all for accuracy, since I believe that there is a kind of poetry, even a kind of truth, in simple fact. But the desert is a vast world, an oceanic world, as deep in its way and complex and various as the sea. Language makes a mighty loose net with which to go fishing for simple facts, when facts are infinite. If a man knew enough he could write a whole book about the juniper tree. Not juniper trees in general but that one particular juniper tree which grows from a ledge of naked sandstone near the old entrance to Arches National Monument. What I have tried to do then is something a bit different. Since you cannot get the desert into a book any more than a fisherman can haul up the sea with his nets, I have tried to create a world of words in which the desert figures more as medium than as material. Not imitation but evocation has been the goal.

Aside from this modest pretension the book is fairly plain and straight. Certain faults will be obvious to the general reader, of course, and for these I wish to apologize. I quite agree that much of the book will seem coarse, rude, bad-tempered, violently prejudiced, unconstructive—even frankly antisocial in its point of view. Serious critics, serious librarians, serious associate professors of English will if they read this work dislike it intensely; at least I hope so. To others I can only say that if the book has virtues they cannot be disentangled from the faults; that there is a way of being wrong which is also sometimes necessarily right.

It will be objected that the book deals too much with mere appearances, with the surface of things, and fails to engage and reveal the patterns of unifying relationships which form the true underlying reality of existence. Hence I must confess that I know nothing whatever about true underlying reality, having never met any. There are many people who say they have, I know, but they've been luckier than I.

For my own part I am pleased enough with surfaces—in fact they alone seem to me to be of much importance. Such things for example as the grasp of a child's hand in your own, the flavor of an apple, the embrace of friend or lover, the silk of a girl's thigh, the sunlight on rock and leaves, the feel of music, the bark of a tree, the abrasion of granite and sand, the plunge of clear water into a pool, the face of the wind—what else is there? What else do we need?

Regrettably I have found it unavoidable to write some harsh words about my seasonal employer the National Park Service, Department of the Interior, United States Government. Even the Government itself has not entirely escaped censure. I wish to point out therefore that the Park Service has labored under severe pressure from powerful forces for many decades and that under the circumstances and so far it has done its work rather well. As governmental agencies go the Park Service is a good one, far superior to most. This I attribute not to the administrators of the Park Service—like administrators everywhere they are distinguished chiefly by their ineffable mediocrity—but to the actual working rangers in the field, the majority of whom are capable, honest, dedicated men. Preeminent among those I have known personally is Mr. Bates Wilson of Moab, Utah, who might justly be considered the founder of Canyonlands National Park. He cannot be held responsible for any of the opinions expressed herein, but he is responsible for much of what understanding I have of a country we both love.

A note on names. All of the persons and places mentioned in this book are or were real. However for the sake of their privacy I have invented fictitious names for some of the people I once knew in the Moab area and in a couple of cases relocated them in space and time. Those who read this will, I hope, understand and forgive me; the others will not mind.

Finally a word of caution:

Do not jump into your automobile next June and rush out to the canyon country hoping to see some of that which I have attempted to evoke in these pages. In the first place you can't see *anything* from a car; you've got to get out of the goddamned contraption and walk, better yet crawl, on hands and knees, over the sandstone and through the thornbush and cactus. When traces of blood begin to mark your trail you'll see something, maybe. Probably not. In the second place most of what I write about in this book is already gone or going under fast. This is not a travel guide but an elegy. A memorial. You're holding a tombstone in your hands. A bloody rock. Don't drop it on your foot—throw it at something big and glassy. What do you have to lose?

> E. A.
> April 1967
> Nelson's Marine Bar
> Hoboken

The First Morning

THIS IS the most beautiful place on earth.

There are many such places. Every man, every woman, carries in heart and mind the image of the ideal place, the right place, the one true home, known or unknown, actual or visionary. A houseboat in Kashmir, a view down Atlantic Avenue in Brooklyn, a gray gothic farmhouse two stories high at the end of a red dog road in the Allegheny Mountains, a cabin on the shore of a blue lake in spruce and fir country, a greasy alley near the Hoboken waterfront, or even, possibly, for those of a less demanding sensibility, the world to be seen from a comfortable apartment high in the tender, velvety smog of Manhattan, Chicago, Paris, Tokyo, Rio or Rome—there's no limit to the human capacity for the homing sentiment. Theologians, sky pilots, astronauts have even felt the appeal of home calling to them from up above, in the cold black outback of interstellar space.

For myself I'll take Moab, Utah. I don't mean the town itself, of course, but the country which surrounds it—the canyonlands. The slickrock desert. The red dust and the burnt cliffs and the lonely sky—all that which lies beyond the end of the roads.

The choice became apparent to me this morning when I stepped out of a

From *Desert Solitaire: A Season in the Wilderness* (1968)

Park Service housetrailer—my caravan—to watch for the first time in my life the sun come up over the hoodoo stone of Arches National Monument.

I wasn't able to see much of it last night. After driving all day from Albuquerque—450 miles—I reached Moab after dark in cold, windy, clouded weather. At park headquarters north of town I met the superintendent and the chief ranger, the only permanent employees, except for one maintenance man, in this particular unit of America's national park system. After coffee they gave me a key to the housetrailer and directions on how to reach it; I am required to live and work not at headquarters but at this one-man station some twenty miles back in the interior, on my own. The way I wanted it, naturally, or I'd never have asked for the job.

Leaving the headquarters area and the lights of Moab, I drove twelve miles farther north on the highway until I came to a dirt road on the right, where a small wooden sign pointed the way: Arches National Monument Eight Miles. I left the pavement, turned east into the howling wilderness. Wind roaring out of the northwest, black clouds across the stars—all I could see were clumps of brush and scattered junipers along the roadside. Then another modest signboard:

WARNING: QUICKSAND
DO NOT CROSS WASH
WHEN WATER IS RUNNING

The wash looked perfectly dry in my headlights. I drove down, across, up the other side and on into the night. Glimpses of weird humps of pale rock on either side, like petrified elephants, dinosaurs, stone-age hobgoblins. Now and then something alive scurried across the road: kangaroo mice, a jackrabbit, an animal that looked like a cross between a raccoon and a squirrel—the ringtail cat. Farther on a pair of mule deer started from the brush and bounded obliquely through the beams of my lights, raising puffs of dust which the wind, moving faster than my pickup truck, caught and carried ahead of me out of sight into the dark. The road, narrow and rocky, twisted sharply left and right, dipped in and out of tight ravines, climbing by degrees toward a summit which I would see only in the light of the coming day.

Snow was swirling through the air when I crossed the unfenced line and passed the boundary marker of the park. A quarter-mile beyond I found the ranger station—a wide place in the road, an informational display under a lean-to shelter, and fifty yards away the little tin government housetrailer where I would be living for the next six months.

A cold night, a cold wind, the snow falling like confetti. In the lights of the truck I unlocked the housetrailer, got out bedroll and baggage and moved in. By flashlight I found the bed, unrolled my sleeping bag, pulled off my boots and crawled in and went to sleep at once. The last I knew was the shaking of the trailer in the wind and the sound, from inside, of hungry mice scampering around with the good news that their long lean lonesome winter was over— their friend and provider had finally arrived.

This morning I awake before sunrise, stick my head out of the sack, peer through a frosty window at a scene dim and vague with flowing mists, dark fantastic shapes looming beyond. An unlikely landscape.

I get up, moving about in long underwear and socks, stooping carefully under the low ceiling and lower doorways of the housetrailer, a machine for living built so efficiently and compactly there's hardly room for a man to breathe. An iron lung it is, with windows and venetian blinds.

The mice are silent, watching me from their hiding places, but the wind is still blowing and outside the ground is covered with snow. Cold as a tomb, a jail, a cave; I lie down on the dusty floor, on the cold linoleum sprinkled with mouse turds, and light the pilot on the butane heater. Once this thing gets going the place warms up fast, in a dense unhealthy way, with a layer of heat under the ceiling where my head is and nothing but frigid air from the knees down. But we've got all the indispensable conveniences: gas cookstove, gas refrigerator, hot water heater, sink with running water (if the pipes aren't frozen), storage cabinets and shelves, everything within arm's reach of every-thing else. The gas comes from two steel bottles in a shed outside; the water comes by gravity flow from a tank buried in a hill close by. Quite luxurious for the wilds. There's even a shower stall and a flush toilet with a dead rat in the bowl. Pretty soft. My poor mother raised five children without any of these luxuries and might be doing without them yet if it hadn't been for Hitler, war and general prosperity.

Time to get dressed, get out and have a look at the lay of the land, fix a breakfast. I try to pull on my boots but they're stiff as iron from the cold. I light a burner on the stove and hold the boots upside down above the flame until they are malleable enough to force my feet into. I put on a coat and step outside. Into the center of the world, God's navel, Abbey's country, the red wasteland.

The sun is not yet in sight but signs of the advent are plain to see. Laven-der clouds sail like a fleet of ships across the pale green dawn; each cloud, planed flat on the wind, has a base of fiery gold. Southeast, twenty miles by line of sight, stand the peaks of the Sierra La Sal, twelve to thirteen thousand feet above sea level, all covered with snow and rosy in the morning sunlight. The air is dry and clear as well as cold; the last fogbanks left over from last night's storm are scudding away like ghosts, fading into nothing before the wind and the sunrise.

The view is open and perfect in all directions except to the west where the ground rises and the skyline is only a few hundred yards away. Looking toward the mountains I can see the dark gorge of the Colorado River five or six miles away, carved through the sandstone mesa, though nothing of the river itself down inside the gorge. Southward, on the far side of the river, lies the Moab valley between thousand-foot walls of rock, with the town of Moab somewhere on the valley floor, too small to be seen from here. Beyond the Moab valley is more canyon and tableland stretching away to the Blue Mountains fifty miles south. On the north and northwest I see the Roan Cliffs and the Book Cliffs, the two-level face of the Uinta Plateau. Along the foot of those cliffs, maybe thirty miles off, invisible from where I stand, runs U.S. 6-50, a major east-west artery of commerce, traffic and rubbish, and the main line of the Denver–Rio Grande Railroad. To the east, under the spreading sunrise, are more mesas, more canyons, league on league of red cliff and arid tablelands, extending through purple haze over the bulging curve of the planet to the ranges of Colorado—a sea of desert.

Within this vast perimeter, in the middle ground and foreground of the picture, a rather personal demesne, are the 33,000 acres of Arches National Monument of which I am now sole inhabitant, usufructuary, observer and custodian.

What are the Arches? From my place in front of the housetrailer I can see several of the hundred or more of them which have been discovered in the park. These are natural arches, holes in the rock, windows in stone, no two alike, as varied in form as in dimension. They range in size from holes just big enough to walk through to openings large enough to contain the dome of the Capitol building in Washington, D.C. Some resemble jug handles or flying buttresses, others natural bridges but with this technical distinction: a natural bridge spans a watercourse—a natural arch does not. The arches were formed through hundreds of thousands of years by the weathering of the huge sandstone walls, or fins, in which they are found. Not the work of a cosmic hand, nor sculptured by sand-bearing winds, as many people prefer to believe, the arches came into being and continue to come into being through the modest wedging action of rainwater, melting snow, frost and ice, aided by gravity. In color they shade from off-white through buff, pink, brown and red, tones which also change with the time of day and the moods of the light, the weather, the sky.

Standing there, gaping at this monstrous and inhuman spectacle of rock and cloud and sky and space, I feel a ridiculous greed and possessiveness come over me. I want to know it all, possess it all, embrace the entire scene intimately, deeply, totally, as a man desires a beautiful woman. An insane wish? Perhaps not—at least there's nothing else, no one human, to dispute possession with me.

The snow-covered ground glimmers with a dull blue light, reflecting the sky and the approaching sunrise. Leading away from me the narrow dirt road, an alluring and primitive track into nowhere, meanders down the slope and toward the heart of the labyrinth of naked stone. Near the first group of arches, looming over a bend in the road, is a balanced rock about fifty feet high, mounted on a pedestal of equal height; it looks like the head from Easter Island, a stone god or a petrified ogre.

Like a god, like an ogre? The personification of the natural is exactly the tendency I wish to suppress in myself, to eliminate for good. I am here not only to evade for a while the clamor and filth and confusion of the cultural apparatus but also to confront, immediately and directly if it's possible, the bare bones of existence, the elemental and fundamental, the bedrock which sustains us. I want to be able to look at and into a juniper tree, a piece of quartz, a vulture, a spider, and see it as it is in itself, devoid of all humanly ascribed qualities, anti-Kantian, even the categories of scientific description. To meet God or Medusa face to face, even if it means risking everything human in myself. I dream of a hard and brutal mysticism in which the naked self merges with a nonhuman world and yet somehow survives still intact, individual, separate. Paradox and bedrock.

Well—the sun will be up in a few minutes and I haven't even begun to make coffee. I take more baggage from my pickup, the grub box and cooking gear, go back in the trailer and start breakfast. Simply breathing, in a place like this, arouses the appetite. The orange juice is frozen, the milk slushy with ice. Still chilly enough inside the trailer to turn my breath to vapor. When the first rays of the sun strike the cliffs I fill a mug with steaming coffee and sit in the doorway facing the sunrise, hungry for the warmth.

Suddenly it comes, the flaming globe, blazing on the pinnacles and minarets and balanced rocks, on the canyon walls and through the windows in the sandstone fins. We greet each other, sun and I, across the black void of ninety-three million miles. The snow glitters between us, acres of diamonds almost painful to look at. Within an hour all the snow exposed to the sunlight will be gone and the rock will be damp and steaming. Within minutes, even as I watch, melting snow begins to drip from the branches of a juniper nearby; drops of water streak slowly down the side of the trailerhouse.

I am not alone after all. Three ravens are wheeling near the balanced rock, squawking at each other and at the dawn. I'm sure they're as delighted by the return of the sun as I am and I wish I knew the language. I'd sooner exchange ideas with the birds on earth than learn to carry on intergalactic communications with some obscure race of humanoids on a satellite planet from the world of Betelgeuse. First things first. The ravens cry out in husky voices, blue-black wings flapping against the golden sky. Over my shoulder comes the sizzle and smell of frying bacon.

That's the way it was this morning.

The Serpents of Paradise

THE APRIL MORNINGS are bright, clear and calm. Not until the afternoon does the wind begin to blow, raising dust and sand in funnel-shaped twisters that spin across the desert briefly, like dancers, and then collapse—whirlwinds from which issue no voice or word except the forlorn moan of the elements under stress. After the reconnoitering dust-devils comes the real the serious wind, the voice of the desert rising to a demented howl and blotting out sky and sun behind yellow clouds of dust, sand, confusion, embattled birds, last year's scrub-oak leaves, pollen, the husks of locusts, bark of juniper. . . .

Time of the red eye, the sore and bloody nostril, the sand-pitted windshield, if one is foolish enough to drive his car into such a storm. Time to sit indoors and continue that letter which is never finished—while the fine dust forms neat little windrows under the edge of the door and on the windowsills. Yet the springtime winds are as much a part of the canyon country as the silence and the glamorous distances; you learn, after a number of years, to love them also.

The mornings therefore, as I started to say and meant to say, are all the sweeter in the knowledge of what the afternoon is likely to bring. Before be-

From *Desert Solitaire: A Season in the Wilderness* (1968)

ginning the morning chores I like to sit on the sill of my doorway, bare feet planted on the bare ground and a mug of hot coffee in hand, facing the sunrise. The air is gelid, not far above freezing, but the butane heater inside the trailer keeps my back warm, the rising sun warms the front, and the coffee warms the interior.

Perhaps this is the loveliest hour of the day, though it's hard to choose. Much depends on the season. In midsummer the sweetest hour begins at sundown, after the awful heat of the afternoon. But now, in April, we'll take the opposite, that hour beginning with the sunrise. The birds, returning from wherever they go in winter, seem inclined to agree. The pinyon jays are whirling in garrulous, gregarious flocks from one stunted tree to the next and back again, erratic exuberant games without any apparent practical function. A few big ravens hang around and croak harsh clanking statements of smug satisfaction from the rimrock, lifting their greasy wings now and then to probe for lice. I can hear but seldom see the canyon wrens singing their distinctive song from somewhere up on the cliffs: a flutelike descent—never ascent—of the whole-tone scale. Staking out new nesting claims, I understand. Also invisible but invariably present at some indefinable distance are the mourning doves whose plaintive call suggests irresistibly a kind of seeking-out, the attempt by separated souls to restore a lost communion:

Hello . . . they seem to cry, *who . . . are . . . you?*

And the reply from a different quarter. *Hello* . . . (pause) *where . . . are . . . you?*

No doubt this line of analogy must be rejected. It's foolish and unfair to impute to the doves, with serious concerns of their own, an interest in questions more appropriate to their human kin. Yet their song, if not a mating call or a warning, must be what it sounds like, a brooding meditation on space, on solitude. The game.

Other birds, silent, which I have not yet learned to identify, are also lurking in the vicinity, watching me. What the ornithologist terms l.g.b.'s—little gray birds—they flit about from point to point on noiseless wings, their origins obscure.

As mentioned before, I share the housetrailer with a number of mice. I don't know how many but apparently only a few, perhaps a single family. They don't disturb me and are welcome to my crumbs and leavings. Where they came from, how they got into the trailer, how they survived before my arrival (for the trailer had been locked up for six months), these are puzzling matters I am not prepared to resolve. My only reservation concerning the mice is that they do attract rattlesnakes.

I'm sitting on my doorstep early one morning, facing the sun as usual, drinking coffee, when I happen to look down and see almost between my bare feet, only a couple of inches to the rear of my heels, the very thing I had in mind. No mistaking that wedgelike head, that tip of horny segmented tail peeping out of the coils. He's under the doorstep and in the shade where the ground and air remain very cold. In his sluggish condition he's not likely to strike unless I rouse him by some careless move of my own.

There's a revolver inside the trailer, a huge British Webley .45, loaded, but it's out of reach. Even if I had it in my hands I'd hesitate to blast a fellow creature at such close range, shooting between my own legs at a living target flat on solid rock thirty inches away. It would be like murder; and where would I set my coffee? My cherrywood walking stick leans against the trailerhouse wall only a few feet away but I'm afraid that in leaning over for it I might stir up the rattler or spill some hot coffee on his scales.

Other considerations come to mind. Arches National Monument is meant to be among other things a sanctuary for wildlife—for all forms of wildlife. It is my duty as a park ranger to protect, preserve and defend all living things within the park boundaries, making no exceptions. Even if this were not the case I have personal convictions to uphold. Ideals, you might say. I prefer not to kill animals. I'm a humanist; I'd rather kill a *man* than a snake.

What to do. I drink some more coffee and study the dormant reptile at my heels. It is not after all the mighty diamondback, *Crotalus atrox*, I'm confronted with but a smaller species known locally as the horny rattler or more precisely as the Faded Midget. An insulting name for a rattlesnake, which may explain the Faded Midget's alleged bad temper. But the name is apt: he is small and dusty-looking, with a little knob above each eye—the horns. His bite though temporarily disabling would not likely kill a full-grown man in normal health. Even so I don't really want him around. Am I to be compelled to put on boots or shoes every time I wish to step outside? The scorpions, tarantulas, centipedes and black widows are nuisance enough.

I finish my coffee, lean back and swing my feet up and inside the doorway of the trailer. At once there is a buzzing sound from below and the rattler lifts his head from his coils, eyes brightening, and extends his narrow black tongue to test the air.

After thawing out my boots over the gas flame I pull them on and come back to the doorway. My visitor is still waiting beneath the doorstep, basking in the sun, fully alert. The trailerhouse has two doors. I leave by the other and get a long-handled spade out of the bed of the government pickup. With this tool I scoop the snake into the open. He strikes; I can hear the click of the fangs against steel, see the stain of venom. He wants to stand and fight, but I am patient; I insist on herding him well away from the trailer. On guard, head aloft—that evil slit-eyed weaving head shaped like the ace of spades—tail whirring, the rattler slithers sideways, retreating slowly before me until he reaches the shelter of a sandstone slab. He backs under it.

You better stay there, cousin, I warn him; if I catch you around the trailer again I'll chop your head off.

A week later he comes back. If not him, his twin brother. I spot him one morning under the trailer near the kitchen drain, waiting for a mouse. I have to keep my promise.

This won't do. If there are midget rattlers in the area there may be diamondbacks too—five, six or seven feet long, thick as a man's wrist, dangerous. I don't want *them* camping under my home. It looks as though I'll have to trap the mice.

However, before being forced to take that step I am lucky enough to capture a gopher snake. Burning garbage one morning at the park dump, I see a long slender yellow-brown snake emerge from a mound of old tin cans and plastic picnic plates and take off down the sandy bed of a gulch. There is a burlap sack in the cab of the truck which I carry when plucking Kleenex flowers from the brush and cactus along the road; I grab that and my stick, run after the snake and corner it beneath the exposed roots of a bush. Making sure it's a gopher snake and not something less useful, I open the neck of the sack and with a great deal of coaxing and prodding get the snake into it. The gopher snake, *Drymarchon corais couperi,* or bull snake, has a reputation as the enemy of rattlesnakes, destroying or driving them away whenever encountered.

Hoping to domesticate this sleek, handsome and docile reptile, I release him inside the trailerhouse and keep him there for several days. Should I attempt to feed him? I decide against it—let him eat mice. What little water he may need can also be extracted from the flesh of his prey.

The gopher snake and I get along nicely. During the day he curls up like a cat in the warm corner behind the heater and at night he goes about his business. The mice, singularly quiet for a change, make themselves scarce. The snake is passive, apparently contented, and makes no resistance when I pick him up with my hands and drape him over an arm or around my neck. When I take him outside into the wind and sunshine his favorite place seems to be inside my shirt, where he wraps himself around my waist and rests on my belt. In this position he sometimes sticks his head out between shirt buttons for a survey of the weather, astonishing and delighting any tourists who may happen to be with me at the time. The scales of a snake are dry and smooth, quite pleasant to the touch. Being a cold-blooded creature, of course, he takes his temperature from that of the immediate environment—in this case my body.

We are compatible. From my point of view, friends. After a week of close association I turn him loose on the warm sandstone at my doorstep and leave for a patrol of the park. At noon when I return he is gone. I search everywhere beneath, nearby and inside the trailerhouse, but my companion has disappeared. Has he left the area entirely or is he hiding somewhere close by? At any rate I am troubled no more by rattlesnakes under the door.

The snake story is not yet ended.

In the middle of May, about a month after the gopher snake's disappearance, in the evening of a very hot day, with all the rosy desert cooling like a griddle with the fire turned off, he reappears. This time with a mate.

I'm in the stifling heat of the trailer opening a can of beer, barefooted, about to go outside and relax after a hard day watching cloud formations. I happen to glance out the little window near the refrigerator and see two gopher snakes on my verandah engaged in what seems to be a kind of ritual dance. Like a living caduceus they wind and unwind about each other in undulant, graceful, perpetual motion, moving slowly across a dome of sandstone. Invisible but tangible as music is the passion which joins them—sexual? combative? both? A shameless *voyeur,* I stare at the lovers, and then to get a closer view run outside and around the trailer to the back. There I get down on hands and knees and creep toward the dancing snakes, not wanting to frighten or disturb them. I crawl to within six feet of them and stop, flat on my belly, watching from the snake's-eye level. Obsessed with their ballet, the serpents seem unaware of my presence.

The two gopher snakes are nearly identical in length and coloring; I cannot be certain that either is actually my former household pet. I cannot even be sure that they are male and female, though their performance resembles so strongly a *pas de deux* by formal lovers. They intertwine and separate, glide side by side in perfect congruence, turn like mirror images of each other and glide back again, wind and unwind again. This is the basic pattern but there is a variation: at regular intervals the snakes elevate their heads, facing one another, as high as they can go, as if each is trying to outreach or overawe the other. Their heads and bodies rise, higher and higher, then topple together and the rite goes on.

I crawl after them, determined to see the whole thing. Suddenly and simultaneously they discover me, prone on my belly a few feet away. The dance stops. After a moment's pause the two snakes come straight toward me, still in flawless unison, straight toward my face, the forked tongues flickering, their intense wild yellow eyes staring directly into my eyes. For an instant I am paralyzed by wonder; then, stung by a fear too ancient and powerful to overcome I scramble back, rising to my knees. The snakes veer and turn and race away from me in parallel motion, their lean elegant bodies making a soft hissing noise as they slide over the sand and stone. I follow them for a short distance, still plagued by curiosity, before remembering my place and the requirements of common courtesy. For godsake let them go in peace, I tell myself. Wish them luck and (if lovers) innumerable offspring, a life of happily ever after. Not for their sake alone but for your own.

In the long hot days and cool evenings to come I will not see the gopher snakes again. Nevertheless I will feel their presence watching over me like totemic deities, keeping the rattlesnakes far back in the brush where I like them best, cropping off the surplus mouse population, maintaining useful connections with the primeval. Sympathy, mutual aid, symbiosis, continuity.

How can I descend to such anthropomorphism? Easily—but is it, in this case, entirely false? Perhaps not. I am not attributing human motives to my snake and bird acquaintances. I recognize that when and where they serve purposes of mine they do so for beautifully selfish reasons of their own. Which is exactly the way it should be. I suggest, however, that it's a foolish, simpleminded rationalism which denies any form of emotion to all animals but man and his dog. This is no more justified than the Moslems are in denying souls to women. It seems to me possible, even probable, that many of the nonhuman undomesticated animals experience emotions unknown to us. What do the coyotes mean when they yodel at the moon? What are the dolphins trying so patiently to tell us? Precisely what did those two enraptured gopher snakes have in mind when they came gliding toward my eyes over the naked sandstone? If I had been as capable of trust as I am susceptible to fear I might have learned something new or some truth so very old we have all forgotten it.

They do not sweat and whine about their condition,
They do not lie awake in the dark and weep for their sins. . . .

All men are brothers, we like to say, half-wishing sometimes in secret it were not true. But perhaps it is true. And is the evolutionary line from protozoan to Spinoza any less certain? That also may be true. We are obliged, therefore, to spread the news, painful and bitter though it may be for some to hear, that all living things on earth are kindred.

Polemic: Industrial Tourism
and the National Parks

I LIKE MY JOB. The pay is generous; I might even say munificent: $1.95 per hour, earned or not, backed solidly by the world's most powerful Air Force, biggest national debt and grossest national product. The fringe benefits are priceless: clean air to breathe (after the spring sandstorms); stillness, solitude and space; an unobstructed view every day and every night of sun, sky, stars, clouds, mountains, moon, cliffrock and canyons; a sense of time enough to let thought and feeling range from here to the end of the world and back; the discovery of something intimate—though impossible to name—in the remote.

The work is simple and requires almost no mental effort, a good thing in more ways than one. What little thinking I do is my own and I do it on government time. Insofar as I follow a schedule it goes about like this:

For me the work week begins on Thursday, which I usually spend in patrolling the roads and walking out the trails. On Friday I inspect the campgrounds, haul firewood and distribute the toilet paper. Saturday and Sunday are my busy days as I deal with the influx of weekend visitors and campers, answering questions, pulling cars out of the sand, lowering children down off

From *Desert Solitaire: A Season in the Wilderness* (1968)

the rocks, tracking lost grandfathers and investigating picnics. My Saturday night campfire talks are brief and to the point. "Everything all right?" I say, badge and all, ambling up to what looks like a cheerful group. "Fine," they'll say; "how about a drink?" "Why not?" I say.

By Sunday evening most everyone has gone home and the heavy duty is over. Thank God it's Monday, I say to myself the next morning. Mondays are very nice. I empty the garbage cans, read the discarded newspapers, sweep out the outhouses and disengage the Kleenex from the clutches of cliffrose and cactus. In the afternoon I watch the clouds drift past the bald peak of Mount Tukuhnikivats. (*Someone* has to do it.)

Tuesday and Wednesday I rest. Those are my days off and I usually set aside Wednesday evening for a trip to Moab, replenishing my supplies and establishing a little human contact more vital than that possible with the tourists I meet on the job. After a week in the desert, Moab (pop. 5,500, during the great uranium boom), seems like a dazzling metropolis, a throbbing dynamo of commerce and pleasure. I walk the single main street as dazed by the noise and neon as a country boy on his first visit to Times Square. (Wow, I'm thinking, this is great.)

After a visit to Miller's Supermarket, where I stock up on pinto beans and other necessities, I am free to visit the beer joints. All of them are busy, crowded with prospectors, miners, geologists, cowboys, truckdrivers and sheepherders, and the talk is loud, vigorous, blue with blasphemy. Although differences of opinion have been known to occur, open violence is rare, for these men treat one another with courtesy and respect. The general atmosphere is free and friendly, quite unlike the sad, sour gloom of most bars I have known, where nervous men in tight collars brood over their drinks between out-of-tune TV screens and a remorseless clock. Why the difference?

I have considered the question and come up with the following solution:

1. These prospectors, miners, etc. have most of them been physically active all day out-of-doors at a mile or more above sea level; they are comfortably tired and relaxed.

2. Most of them have been working alone; the presence of a jostling crowd is therefore not a familiar irritation to be borne with resignation but rather an unaccustomed pleasure to be enjoyed.

3. Most of them are making good wages and/or doing work they like to do; they are, you might say, happy. (The boom will not last, of course, but this

is forgotten. And the ethical and political implications of uranium exploitation are simply unknown in these parts.)

4. The nature of their work requires a combination of skills and knowledge, good health and self-reliance, which tends to inspire self-confidence; they need not doubt their manhood. (Again, everything is subject to change.)

5. Finally, Moab is a Mormon town with funny ways. Hard booze is not sold across the bar except in the semiprivate "clubs." Nor even standard beer. These hard-drinking fellows whom I wish to praise are trying to get drunk on three-point-two! They rise somewhat heavily from their chairs and barstools and tramp, with frequency and a squelchy, sodden noise, toward the pissoirs at the back of the room, more waterlogged than intoxicated.

In the end the beer halls of Moab, like all others, become to me depressing places. After a few games of rotation pool with my friend Viviano Jacquez, a reformed sheepherder turned dude wrangler (a dubious reform), I am glad to leave the last of those smoky dens around midnight and to climb into my pickup and take the long drive north and east back to the silent rock, the unbounded space and the sweet clean air of my outpost in the Arches.

Yes, it's a good job. On the rare occasions when I peer into the future for more than a few days I can foresee myself returning here for season after season, year after year, indefinitely. And why not? What better sinecure could a man with small needs, infinite desires and philosophic pretensions ask for? The better part of each year in the wilderness and the winters in some complementary, equally agreeable environment—Hoboken perhaps, or Tiajuana, Nogales, Juarez . . . one of the border towns. Maybe Tonopah, a good tough Nevada mining town with legal prostitution, or possibly Oakland or even New Orleans—some place grimy, cheap (since I'd be living on unemployment insurance), decayed, hopelessly corrupt. I idle away hours dreaming of the wonderful winter to come, of the chocolate-covered mistress I'll have to rub my back, the journal spread open between two tall candles in massive silver candlesticks, the scrambled eggs with green chile, the crock of homebrew fermenting quietly in the corner, etc., the nights of desperate laughter with brave young comrades, burning billboards and defacing public institutions. . . . Romantic dreams, romantic dreams.

For there is a cloud on my horizon. A small dark cloud no bigger than my hand. Its name is Progress.

The ease and relative freedom of this lovely job at Arches follow from the comparative absence of the motorized tourists, who stay away by the millions.

And they stay away because of the unpaved entrance road, the unflushable toilets in the campgrounds and the fact that most of them have never even heard of Arches National Monument. (Could there be a more genuine testimonial to its beauty and integrity?) All this must change.

I'd been warned. On the very first day Merle and Floyd had mentioned something about developments, improvements, a sinister Master Plan. Thinking that *they* were the dreamers, I paid little heed and had soon forgotten the whole ridiculous business. But only a few days ago something happened which shook me out of my pleasant apathy.

I was sitting out back on my 33,000-acre terrace, shoeless and shirtless, scratching my toes in the sand and sipping on a tall iced drink, watching the flow of evening over the desert. Prime time: the sun very low in the west, the birds coming back to life, the shadows rolling for miles over rock and sand to the very base of the brilliant mountains. I had a small fire going near the table—not for heat or light but for the fragrance of the juniper and the ritual appeal of the clear flames. For symbolic reasons. For ceremony. When I heard a faint sound over my shoulder I looked and saw a file of deer watching from fifty yards away, three does and a velvet-horned buck, all dark against the sundown sky. They began to move. I whistled and they stopped again, staring at me. "Come on over," I said, "have a drink." They declined, moving off with casual, unhurried grace, quiet as phantoms, and disappeared beyond the rise. Smiling, thoroughly at peace, I turned back to my drink, the little fire, the subtle transformations of the immense landscape before me. On the program: rise of the full moon.

It was then I heard the discordant note, the snarling whine of a jeep in low range and four-wheel-drive, coming from an unexpected direction, from the vicinity of the old foot and horse trail that leads from Balanced Rock down toward Courthouse Wash and on to park headquarters near Moab. The jeep came in sight from beyond some bluffs, turned onto the dirt road and came up the hill toward the entrance station. Now operating a motor vehicle of any kind on the trails of a national park is strictly forbidden, a nasty bureaucratic regulation which I heartily support. My bosom swelled with the righteous indignation of a cop: by God, I thought, I'm going to write these sons of bitches a ticket. I put down the drink and strode to the housetrailer to get my badge.

Long before I could find the shirt with the badge on it, however, or the ticket book, or my shoes or my park ranger hat, the jeep turned into my driveway and came right up to the door of the trailer. It was a gray jeep with a U.S. Government decal on the side—Bureau of Public Roads—and covered with dust. Two empty water bags flapped at the bumper. Inside were three sun-burned men in twill britches and engineering boots, and a pile of equipment: transit case, tripod, survey rod, bundles of wooden stakes. (*Oh no!*) The men got out, dripping with dust, and the driver grinned at me, pointing to his parched open mouth and making horrible gasping noises deep in his throat.

"Okay," I said, "come on in."

It was even hotter inside the trailer than outside but I opened the refrig-erator and left it open and took out a pitcher filled with ice cubes and water. As they passed the pitcher back and forth I got the full and terrible story, confirming the worst of my fears. They were a survey crew, laying out a new road into the Arches.

And when would the road be built? Nobody knew for sure; perhaps in a couple of years, depending on when the Park Service would be able to get the money. The new road—to be paved, of course—would cost somewhere be-tween half a million and one million dollars, depending on the bids, or more than fifty thousand dollars per linear mile. At least enough to pay the salaries of ten park rangers for ten years. Too much money, I suggested—they'll never go for it back in Washington.

The three men thought that was pretty funny. Don't worry, they said, this road will be built. I'm worried, I said. Look, the party chief explained, you *need* this road. He was a pleasant-mannered, soft-spoken civil engineer with an unquestioning dedication to his work. A very dangerous man. Who *needs* it? I said; we get very few tourists in this park. That's why you need it, the engineer explained patiently; look, he said, when this road is built you'll get ten, twenty, thirty times as many tourists in here as you get now. His men nodded in solemn agreement, and he stared at me intently, waiting to see what possible answer I could have to that.

"Have some more water," I said. I had an answer all right but I was saving it for later. I knew that I was dealing with a madman.

AS I TYPE these words, several years after the little episode of the gray jeep and the thirsty engineers, all that was foretold has come to pass. Arches National Monument has been developed. The Master Plan has been fulfilled. Where once a few adventurous people came on weekends to camp for a night or two and enjoy a taste of the primitive and remote, you will now find ser-pentine streams of baroque automobiles pouring in and out, all through the spring and summer, in numbers that would have seemed fantastic when I worked there: from 3,000 to 30,000 to 300,000 per year, the "visitation," as they call it, mounts ever upward. The little campgrounds where I used to putter around reading three-day-old newspapers full of lies and watermelon seeds have now been consolidated into one master campground that looks, during the busy season, like a suburban village: elaborate housetrailers of quilted aluminum crowd upon gigantic camper trucks of Fiberglas and molded plastic; through their windows you will see the blue glow of television and hear the studio laughter of Los Angeles; knobby-kneed oldsters in plaid Bermudas buzz up and down the quaintly curving asphalt road on motor-bikes; quarrels break out between campsite neighbors while others gather around their burning charcoal briquettes (ground campfires no longer per-mitted—not enough wood) to compare electric toothbrushes. The Comfort Stations are there, too, all lit up with electricity, fully equipped inside, though the generator breaks down now and then and the lights go out, or the sewage backs up in the plumbing system (drain fields were laid out in sand over a solid bed of sandstone), and the water supply sometimes fails, since the 3,000-foot well can only produce about 5 gpm—not always enough to meet the demand. Down at the beginning of the new road, at park headquarters, is the new entrance station and visitor center, where admission fees are collected and where the rangers are going quietly nuts answering the same three basic ques-tions five hundred times a day: (1) Where's the john? (2) How long's it take to see this place? (3) Where's the Coke machine?

Progress has come at last to the Arches, after a million years of neglect. Industrial Tourism has arrived.

What happened to Arches Natural Money-Mint is, of course, an old story in the Park Service. All the famous national parks have the same problems on a far grander scale, as everyone knows, and many other problems as yet un-known to a little subordinate unit of the system in a backward part of south-eastern Utah. And the same kind of development that has so transformed Arches is under way, planned or completed in many more national parks and national monuments. I will mention only a few examples with which I am personally familiar:

The newly established Canyonlands National Park. Most of the major points of interest in this park are presently accessible, over passable dirt roads, by car—Grandview Point, Upheaval Dome, part of the White Rim, Cave Spring, Squaw Spring campground and Elephant Hill. The more difficult places, such as Angel Arch or Druid Arch, can be reached by jeep, on horse-back or in a one- or two-day hike. Nevertheless the Park Service had drawn up the usual Master Plan calling for modern paved highways to most of the places named and some not named.

Grand Canyon National Park. Most of the south rim of this park is now closely followed by a conventional high-speed highway and interrupted at numerous places by large asphalt parking lots. It is no longer easy, on the South Rim, to get away from the roar of motor traffic, except by descending into the canyon. Toroweap Point in the remote northwest corner of the park, at present still unimpaired (though accessible), has not been forgotten; the plans are in the files for developing even that wild and lovely corner.

Navajo National Monument. A small, fragile, hidden place containing two of the most beautiful cliff dwellings in the Southwest—Keet Seel and Betatakin. This park will be difficult to protect under heavy visitation, and for years it was understood that it would be preserved in a primitive way so as to screen out those tourists unwilling to drive their cars over some twenty miles of dirt road. No longer so: the road has been paved, the campground enlarged and "modernized," and the old magic destroyed.

Natural Bridges National Monument. Another small gem in the park system, a group of three adjacent natural bridges tucked away in the canyon country of southern Utah. Formerly you could drive your car (over dirt roads, of course) to within sight of and easy walking distance—a hundred yards?—of the most spectacular of the three bridges. From there it was only a few hours walking time to the other two. All three could easily be seen in a single day. But this was not good enough for the developers. They have now constructed a paved road into the heart of the area, *between* the two biggest bridges.

Zion National Park. The northwestern part of this park, known as the Kolob area, has until recently been saved as almost virgin wilderness. But a broad highway, with banked curves, deep cuts and heavy fills, that will invade this splendid region, is already under construction.

Capitol Reef National Monument. Grand and colorful scenery in a rugged land—south-central Utah. The most beautiful portion of the park was the canyon of the Fremont River, a great place for hiking, camping, exploring. And what did the authorities do? They built a state highway through it.

Lee's Ferry. Until a few years ago a simple, quiet, primitive place on the shores of the Colorado, Lee's Ferry has now fallen under the protection of the Park Service. And who can protect it against the Park Service? Powerlines now bisect the scene; a 100-foot pink water tower looms against the red cliffs; tract-style houses are built to house the "protectors"; natural campsites along the river are closed off while all campers are now herded into an artificial steel-and-asphalt "campground" in the hottest, windiest spot in the area; historic buildings are razed by bulldozers to save the expense of maintaining them while at the same time hundreds of thousands of dollars are spent on an unneeded paved entrance road. And the administrators complain of *vandalism*.

I could easily cite ten more examples of unnecessary or destructive development for every one I've named so far. What has happened in these particular areas, which I chance to know a little and love too much, has happened, is happening or will soon happen to the majority of our national parks and national forests, despite the illusory protection of the Wilderness Preservation Act, unless a great many citizens rear up on their hind legs and make vigorous political gestures demanding implementation of the Act.

THERE MAY BE some among the readers of this book, like the earnest engineer, who believe without question that any and all forms of construction and development are intrinsic goods, in the national parks as well as anywhere else, who virtually identify quantity with quality and therefore assume that the greater the quantity of traffic, the higher the value received. There are some who frankly and boldly advocate the eradication of the last remnants of wilderness and the complete subjugation of nature to the requirements of—not man—but industry. This is a courageous view, admirable in its simplicity and power, and with the weight of all modern history behind it. It is also quite insane. I cannot attempt to deal with it here.

There will be other readers, I hope, who share my basic assumption that wilderness is a necessary part of civilization and that it is the primary responsibility of the national park system to preserve *intact and undiminished* what little still remains.

Most readers, while generally sympathetic to this latter point of view, will feel, as do the administrators of the National Park Service, that although wilderness is a fine thing, certain compromises and adjustments are necessary in order to meet the ever-expanding demand for outdoor recreation. It is precisely this question which I would like to examine now.

The Park Service, established by Congress in 1916, was directed not only to administer the parks but also to "provide for the enjoyment of same in such manner and by such means as will leave them unimpaired for the enjoyment of future generations." This appropriately ambiguous language, employed long before the onslaught of the automobile, has been understood in various and often opposing ways ever since. The Park Service, like any other big organization, includes factions and factions. The Developers, the dominant faction, place their emphasis on the words *"provide for the enjoyment."* The Preservers, a minority but also strong, emphasize the words *"leave them unimpaired."* It is apparent, then, that we cannot decide the question of development versus preservation by a simple referral to holy writ or an attempt to guess the intention of the founding fathers; we must make up our own minds and decide for ourselves what the national parks should be and what purpose they should serve.

The first issue that appears when we get into this matter, the most important issue and perhaps the only issue, is the one called *accessibility*. The Developers insist that the parks must be made fully accessible not only to people but also to their machines, that is, to automobiles, motorboats, etc. The Preservers argue, in principle at least, that wilderness and motors are incompatible and that the former can best be experienced, understood and enjoyed when the machines are left behind where they belong—on the superhighways and in the parking lots, on the reservoirs and in the marinas.

What does accessibility mean? Is there any spot on earth that men have not proved accessible by the simplest means—feet and legs and heart? Even Mt. McKinley, even Everest, have been surmounted by men on foot. (Some of them, incidentally, rank amateurs, to the horror and indignation of the professional mountaineers.) The interior of the Grand Canyon, a fiercely hot and hostile abyss, is visited each summer by thousands and thousands of tourists of the most banal and unadventurous type, many of them on foot—self-propelled, so to speak—and the others on the backs of mules. Thousands climb each summer to the summit of Mt. Whitney, highest point in the forty-eight United States, while multitudes of others wander on foot or on horseback through the ranges of the Sierras, the Rockies, the Big Smokies, the Cascades and the mountains of New England. Still more hundreds and thousands float or paddle each year down the currents of the Salmon, the Snake, the Allagash, the Yampa, the Green, the Rio Grande, the Ozark, the St. Croix and those portions of the Colorado which have not yet been destroyed by the dam builders. And most significant, these hordes of nonmotorized tourists, hungry for a taste of the difficult, the original, the real, do not consist solely of people young and athletic but also of old folks, fat folks, pale-faced office clerks who don't know a rucksack from a haversack and even children. The one thing they all have in common is the refusal to live always like sardines in a can—they are determined to get outside of their motorcars for at least a few weeks each year.

This being the case, why is the Park Service generally so anxious to accommodate that other crowd, the indolent millions born on wheels and suckled on gasoline, who expect and demand paved highways to lead them in comfort, ease and safety into every nook and corner of the national parks? For the answer to that we must consider the character of what I call Industrial

Tourism and the quality of the mechanized tourists—the Wheelchair Explorers—who are at once the consumers, the raw material and the victims of Industrial Tourism.

Industrial Tourism is a big business. It means money. It includes the motel and restaurant owners, the gasoline retailers, the oil corporations, the road-building contractors, the heavy equipment manufacturers, the state and federal engineering agencies and the sovereign, all-powerful automotive industry. These various interests are well organized, command more wealth than most modern nations and are represented in Congress with a strength far greater than is justified in any constitutional or democratic sense. (Modern politics is expensive—power follows money.) Through Congress the tourism industry can bring enormous pressure to bear upon such a slender reed in the executive branch as the poor old Park Service, a pressure which is also exerted on every other possible level—local, state, regional—and through advertising and the well-established habits of a wasteful nation.

When a new national park, national monument, national seashore or whatever it may be called is set up, the various forces of Industrial Tourism, on all levels, immediately expect action—meaning specifically a road-building program. Where trails or primitive dirt roads already exist, the Industry expects—it hardly needs to ask—that these be developed into modern paved highways. On the local level, for example, the first thing that the superintendent of a new park can anticipate being asked, when he attends his first meeting of the area's Chamber of Commerce, is not "Will roads be built?" but rather "When does construction begin?" and "Why the delay?"

(The Natural Money-Mint. With supersensitive antennae these operatives from the C. of C. look into red canyons and see only green, stand among flowers snorting out the smell of money and hear, while thunderstorms rumble over mountains, the fall of a dollar bill on motel carpeting.)

Accustomed to this sort of relentless pressure since its founding, it is little wonder that the Park Service, through a process of natural selection, has tended to evolve a type of administration which, far from resisting such pressure, has usually been more than willing to accommodate it, even to encourage it. Not from any peculiar moral weakness but simply because such well-adapted administrators are themselves believers in a policy of economic development. "Resource management" is the current term. Old foot trails may be neglected, back-country ranger stations left unmanned and interpretive and protective services inadequately staffed, but the administrators know from long experience that millions for asphalt can always be found; Congress is always willing to appropriate money for more and bigger paved roads, anywhere—particularly if they form loops. Loop drives are extremely popular with the petroleum industry—they bring the motorist right back to the same gas station from which he started.

Great though it is, however, the power of the tourist business would not in itself be sufficient to shape Park Service policy. To all accusations of excessive development the administrators can reply, as they will if pressed hard enough, that they are giving the public what it wants, that their primary duty is to serve the public not preserve the wilds. "Parks are for people" is the public-relations slogan, which decoded means that the parks are for people-in-automobiles. Behind the slogan is the assumption that the majority of Americans, exactly like the managers of the tourist industry, expect and demand to see their national parks from the comfort, security and convenience of their automobiles.

Is this assumption correct? Perhaps. Does that justify the continued and increasing erosion of the parks? It does not. Which brings me to the final aspect of the problem of Industrial Tourism: the Industrial Tourists themselves.

They work hard, these people. They roll up incredible mileages on their odometers, rack up state after state in two-week transcontinental motor marathons, knock off one national park after another, take millions of square yards of photographs and endure patiently the most prolonged discomforts: the tedious traffic jams, the awful food of park cafeterias and roadside eateries, the nocturnal search for a place to sleep or camp, the dreary routine of One-Stop Service, the endless lines of creeping traffic, the smell of exhaust fumes, the ever-proliferating Rules & Regulations, the fees and the bills and the service charges, the boiling radiator and the flat tire and the vapor lock, the surly retorts of room clerks and traffic cops, the incessant jostling of the anxious crowds, the irritation and restlessness of their children, the worry of their wives and the long drive home at night in a stream of racing cars against the lights of another stream racing in the opposite direction, passing now and then the obscure tangle, the shattered glass, the patrolman's lurid blinker light, of one more wreck.

Hard work. And risky. Too much for some, who have given up the struggle on the highways in exchange for an entirely different kind of vacation—out in the open, on their own feet, following the quiet trail through forest and mountains, bedding down at evening under the stars, when and where they feel like it, at a time when the Industrial Tourists are still hunting for a place to park their automobiles.

Industrial Tourism is a threat to the national parks. But the chief victims of the system are the motorized tourists. They are being robbed and robbing themselves. So long as they are unwilling to crawl out of their cars they will not discover the treasures of the national parks and will never escape the stress and turmoil of those urban-suburban complexes which they had hoped, presumably, to leave behind for a while.

How to pry the tourists out of their automobiles, out of their back-breaking upholstered mechanized wheelchairs and onto their feet, onto the strange warmth and solidity of Mother Earth again? This is the problem which the Park Service should confront directly, not evasively, and which it cannot resolve by simply submitting and conforming to the automobile habit. The automobile, which began as a transportation convenience, has become a bloody tyrant (50,000 lives a year), and it is the responsibility of the Park Service, as well as that of everyone else concerned with preserving both wilderness and civilization, to begin a campaign of resistance. The automotive combine has almost succeeded in strangling our cities; we need not let it also destroy our national parks.

It will be objected that a constantly increasing population makes resistance and conservation a hopeless battle. This is true. Unless a way is found to stabilize the nation's population, the parks cannot be saved. Or anything else worth a damn. Wilderness preservation, like a hundred other good causes, will be forgotten under the overwhelming pressure of a struggle for mere survival and sanity in a completely urbanized, completely industrialized, ever more crowded environment. For my own part I would rather take my chances in a thermonuclear war than live in such a world.

Assuming, however, that population growth will be halted at a tolerable level before catastrophe does it for us, it remains permissible to talk about such things as the national parks. Having indulged myself in a number of harsh judgments upon the Park Service, the tourist industry and the motoring public, I now feel entitled to make some constructive, practical, sensible proposals for the salvation of both parks and people.

(1) No more cars in national parks. Let the people walk. Or ride horses, bicycles,° mules, wild pigs—anything—but keep the automobiles and the motorcycles and all their motorized relatives out. We have agreed not to drive our automobiles into cathedrals, concert halls, art museums, legislative as-

---

° Abbey did not anticipate the mountain biker who moves across wild lands like a steamroller flattening every living thing in his path.—Ed.

semblies, private bedrooms and the other sanctums of our culture; we should treat our national parks with the same deference, for they, too, are holy places. An increasingly pagan and hedonistic people (thank God!), we are learning finally that the forests and mountains and desert canyons are holier than our churches. Therefore let us behave accordingly.

Consider a concrete example and what could be done with it: Yosemite Valley in Yosemite National Park. At present a dusty milling confusion of motor vehicles and ponderous camping machinery, it could be returned to relative beauty and order by the simple expedient of requiring all visitors, at the park entrance, to lock up their automobiles and continue their tour on the seats of good workable bicycles supplied free of charge by the United States Government.

Let our people travel light and free on their bicycles—nothing on the back but a shirt, nothing tied to the bike but a slicker, in case of rain. Their bedrolls, their backpacks, their tents, their food and cooking kits will be trucked in for them, free of charge, to the campground of their choice in the Valley, by the Park Service. (Why not? The roads will still be there.) Once in the Valley they will find the concessioners waiting, ready to supply whatever needs might have been overlooked, or to furnish rooms and meals for those who don't want to camp out.

The same thing could be done at Grand Canyon or at Yellowstone or at any of our other shrines to the out-of-doors. There is no compelling reason, for example, why tourists need to drive their automobiles to the very brink of the Grand Canyon's south rim. They could *walk* that last mile. Better yet, the Park Service should build an enormous parking lot about ten miles south of Grand Canyon Village and another east of Desert View. At those points, as at Yosemite, our people could emerge from their steaming shells of steel and glass and climb upon horses or bicycles for the final leg of the journey. On the rim, as at present, the hotels and restaurants will remain to serve the physical needs of the park visitors. Trips along the rim would also be made on foot, on horseback or—utilizing the paved road which already exists—on bicycles. For those willing to go all the way from one parking lot to the other, a distance of some sixty or seventy miles, we might provide bus service back to their cars, a service which would at the same time effect a convenient exchange of bicycles and/or horses between the two terminals.

What about children? What about the aged and infirm? Frankly, we need waste little sympathy on these two pressure groups. Children too small to ride bicycles and too heavy to be borne on their parents' backs need only wait a few years—if they are not run over by automobiles they will grow into a lifetime of joyous adventure, if we save the parks and *leave them unimpaired for the enjoyment of future generations.* The aged merit even less sympathy: after all they had the opportunity to see the country when it was still relatively un-spoiled. However, we'll stretch a point for those too old or too sickly to mount a bicycle and let them ride the shuttle buses.

I can foresee complaints. The motorized tourists, reluctant to give up the old ways, will complain that they can't see enough without their automobiles to bear them swiftly (traffic permitting) through the parks. But this is non-sense. A man on foot, on horseback or on a bicycle will see more, feel more, enjoy more in one mile than the motorized tourists can in a hundred miles. Better to idle through one park in two weeks than try to race through a dozen in the same amount of time. Those who are familiar with both modes of travel know from experience that this is true; the rest have only to make the exper-iment to discover the same truth for themselves.

They will complain of physical hardship, these sons of the pioneers. Not for long; once they rediscover the pleasures of actually operating their own limbs and senses in a varied, spontaneous, voluntary style, they will complain instead of crawling back into a car; they may even object to returning to desk and office and that dry-wall box on Mossy Brook Circle. The fires of revolt may be kindled—which means hope for us all.

(2) No more new roads in national parks. After banning private automo-biles the second step should be easy. Where paved roads are already in exis-tence they will be reserved for the bicycles and essential in-park services, such as shuttle buses, the trucking of camping gear and concessioners' sup-plies. Where dirt roads already exist they too will be reserved for nonmotor-ized traffic. Plans for new roads can be discarded and in their place a program of trail building begun, badly needed in some of the parks and in many of the national monuments. In mountainous areas it may be desirable to build emer-gency shelters along the trails and bike roads; in desert regions a water supply might have to be provided at certain points—wells drilled and handpumps installed if feasible.

Once people are liberated from the confines of automobiles there will be a greatly increased interest in hiking, exploring and back-country packtrips. Fortunately the parks, by the mere elimination of motor traffic, will come to seem far bigger than they are now—there will be more room for more per-sons, an astonishing expansion of space. This follows from the interesting fact that a motorized vehicle, when not at rest, requires a volume of space far out of proportion to its size. To illustrate: imagine a lake approximately ten miles long and on the average one mile wide. A single motorboat could easily circumnavigate the lake in an hour; ten motorboats would begin to crowd it; twenty or thirty, all in operation, would dominate the lake to the exclusion of any other form of activity; and fifty would create the hazards, confusion and turmoil that make pleasure impossible. Suppose we banned motorboats and allowed only canoes and rowboats; we would see at once that the lake seemed ten or perhaps a hundred times bigger. The same thing holds true, to an even greater degree, for the automobile. Distance and space are functions of speed and time. Without expending a single dollar from the United States Treasury we could, if we wanted to, multiply the area of our national parks tenfold or a hundredfold—simply by banning the private automobile. The next generation, all 250 million of them, would be grateful to us.

(3) Put the park rangers to work. Lazy scheming loafers, they've wasted too many years selling tickets at toll booths and sitting behind desks filling out charts and tables in the vain effort to appease the mania for statistics which torments the Washington office. Put them to work. They're supposed to be rangers—make the bums range; kick them out of those overheated air-conditioned offices, yank them out of those overstuffed patrol cars and drive them out on the trails where they should be, leading the dudes over hill and dale, safely into and back out of the wilderness. It won't hurt them to work off a little office fat; it'll do them good, help take their minds off each other's wives and give them a chance to get out of reach of the boss—a blessing for all concerned.

They will be needed on the trail. Once we outlaw the motors and stop the road-building and force the multitudes back on their feet, the people will need leaders. A venturesome minority will always be eager to set off on their own, and no obstacles should be placed in their path; let them take risks, for Godsake, let them get lost, sunburnt, stranded, drowned, eaten by bears, buried alive under avalanches—that is the right and privilege of any free American. But the rest, the majority, most of them new to the out-of-doors, will need and welcome assistance, instruction and guidance. Many will not know how to saddle a horse, read a topographical map, follow a trail over slickrock, memorize landmarks, build a fire in rain, treat snakebite, rappel down a cliff, glissade down a glacier, read a compass, find water under sand, load a burro, splint a broken bone, bury a body, patch a rubber boat, portage a waterfall, survive a blizzard, avoid lightning, cook a porcupine, comfort a girl during a thunderstorm, predict the weather, dodge falling rock, climb out of a box canyon or pour piss out of a boot. Park rangers know these things, or should know them, or used to know them and can relearn; they will be needed. In addition to this sort of practical guide service the ranger will also be a bit of a naturalist, able to edify the party in his charge with the natural and human history of the area, in detail and in broad outline.

Critics of my program will argue that it is too late for such a radical reformation of a people's approach to the out-of-doors, that the pattern is too deeply set, and that the majority of Americans would not be willing to emerge from the familiar luxury of their automobiles, even briefly, to try the little-known and problematic advantages of the bicycle, the saddle horse and the footpath. This might be so; but how can we be sure unless we dare the experiment? I, for one, suspect that millions of our citizens, especially the young, are yearning for adventure, difficulty, challenge—they will respond with enthusiasm. What we must do, prodding the Park Service into the forefront of the demonstration, is provide these young people with the opportunity, the assistance and the necessary encouragement.

How could this most easily be done? By following the steps I have proposed, plus reducing the expenses of wilderness recreation to the minimal level. Guide service by rangers should, of course, be free to the public. Money saved by *not* constructing more paved highways into the parks should be sufficient to finance the cost of bicycles and horses for the entire park system. Elimination of automobile traffic would allow the Park Service to save more millions now spent on road maintenance, police work and paper work. Whatever the cost, however financed, the benefits for park visitors in health and happiness—virtues unknown to the statisticians—would be immeasurable.

Excluding the automobile from the heart of the great cities has been seriously advocated by thoughtful observers of our urban problems. It seems to me an equally proper solution to the problems besetting our national parks. Of course it would be a serious blow to Industrial Tourism and would be bitterly resisted by those who profit from that industry. Exclusion of automobiles would also require a revolution in the thinking of Park Service officialdom and in the assumptions of most American tourists. But such a revolution, like it or not, is precisely what is needed. The only foreseeable alternative, given the current trend of things, is the gradual destruction of our national park system.

Let us therefore steal a slogan from the Development Fever Faction in the Park Service. The parks, they say, are for people. Very well. At the main entrance to each national park and national monument we shall erect a billboard one hundred feet high, two hundred feet wide, gorgeously filigreed in brilliant neon and outlined with blinker lights, exploding stars, flashing prayer wheels and great Byzantine phallic symbols that gush like geysers every thirty seconds. (You could set your watch by them.) Behind the fireworks will loom the figure of Smokey the Bear, taller than a pine tree, with eyes in his head that swivel back and forth, watching YOU, and ears that actually twitch. Push a button and Smokey will recite, for the benefit of children and government officials who might otherwise have trouble with some of the big words, in a voice ursine, loud and clear, the message spelled out on the face of the billboard. To wit:

HOWDY FOLKS. WELCOME. THIS IS YOUR NATIONAL PARK, ESTABLISHED FOR THE PLEASURE OF YOU AND ALL PEOPLE EVERYWHERE. PARK YOUR CAR, JEEP, TRUCK, TANK, MOTORBIKE, MOTORBOAT, JETBOAT, AIRBOAT, SUBMARINE, AIRPLANE, JETPLANE, HELICOPTER, HOVERCRAFT, WINGED MOTORCYCLE, ROCKETSHIP OR ANY OTHER CONCEIVABLE TYPE OF MOTORIZED VEHICLE IN THE WORLD'S BIGGEST PARKING LOT BEHIND THE COMFORT STATION IMMEDIATELY TO YOUR REAR. GET OUT OF YOUR MOTORIZED VEHICLE, GET ON YOUR HORSE, MULE, BICYCLE OR FEET, AND COME ON IN. ENJOY YOURSELVES. THIS HERE PARK IS FOR *PEOPLE*.

The survey chief and his two assistants did not stay very long. Letting them go in peace, without debate, I fixed myself another drink, returned to the table in the backyard and sat down to await the rising of the moon.

My thoughts were on the road and the crowds that would pour upon it as inevitably as water under pressure follows every channel which is opened to it. Man is a gregarious creature, we are told, a social being. Does that mean he is also a herd animal? I don't believe it, despite the character of modern life. The herd is for ungulates, not for men and women and their children. Are men no better than sheep or cattle, that they must live always in view of one another in order to feel a sense of safety? I can't believe it.

We are preoccupied with time. If we could learn to love space as deeply as we are now obsessed with time, we might discover a new meaning in the phrase *to live like men*.

At what distance should good neighbors build their houses? Let it be determined by the community's mode of travel: if by foot, four miles; if by horseback, eight miles; if by motorcar, twenty-four miles; if by airplane, ninety-six miles.

Recall the Proverb: "Set not thy foot too often in thy neighbor's house, lest he grow weary of thee and hate thee."

The sun went down and the light mellowed over the sand and distance and hoodoo rocks "pinnacled dim in the intense inane." A few stars appeared, scattered liberally through space. The solitary owl called.

Finally the moon came up, a golden globe behind the rocky fretwork of the horizon, a full and delicate moon that floated lightly as a leaf upon the dark slow current of the night. A face that watched me from the other side.

The air grew cool. I put on boots and shirt, stuffed some cheese and raisins in my pocket and went for a walk. The moon was high enough to cast a good light when I reached the place where the gray jeep had first come into view. I could see the tracks of its wheels quite plainly in the sand and the route was well marked, not only by the tracks but by the survey stakes planted in the ground at regular fifty-foot intervals and by streamers of plastic ribbon tied to the brush and trees.

Teamwork, that's what made America what it is today. Teamwork and initiative. The survey crew had done their job; I would do mine. For about five miles I followed the course of their survey back toward headquarters, and as I went I pulled up each little wooden stake and threw it away, and cut all the bright ribbons from the bushes and hid them under a rock. A futile effort, in the long run, but it made me feel good. Then I went home to the trailer, taking a shortcut over the bluffs.

Tukuhnikivats, the Island
in the Desert

L ATE IN AUGUST the lure of the mountains becomes irresistible. Seared by the everlasting sunfire, I want to see running water again, embrace a pine tree, cut my initials in the bark of an aspen, get bit by a mosquito, see a mountain bluebird, find a big blue columbine, get lost in the firs, hike above timberline, sunbathe on snow and eat some ice, climb the rocks and stand in the wind at the top of the world on the peak of Tukuhnikivats.

On a Monday evening before my two days off I load bedroll, rucksack, climbing boots and grub box into the pickup and drive away, turning my back on the entrance station and housetrailer and ramada, the lone juniper and all the hoodoo rocks. Take care of yourselves as best you can, I'm thinking— your slave is off to the high country. Cousin buzzard, keep an eye peeled for trouble.

Over the rocky wagon road—that trail of dust and sand and washouts which I love, which the tourists hate so deeply—I go jouncing, banging, clattering in the old Chevy, scaring the daylights out of the lizards and beetles trying to cross the road.

Stepping harder on the gas I speed over the sand flats at sixty-five mph, trailing a funnel of dust about a mile and a half long. Washout ahead: playing

From *Desert Solitaire: A Season in the Wilderness* (1968)

the brakes lightly, fishtailing over the sand ripples, I gear down into second, into low and when I hit the new gulch slam the brakes hard and shift into compound low—creeper gear—to negotiate the rocks and logs strewn over the roadway. A hundred yards down the wash I can see the culvert, displaced by the flood and half-buried in quicksand—ought to anchor that thing. Into low, into second, up to the surface of a long ledge of sandstone dotted here and there with stunted junipers and the iridescent silver-blue sage; from there in high at highest feasible velocity—thirty mph—through a slalom course of boulders, trees and tight curves to the bank of Courthouse Wash, where a sliver of metallic-looking water snakes from pool to pool over the gravel, quicksand and mud. On the shores of the wash are reeds and rushes all bowed downstream under the weight of silt. In low gear at full throttle I gun the truck across the wash, anxious not to get bogged down, and roar up over the rocks and ruts on the far side. Easy enough: from here it's only a mile of dust, pot-holes and dunes of blowsand to the paved highway, which I reach without difficulty.

I look at my watch. I've driven the eight miles from park entrance to highway in only seventeen minutes or at an average rate of nearly thirty miles an hour. Very good, considering the obstacles. Why the tourists complain so much about this road I cannot understand: every foot of it offers some kind of challenge to nerve and skill and the drive as a whole is nothing less than a small adventure for man and machine. With brilliant scenery all the way, com-ing or going—what more could they want?

Well, damn the lot of them, I think, rolling down the broad asphalt trail to Moab at a safe and sane eighty-five, not forgetting to keep one eye skinned for a sign of Fred Burkett the local highway patrolman, whose favorite hiding place north of town was behind a Chamber of Commerce billboard welcom-ing tourists to "Moab, Uranium Capital of the World"—was until I leveled the billboard to the ground one night with a bucksaw which I had borrowed for the job from the United States National Park Service, Department of the Interior (Help Keep America Beautiful)—good thing Fred wasn't there at the time; his new Plymouth Interceptor would've got badly wrinkled—as-suming he was asleep as usual.

Yes, I say, let them all SQUEEZE TO RIGHT FORM SINGLE LANE REMOVE SUNGLASSES TURN ON LIGHTS REDUCE SPEED OBEY SIGNALS MERGING TRAFFIC AHEAD as they supinely gas themselves dead (passive nonresistance) tunneling into Hoboken Manhattan Jersey City Brooklyn New Haven Boston Baltimore Oakland Berkeley San Francisco Washington Seattle Chicago Pittsburgh L.A. San Diego etc. Atlanta Birming-

ham Miami etc. etc. Denver Phoenix Sacramento Salt Lake Tulsa OK City
etc. etc. etc. Houston etc. & Hell. . . . But not here please. Not at my own
Arches Natural Money-Mint National Park.

I drive swiftly on thinking the unthinkable, past Arches headquarters
where I glimpse the superintendent mowing his front lawn, and across the
bridge over the Colorado River, rich and red as beet soup with a load of Moenkopi mud flushed by yesterday's deluge out of Onion Creek Canyon. Poison
water—selenium, arsenic, radon in solution. Into Moab and the bright lights,
the jostling throng of kids, cowboys, miners, young bronzed hoods with side-
burns and the sleeves removed from their shirts, through the blaring traffic
and under the nervous neon—ATOMIC CAFE!—to the liquor store. Just in
time; they close at seven here. A bottle of *Liebfraumilch* and then to the market for meat, fruit. Gasoline for my machine.

Getting late: the sun is down beyond Back-of-the-Rocks, beyond the es-
carpment of Dead Horse Point. A soft pink mist of light, the alpenglow, lies
on the mountains above timberline. I hurry on, south from Moab, off the
highway on the gravel road past the new airport, past the turnoff to old Roy's
place and up into the foothills. Getting dark: I switch on the lights and keep
moving. I know exactly where I want to camp tonight and will keep driving till
I get there.

Up to the top of Wilson's Mesa and eastward and upward through the
pygmy forest of juniper and pinyon pine. Pale phantom deer leap across the
road through the beams of my lights—a four-point buck and one, two, three
does. Climbing steadily in second gear I leave the pinyon-juniper zone and
enter the scrub-oak jungles, the manzanita, sumac and dogbane; higher still
appear stands of jackpine and yellowpine, common though not abundant in
the La Sal range.

I turn off the main dirt road and take one narrower, rougher, with a high
grass-grown center, drive through a meadow where the golden eyes of more
deer gleam in my headlights and enter groves of quaking aspen, tall straight
slim trees with bark as white as that of birches, easy to cut with a knife, much
in favor among sheepherders, hunters, lovers.

A bunch of cattle in the road. Too dull-witted to get out of the way, they
trot along in front of the truck for a quarter of a mile before I can pass them.
The road gets tougher, resembling a cobblestone alley—but here every cob-
ble is loose and no two the same size or shape. When I come to a very steep
pitch the rear wheels spin, the motor stalls. I get out and load rocks into the
back of the bed, adding weight and traction enough to climb the grade.

In compound low, engine overheating, radiator at boiling point, I keep going, looking for a certain dim trail off to the right into the aspens; it comes, I turn off the road and drive through an opening in a derelict rail fence, brush beneath leafy boughs and emerge in a small grassy glade surrounded on all sides but one by solid ranks of aspens. Here I stop, turn off the lights, let the motor idle for a minute and then shut it off.

After the droning mechanical grind of the long pull up the mountain the silence of the forest seems startling, deafening, most welcome. I get out, stretch, relieve myself. The air is chill and I put on a jacket.

As my ears and nerves recover from the long oppression of the drive I can hear the flutter of aspen leaves above my head and the ripple of running water not far away. In the light of the stars I walk through tall, dewy grass past a stone fireplace which I remember well, for I am the one who built it, to the edge of a brook.

The water is gushing over roots, splashing among stones. It mills in a pool at my feet and races on into the darkness. On the surface of the pool I see fragmented stars, glints of light on the whirling water. Cupping my hands I take a drink. Fresh from melting snowbanks on the peak above, the water is cold as ice. My hands tingle, burning with cold.

I find some dry sticks, build a little fire in the fireplace, uncork the wine. Excellent. Waiting for the fire to settle down to exactly where I want it, I spread a tarp on the ground close to the fire and place my bedroll on it for a cushion, sitting like a tailor. I'll not unroll the sleeping bag until I'm ready to sleep; I want to save that desert warmth stored up inside it.

The fire is right. I set a light grill over the flames and on the grill roll out a big thin tough beefsteak, which happens to be the kind of beefsteak I prefer. I reach for the bottle.

Very quietly and selfishly, all by my lonesome, I cook and drink and eat my supper, smoke a cigar for dessert, finish the wine. The stars look kindly down. Drunk as a Navajo I pull off my boots and crawl into the snug warm down-filled womblike mummy bag. The night is cold, perhaps freezing—should I drain the radiator? To hell with it. High on the lap of Tukuhnikivats the King, wrapped in the sack in my home away from home, I close my eyes and go to sleep.

IN THE SWEET CHILL of the dawn I wake up, hearing the ratchetlike screech of a squirrel. I open my eyes and see first a tall stem of grass bending over my face, weighed down by a drop of dew that glistens like a pearl on its tip. Beyond the grass the pale trunks of the aspens stand in serried formation, thick as corn, blue-white and ghostly, their leafy crowns in perpetual motion. The trees are in shadow but above the forest shafts of sunlight fan out across the blue. Deep in the sky rises the bald peak of Tukuhnikivats, sunlit. Time to get up there.

I wash my face in the icy stream, shocking myself wide awake. Make a fire, put water on to boil for tea, lay thick slices of bacon tenderly across the grill. While the bacon broils above the coals I crack eggs in a skillet—five eggs—add slices of green chile and scramble. Hunger stirs within me like a great music. Turning the bacon with a fork, I watch the light deepen on the mountain, am watched in turn by a bluejay, a redheaded woodpecker, the gray squirrel. In the bark of the nearest aspen, deeply inscribed, are the initials "C.E.M.," without a date. I squat close to the fire, lean half over it inhaling aspen smoke, trying to keep warm, and eat my breakfast.

After the meal I pack fruit, nuts, cheese and raisins into the rucksack, take my cherrywood stick and start up the mountain. I follow the little stream, keeping close to its course up through the clear green shade of the aspens. Though resembling the birch, the quaking aspen like the cottonwood is a member of the willow family, and reveals its kinship by the delicate suspension of the leaves. Like that of the cottonwood, the foliage of the aspen responds to the slightest movement of air—even a blow on the trunk with my stick makes the leafy assembly vibrate like bangles. In autumn the leaves turn a bright, uniform yellow, glorifying entire mountainsides with bands and slashes of gold.

I hear and see a few birds—woodpecker, flicker, bluejay, phainopepla— but no sign of any animal life except squirrel and deer. According to reputation there are still a few mountain lions in the Sierra La Sal, ranging through from time to time, and possibly even bear, but it's not my kind of luck today to find their tracks. But if the animals are few the flowers are plentiful, especially in the open glades and along the brook, where I find clusters of larkspur, blue flax and Sego lilies.

The larkspur is of the species called Subalpine or Barbey (*Delphinium barbeyi*), with a thick stem, deep blue petals and a toxic content of delphinine. Too much larkspur and the flower-eating cow or sheep turns belly up, legs in the air, dead as a log and crawling with maggots.

Equally beautiful and not so potent is the blue flax with its pale sky-blue petals veined in violet, and the Sego lily or Mariposa lily, state flower of Utah. *Calochortus nuttalli* . . . "beautiful herb." Each deep cup-shaped bloom sparkles with morning dew. The Sego lily grows from an onionlike bulb and if I were hungry or the flower more abundant I'd dig one up and try the thing for flavor. Instead I content myself with a stem of grass.

Climbing higher, I enter by degrees into the Hudsonian life zone, leaving behind the Canadian with its aspen and Douglas fir, and find myself in the dark cool depths of the silver fir and spruce forest. The shade grows darker, the silence deeper; gracing the air is the subtle fragrance of sun-warmed, oozing resin. There is no trail and the many dead and fallen trees make progress difficult. I leave the stream and work my way directly up the mountainside toward the light of timberline.

As I ascend the trees become smaller and at the edge of the woods, on the margin of the scree that leads to the summit, the trees are little more than shrubs, gnarled, twisted and storm-blasted, with matlike tangles of Engelmann spruce growing over the rock. I stop to orient myself and to look for the best route to the top.

I stand on broken rock, slabs of granite veined with feldspar and quartz, colored with patches of green and auburn lichens. I am on the north face of Tukuhnikivats; blocking the view to the east and northeast are Mounts Peale and Mellanthin but north and west and southwest the world is open and I can see the knobs and domes of the Arches, the gray-blue Roan Cliffs beyond, the town and valley of Moab 7,000 feet below, the looming headlands of Hatch Point, Dead Horse Point and Grandview Point, and farther away, farthest of all, wonderfully remote, the Orange Cliffs, Land's End and The Maze, an exhilarating vastness bathed in morning light, room enough for a lifetime of exploration.

I look up to the peak. Timberline at this latitude is in the neighborhood of 11,000 feet; therefore I have about 2,000 vertical feet to climb. There is no trail to the summit and from where I stand no ridge of solid rock to make the climb easier. Nothing but the immense talus slopes of loose, jumbled, broken slabs, a few islands of tundra, and up the middle a long couloir partly filled with snow. I start toward that.

Munching raisins, I climb and scramble over the rocks, which sometimes seesaw under my weight or start sliding, adding the hazards of surprise, twisted knee, sprained ankle or crushed foot to the general interest of the ascent. Aside from the awkward footing the climb is simple enough, requiring no special equipment except heart and legs. In the technical sense of the mountaineer not a *climb* at all but only a *scramble*. Not that such distinctions matter to me; the easier the better so far as I'm concerned. I am more interested in the pikas squealing under the rocks, in the subalpine buttercups on the grassy patches, in the furtive elusive gray spiders that dance over the slabs before me than in engineering exercises with nylon rope, carabiners, brakebars, pitons, slings, crampons, star drills and expansion bolts. For the present, anyway.

I can hear the pikas all around me signaling each other with their whistles but never catch a glimpse of one. They stay in their tunnels and lairs under the rock, listening to the strange two-legged monster stumbling over their homes. Pika: a harelike mammal, a lagomorph, having two pairs of upper incisors, one set behind the other—why? The better to gnaw the tough roots of the scrubby tundra plants.

When I reach one of the islandlike areas of solid rock in the midst of the scree I lie down for a while to catch my breath and examine at close range, six inches, the buttercups, the Sticky Polemonium, the moss campion (lovely name) and the miniature alpine violets with their flowers no bigger than the head of a thumbtack. I also hope to find the flower called Rocky Mountain Pussytoes, a favorite of mine for no better reason than the name.

Here are the buttercups, alpine or subalpine, with their hairy sepals, divided leaves, shiny yellow petals: hold one close to your nose, the old wives say, and if your nose reflects the yellow you are a butter-lover. I have no mirror with me except a knifeblade and do not perform the experiment. In any case the game was not meant for the solitary but for two alone—lad and lass, man and maid.

Sticky Polemonium has an engaging sound. It is a tiny tubular purplish flower with orange anthers, clusters of them on fuzzy stalks about ten inches high; *Polemonium viscosum,* alias Sky Pilot, for it often lives at 13,000 feet or more. As for the moss campion I am lying on it; it makes a pleasant cushioning on the rock and the small pink flowers will not be damaged by my temporary sojourn here.

It won't do to pause for long on a mountain climb. The longer you rest the harder it is to get up and go on. The steady oxlike plod is best. I rise from the flowerbed and continue, moving up from rock to shaky rock, sliding, slipping, sometimes losing ground but gaining in the long run. The long field of snow looks good and I make straight for it, hoping the snow will be firm enough to climb, soft enough to kick toeholds in.

I am also eager for a drink of water; the keen chill air of the upper world whets my thirst and I'm carrying no water in my pack. I am already close enough to the snowfield to hear the muted roar, as of an underground waterfall, of the melted snow rushing downward through the piled slabs over which I struggle.

Coming near the edge of the snowfield I find running water close to the surface, visible among the rocks. I stop to drink. The water is bitterly, brilliantly cold, with particles of glacial grit—utterly delicious.

A few more steps and I reach the snowfield, which extends for a thousand feet, bell-curved, up through the couloir toward the summit. It looks like it might go. I advance upon it slowly and carefully, kicking out footholds as I climb. The snow is firm, solid, as expected, and at first it seems easier to go this way. But the kicking of niches becomes tiring; an ice axe would be handy now. Also one false step, one slip, and I'll be back down at my starting point in seconds. Somewhat regretfully I decide to leave the snow and traverse over to the rocks, continuing the climb up those unstable fragments.

It seems odd that the mountainside should be covered with this loose debris but so it is with Tukuhnikivats; nearly symmetrical, like a volcano, it has weathered evenly on all sides, unlike its neighbor Mount Peale for instance, which can be reached over spurs and ridges of solid base rock. Which is also for that matter a little bit higher, according to the surveyors.

Then why climb Tukuhnikivats? Because I prefer to. Because no one else will if I don't—and *somebody has to do it.* Because it is the most dramatic in form of the La Sals, the most conspicuous and beautiful as seen from my terrace in the Arches. Because, finally, I like the name. Tukuhnikivats—in the language of the Utes "where the sun lingers."

The mountain resists me. Slowly, laboriously I struggle upward, clambering over the tricky slabs. Halfway up, the mountain hits me with a sudden storm. First the wind and a sinister clot of gray scud crawling over the peak; then a rain of sleet followed by hailstones that bombard me like a cascade of marbles. I have put on my jacket, pulled my hat tight on my skull—I keep on climbing. What else can I do? There's no shelter and little comfort in simply standing still and suffering.

In a few minutes the storm melts away, the clouds break, the sun comes out to warm my body and melt the hailstones that are piled like mothballs in every cranny among the rocks. As the weather improves so does the terrain. The scree gives way to outcroppings of solid country rock which I climb to reach the firm, grass-covered dome of the peak. A cairn of stones over the brass-headed benchmark of the Geodetic Survey marks the highest point and there I sit to eat my lunch, shielded from the wind by the cairn and drenched in warmth from a sun that has never seemed so close, so dazzling, in such a dark and violet sky.

The sun in fact has changed color. Seen from the desert it is a golden glare and sometimes, on the horizon or during a sandstorm, red as blood. But from

here, at 13,000 feet above sea level, the sun is a white star, a white fire fierce
as radium, burning in a sky of deeper, darker blue.

Peeling an orange I survey the larger globe below. All around the peaks of
the Sierra La Sal lies the desert, a sea of burnt rock, arid tablelands, barren
and desolate canyons. The canyon country is revealed from this magnificent
height as on a map and I can imagine, if not read, the names on the land. The
folk poetry of the pioneers:

Desolation Canyon, Labyrinth Canyon, Stillwater Canyon, Dark Can-
yon, Happy Canyon, Cohabitation Canyon, Nigger Bill Canyon, Recapture
Canyon;

Mollie's Nipple, The Bishop's Prick, Queen Anne's Bottom;

Dirty Devil River, Onion Creek, Last Chance Creek, Salvation Creek,
Moonlight Wash, Grand Gulch;

Cigarette Spring, Stinking Spring, Hog Spring, Squaw Spring, French-
man's Spring, Matrimony Spring, Arsenic Spring;

Woodenshoe Butte, Windowblind Peak, Looking Glass Rock, Lizard
Rock, Elephant Hill, Turk's Head, Candlestick Spire, Cleopatra's Chair, Jacob's Ladder, Copper Globe, Black Box;

Waterpocket Fold, Sinbad Valley, Beef Basin, Fable Valley, Ruin Park,
Devil's Pocket, Robbers' Roost, Goblin Valley, Soda Springs Basin, Potato
Bottom Basin, Cyclone Lane, Buckhorn Flat, Surprise Valley, The Big Draw,
Professor Valley, Kodachrome Flats, Calamity Mesa, Upheaval Dome;

Poison Strip, Yellowcat, Hidden Splendor, Happy Jack, Rattlesnake, Mi
Vida (all uranium mines);

Ernie's Country, Pete's Mesa, Zeke's Hole, Pappy's Pasture;

Wolf Hole and Poverty Knoll;

Pucker Pass (where the canyon puckers up) and Hooray Pass (hooray we
made it);

Tavaputs, Kaiparowits, Toroweap, Owachomo, Hovenweap, Dinne-
hotso, Hoskinnini, Dot Klish, Betatakin, Keet Seel, Tes-Nos-Pas, Kayenta,
Agathla, Tukuhnikivats;

Grand Mesa, Thunder Mesa, Wild Horse Mesa, Horsethief Point, Dead
Horse Point, Grandview Point, Land's End;

Capitol Reef, San Rafael Swell, Dandy Crossing (a dandy place to cross
the river), Hell's Backbone, Big Rock Candy Mountain, Book Cliffs;

Hondoo Arch, Angel Arch, Druid Arch, Delicate Arch;

The Needles, The Standing Rocks, The Maze;

Dugout Ranch, Lonesome Beaver Camp, Paria, Bundyville, Hanksville,

Bluff, Mexican Hat, Mexican Water, Bitter Springs, Kanab; Bedrock and
Paradox;

Moab (cf. Kings II:iii, *The Holy Bible*).

THE WIND STOPS, completely, as I finish my lunch. I strip and lie back
in the sun, high on Tukuhnikivats, with nothing between me and the universe
but my thoughts. Deliberately I compose my mind, quieting the febrile buzzing of the cells and circuits, and strive to open my consciousness directly,
nakedly to the cosmos. Under the influence of cosmic rays I try for cosmic
intuitions—and end up earthbound as always, with a vision not of the universal but of a small and mortal particular, unique and disparate . . . her smile,
her eyes in firelight, her touch.

Well, let it be. You'll find no deep thinkers at 13,000 feet anyway. The
wind comes up again, I get to my feet and dance along the cornice of a snow-
bank that hangs above the void. Down there in the forest, somewhere, is my
camp, my old truck, my fireplace—home. I look for a quick and easy way to
return.

The climb up from timberline had taken about two hours. Looking down
at the graceful curve of the thousand-foot snowfield it seems to me that the
descent should not require more than five minutes. I put on my clothes, shoulder the rucksack and work down over the rock to the couloir and the upper
end of the slide.

It looks too steep. Experimentally I push a slab onto the snow and let it
go. It drops away rapidly, picking up speed and throwing a spray of snow into
the air, turns on edge and rolls and bounds like a clumsy wheel all the way to
the bottom, shattering on the rocks below. A certain length of time passes
before I hear the sound of the explosion.

What I need is a braking device. An ice axe now would be the thing; I
could squat on my heels and glissade down the snowfield in good form, con-
trolling direction and velocity by dragging the blade in the snow.

I launch a second big stone and watch it go down, sliding then skimming
over the hard snow, faster and faster until, like the first, it catches on something, turns on its edge and bounces like a wheel the rest of the way down. I
see it now; the point is to stay flat. The pitch of the snowfield is less steep
toward the bottom; it should be possible to slow down or stop before smash-
ing into the rocks at the lower edge.

I choose a third flat rock and drag it to the margin of the snowfield. Facing
downhill with my heels braced in the snow, I straddle the rock, grasp and

elevate its forward edge with both hands (my stick tucked under my arm) and sit down firmly, taking a deep breath.

Nothing happens. My feet are still dug in and seem unwilling to obey my command to rise—instinct more powerful than reason. I urge them again; grudgingly they come up. Look at it this way, fellows—nobody lives forever. The descent begins.

Too late for arguments now and as usual not enough time for panic. We're sledding down the mountain at a sensational clip, accelerating according to formula. I brake my speed with my boot heels as best I can but can't see a thing because of the gush of snow flying in my face. Halfway down I lose the slab I'm riding and go on for a piece without it. The rock follows hard upon me, almost at my neck. I manage to recapture it and climb partway back on but before I can get comfortable again I see an outcrop of immovable granite, which I hadn't noticed before, rising in our path. I abandon the slab, roll to the side and go skidding past the obstacle by an adequate margin. Things are out of control at this point but fortunately the snowfield begins to level off. I get my boots in front of my body, dig in and coast to a stop a few feet short of the broken rocks at the bottom of the couloir. As I sit there resting another loose object thunders by on my left, perhaps the same rock or part of it that I had started down with. A moment later comes my walking stick.

Everything seems to be in good shape except my hands, which are bruised and numb, and the heels and soles of my boots, which are hanging to the uppers by a few threads and a couple of bent nails. I hammer them back together with a stone and continue my descent the hard way, crawling over the rubble until I reach the scrub spruce and the fringe of the forest.

The ascent of Tukuhnikivats has taken me half the day, the descent from summit to timberline less than half an hour. I have plenty of time before sundown for another hike. But the boots are in a bad way, soles flapping like loose tongues at every step, my frozen toes sticking out, the heels twisted out of line. I limp back to camp to exchange them for something else.

On the way, in an area where spruce and fir mingle with quaking aspen, in a cool shady well-watered place, I discover a blue columbine, rarest and loveliest of mountain flowers. This one is growing alone—perhaps the deer have eaten the others—there must have been others—and wears therefore the special beauty of all wild and lonely things. Silently I dedicate the flower to a girl I know and in honor both of her and the columbine open my knife and carve something appropriate in the soft white bark of the nearest aspen. Fifty years from now my inscription will still be there, enlarged to twice its present size by the growth of the tree. May the love I feel at this moment for columbine, girl, tree, symbol, grass, mountain, sky and sun also stay, also grow, never die.

Back to camp. My feet are wet and cold. I build a fire and toast my bare feet lightly in the flames until sensation is restored. The glade is quiet except for the whisper of aspen leaves and running water, the air warm in the late afternoon sunlight. There is no wind here, though I can see by the streamers of cloud off the peaks that it is still blowing up above. I put on dry socks and moccasins, and cook my supper: refried pinto beans with chile and a number of eggs, a potato baked in tinfoil. I am very hungry. Tea and cigar for the final course.

The quiet forest. There are few birds in the high woods, less wildlife it seems than down below in the sunbaked desert. Probably because at this altitude the summer is so brief—"much too beautiful to last"—and the winter long.

One bird, however, is singing, if you could call it singing. The song is so laconic and melancholic that it very nearly takes all the joy out of my smoke. I don't know what kind of bird it is, if it is a bird, but the song goes like this, repeated over and over, *lentissimo*:

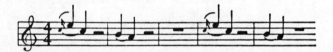

When I've had enough of this sentiment (there is a bird called the Townsend Solitaire) I get up and walk away, out to the dirt road beyond the old rail fence and up the road to a wide meadow from which I can watch the sun go down over the western world. Mesa, canyon and plateau, the pacific desert lies in whiskey-colored light and lilac dusk, a sea of silence. Clouds edged with fire sail on the clear horizon.

Somebody's goddamned cows, Scobie's perhaps or McKee's, I can't see the brand, gape at me from the lower side of the meadow. I wave my arm and stick at them and they bolt suddenly for the trees, like deer. I walk among thistles and coarse dying goldenrod (signs of overgrazing) and a kind of sunflower called Five-Nerve Helianthella, knock a few heads off—helping to spread the seed—and ponder the meaning of my solitude. Reaching no conclusions.

Tomorrow morning, *Deo volente*, I plan a walk to the summit of the pass between Tukuhnikivats and Mount Tomaski. There is a little lake not far over the saddle, a tarn really, a mountain pond bordered in marsh marigold and yarrow, with water black and glassy as obsidian. Bottomless? Certainly. There are some old friends living there whom I haven't seen for a long time.

Afterwards . . . back to Moab. Back to the juniper, the red sand and the fanatic rocks. Into September, the final month.

Appalachian Pictures

Going back to the Big Smokies always reminds me of coming home. There was the town set in the cup of the green hills. In the Alleghenies. A town of trees, two-story houses, red-brick hardware stores, church steeples, the clock tower on the county courthouse, and over all the thin blue haze—partly dust, partly smoke, but mostly moisture—that veils the Appalachian world most of the time. That diaphanous veil that conceals nothing. And beyond the town were the fields, the zigzag rail fences, the old gray barns and gaunt Gothic farmhouses, the webwork of winding roads, the sulfurous creeks and the black coal mines and—scattered everywhere—the woods.

The trees. Vegetation cradle of North America. All those trees transpiring patiently through the wet and exhilarating winds of spring, through the heavy, sultry, sullen summers into the smoky autumns. Through the seasons, years, millennia. Sensitive and sensible plants, with who knows what aspirations of their own.

Through town and into the hills, I'd follow a certain road for about ten miles until I came to a church and a graveyard on top of a tall hill. (I worked

From *Appalachian Wilderness: The Great Smoky Mountains* (1970)

there once, tending that graveyard and the dead, firing the furnace in the church on winter Sunday mornings, me the sexton, best job I ever had, all that rich grass, all that meditation, all those ghosts that haunt the human mind, all that deep dark dank earth rich in calcium, all those lonely clouds with rosy bottoms drifting pensively on the horizon for a while after sundown, inviting questions, when it was time to go home.)

Time to go home. From the top of the hill you can look down into a long emerald valley where a slow stream meanders back and forth, back and forth, in long lazy loops like somebody's intestines strewn casually over the ground, through overgrazed pastures in which cows drift along the contours of the slope as slowly as clouds. All facing in the same direction. Beyond the end of that particular valley, not in it, in the mostly woods and submarginal corn-fields that lay beyond, was my home.

You go down into that valley, an easy, pleasant sort of walk, past the little farms, barns, tile springhouses, pickup trucks, hayrakes and mowing ma-chines, until you come to a big creek—that's Crooked Creek, glowing with golden acids from the mines upstream—and across the creek and up a red-dog road under a railroad trestle through a tunnel in the woods. I call it a tunnel because the road there is so narrow and winding that the trees on either side interlace their branches overhead, forming a canopy that in win-ter, under the typical gray sky of winter in that country, looks like a network of fine, artistic cracks in a decaying plaster ceiling, and in spring and summer like an underwater vision of translucent algal green, and in the fall, naturally, like the scales of a fire dragon. From shady green to dying flame.

At the far end of the living tunnel, beyond it and in the open, under a shimmer of summer sun or behind a curtain of whirling snow or within a lavender mist of twilight condensing toward darkness, stood the house. An austere and ancient clapboarded farmhouse, taller than wide when seen from the road, it had filigreed porchwork, a steep-pitched roof and on the roof lightning rods pointing straight up at the sun or stars; half the year there would be smoke winding out of the chimney and amber lamps burning behind the curtains of the windows.

Slinking toward me across the damp grass would come a familiar dog, always older, always more arthritic than she was ten years before. Too timid to growl, too shy to bark, she always remembered me. Her job was to guard those doors that, in nearly thirty years, had never been locked. Nobody even knew if there was a key.

Home again. Time to slop the hogs, Paw.

That's what going back to the Big Smokies always reminded me of. That hill country in North Carolina, eastern Kentucky and eastern Tennessee seems today something like Punxsutawney, Pennsylvania, thirty years ago. Like Seneca and Powhatan, like Home, Pa., where many of us were once brung up. All of it Appalachian, winter or summer, then and now. Land of the breathing trees, the big woods, the rainy forests.

TREAT YOURSELF TO THE BEST

That's what it says on the side of most any barn in these parts. "Chew Mail Pouch," it says. "Treat Yourself to the Best." That way a farmer gets at least one wall of his barn painted free, by the tobacco company. Coming down through the extreme southwest corner of Virginia into Tennessee, we saw that legend many times, as often as "Jesus Saves" and "Get Right with God."

When I saw the red claybanks, though, I knew I was in the South for sure. Land of romance and myth, of chitlin and chigger, of country-cured ham, Dr. Pepper and Colonel Sanders' Kentucky Fried Chicken, finger-lickin' good. Of good poets, too, like Newton Smith of Tuckasegee, for example, and brave good men like Harry Caudill of Letcher County. Homeland too and burial place of Thomas Wolfe. That alone justifies the existence of North Carolina.

Approaching Gatlinburg, Gateway to the Big Smokies, we drive down a highway whose shoulders are sprinkled and ditches lined with glittering aluminum litter. Immortal beer can, immutable chicken basket, eternal plastic picnic spoon. At night the round ends of the cans gleam in your headlights like the glowing eyes of foxes. The hillsides are carpeted with a layer of automobile hulks. Trentville, Tennessee, where all old cars come to die, explained a man at a filling station. Poor hillbillies buy them used in Cleveland and Detroit, get laid off and come home, abandon them when the clutch gives out, the valves burn up, the retreads peel off, the pistons freeze within the worn-out rings.

Orphans. Another thing we notice coming into the South is this: while most of the farmhouses get smaller and flimsier, a few of them get bigger and fancier. Along the road, unpainted frame shacks one story high, but here and there, now and then on a hilltop, you see a grand brick plantation house with white columns framing its entrance, the house centered in a spacious park of lawn and shrub and tree, approached by a winding asphalt drive. Power.

Comical, conical hills appear, like the hills in hillbilly comic strips—Snuffy Smith, Li'l Abner—with sagging gray shacks snagged on their summits. The leafless trees of winter, looking like the bristles on a brush, stand against the skyline. In each yeoman's frontyard there is a great pile of coal. Prepared for winter. The deadly fumes of coal smoke float on the breeze. Somewhere nearby, somebody's home and farm is being disemboweled by dragline, Euclid and power shovel to provide such fuel for this person in the shack, for TVA and Oak Ridge ("sub-capital of Death"), for Con Edison, etc., for you and me. Vast crimes are being committed in this region, whole hillsides raped and robbed, life systems that required ages for their weaving ripped apart.

But it's all legal. As local boosters eagerly point out, strip mining does provide jobs as well as fuel the turbines. What would you have those men do, weave baskets? fire bricks? bake biscuits? We'll have more on this matter later. And who, you might be thinking, is "they"? That referenceless pronoun. Nobody knows exactly who "they" are, that's part of the trouble. They is It, that's all I know, that fantastic labyrinthine sky-towering ziggurat of iron and stone, paper and wire, glass and aluminum and cement, habit and obedience through which we creep and scurry in our channeled runways, us 200 million nice, neat mice. Call it The Leaning Tower of Babel. Call it what you will, it's the greatest thing since Atlantis went down with all aboard, explosions in the boiler room and rockets firing at the moon.

We drive through fields of dead goldenrod in the gray chill air of December. Snow gleams in bald patches on the blue mountains beyond. We pass tawny hills, more ramshackle shacks and pause for a while at a deserted crossroads to contemplate an abandoned country store.

The store just sits there in the cloud-filtered daylight, its old silvery clapboards warped and sprung, shakes dangling from the edge of the roof, screendoor ajar and hanging by one rusty hinge, the long front porch sagging in the middle, the whole aching creaking vacant structure canted to the east, in line I suppose with the prevailing winds.

We read and photograph the messages placarded in tin on the walls:

CHESTERFIELDS ARE BEST FOR YOU

DRINK DR. PEPPER

DRINK COCA-COLA

DRINK NESBITT'S CALIFORNIA ORANGE

TAKE HOME KERN'S BREAD

TRY W. E. GARRETT & SONS' SWEET, MILD SNUFF:

A TASTE TREAT

BUY MERITA BREAD VITAMIN-ENRICHED

Failure. Capitalism sounds good in theory but look at this old store. Heartbreak and bankruptcy. The metal signs are rusting, they are loose, they flap and rattle in the wind. We pass on.

Past rocky pastures. Beautiful gray-green boulders mottled with lichen rise from, or sink into, the tough winter grass. Cows lounge about in the vicinity, picking their teeth, not getting much accomplished. Sumac and willow stand with glowing leaves and glowing skin along the fencerows. Mighty white oaks grow on the higher ground, their dried-out red leathery leaves still clinging to the stems.

Dead trees and dying trees draped in vine come into view on both sides of the road. They are victims of the creeping kudzu, *Pueraria lobata*, a parasitic vine imported from the Orient back in the late 1920s. Entire trees are enmeshed in the smothering stuff, trapped and wrapped like flies in a spiderweb. A gift, like karate and kamikaze, from Japan, this fast-growing exotic has spread over much of the Smoky Mountain area, creating expensive eradication problems both for home owners and for the National Park Service.

More trees and different trees, a bewildering variety of trees, display themselves and we're not even in the mountains yet. Hemlock, white pine, pitch pine and other conifers, and rows of planted Scotch pine for the Christmas tree market.

Here's an ancient country church, painted white but faded to gray, with a high cupola on the roof and the bell missing. The New Era Baptist Church—like the store we had passed a mile before, this church looks derelict. Christ Was Here. Religion and the failure of capitalism. Soul food for thought. Who stole the bell? Some Baptist, probably. May he be totally immersed in Hell, that'll learn him.

Into the hills we roll on joyous wheels, into the past. Way up yonder on the mountainside hangs a real log cabin with real blue smoke coming from the chimney. Near the road we pass an old barn made of squared-off logs. But it has a sheet-metal roof, not shakes. Close by, underneath a handy pine, is a Farmall tractor, a 1940s model, rusting away. The barn is covered with vinery, but not kudzu; looks more like *Wisteria frutescens*, an attractive plant even when not in flower.

Into a little valley. Here we find farms that appear to be actually inhabited and worked. Some of the houses are painted. Some of the Chevies are new. Some of the barns, while not nearly so grand as Pennsylvania barns, look fairly well kept up; they have gambrel roofs and overhanging eaves at one end to shield the open gable from rain; through that opening under the end of the roof hay is carried by hayfork and pulley from outside up, and into the mow.

Prosperity. High on a graded, grassy hill stands another red-brick chateau: Ole Massa's house; it makes a lovely picture from the road below with its white fluted pillars two stories high, the classic pediment, the tall windows flanked by shutters. It must be good to live in a home like that, watching the peasants toiling in the fields, junkyards and gas stations down there in the bottoms. It's got to be good living up there, otherwise what's the point of all the rest of us dying down here? If only passing through on our way to the park. (We are all merely tourists in this world. Just poor wayfaring tourists. Sextons out of work, seeking new graveyards.)

Beyond the happy valley, we enter the foothills again. More hillbilly shacks appear, with smoking chimneys and staring children. Why aren't those children in school? I ask, scenting something sociological. Because it's Saturday, says Judy. A stickler for objective fact, she'll come in handy here.

We see a stand of trees that look like a type of juniper. On closer inspection, we see that they actually *are* junipers, or what is called here eastern red cedar, *Juniperus virginiana.* There is no true cedar in the Western Hemisphere, the botanists assure us. But I'm thinking of an old song I heard somewhere:

> *You just lay there by the juniper*
> *When the moon is shining bright,*
> *And watch them jugs a-fillin'*
> *In the pale moonlight . . .*

Clair de lune. Pommes de terre. One thinks of Debussy and his big hit. Of white lightning, lead poisoning and rusty-red radiators. Shine on, harvest moon.

And then we come to the main highway.

THE FAILURE OF CAPITALISM

Here we are, me and Judy and Suzie,* trying to get to the national park, and what happens, we have to run a gauntlet of raw capitalism.

We'd forgotten what Industrial Tourism is like. Having got lost about fifty miles ago, on purpose, staying off the Superstate Interstate so far as possible, we were happily following this narrow winding rural road that led us up hill and down dale, through farmyards and mountain meadows, through potato field, woodlot and corn patch.

* Abbey's third wife, Judy, and third child, Suzie.—Ed.

We were out in the country, out there where the *people* used to live. Picnic country, good place to throw beer cans, out there among the forgotten general stores and the deconsecrated churches. Hysterical hens tearing across the path of the car, hogs rooting in the oak groves, an old horse resting his chin in the crotch of a butternut tree and watching life pass him by. We saw hand-built WPA bridges arching polluted but pretty streams where great old leprous-skinned sycamores lean above the water. We passed slightly crumpled farmhouses with swings hanging by chains on their front porches (for the old folks and for lovers), and the frontyards where threadbare auto tires hang on ropes from the boughs of sugar maples (for the kids to swing on). We saw an antique John Deere tractor, the kind with iron lugs instead of rubber on the wheels, and a flatbed Ford truck with two flat tires, and recently completed autumn plowing on the tilted hillside and cornfields with the fodder still in the shock. Yes—scenes of melancholy beauty and bucolic melancholy, under the ivory, pearl-gray sky of December, where Jefferson's agrarian America makes its final stand. In the pastures of remembrance.

And then, following this road, at a safe and sane distance behind some reckless rustic who was tooling his Plymouth into eternity at thirty mph, we come barreling round a turn into the Knoxville-Gatlinburg highway and the mainstream of the way things are. By this I mean Sevierville, Tennessee, and the Little Pigeon River, full of filth, and the walls of billboards on either side of the pavement, busy selling something fake:

GOLDRUSH JUNCTION—Cowboys, Indians & Outlaws: Gunfights Every Day

FORT APACHE—Gunfights Hourly—Live Saloon Shows

FRONTIERLAND [illustrated with a picture of a Sioux Indian in full ceremonial regalia]—Cherokee, N.C.

Don't Miss the New WAX MUSEUM—See Alan Shepard, Sgt. York real-as-life

See GHOST TOWN, MAGGIE VALLEY, N.C.—Real Life Gun Battles!

FABULOUS FAIRYLAND—Exciting Fun Rides for All Ages

MYSTERY HILL—Amazing Force of Gravity

GHOST TOWN IN THE SKY—Realistic Indian Battles

HILLBILLY VILLAGE—Copter Rides, Flea Market, Souvenirs

CAR MUSEUM & KAMP GROUND

JUNGLE CARGO—Indian Mocassins, Ice Cold Cider, Thick Rich Malts

CHRISTUS GARDENS—Outstanding All-Year All-Weather At-
   traction
GATLINBURG SKY LIFT—Your Shortcut to Heavenly Delight

Oh, well, it's only innocent fun. Like any fungus. No harm in it. We proceed past the motels, filling stations and Frigid Queen shake-and-burger
joints—about ten miles of them—to the bright clean tourist town called
Gatlinburg. The Gateway to the Park. Here we make camp for the night in a
pleasant motel room with a wood fire burning in a genuine fireplace. (Small
extra charge for use of firewood says a sneaky notice on the door.)

Tomorrow we shall conquer Clingman's Dome. By Volkswagen. Looking
up from the side of the motel swimming pool—water the color of antifreeze—
through the chill pellucid air, we can see the Big Smokies all covered with
snow. They look like real mountains.

In the meantime, however, we make a tour of Gatlinburg. The town looks
so sharp and neat it's obvious the inhabitants take great pride in the place. The
motels and hotels are big, handsome, all new and all, no doubt, comfortable.
(Extra charge for firewood?) Over the course of several evenings, we sample
the food in various restaurants and find it uniformly good. I'm no gour-
met—my favorite meal here is country-cured ham and red-eye gravy, with
yams, black-eyed peas, mashed potatoes and a pitcher of Budweiser—but I
do know the difference between honest food and thawed-out ersatz, no matter how hungry I get.

Gatlinburg lies in a dry county, so I suppose some might lament the lack
of legal booze. But one can learn to live without it, at least for a few days at a
time. In the wintertime, the off-season, with half the public places closed,
there is no entertainment of any kind, not even a movie theater, but this too is
an irrelevant concern. We're here to see the Great Smokies not the films or
cabarets. Newspapers are available, if you like to read newspapers. And
there's TV IN EVERY ROOM.

Also curio shops. Gas stations. Drugstores. Laundromats. Everything
the heart desires. A discreet and limited use of neon tubing. No pig-iron
mills rumbling night and day and belching garbage into the air. No roar
of traffic, no thunder of jets, no machine-gun rattle of air hammers
in the streets. Gatlinburg, at least in winter, is as tidy and efficient and
quiet and sanitary as a Swiss ski village. The blatant and vulgar commercial-
ism of Sevierville, only a few miles back the way we came, is not in evidence here.

The Compleat Tourist Town. In the restaurants blue gas fires burning under stacks of ceramic logs that look almost real until you get close. Omnipresent in the background that bland tapioca-like sound my wife calls "department-store music." Decor by Holiday Inn—all the motel lobby furnishings, all the restaurant tables and chairs and lighting fixtures, look as though they came from the same factory somewhere in Southern California. Everything designed by a neurotic suffering from a severe case of social irrelevance.

What's the alternative to this comfortable mediocrity? A grand European-style luxury that most of us would not be able to afford? Or a return to the mode of a century ago, coming into a mountain village on horseback, having a cold supper by lamplight in the cabin-kitchen of some morose mountaineer, while savage coon dogs howl, slaver and snarl on the other side of the door, and going to sleep in the early dark on a cornshuck mattress, prey to a host of bloodsucking vermin?

Which would you really prefer? Which would I really prefer?

You won't believe me but I'll tell you: I fancy the latter, i.e., the horse, cabin, dogs and bugs.

Thus we see the secret failure of American capitalism. For all of its obvious successes and benefits (this book, for example, is being published by Jack Macrae, a maverick capitalist friend of mine), capitalism has failed to capture our hearts. Our souls, yes, but not our hearts.

So much for political economy. Walking at night through the quiet streets of Gatlinburg—where have all the tourists gone?—I look up, above the motel-hotel rooftops, and see the dark forms of the mountains bulking beyond, snow gleaming in the starlight.

Real mountains.

Appalachia, Good-bye

T IME TO CHECK out of the Bearskin Motel. Churlishly I refuse to pay the extra charge for use of firewood, implying that I think it immoral and unethical for a hotel, even a motel, to advertise as this one does—"YUP, REAL FIREPLACES"—and then penalize the unwary lodger for not bringing his own firewood. The clerk, an insouciant Southerner, smiles and graciously accepts my refusal. The Great Refusal.

Judy salvages our laundry from the Snow White & The Seven Dwarfs Washateria (free Baptist literature on the walls) and we are off, once more up the mountain to Newfound Gap and down the other side into North Carolina and the town of Cherokee, Cherokee Capital of the World.

More charming and picturesque philistinism: The Wigwam Motel, with wigwams made of steel and concrete (try dragging *that* down the Platte, Mrs. Crazy Horse); a green stegosaurus made of chicken wire and plaster, leering at the passing motorist from the doorway of a curio shop where authentic Indian spears, made in Hong Kong, are offered for sale; The Mystery House, Closed for the Season; Frontierland—20 Rides & Shows, One Price; Deadwood Gulch; Fort Cherokee; Redskin Motel—50 Ultra-Modern Units; Hon-

From *Appalachian Wilderness: The Great Smoky Mountains* (1970)

est Injun Trading Post (behind a gateway of totem poles); and the Twin Tepee Craft Shop. Exhilarating.

Accelerating, we come next to Sylva where I had lived the year before while teaching at the nearby University of Western Carolina.

Sylva must have once been a lovely town. Small, with a population of perhaps five thousand, nestled in the green hills below the Great Smokies, full of beautiful old houses, laved as they say by the sparkling waters of the Tuckasegee River, with the life of a market center and the dignity of county seat, Sylva must have been beautiful. Now it is something else, for the streets are grimy and noisy, jammed always with motor traffic, the river is a sewer, and the sky a pall of poisonous filth. The obvious villain in the picture is the local Mead's Paper Mill, busily pumping its garbage into the air and into the river, but general traffic and growth must bear the rest of the blame.

When I commented to one of the town's leading citizens, a fine old Southern gentleman, about the perpetual stink in the air, he replied, "Why, son, that there smells lahk *money* to me." Smug and smiling all the way to the bank, where—I hope—he drops dead on the doorstep. Pascal said somewhere in words to this effect that in order to grasp the concept of the infinite we need only meditate for a while upon human stupidity.

Looking at the foul mess industry has made of a town like Sylva, I am also moved to reflect, once again, that capitalism, while it sounds good in theory, just doesn't work. Look about you and see what it has done to our country. *Mene, mene, tekel . . .*

I don't know. One suffers from hope. Maybe we can learn something from what we have done to this land. Probably not. And in any case, is it any better elsewhere? No matter in what nation I lived I am certain I would find much to detest. All big social organizations are ugly, brutal, inhuman—prone to criminal acts which no man or *community* of men, on their own, would even think of. But just the same I despise my own nation most. Because I know it best. Because I still love it, suffering from hope. For me that's patriotism.

Enough of these gloomy thoughts. We must hasten on to Tuckasegee, Judy and Suzie and I, to visit old Newt Smith and his marvelous chestnut pigpen again. And after that—home.

And where might that be? Where is home? That old gray gaunt Gothic farmhouse along a red-dog road in the hills of northern Appalachia? No more; never again. Where then?

A Russian writer named Prishvin said that "Home is where you have

found your happiness." I think I know where that may be, at least for myself.
I'll reveal this much: it has something to do with those mountains, those forests, those wild, free, lost, full-of-wonder places that rise yet (may they always!) above the squalor of the towns.

Appalachia, we'll be back.

My Life as a P.I.G.,
or The True Adventures of
Smokey the Cop

THE SMOKEY we're talking about is not the natty chap in the sharp sombrero, bane of truck drivers, who lurks behind billboards along the Interstate. No, the one under discussion here is the fellow in the suit of forest green who hands you the ticket, leaning out of his box office, when you buy your admission to Yosemite, Grand Canyon, Yellowstone, Great Smokies or any one of our many national parks. The Crown Jewels of America, as someone once said. No doubt. Guarded, patrolled, looked after, explained more or less by the rangers of the National Park Service. Also known, formerly, as tree fuzz, tree pigs or Smokey Bears—no kin of that other Smokey Bear (the famous ursine bore) who used to serve as a fire-fighting symbol of the Forest Service until he died (of tertiary syphilis) in a Washington, D.C., zoo.

Perhaps there are still some people who don't know the difference between the National Park Service and the U.S. Forest Service. Let us review the question one more time. The Park Service is an agency of the Department of the Interior, entrusted with the care and management of the national parks, national monuments (such as Death Valley and the Statue of Liberty) and what are called National Recreation Areas—Lake Mead, Lake Powell, etc. The Forest Service is a branch of the Department of Agriculture, alas, and

From *Abbey's Road* (1979)

was given charge, long ago, by Congress, of our national forests. The parks were established primarily as wilderness areas, to be kept so far as possible in a state of nature, but open (in some manner) to the enjoyment of the people. The forests, on the other hand, have been meant for various uses—watershed protection, wildlife habitat, human recreation, livestock grazing, logging, even mining. Since World War II the last three uses have become predominant, usually at the expense of the first three.

There is a certain built-in antagonism between the two agencies. Park rangers sometimes refer to forest rangers as "tree farmers" (this was once considered an insult); while the latter like to call the former "turkey herders" or "posie sniffers." No matter. The difference between one service and the other, and between national parks and national forests, is not so great as it once was. With mass motorized recreation becoming a bigger and bigger industry in itself, the national parks have been subjected to increasing commercial development: paved roads, motels, hotels, marinas, gas stations, stores, banks, hospitals, cloverleaf intersections, parking lots, traffic lights, even jails. I know of no place in the national forests that has suffered the grotesque and incongruous development of Yosemite, Grand Canyon, Yellowstone, Great Smokies.

In any case, I myself have worked for both agencies, in both kinds of places, and can testify from ample personal experience that the difference between the Park Service and the Forest Service is more nominal than real: both labor under the domination of the GNP, the NAM, the corporate pursuit of pecuniary happiness. "Business means America and America means business," says your friendly U.S. Chamber of Commerce. "America's business is business," says John Calvin Coolidge, our last honest president, and he was never more right than now, here, in the Sick Seventies, when even sex therapy and spiritual fulfillment have become growth industries. (My cousin Gus told me the other day, with barely subdued excitement, that he has nailed down the Transcendental Meditation franchise for Winkelman, Arizona. Better than Pizza Parlor or Midas Muffler—a gold mine.)

What has all this whining and complaining to do with Smokey the Cop or the out-of-doors, that other world *out there,* beyond the expanding labyrinth of walls that cuts us off from what we long for, more and more, as it recedes into our past? Not much. Very little. But some.

For seventeen seasons, off and on, I have worked as a ranger, as a fire lookout, as a garbage collector, for the Park Service, occasionally for the Forest Service. Since most of these jobs involved, to some extent, what is called "protection" (law enforcement) as well as "interpretation," I too have played the role, or more exactly played *at* the role, of Smokey the Cop. I wore a uniform and a badge, I carried a .38 in the glove compartment of a government pickup, I sometimes harassed people, especially hippies. And shot two dogs and a number of beer cans. In self-defense.

An odd part to play, you might think, for one who fancies himself a libertarian, an anarchist, a dedicated scofflaw. Perhaps not. I've never known a serious policeman who had much respect for the law; in any well-organized society the police constitute the most lawless element. Policemen are not legalists; they are moralists, stern believers in good and bad, right and wrong. I too am a moralist, not a legalist, and thus fulfill the basic qualification for cophood.

My career as a PIG (Pride, Integrity, Guts) began not with the Park Service, however, but during my stint with another overgrown governmental bureaucracy affiliated with the Department of Commerce—I refer of course to the U.S. Army. One morning I was coming down off a boat onto the bomb-wrecked docks of Naples, Italy, when this man I'd never seen before tapped me on the shoulder and asked how tall I was. I told him I was six foot two on a warm day but contracted a bit in cold weather. "You're a cop now, wiseass," said the man. He was a second lieutenant in the military police; the boat I'd just left (traveling tourist class) was a troop ship; I was an eighteen-year-old acne-haunted draftee rifleman in the infantry; and on that particular day every replacement six feet tall or taller was being shunted, willing or not, into the military police.

Typical of the army; keep the big men in the rear; let the little guys do the fighting. Actually the war was over; the Japanese had surrendered the day I finished basic training; but our wise, spunky Harry Truman was doing his best to get a fresh war started with Russia, Yugoslavia, Korea, Arkansas, anyone available.

My feelings were hurt at being assigned to the MPs, since my true military ambition was to become a clerk-typist like James Jones and Norman Mailer. But it did no good to object. Some sergeant put a black and white Nazi-like armband on my sleeve, a white helmet liner on my head, a nifty red scarf around my neck and a club and a .45 automatic in my hands. At once I began to feel mean, brutal, arbitrary, righteous. "Let's stop coddling criminals," I wrote home to mother, that first night in Napoli; "let's put father in jail where he belongs." (My father was the village Socialist back in Home, Pennsylvania.)

After that first day I never saw an MP officer. The officers were down in Sorrento, shacking up with contessas, living off their black market profits.

Our boss was Sergeant Smitty, a lifer and a drunk, who'd received his police
science training, like most other MP noncoms, in the army's Disciplinary
Training Center at Pisa. There he had served first as an ordinary inmate (rape,
larceny, assault, murder), then as a trusty, then as a guard, emerging fully
qualified to enforce the law. Smitty was proud of the two years he'd put in at
Pisa; not only had he avoided front-line combat, but he had also learned, as a
routine part of the required training there, how to polish his mess kit with a
needle. With a needle? Why yes, with a needle. That's the way it was done at
old ivy-covered DTC.

Smitty became my hero. "Did you ever kill a man, Smitty?" I asked him
once, stars in my eyes. He grinned his evil, wolfish, yellow grin. "Naw," he
said modestly, "not really. Couple of niggers, that's all. A few Germans. I'm
kind of a tender-hearted fella." And he gave me the fearsome grin again and
put me down for the vice squad.

"Dear Mother," I wrote home after my third day in Napoli, "last night I
raided my first whorehouse." Not entirely true, I wrote no such thing. But I
did raid the whorehouse, and it was certainly my first. In fact I was still a
virgin. In many ways. I had never before seen, for example, one man beat
another with a club. Sergeant Smitty showed us—me and another rookie—
how it is done. We arrested several whores and one AWOL soldier, the black
man Smitty had clubbed into unconsciousness. That soldier, I later learned,
was sent to Pisa, where he too would learn to polish his mess kit with a needle.

I requested a transfer to the motorcycle squad. "What's the matter, kid,
you cherry?" Smitty asked. "Yellow?"

"Well, sir," I said, "that night work . . . I don't know."

"Can you handle a Harley?" he said.

"No problem," I said. I wasn't sure what a Harley was, but figured that
anyone, like me, who knew how to harness a team of horses or crank up a
Farmall could probably put a bridle on a Harley.

"Well, stick around," Smitty said, "we're having the tryouts in a few days."

There were three positions open on the bike squad. Six of us showed up
for the tryouts, which were held on a racetrack outside the city. Sergeant
Smitty—wreathed in whisky fumes—wrote our names down on his clipboard
sheet. "Okay, Abbey," he said, "you're first." (I was at the head of every list in
the army.)

I approached this olive drab machine parked on the cinders, a huge
Harley-Davidson loaded with red lights, a siren, chrome-plated crash bars
and a tailpipe fashioned from a German 88-mm cannon shell, the brass polished to a golden gleam. I straddled the seat and turned the switch. I'd been

doing some homework and sneaking around and was pretty certain I knew how to start this type of machine. Spark in the left grip, throttle in the right, kick starter, gear shift lever and clutch pedal just like a car. Easy. Nothing to it. Nervous all the same, my sweaty thumb slipped onto a button on the handlebar. The siren began to growl. "Shut that thing off!" Smitty bellowed. Okay, okay. I fumbled around, got the shift lever into neutral, my foot on the starter, and kicked. The motor roared like a dinosaur. Frightened but determined, revving the engine, I slipped the lever forward into first (*clunk!*) and slowly, cautiously engaged the clutch (*clang!*). The bike leaped forward like a spooked horse, bearing straight ahead.

Paralyzed with terror, I clung to the handlebars, trying to think what I was supposed to do next. Shift into second? Of course. But we were already approaching the first turn in the track. How do you steer this thing? To me the handlebars seemed rigid, welded to the frame. It never occurred to me that I must lean into the turn. Locked together, the Harley and I crashed through the wooden fence on the outside of the track, plowed into a dirt bank, stalled out, keeled over. Still gripping the handlebars, I heard, above the scream of the siren, the outraged bellowing of Sergeant Smitty staggering down the track toward me. "Back to the vice squad, Abbey! Back to the whorehouse for you!"

One week later I was riding my Hog, loaded with siren and chrome, up the wide streets and down the cobbled alleyways of Napoli, a proud, full-fledged member of the motorcycle squad. A traffic cop. A bona fide Smokey. A genuine Pig.

How did I do it? Simple. On the day of the tryouts, after my disastrous debut, while Smitty was watching the others (he flunked them all), I crept back to the bench where he had left his clipboard and when he wasn't looking wrote in "passed" after my name. Shit-faced and falling-down drunk, he never knew the difference. A few secret hours of practice and I was on the squad.

My eight months as a motorcycle cop in the balmy, crazy, sunny, utterly depraved city of Naples was the most educational time of my life, so far. Glorious days breezing along the bay and up the Via Roma toward Salerno, charging up and down marble stairways on our bikes into Mussolini's Palazzo di Esporza where we made our barracks, weekend passes to Capri, Ischia, Amalfi, Vesuvius, Pompeii. Long siestas with my girl friend in her filthy villa high on Posillipo, the Harley hidden under the orange trees. Yes, I'd finally discovered sex. (I was a retarded child.) And the black market. And the pizza pie. And grand opera: Puccini! Rossini! Verdi! Ravioli! Claudio Monteverdi and His Green Mountain Boys! And good wine. Real cheese. Honest bread.

Once stopped and cited an air corps colonel—and his dark-eyed sweet-heart—for speeding (85 in a 15 mph zone) and driving one-handed. "Use both hands, sir," I reminded him, leering at his girl. "I'd like to," he replied, "but I need one hand to steer with." I wish we could have another war like that one. Whatever happened to Hitler and Tojo anyhow?

There were little catches to the hitch. The weekly quota of traffic tickets, for instance. But I learned to solve that problem. Once a week I'd stop a military supply convoy outside the city, give the first thirty truck drivers citations for some violation or other—dust on the headlights, dirt on the bumper markings, worn windshield wipers, etc. The drivers didn't give a damn; most of them didn't speak English; they were Germans, POWs, Nazis. If I'd managed to catch Himmler or Hess or Bormann or Ehrlichman (excuse me, Eichmann) among them, I'd have written him up too, just like anybody else. I was a good cop.

But it couldn't last. Something went wrong. Various things. Foolish mistakes, like giving Italy back to the Italians—once the Allied High Command had made certain the Italian working people would not be allowed to take over the country. And personal mistakes. Like getting caught once too often failing to salute an officer. You're saluting the uniform not the man, they had taught us in basic. Really? I'll salute a *man* anytime, but damned if I'll salute a *uniform*.

The war ended for me much as it began, mopping floors and peeling potatoes in an army mess hall. From the military police back to the kitchen police. And then—discharge. Out. I never did get to be a corporal like Norman Mailer or James Jones. All I salvaged from my career as a military cop was one Colt automatic, chrome-plated by skilled Ginzo craftsmen in Naples, which I smuggled past the MPs at the exit gate of Fort Dix, New Jersey. Good thing I got it past; otherwise, I'd have been polishing mess gear with a needle myself.

Well sir, about ten years later, armed with my more or less honorable discharge and my five-point veteran's preference, I began a long series of sometime seasonal jobs as a ranger with the National Park Service. (I am one of the few veterans of World War II who has yet to find a steady job.) My first was in Arches National Park in Utah, then quite a primitive place, where I enforced the law (natural law) by pulling up survey stakes from a new road the Park Service was attempting to build into *my park*. That didn't do much good; I moved on.

I spent three winters as a ranger in Organ Pipe Cactus National Monument in southwest Arizona, a lovely place swarming with rattlesnakes, Gila monsters, scorpions, wild pigs and illegal Mexicans. The only useful work I did there was rescuing rattlesnakes discovered in the campground, catching them alive with my wooden Kleenex-picker before some tourist could cause them harm, dumping them in a garbage can and relocating them by stuffing them down a gopher hole six miles out in the desert.

At Petrified Forest, the worst job I ever held in our National Park Service, I worked the box office. That is, I sold tickets to tourists entering the park and interrogated those departing. The latter task we carried out in this manner: the tourist, obeying the stop sign, would rein his car to a halt beside my station; looking him straight in the eye I would say, "Sir, have you or any members of your party removed any rocks or other objects from this National Park?" Looking me straight in the eye, the man at the wheel would reply, "Oh no, just looking," and his wife, at his side, would nod in solemn agreement. Then one of the little kids in the back seat would say, "But Daddy, what about that big log we put in the trunk?"

So that's why the rear bumper was scraping the asphalt; and here I'd thought it was just another Punkmobile. I'd radio at once for reinforcements; we'd open the trunk, remove the petrified log (worth about $3,000 on the curio dealer black market), club the driver into insensibility while his family stood around screaming, arrest them all, generally have the husband and wife locked up for five to fifteen years and pack the kids off to an orphanage where they'd probably get better balanced meals anyway. But such diversions seldom occurred more than two or three times a day. In general, the job was a bore; if it had not been for the financial rewards I would have quit much sooner. Financial rewards? True, a seasonal park ranger then was paid about $2.50 an hour. But the tickets! Each time I sold a tourist his admission ticket, I would remind him to keep that piece of paper in plain view at all times, verifying his right to be in the park. (Really. For Petrified Forest, like Grand Canyon or Yosemite, is a *national* park—not a people's park.) When the tourist was leaving the park, I would lean out my window, extend my hand and say, "May I see your pass, sir?" The tourist would give me his ticket, I'd look it over, say, "Okay sir, thank you," and he'd drive away, glad to be gone, and I would resell the same ticket to the next mark coming in off the Interstate. In that way I'd clean up about $500 to $600 on a good day, sometimes more on weekends when the action was lively.* But as I said, the job was a bore; I moved on.

---

* This actually happened—once—at Grand Canyon National Park. The culprit (not me) was caught, I am happy to say, convicted and duly electrocuted at the federal penitentiary in Leavenworth, Texas.

On, to Everglades National Park down in Florida, where I was given a souped-up Plymouth Interceptor with siren concealed behind the grill and a big red light on the roof. Once again I found myself a traffic cop, a highway patrolman. Night shift. I wrote a few warning tickets, out of meanness, but spent more time careering down the Pine Island–Flamingo Park highway, late at night, lights flashing, to see what the Interceptor would do (115 mph). Sometimes I had to halt traffic on the highway for a few minutes in order to assist one of those eight-foot sawgrass diamondbacks across the pavement. A routine chore was checking doors at the visitor center, chasing skunks and drunks and alligators out of the rest rooms, which were left unlocked at night. But the best part of the job was lying in wait for 'Gator Roberts, the most famous alligator poacher in the state of Florida, maybe in the whole Southeast; a legendary figure, phantom outlaw, folk hero and a bone in the throat of Everglades park rangers. We hated him.

We had an informant, a waitress who worked at the Redneck Café near Pine Island; she had connections with the alligator underworld and would tell us from time to time (for a price) exactly where old 'Gator Roberts was planning to strike next. We'd stake out the place—some stinking, stagnant slough deep in the dismal swamp—and wait there through the night, sweating, cursing, scratching chigger bites, slapping mosquitoes, fondling our guns. He never appeared. Next morning we'd learn that sixteen skinned alligator carcasses had been found at the other end of the park, forty miles away, with a note attached: "You Smokies aint got the brains Gawd give a spoonbill duck, regards, Gator."

One winter in that low-rent bog was enough. Retiring phase by phase from the law enforcement business I returned to Arizona and got myself a job as a fire lookout up in a sixty-foot tower on the North Rim of the Grand Canyon. The good rim, where the Mormon girls come every summer to work at the lodge. Strictly forbidden all vices but one, those bountiful handsome girls always make the most of that one, which may be the reason Utah has the highest birth rate and the highest VD rate in the nation. Strict family types, those Utahns, stern believers in woman's traditional role. "Woman's place?" said Joseph Smith; "why woman's place—is in my bed!"

I'd sit there in my lookout waiting for Kathy or Susan or Sharon—all those girls seemed to be named Kathy or Susan or Sharon—waiting for one or the other to come and climb my tower. As far as I can tell, it never did any of us harm. Although now that I think about it, looking over what I've written here so far, I'm not so sure. (Were you ever awakened at night by the sound of crashing brain cells, whole tiers and entire galleries of corroded gray matter coming loose and thundering like an avalanche down into the abyss of your cerebellum?)

The last I heard of Smokey the Cop was over the short airwaves, through the Park Service radio in my lookout tower. It seemed that some scruffy types from California, degenerate hippies, were smoking a controlled substance somewhere in the vicinity of Indian Gardens under the South Rim. Far out in the wilds, as they doubtless imagined, far from the fuzz, the law and those who call themselves "the authorities." So they thought. But they were wrong. A humble maintenance man, fixing a waterline, saw them, smelled the sweet stink of *Cannabis* and radioed park headquarters. Minutes later a helicopter—a helicopter!—with armed rangers inside was sent down to make the bust. I can see those hippies now, in my mind's eye, sitting naked and cross-legged in their little circle under the shade of a juniper, passing the pipe of peace from hand to hand, each one far out in the cool of inner space; I see them becoming gradually aware of a giant dark bird with whirling wings hovering above, shrieking at them in the voice of steel and power and outrage— God is the great black spider in the sky!—coming down, down, down upon them. . . .

Was it then I finally gave away my Smokey Bear hat? The one with the four dimples in the high crown and that wide, flat, rigid brim, hard as iron, with which you could chop a man's head off if necessary? (We kept the brim flat by installing the hat under the seat of a toilet bowl each night; the same way your friendly state police do it.) Don't remember. Can't seem to recall things as good as I used to. As the French say, *quel dommage du brains.* But I did give it away, to a short boatman with a big head. Fellow named Stewart, I think. He ruined it by wearing it head-first through the Big Drop in Cataract Canyon down in Utah.

But I still remember some things. I remember the old Park Service Bizet-inspired fight song that we sang at night around the campfire at the Horace Albright Training Center (not quite the same thing as DTC in Pisa):

> *Toreadora*
> *Don't piss on the flora*
> *Save our wild decóra.*
> Etc.

And I remember a few other things I'd rather forget. Only a few but they're enough. That's why I live out here where I do, where none but the wedgetail eagles and the buzzards will ever find me, here on this rocky butte with the

200-mile view in all directions, here in the heart (but the desert has no heart),
here in the skull of the Hoodoo Desert. Paranoid? Yes, I'm paranoid; anyone
who's not should have his head examined. What? What's that, Doctor? Well,
yes sir, you're right, I don't know *exactly* who my enemies are, I can't *name*
them, if that's what you mean. But Doctor, can't you see?—that's what fright-
ens me: *I don't know who they are.*

As for Smokey the Cop and all his friends—those jolly policemen of various types—state, federal, secret, private, uniformed, plainclothes, foreign
and domestic—I stay away from them. I also avoid muggers, rapists, hijack-
ers, terrorists, politicians, murderers and other lunatics. And for precisely the
same reason.

III

Ed Moves On

ABBEY'S ENDLESS FASCINATION with young, beautiful women—in life and art—can be glimpsed directly in *Black Sun*. The slim novel's funniest, sexiest, most outrageous pages (chapter 6) have been placed alongside the poignant and bittersweet fragment from *The Fool's Progress* entitled "Henry in Love—An Interlude."

With a flair for simplicity that feminists never forgot (nor forgave), Ed dismissed Gloria Steinem's product (which he spelled "Miz") and repeatedly mocked the "manliness" of East Coast intellectuals of both genders. Among other targets, some deserving, some not, that attracted Abbey's incendiary arrows: U.S. immigration policy ("Immigration and Liberal Taboos," p. 373) and the ranchers' practice of running cattle on public lands ("Free Speech: The Cowboy and His Cow," p. 358).

In the summer of 1970, as he was coming to terms with the death of Judy Pepper, his third wife, from leukemia, Abbey put in time as a park ranger while caring for his three-year-old daughter, Suzie. It was the summer Abbey was completing *Black Sun*, and once again, he depended heavily on the kindness of Ingrid, the same woman who had seen him through the final chapters of *Desert Solitaire* four years earlier. By early fall a smart, attractive New York editor entered Abbey's life. She persuaded him to publish the novel *Black Sun*—more like a novella, I thought at the time—with Simon & Schuster

without benefit of Don Congdon, Ed's longtime agent. The publishing relationship with Simon & Schuster was to last only one book, yet it's my guess
that the attentions of Ed's friend within the house helped to position *Desert
Solitaire*, which was then considered a title of limited appeal, in the paperback market. Touchstone, a reprint arm of Simon & Schuster, had purchased
a paperback license to *Desert Solitaire* from McGraw-Hill in 1968;° the paperback, published in the fall of 1969, loped around the Simon & Schuster
stable like an unclaimed Thoroughbred until 1971, when it took off, never to
falter again.

Bob Gutwillig, then a hotshot editor, had signed Abbey to a two-book
contract in 1966; as with many such hotshots in book publishing, Gutwillig
had departed his job before the first book, *Desert Solitaire*, was published.
The manuscript languished in a pile of contracted but unread manuscripts in
a small office at McGraw taken over by Walter Clemons. In 1968, new to my
job running Dutton, I had met Walter while on the lookout for literary editors. When he sent me a galley of *Desert Solitaire*, I misunderstood Walter's
gesture and thought he and McGraw wanted me to take the book off their
hands (he simply wanted my help in getting names of appropriate Abbey supporters). As it soon became clear, Clemons was dazzled by Abbey's prose
style; it was also clear to me that the concerns Ed raised in the book failed to
capture the editor's interest. Within a few months Clemons, too, had departed McGraw-Hill; in his case it was a career change, and *Newsweek* magazine was to be the beneficiary of Walter's twenty-year run as a book critic.
Before his departure, Walter and others had received enthusiastic support
for *Desert Solitaire* from the likes of Tom Lea, Walter Van Tilburg Clark,
A. B. Guthrie, Jr., and Joseph Wood Krutch.

As the book's shepherd, Walter had persuaded artist Peter Parnall to
scratch out handsome pictographlike line drawings to add a touch of timeless
mystery to each chapter opening page. These drawings were "based on the
author's copies of prehistoric Indian petroglyphs and pictographs found in
southern Utah and northern Arizona," as noted on the book's copyright page.

The legendary Krutch, desert rat to the core, formerly the drama critic of
the *New York Times*, had this to say on the book's jacket: "Some years ago,
Edward Abbey sought solitude and reflection as an isolated ranger in Arches

---

° Ballantine Books had acquired the rights to publish a lower-priced edition. At the time it was
not uncommon for the original publisher to license two paperback reprint editions simultaneously: one trade, the other mass market. The mass-market Ballantine edition did not reach
full stride until 1974.

National Monument. But he had hardly got settled before the advance guard of 'developers' began to arrive. His book is a passionate celebration of what he sought and a hymn of hate against those who deprived him of it. He is eloquent, bitter, and extravagant, but those of us on his side will not like him any less for that."

Soon after publication, the book died a silent death, or so it seemed.

Ed Abbey had come by to see me at Dutton soon after *Desert Solitaire*'s publication. Until I took him downstairs to Max's Kansas City, a hip nighttime dive that offered the previous evening's stale smoke and grime as its lunchtime ambience, Abbey had said almost nothing. Awakened by steak and eggs, chick-peas and liberal servings of Jack Daniel's, he and I talked of words and writers, especially about Pablo Neruda and Jorge Luis Borges, whom I was publishing in English. Sweet, shy, polite—courtly, in fact—Ed in person was a different man from the Abbey persona in print.

It wasn't long before he agreed to write a book on the Appalachian wilderness (two chapters are included in part II pp. 141–152), the first of nine books we were to publish together. A relationship developed that was close but guarded—Ed's way; we roamed the rocky gorge known as Aravaipa Canyon near Ed's trailer, took trips together, drank from the same bottle; stayed up until dawn around my kitchen table in Rockland County, gabbing with Willie Gaddis, one of Ed's favorite novelists, or with Bill Eastlake in Tucson.

Another friend of Ed's, the writer Edward Hoagland, identified what's special about Abbey's writing in a telephone conversation we had five years after Ed's death: "He'll outlast all the others," Hoagland began, without a stutter. "The others—Peter Matthiessen, John McPhee, Dillard, Lopez, they're all good writers, but it's character that distinguishes Abbey. The cranky, authentic personality comes through. That's why he'll last."

J.M.

From <u>Black Sun</u>

"G ATLIN, YOU BUM, where the hell are you?" The great voice thunders through the woods as Art Ballantine marches into the clearing. Red
curls on his forehead, a red fat neck, the curly hairs of his chest revealed in the
open collar above the loosened tie. Panting from the climb, he strides to the
door of the cabin.

"I say there, Gatlin, for christsake where are you?" He peers into the
open door, blinking. "Reveal yourself. Break out the ice, man."

He holds a jug in his large, hairy, freckled hand, a quart of something
potable clutched in a paper sack.

"Speak, O vocalissimus," he roars.

Gatlin comes out on the catwalk of the tower and looks down. Grins, says
nothing, but at once begins to descend the stairway. Ballantine looks up, shading his eyes against the glare of the sun.

"Hey! You're up there. Get on down here. God damn it to hell, come
down."

They sit at the old picnic table near the pump, beside the rusted horse-
shoe pegs and the chopping block. The bottle between them, a glass in Ballantine's hand, a tin cup before Gatlin. Canteen of branch water on the
boards.

"Actually don't drink much of this stuff anymore."

"I've noticed you're sipping rather daintily, man. For the love of God's bod, drink up. This is a great occasion."

"I am glad to see you again, Art."

"Glad? Rejoice! I've come to rescue you from exile. To drag you out of this Godforsaken wilderness. How much longer can you let yourself rot in this unspeakable, slovenly"—Ballantine waves his big hand at the surrounding and nearly silent forest—"this *blague* of nothingness?"

"I like it."

"You look good. But your mind is starving. For the sake of your nerves you're starving your mind and drying up your soul. You're becoming a spinster. Will Gatlin, our maiden aunt."

"It's nature."

"Fuck nature. Where we throw our empty beer cans on a Sunday afternoon. Man, get out of here before you die. If you live that long."

Neglecting the drink, Gatlin reloads his short evil pipe. Strikes a match on the tabletop.

Ballantine watches the steady hands. "Yes, you look well. But by God, Will, how many years at this now? Six? Seven?"

"Six."

"Six years in the primeval bog."

"Not all of it here. Various places."

Ballantine laughs. "Various places, he says. Christ, man, what kind of places? Some of them worse than this. That hellish sandtrap you were in two years ago. What did they call it? Death Valley? Good God, what a hole! Those others. And now this . . . a rotting forest. What do you do for women? Make love to your fist?"

He grins. "Whatever's handy."

"You're becoming a freak, Will. A fanatic. A weird queer kind of anchorite. You're dreaming your life away."

"Oh no, it's not that bad."

"Drink." Ballantine half fills his glass, adds water from Gatlin's canteen. "Not that bad, eh? You ever hear from the ex?"

"No. She doesn't write."

"The kid ever write you?"

"Yes."

"Thank God for that. Support payments?"

"I do what I can."

"Thank God for that too. I'd hate to see you escape scot-free, man, when all the rest of us are paying blood. Through the nose. Through the nose, Will. Visualize. O pussy-whipped men of America, visualize."

"I'm trying."

"But don't let her bleed you to death. The ex-wife is like a succubus. The bitter half. The older they get the more bitter; they never forget and they never forgive. They'll bleed a man to death if they can. And then throw the empty shell into the garbage can and cash in his life insurance. And hang his picture upside down, face to the wall, behind the water heater. And sow salt on his grave. Adding salt to insult. Don't let her do that to you, Will. But you've got to make a fresh start. Get out of the woods here, shape up a bit, take a decent sort of job—you could always go back to teaching, you know, man, it pays better than ever now, they're screaming for instructors, assistant professors, yes and the girls are better than ever—and then, when you're set, find yourself a good strong simple-minded wench, like my new one, for example, Elsie I mean, and *hurl yourself upon her*. In fact you can have Elsie if you want her."

"She's a fine woman."

"She's a bitch." Ballantine drinks deep, lowers the glass. Wipes his broad mouth. "But a good one, mind, a good bitch. In her goddamned cockeyed way she loves me, I'll say that much for her. The kid has judgment. If only she weren't so ugly. One thing I cannot and will not suffer is an ugly woman. There's no excuse for it."

He thinks, *Dishonoring his wife, he dishonors himself. Spare us, old friend, these reductions.*

"Of course," Ballantine goes on, "I know what you're thinking. In the dark it's all the same, the standing cock hath no conscience, let alone the power of making aesthetic discriminations." He pauses, grins. "Maybe that's why I suffer from penis envy. My penis has more fun than I do."

He adds bourbon and water to his glass, offers the same to Gatlin. Who shakes his head. "Will, get out of this. Do you know the etymology of the word 'idiot'? No? What kind of philologist have we got here? Idiot: from the Greek *idiotes*, meaning a 'private' person, one who is alone. By extension, one who lives alone."

"I'm not alone."

"You're not?"

"I have excellent company."

Ballantine frowns. "Yourself, I suppose. Don't give me that Thoreauvian bullshit, man. Listen, leave this Smokey Bear stuff for the local jokels. They can hack it, they've got nothing to begin with anyway. But outside there's a world, Will. The great world. All yours. Full of fruit, wine, beautiful ideas, lovely and lascivious ladies, enchanted cities, gardens of electricity and light."

"I've been there."

"Hah! listen to the—"

"Well quit of all that."

"Ah, listen to the sonofabitch. He's been there before. Well quit of the world. Jesus. Jesus. Jesus X. Christ. Where have I heard all this crap before? Where haven't I heard it all before?"

Gatlin, patiently smoking his pipe, says nothing.

"Will, you need a woman."

He lifts one eyebrow.

"Yes, a woman. Sex."

"Love?"

"No, not love for godsake. Who said anything about love? Love is a disease. A social disease. A romantic, venereal, medieval disease. A hangover from the days of the fornicating troubadours and the gentlemen in iron britches. A disease for which marriage is the perfect cure. Never confuse love and sex. Fatal mistake."

"I do not get them mixed up."

"Yes, you do. I'm sure you do. That's your trouble, man. So you've got to get out of here, get a job, a real job, a man's job—"

"Become a professor like you."

"That's it. And grab a woman. Help the movement. Liberate a woman tonight. You'll get stale out here in the woods, living like a bear. Your balls will shrink, your tongue grow stiff and heavy. Your mind will wither away. Whatever became of William Gatlin? Went mad flogging his bloody duff."

"Poor Willy."

"Poor Will, poor Will, poor Will, sick ghost of a dead bird haunting the woods of nowhere."

Sad, sad . . .

"Prematurely middle-aged. Evading life. Wasting away. Look at you, flat as a board, you don't get enough to eat for christsake. When's the last time you had a full dinner, served by the woman who loves you?"

"Art, you shake me."

"Just trying to wake you up, old buddy. Life is short."

"Life is long."

"Life is too short."

"Life is very long."

And now melancholy, like the shadow of a cloud, passes over them both. In the quiet forest.

The gaunt and hungry mule deer, Gatlin's parasites, stand in the shadow waiting for sundown. Ballantine's roving eyes seek them out, while his hands refill his glass.

"Your friends are here again. God, look at those scroungy brutes. Like gigantic . . . Yes, they remind me of gigantic stuffed rabbits."

"The deer? They're starving. Too many for the range."

"Feed them."

"They're spoiled enough already."

"Shoot them."

"I'll take a couple in the fall. They're no good now."

"So what's the solution?"

"We need more lions, wolves and coyotes."

Ballantine turns his back on the deer. "Outside we have plenty of wolves."

"Yes, I remember."

"Another reason why we need you, Will, out there. You've got no right to hide in here like a monk in a monastery. It's cowardly."

"No right? Well, I was sick of all the talk. The petitions and the protests. When the shooting starts I'll come out."

"Then it will be too late."

His pipe is dead, he's trying to smoke the bottom of the bowl. Sun sinking in a reef of clouds. Gatlin excuses himself, hurries up the tower for an evening look at things. Ballantine hauls his heavy bulk up from the bench, steps towards the edge of the clearing, unzips and pisses heartily on the fallen leaves, the dust, the pine needles. Zips and backs off. Some of the deer approach. Ballantine clambers slowly up the stairway. The tower shakes.

Joins Gatlin on the catwalk.

"Whew! Christ! Jesus, how many times a day you climb this goddamned thing?"

Gatlin peers into the northwest, shading his eyes. The binoculars hang by a strap from his neck.

Ballantine sags over the rail and stares down at the ground far below, where the deer are now moving slowly through the clearing, heads lowered, nuzzling the earth. Two of them circle the stain of Ballantine's urine, striking at each other; one retires. All does and fawns. Thin gray shapes, silent as shadows. Tiring of them, he looks where Gatlin is looking.

"What do you see?"

"Nothing."

"What are you looking at then?"

Gatlin does not answer.

"I don't see it," Ballantine says. He smiles to himself, hums a tune. "What happens to this tower when the wind blows hard?"

"It sways."

"And lightning? St. Elmo's fire?"

"Yes, there's some of that too."

"You're mad. You're a madman, Will. This place is driving you out of your mind. Let's go down to the lodge and have a big dinner."

"Stay here tonight. I was about to start supper."

"I know your suppers. Thanks anyway. And Elsie's waiting for me at the lodge. She'd love to see you. Come and eat with us. We have to get an early start tomorrow."

"Back to California?"

"Yes. Summer session begins in three days. They need me. They're calling."

"Stay here, both of you. Take a summer off."

Ballantine smiles. "Can't do it, man. Can't do it."

"You owe it to yourself, Art. I think you've earned it, Art."

"He mocks me. He jests at my burdens. Why don't you come with *us*?"

"I can't leave the job."

"Job? You call this a job? This Boy Scout stuff?"

"Someone's got to do it."

"So. But why you?"

He makes no reply. Ballantine waits. Tries again.

"Will?"

"Yeah?"

"Why are you here?"

No reply.

"What in God's name do you think you're doing here? What do you *really* want to do anyway?"

"Really want to do," Gatlin repeats softly, still gazing out over the forest. Toward the desert. A pause. "Stare at the sun," he says.

"What?"

"Stare it down."

Ballantine sighs. "Will, you're crazy."

"Stare it out," says Gatlin, smiling. "Stand on this tower and stare at the sun until the sun goes . . . black."

"Let's get out of here. You need a drink. No, I need a drink. We all need a drink. I'm sorry I asked."

They descend the tower. They walk down the darkening pathway. The deer watch, the mule ears alert; in silhouette they look like giant hares. Down the trail, under the breathing and whispering trees, through a grove of crooked aspen in a green-gold fading light. The hermit thrush. Two men walking beneath the glowing and heartbreaking sky, where mountainous clouds drift against the wheeling spokes of evening, toward the evening star. One talking.

His arm on Gatlin's shoulders, Ballantine speaks of love. A two-time loser, he speaks of marriage. A doctor of philosophy, he speaks of duty, honor, obligation and the world. He speaks of choice, of decision, of creation and significance. Of purpose and meaning. Of happiness. Of joy.

Gatlin swings his stick. He stops for a moment, pointing at something deep in the shadows among the trees.

"What?" Ballantine stares. "Yes? What is it, Will?"

Gatlin points.

"What do you see, Will?"

SAW HER smiling reflection rise beside his. The sunlight shone through her hair. He felt her hands move up his back, onto his shoulders, into his hair.

She started to laugh, and with the sudden strength that always surprised him she pushed his head down, into the water. And ran away, laughing, towards the aspen trees, through the silken knee-high green rice grass. Those slim brown legs, bare beneath the short kilt, flashing through the shining grass. Her long hair, gleaming like copper, streamed out behind her.

He pounded after her but she ran like a startled doe, quick with life, sprang over a log and was into the trees before he even began to gain on her. In the green gloom she raced before him, laughing. He yelled, she looked back, veered to one side, then the other. Each time she changed direction he crossed the angle of her course and closed the gap. She collapsed suddenly on the edge of another grassy place, a small and sunlit opening deep in the forest. He sprawled upon her.

"Got you now, rabbit."

"You got me."

"You run like a rabbit." His heart was beating furiously. "First like a doe. Then like a rabbit."

"Dirty old man."

"Aye, lass."

"Dirty filthy hairy old beast."

"Aye, lassie. Old enough."

His hand moved upon her and she shivered, turned, twisted beneath him. He kissed her long and deep, caressed her, gasped with pleasure when he found her naked beneath the kilt.

"You were expecting me."

"Yes. There."

He kissed her hair, her forehead, her darkened eyelids, closing the bright and expectant eyes. Raising his lips, he drew back for a moment and she gazed steadily at him. In the green and gold and hazel of her eyes he saw a brief reflection of the trees, the sky.

" 'Your eyen two wol slee me sodenly . . .' "

"Chaucer wrote that."

"You're right, lass."

"What else do you know?"

" 'I may the beauté of them not sustene.' "

"Slay me."

"Yes."

"Kiss me."

"Yes. Shut up and I'll kiss you."

He kissed her mouth, unbuttoned her blouse and stroked the small soft breasts, feeling the nipples rise and harden under his touch.

"Yes. There. Kiss me there."

He kissed them, nibbled on them. Her arms tightened fiercely around his neck. He touched her knee, the silken skin above. Her thighs parted slowly before his hand.

"Yes, oh Will. There, there . . ."

Her warm sex was soft and sleek as velvet when he slipped a finger into her.

"Oh Will. Please. Oh God. Oh Will, I want to say all the words."

"Say them."

"I don't know how."

"Say fuck."

"Fuck. Fuck me."

"Yes. Say cock. Say cunt."

"Cock. Cunt. Cock. Oh Will . . ."

"Say cocksucker."

"Cocksucker. Will. Oh God. Oh Jesus."

"Jesus? Jesus who?"

"Jesus H. Christ."

"Thatta girl. Say the words."

"Cock. Cunt. Fuck. Jesus H. Christ." She was turning, trembling, opening for him. "Oh God, Will. Now. Fuck me. Fuck me."

"Where?"

"Oh God. Please."

"Where?"

"In my. In my."

The sun sparkled through the shaking shimmering trim translucent leaves. The warm grass surrounded them, bedded them, embraced them. An orange-black butterfly danced in the air, in the light. Monarch of the moment.

Dear heart how like you this

1971–77:

Henry in Love—An Interlude

I AM A SCOUNDREL, he reflected, dialing the sacred number. This girl's young enough to be my daughter. So what? Let's make the most of it.

"Yes?" inquired a gentle voice on the other end of the line. She sounded sweet enough to eat with a spoon.

"Claire? This is Henry." He felt the first drops of sweat begin to trickle from his armpits, the first involuntary twitching in his groin.

"Henry? Henry who?"

He hesitated. "Is this Claire? Claire Mellon?"

"No, this is Grace Mellon. Just a moment, please."

Long pause. Must be her sister. Henry waited, gripped in terror. How to begin? Would she even remember? She must have got his letters. Letters she never answered. Must have read them. But then what? What then?

A second voice vibrated in his ear, a voice sweeter, younger, even more delicious than the first. "Hello, Henry."

"Claire. It's me."

"Yes, Henry, it's you."

"Henry the Ranger. Remember?"

"Henry the Ranger. Yes, I remember."

From *The Fool's Progress: An Honest Novel* (1988)

"I'm in Denver, Claire. Only ten blocks away. I want to see you."

"That's sweet of you, Henry. But we're going to a concert. We have to leave in a few minutes."

"Oh." He stopped. Now what? "Well—I'll go with you. I'll buy the tickets."

She laughed. An angel's laugh, it seemed to him. "But Henry, I'm in the orchestra."

"In the orchestra?"

"String section. Second violin."

"Oh." What now. "Well—I'll come and watch."

"You're not supposed to watch, Henry, you're supposed to listen. Both, rather. But yes, do come. Meet me at the reception afterward."

His heart swelled with relief. She does remember me. Joyously he said, "I'll bring my harmonica. And my Jew's harp. And my Paiute foreskin fertility dance drum."

"What?"

"Dogskin." Giddy with sudden happiness, he barely heard her instructions. But he found the place, the concert hall—after a quick stop at a gas station to bathe, change shirt, whip on necktie and jacket—and bought a cheap seat high in the peanut gallery, among the music students. He noticed a few of them adjusting opera glasses. The orchestra had not yet come onstage. Henry hurried out to his truck and returned with his 7×50 U.S. government official forest ranger binoculars. The tympani leaped to his eyes. The harp stood five feet before him. He could read the lettering of the open score on the conductor's podium: *Leonore* Overture no. 2. Henry was so excited he could barely restrain himself from turning to the young people around him and announcing in bold frank supercharged tones that he, Henry Holyoak Lightcap, was boldly frankly candidly in love with a girl, with a violinist, with the whole string section, with the entire Denver Fucking Symphony Orchestra, with Leonore too and Ludwig Whatshisname. . . .

He waited, waited.

The members of the orchestra began to file in—first the percussionists (how he envied the man at the great copper bowls of the kettledrums) then the brass then the woodwinds then finally the string folk: the bass viols, the violoncellos, the violas, the violins—including yes, yes, there she was a slender figure holding her dainty instrument (and later mine, hoped Henry) in one hand, plucking up the long skirt of her formal blue-black velvet gown, trimmed at neck and sleeve with snowy lace, as she picked her way on slick black glossy pointy shoes among assorted elbows, cellos, legs and feet toward her chair. Henry stood up, the better to see her—and as he did so a number of others around him also stood, following his lead, assuming the advent of an important personage onstage—and waved at Claire. Already tuning her fiddle, however, she failed to notice Henry, failed even to look up. Henry sat down, disappointed. Those around him sat down. He remembered the giant field glasses hanging from his neck. He raised the eyepieces to his eyes, adjusted the focus and grazed with greedy looks upon the radiance of her flowing butter-colored hair (no braids tonight), the rosy luster of her cheeks, the bare glowing flesh of neck, bosom, arms . . .

Entered the concertmeister and took his place. A man with a pickled face and a nut-brown oboe sounded his nasaline keynote. The other players took up the note, converged upon consonance, groped closer and closer until the entire Denver Symphony Orchestra was braying forth one sustained and mighty A. (Often the highlight of an entire concert.) Satisfied, the first violinist nodded his sleek rodentine Central European head. The musicians fell into silence.

Pause.

Then applause, beginning with a tentative few, catching on with more, bursting out from the entire hall as the members of the orchestra rose to their feet and the conductor marched onstage. Smiling, the maestro—a brusque fellow named Fritz—bowed once to the audience, turned briskly to his reseated orchestra, faced the music, uplifted his baton . . .

Now what?

Two hours of bliss, by the clock. An eternal moment, in Henry's soul.

The question of temporal sequence hardly entered into the matter. With Henry H. Lightcap the dance of love began as a mad impulse followed, in due course, by leisurely regret. Events in between proceeded by quantum jumps, often without traversing the intervening space, sometimes jogging through time in reverse. Each particle indeterminate and unpredictable but the aggregate bound tighter than a bull's asshole in flytime to the iron laws of probability. As Henry would have phrased it, composing his footnote to Plato.

He found the reception, smuggling himself in when challenged by affecting a Continental accent. Smiling, shrugging, spreading his hands—"Mein Hinklish"—an apologetic grimace—"iss how you say?"—tapping his skull, "Not zee best he could be, eh? Je ne c'est pas, non?" He drew a faded card from his jacket pocket, allowing the usher a brief glimpse: "H. Holyoak Lightcap, M.A.; Special Project Consultant."

Working his way politely but firmly through the jostling mass of bald heads, black coats, lacquered hairdos and velvet gowns, he established himself at the vantage point of the punch bowl. He sloshed a champagne glass through the punch, avoiding the fruit, and looked about. Over a bobbing bubbling cumulus of svelte heads he looked for the golden radiant one he sought. And found her, after a moment, trapped within a tight circle of all-male music lovers. Lecherous swine. Henry dipped a second glass into the bowl—the server busy with a queue on the other side of the table—and forged a path through the murmuring mob toward Claire. *Light* was her name, bright star of his soul. The cuffs of his shirt were wet but little he cared about that. Little he knew.

She smiled at his earnest approach, his uncombed head and padded shoulders rising above the crowd, his unsteady hands holding aloft two glasses of punch. He held one toward her, providing her with a pretext for escaping her admirers. My God she's beautiful, thought Henry. The thought left him speechless. Him, Lightcap, speechless.

"Well here you are," she said. He nodded; they touched glasses. "Where's your Smokey Bear suit?" He grinned and nodded, unable to take his eyes from her face, hair, the bare neck and shoulders. Take your eyes off my face for godsake, he imagined her thinking, unable for the moment to imagine what else he could do. "I was hoping you'd be wearing the big hat," she went on.

"Crowded in here."

"It's supposed to be crowded. This is a reception. Our first concert of the season."

"I didn't know you were—so good."

"I'm only a fiddle player. Second fiddle. Besides there's a lot you don't know about me."

"I know. Let's get out of here."

"Don't you want to meet my mother?" A smiling woman stood beside them, looking at her daughter, then up at Henry. She too was beautiful, more beautiful than her daughter: taller, elegantly slender, refulgently blond, with the patrician nose and dramatic cheekbones of an actress.

"Not really," Henry said.

The woman laughed and elevated her little gloved mitt toward his lips. "But now you must."

Blushing, he took the hand in his huge paw, looked down at the thing, squeezed it gently, bent and kissed the fingers.

"Such a gallant ranger. I am Mrs. Mellon. My name is Grace."

Claire said, "Now aren't you sorry? Wouldn't you rather have a date with my mother?"

Slowly, with difficulty, Henry herded his wits together. "You're both beautiful. Let's all three get out of here."

"That's better," the mother said. "Let's do that."

Shit, said Henry. Silently.

"Soon as I make my good-byes," said Claire, moving off. He watched her exchange a smiling kiss with the concertmaster, then bounce on to the drummers, the trumpeters, the little men with the slide trombones. Swine, all of them.

"Claire loves people," the mother explained. "She's the most popular girl in the orchestra." Taking Henry by the elbow, she began guiding him toward the nearest exit. "We'll wait for her outside."

Under the portico, in the cool October air, she took a lengthy cigarette from a gold case in her handbag. She paused. Henry produced a wooden kitchen match from his pocket, ignited it with his thumbnail and lit Mrs. Mellon's cigarette.

"Thank you." She puffed and inhaled and expelled. "That was clever. What else can you do?"

Silently, Henry produced a second match, tautened his right trouser leg by lifting his right knee and struck the match on the seat of his forest green twill ranger pants.

"Dear me. . . ."

He produced a third match and struck it on his teeth. They both stared at the yellow flame.

"You *are* a clever young man. And how young are you, Mr. Lightcap, if I may ask."

About forty-four, he explained.

"About forty-four. Good. You don't look a day over forty. My age." For a moment she mused over the ironies of life. "Claire's new young man. And I understand that you work as—a park ranger?"

Only in the summer.

"Only in the summer? Good. And in the winter . . . ?"

He rested.

"I see. Marvelous. What a marvelous way to set one's course through life. You have a family, Mr. Lightcap?"

He mentioned the Lightcaps of Stump Creek, West Virginia.

"Really? West Virginia? Why we're practically neighbors. My people live in the Old Dominion."

East Virginia?

She laughed. She had a fine grave well-modulated laugh. Highly musical. "And your wife, Mr. Lightcap?"

No wife, he said. Been divorced for many years.

"And her family?"

Henry mentioned the Mishkins of New Rochelle, later Weehawken.

Mishkin, he explained, was a well-known slumlord family in the waterfront district of that urban-surburban North Jersey complex. Or perplex, as they say.

She peered at her smoking cigarette. "I see. . . ."

Claire came bustling up with her violin case, cashmere shawl upon her shoulders. The three walked under the trees, around the corner of the music hall, to a parking lot. Mrs. Mellon unlocked the door of a substantial gray motorcar of recent European extraction. She took the cased violin from Henry's hands, stowed it on the passenger's seat and kissed her daughter on the cheek. "Don't forget, dear, you have classes in the morning."

"I'll be home in an hour, Mother."

"It's eleven already."

"I know that, Mother."

"And you, Mr. Lightcap—" She gave him a thin ironic smile. "I do hope that we meet again someday—perhaps in another of America's splendid national parks or forests."

Henry agreed. For a moment, holding the car door open and observing her form as she eased gracefully into the driver's seat, he imagined the lady spread-eagled on an Indian blanket, nude beneath a canopy of whispering pines as he, Ranger Lightcap, performed his manly duty. Having Grace under pressure.

They watched her drive away.

"Did she give you a hard time?"

"Your mother is a concerned woman."

"She's a prig and a snob but I love her anyway. Let's walk."

They walked through the park near the concert hall. They shared the banalities of tentative love. Whom did she love most? Mozart, she said, and after Mozart, Stravinsky. I don't like either of those guys much, he admitted. I can tell, she said, but if you ever want to be a gentleman you must learn to admire them both. What about Minnie Pearl? he inquired. Minnie's all right in her way, she said, but for real country give me Conway Twitty and Loretta Lynn. They're good, he agreed, but I like Dmitri better. Shostakovich? she asked. No, he said, Kabalevsky. Oh bland, she said, bland as tapioca, oh Henry you must be kidding. I'm kidding, he said.

He slipped an arm around her waist. She leaned toward him. Thigh against thigh, they walked beneath the well-groomed elms. Her moving hip, beneath his hand, felt like warm black velvet. I love this dress you're wearing. It is rather sexy, isn't it?; but all the women in the orchestra were wearing black; you must have noticed. Can't say I did. What a liar you are. Come with me, he said. Where? Anywhere. (Oh my God, Claire, anywhere, he thought, anywhere.) Can't you be more specific, Henry? South, he suggested; let's go down to Tampico, lay on the beach all winter long. Can't, she said.

That was that.

They walked in silence for a while, under the trees, around and around in a meandering loop before the muted glow of the concert hall. Beyond, illuminated by hidden floodlights, the dome of the state capitol shone against the night sky.

You're wondering why I came here? Not at all, she said, not at all. How come you never answered my letters? I apologize; I didn't really think you were serious. Those others? Other men write me letters. Do you think I'm serious now? Yes, right now I think you're serious. What does that mean? It means that I think you're serious right now. You're right. It's a now thing. What does that mean? What else could it mean, Henry?

He stopped at the side of a sycamore, leaned his back against the smooth bole of the trunk and drew the girl gently into his arms. She looked up at him, no longer smiling. He kissed her.

Why did you do that?

That's what you said last time. He kissed her again, seriously. She responded by putting both her hands on the back of his head and pulling down, pressing herself against him, arching her body like a bow.

Let's go somewhere, he suggested. Make love.

Love?

Get this agony over with.

Oh no, Henry, I can't do that. Please don't ask me to do that. One hour together and then I don't see you again for—how long? Six months? A year? Ever?

I could stick around for a few days. We could go camping in the mountains. The aspens are turning gold now. The sunflowers are in full bloom— and the purple asters and the globe mallow. It's beautiful up there, Claire. Cattle gone. Bull elk bugling in the high meadows. Brown trout jumping in the lakes.

She smiled up at him, her eyes misty with pain. No, I can't do it. That would make it even worse for me. I'd be miserable all winter long, thinking about it. Missing you.

It's a now thing, he said.

It's too much of a now thing.

He walked her home, a mile over the sidewalks under the trees through shadowy residential streets. She lived with her mother—father gone—in a fine old brick-and-stucco house, three stories high, behind a wall, in a well-groomed neighborhood of fine old grave Victorian houses. She turned a key in the gate, they said good-bye and kissed once more. She entered and closed the gate, they touched hands through the iron bars, she withdrew. Henry watched her walk to the deep porch of the house, unlock and enter the front door, disappear.

Henry walked back to his pickup truck through the Denver night. At two o'clock in the morning, too restless and agitated for sleep, he started the engine and headed home. Whatever that was. Weehawken? No more. Stump Creek? Not really. Albuquerque, El Culito, San Francisco, Edinburgh, Naples, London, Paris, Madrid? Those days were gone. Back to the park in Utah? That season was over.

He realized with a shock of horror that he was at liberty to go anywhere he wished. Nobody cared where he went.

HE WANTED HER SO MUCH. For so long. He desired her so intensely over such a length of time that the longing became a malaise, a sickness. *Desire*—the word itself, in its very sound, with its dying fall of suspiration, resembled the enchanted misery of his fever. A fever in the blood, fever in the mind, fever of soul.

He tried to telephone her from a town called McCook in Nebraska, two hundred miles east of Denver. Stump Creek was a week behind him when he called the magic number and reached only her mother.

I'm afraid she's not here, Mr. Lightcap. No she's not. I said she's not. She's in Rhode Island now, visiting her grandmother. Spring break, you know. Where in Rhode Island? Does it really matter, Mr. Lightcap? Where are you, if I may ask? On your way to Utah, I suppose? That "seasonal" job, as you call it? I said she's with her grandmother now. In Newport. No, I think I'd rather not divulge the address. There's a quality of *enthusiasm* in you, Mr. Lightcap, that suggests madness. I think you're a dangerous man, Mr. Lightcap, and frankly would prefer that you not see my daughter, frankly. Yes, frankly. I know you appreciate frankness. We have something in common then, don't we? I'm sure that she'll write to you from time to time, if she wishes. I've no control over that. But I will not encourage your interest in her. She sees various young men, you know. Young men, I said. Men her own age. Do you have difficulty hearing me? Your right ear? From what? Guns, you say? Gunnery? Mr. Lightcap, this information does not surprise me in the least, indeed it confirms my worst fears and suspicions. Thank you, sir. Thank you, Mr. Lightcap. Good-bye now. I said good-bye.

Thinking that the mother might be lying, he tried again when he reached the city, slunk about the Mellon house for two days and nights hoping for a glimpse of Claire; she did not appear. He called the secretary of the Symphony Association and learned only that the concert season was over and that Miss Mellon, like other members of the orchestra, had been furloughed for the spring and summer. He visited the music department at the University of Colorado in Boulder but found nobody there except a departmental assistant who refused to reveal any information whatsoever about any student. Henry left a message for her sealed in a departmental envelope:

> Claire—
> Come.
>
> —Henry

THAT DIDN'T WORK.

HE WROTE HER LETTERS, long rambling humorous and pathologic letters, often in blank verse, sometimes in rhyme, from his sun-cooked outpost in the Utah desert. Sent her pictures of himself in ranger suit, Smokey Bear hat, smug smirk, with views beyond of a rearing phallic monument silhouetted against the pure indigo of desert sky. Sent her sketches in his own hand of Navajo hogans, buckboard wagons, tired saddlehorses, sick cowboys vomiting in the horse trough. Sent her a sprig of sagebrush, a corsage of juniper, a mountain lupine wreathed in maidenhair fern. She acknowledged his gifts—some of them—with cryptic notes, highly delayed, that promised nothing.

Finally she agreed to meet him for a day, on his day off, at the town of Glenwood Springs in western Colorado, a midway point between Denver and

Moab, Utah. She would not stay overnight with him, no she would not. Would not or could not? Both. She would arrive on the westbound morning train— Denver, Western & Rio Grande—and depart on the eastbound evening train. She owned no car of her own and preferred not to borrow one from her mother.

Wear that black velvet dress, he begged her on the telephone, with the lacy trim. Henry don't be silly, she replied. . . .

At five o'clock, official quitting time, on the day before the tryst, Henry retired to his plywood ranger hut among the juniper trees, stripped off his sweat-soaked uniform and took a shower. Not in the little trailerhouse, a cramped bug-infested sweatbox with apologetic plumbing, but out back on the rock, in the sun, with two buckets of water, one soapy one clear. He bathed in the soapy bucket and poured the contents of the other over his shaggy head. Shivering with cold goosebumps, at a temperature of 102°F, as a fiery breeze swept down from the rosy, infernal cliffs. The humidity was 6 percent.

He dressed in his sportiest Dacron slacks and loudest Hawaiian shirt, filled his canvas waterbag and hung it on the front bumper of his pickup, loaded buckets, bedroll and cooking gear in bed of truck, tossed in a rag satchel with clean shirt and underwear, toothbrush and razor and comb, locked up his trailer and bolted off like a rabbit for the highway, ten miles away by sand and stone. He paused in Moab for oil, gasoline and beer, then headed northeast up the river road through the gorge past Nigger Bill Canyon, La Sal Creek, Castle Valley, Professor Valley, Onion Creek, Fisher Towers. Flaming with joy, fear, intolerable anticipation, he rumbled—engine faltering—over the Colorado River on the half-century-old one-lane Dewey Bridge. Stopped to fill a bucket and add water to his leaky radiator. Scalding his fingers in the steam. Draped a wet rag over the carburetor to soothe the vapor lock. And waited, walking irritably back and forth in the shade of the cottonwood trees on the riverbank, switching impatiently at the heads of dried cheatgrass with his agave walking stick. Returned to his vehicle, added a quart of reprocessed oil and slammed down the hood, securing it to the grille with the leather latigo that hung from the hood ornament.

Henry drove on, passed the mouth of the Dolores (Sorrows) River, forded a stream that came down from the Roan Cliffs on the north, and entered the ghost slum of Cisco. From there it was but a mile to the paved highway—US 6-50—and an easy roll over the lonely lovely desert to the riverside Mormon towns of Mack, Loma, Fruita and Grand Junction. Only ninety-one miles to Glenwood Springs. And 7:30 P.M.: only fifteen hours before her scheduled arrival.

Air cooling, engine cooling, sun well down behind him, he motored on through Palisade, De Beque, Rulison, Rifle, Antlers and Silt, following the river as the highway did, and entered the fine old resort town of Glenwood Springs. An odor of therapeutic sulfur floated from the baths and through the streets. Henry made sure, first of all, that he could find the railway station and passenger depot. Not hard. The railroad, like the highway, paralleled the river. Anything of any importance in Glenwood Springs ran along the river. He found another clock. He had thirteen hours to wait but at least he was here. Not there. He walked about the streets still flustered a bit from the six cans of beer he'd absorbed during the drive up from Moab but taking care not to attract the eye of the city police. This would be the wrong night to spend in a drunk tank.

Checked a clock in a jewelry store, another in a hotel lobby, a third in a supermarket. Twelve hours to go. He bought a can of sweet corn, some hamburger, an onion, a tomato, a jar of mustard and a package of sesame rolls and drove up into the hills north of town, into White River National Forest, parked his truck facing downhill, cooked his supper over a scrub-oak fire and made camp for the night.

He decided not to eat the onion. He brushed and flossed his teeth, had a long walk in the woods, took a shortcut coming back and got lost for two hours. Near midnight he slid into his sack and tried to sleep. Sleep came hard. About four in the morning, judging by the stance of the Big Dipper, he dozed off, dreaming of a symphony orchestra with one vital violinist missing.

A bird coughed. A daddy longlegs walked across his face. He rolled on his side and saw the bright green leaves on an aspen tree trembling before the morning light. A mountain bluebird swooped like an arc of electricity from the aspen into the shaggy dark arms of a spruce. He heard the sound of mountain water.

A worm fence four aspen poles high, looking fifty years old, zigged and zagged across one corner of the meadow. He thought of West Virginia. For a moment. He looked at the smooth white bark of the aspens and read the names of the sheepherders dead and gone—Garcia, Vargas, Barrutti—and the vague heart-shaped growth-expanded symbols of youthful love, enclosing the initials of brave lads and dark-eyed lasses long forgotten. His heart swelled with joy. Yes, he would bring her here for the day. They'd picnic in the shade at the edge of the trees, they'd drink from the mountain brook, they'd walk up

that soft brown lane that led into the depths of the aspen groves, he'd carve
her name and his own

inside a heart for all the world to see.

My God! He shivered alert, dashed through the goldenrod, morning
glory, dockweed and locoweed to the window of his pickup. A two-dollar
Westclox pocket watch hung on the dashboard, suspended by a leather thong
from the choke rod. The hands on the watch read ten after ten. Impossible.
Horror and panic flashed through his nerves: the train was due at ten-thirty.
He grabbed the watch, held it to his ear: no sound. He shook it, banged it on
the roof of the cab. The thing began to tick then stopped again, dead. He
hurled it over the trees, out of sight.

Glancing again at the sun for reassurance, he skinned on a pair of Levi's
blue jeans. No underwear for Henry. Then remembered the baggy slacks
with the drape shape and the reat pleats at the waistband—only fifteen years
old. His Eisenhower pants, 100 percent virgin Dacron. His wino pants. His
dress-up pants. He peeled off the tight jeans and stepped into the slacks and
tried to see himself in the side mirror of the truck. Wrong. This would not do.
He dropped the slacks, balled them up and stuffed them down a badger hole.
Again he pulled on the Levi's jeans—old and faded and not very clean but at
least they fit. Then reevaluated what he had long ignored, that the crotch was
frayed to a frazzle. If he sat with legs spread his scrotum could be seen, leaking out like some obscure form of marine polyp.

He looked at the badger hole. Decisions. He dug up the slacks, shook off
the dirt, considered and reconsidered. Meanwhile the sun was rising, soaring
like the fire of his hopes well into early morning. That Amtrak train would
already be coming down the grade from Loveland Pass, bearing in its Vista-Vu
dome car the bonniest colleen in the Golden West.

Haste! He counted his money: twenty-one dollars. (No credit card.)
Enough to buy a pair of decent pants at Sears or J.C. Penney maybe, but
what about the feast he planned for her, the imported Danish cheese, the
Prague pilsener, the Swedish flatbread, the grapes, the Italian salami, a pair
of filet mignons (mignones? mignoneaux? mignoni?) with bacon and mush-

rooms or else some lamb, marinated in a garlic lemon wine sauce, skewered with peppers and onions and tomatoes on a spit and broiled over the fire and—and of course the wine, two bottles of a fine Bordeaux perhaps, one red one white, one served at forest temperature the other chilled in ice *pourquoi non?*

He rehearsed the plan, rolling down the mountain toward Glenwood Springs, where he arrived to find that the time of day, Rocky Mountain Daylight Saving Time, was 6:04 A.M. He drove to the railway station anyhow, double-checking, but found the passenger depot locked. Peering through the dusty glass of the windows he read the chalked writing on the blackboard inside, the schedule of arrivals. Ten-thirty, said the board.

He had time for a cup of coffee. He located a cowboy and truckers' café, ordered coffee, flapjacks and pigmeat. Might need the strength later. For what? Who could say? For a rescue operation, perhaps: pretty Claire treed by a bear or frozen with fear on a crag of rock or swept by chance down a raging torrent toward a thundering waterfall, who knows? Henry the Ranger would be prepared.

He left the café. Seven o'clock. Three and a half hours yet to go. He walked around the block five times, drove to the biggest food store in town, parked, waited. Made notes in his diary. Played a few tunes on his harmonica, wondering which might most impress a professional musician. None, probably. He bought a copy of the morning newspaper and read the same old news. Nothing new. Same rotten war dragging on and on, same scoundrels still in office, same derailed freight trains and overturned truck-tankers spreading chlorine gases, flammable fluids, alarums, confusion and terror. What else is new?

Finally the supermarket was opened. Henry entered, first customer of the day, and pushed his cart up and down the quiet aisles. He found most of the items on his list. When the cashier at the check-out counter added things up, Henry had only enough money left for gasoline to return to Moab and his job.

Poverty. Lacking an icebox, he buried the perishables inside his sleeping bag, insulating them from the sun, and drove once again to the railroad station. The passengers' waiting room was open. He entered, looked at the clock on the wall above the ticket windows then at the schedule board. The westbound train would be twenty minutes late. Fifty minutes yet to go. He went into the men's room with his satchel in hand, peeled off his sweaty shirt and bathed himself from the waist up with soap and cold water. He dried himself with paper towels, took out his razor and shaved his bristling jaw, his blue-gray chin and upper lip. Trimmed his eyebrows. With thumb and forefinger plucked a few hairs from his nostrils. He ran a hand through his black hair, finding it greasy again; just another greaseball hillbilly. He shampooed his hair for the second time in less than twenty-four hours and slicked it down with a comb, then fingerwaved his standing pompadour. He brushed his teeth and deodorized his hairy armpits.

Now what?

The pants. He took the slacks from the satchel and held them up to the window. They were so thin at the seat the light shone through. And completely wrinkled—Dacron or not—smeared with damp earth, smelling of roots, rocks, rat turds and badger dung. Unsuitable for the occasion. He would have to wear what he was wearing, the little boy blue jeans with the peekaboo crotch. He stuffed the slacks into a garbage can, thought for a moment, pulled the blue bandana from his hip pocket and lined the inside of the Levi's crotch. The effect was curious but would pass. He put on a fresh white shirt, his finest, and snapped shut the pearly buttons one by one. Looking himself over in the mirror, forcing a grin, tilting his head first right then left, he found little to admire but hoped that little would suffice. He took his spare bandana, a red one, from the satchel and knotted it loosely about his throat. Nice. But it seemed an affectation—with the clean shirt, the lean jeans, the high-heeled pointy-toe boots on his feet, he looked too much like a dude-ranch cowboy. Perhaps she preferred the urban existential type, the sub-bohemian *verité*, a touch of defiant squalor from the student ghetto. Retrieve the Dacron slacks once more?

No! Enough of the waffling. Train's a-coming, boy. Henry joined the crowd outside on the loading docks and watched the train come around the bend uptrack, headlight glaring, power units puffing smoke. A trickle of sweat crept down his ribs. The engines grumbled past, champing steel, smelling of burning oil and hot iron, air brakes hissing. The tall bilevel blue-and-silver passenger cars glided along the platform, slowed, stopped. The conductor's assistant in his brass buttons and suit of navy blue swung down from the gangway holding the steel step-box in hand.

Henry looked for Claire's rosy face, bright eyes, golden head of hair but the tinted windows allowed no positive identification. He saw a few hands waving and waved his own in return. He watched as the first passenger descended the steps—a blue-haired lady in a print dress, followed by a pink-cheeked gentleman wearing a Panama hat. Two little boys in suits got off and rushed into the arms of a waiting mother. Three more elderly couples descended, then a pretty girl with red hair; Henry envied the young man who stepped quickly forward to hug, kiss and take her away—but she was nothing, a drab and a dormouse compared to his Claire, his Honeydew, his radiant ripe and unplucked Mellon.

He waited. He watched. But no one else came out. The conductor was already attending to the tickets of five passengers about to board. Moments later the engine whistled once, twice, thrice, the heavy wheels began to turn. Next stop Thompson Springs, Utah. The Amtrak rumbled off, rattled away and dwindled out of sight, airhorns wailing through the valley. . . .

Slowly, carefully, Henry sat down on a bench, his bag between his feet. He was alone on the platform. He licked his dry lips, felt the shocked slow thumping of his heart. Something like a paralyzing drug spread through his nervous system. He felt dazed, cold, hollow. He felt empty and useless and worthless. He stared at the vacant tracks of the railway, at the trees of the park along the river, at the spas and hotels on the other side and saw nothing. Nothing at all.

He sat there for some time—five minutes? fifteen?—then bestirred himself, picked up his bag and walked on numb legs and nerveless feet into the waiting room. He shuffled to the clerk's window and inquired after a message for Henry H. Lightcap.

The clerk looked. There was nothing.

Henry shuffled outside into the hearty sunlight. He saw dozens of happy people moving about, couples arm in arm, young lovers snuggled close on the front seat of automobiles. He raised his eyes to the dark conifers and pale green aspens crowding the mountainsides, to the gray scree of the peaks, to the snowfields and the first thick clouds forming out of nothing, *ex nihilo,* on the skyline. Stunned, he waited another hour, then drove slowly out of town.

He was ten miles west before he remembered to shift from second into third, twenty miles farther before he remembered the beer and the two bottles of wine, one red one white, wrapped in his bedroll.

Somewhere along the river road to Moab, under the beaked gods and visored goddesses of Fisher Towers, he turned aside up a rocky ravine, plowed firmly into the boughs of a juniper tree and stalled. Little blue-green berries rained down on cab and hood of truck. Henry kicked open the door to let his legs hang out, stretched lengthwise on the bench seat, pillowed his head on his forearm and subsided into the nirvana of unconsciousness.

ON THE AFTERNOON of the following day he checked in at Park Headquarters for mail. Among the letters, bills and junk in his box he found a memo.

Lightcap: Some female named Claire phoned long-distance yesterday to say she could not keep her date. Asked us to relay the message.
We called you on the radio but you were already gone. Hope everything turned out all right.

—Gibbs

HE FOUND other diversions.

But the pain lingered for weeks, months, years. He did not write to her
again until her letter came, a week after his happy journey to Glenwood
Springs and back.

Dear Henry,

Sorry I couldn't make it to the Springs last week. Had a fight with
my mother that day—she still wants me to go to Smith, just because
she went there. What kind of logic is that? Then I found out there was
no return train on the same day. It seemed better to forget the whole
thing. Maybe some other time. I trust that you received my phone
message in time. Do write to me now and then, when you feel like it.
I love your letters. You are the most desperately romantic man I have
ever known, and if I believed half of what you write I'd be a little
worried about your mental health. (Just kidding, Henry.) I appreciate your feelings about me but—you must try to remember that I
don't feel ready to enter into a serious relationship—let alone an "affair"—with any man as of yet. Maybe next year. But you are the funniest one I know and really I do like you a lot. Best regards from your
friend,

Claire

He studied and analyzed that letter for days trying to find solace in its
careless text. "Do write to me . . ." He liked that. But "now and then"? What
good was that? ". . . when you feel like it"? A casual dismissal. But then she
writes "I love your letters." I *love* your letters. How far is that from saying I
love *you*? Well—about a mile. Two miles. Am I indeed "desperately romantic"? Perhaps I frighten her with my ardor. Must cultivate an attitude of ironic
nonchalance. Worries about my mental health. That's all right, so do I. Perfectly reasonable. Appreciates my feelings but not ready for a serious rela-

tionship? What kind of ship does she want? She "likes me a lot." Jejune phrase. No nourishment there. "Your friend . . ." Friend? She dares call herself my friend? After this?

He waited as long as he could before writing to her again. Kept her dangling in agonized suspense for five days—nearly a week. Then wrote her a jaunty note eleven pages long, full of lies. The principal lie was one of omission: he said nothing of his trip to Glenwood Springs. He wrote about the red sands of the desert, the pattern of tracks a dung beetle makes on a dune, the arcs of the wild ricegrass in the wind. He related his more symbolic dreams, hinting of erotic splendors. Described a flash flood pouring like gravy down a chasm in the cliffs. Etc. Inquired politely after the health of Mrs. Mellon, wishing in his heart the woman would get herself flattened by a steamroller while crossing the street to buy a quart of milk, leaving behind only a caricature of the female form stamped on a patch of asphalt paving. Then perhaps, bereft, Claire would come to him in the night, tears streaming down her lovely cheeks, seeking in his arms the warmth of human love. Et cetera.

While waiting for a response to his letter, Ranger Henry journeyed after duty hours to the town of Moab, where he consorted with such old friends as Felicia Hastings, Bliss Quickly and Candy Cotten. Good sweet ladies fresh from the battlefields of divorce and ruptured rapture, ready for fresh adventures.

But his mind was fixed on Claire Mellon. He waited and after two weeks, his letter still unanswered, he decided to give her a ring on the national telephone system. He stacked quarters dimes nickels on the shelf of the public phone in Woody's Bar, dialed the operator and waited.

Your number, sir? The number I'm calling? The number you're calling from. He read the number. And the number you wish to call? He gave that number. A pause. That will be two dollars and eighty-five cents, please. He deposited the coins. Thank you.

He waited, heard the phone begin to ring in the Grace T. Mellon residence. The phone rang and waited, rang and waited, one phone ringing in an empty home. No one answers, sir. Okay operator, I'll try later. Thank you.

He hung up. He waited for his money to come jingling into the return slot. Nothing happened. He pushed the coin-return button. Nothing happened. He hammered on the phone with his fist. Useless. He poked his little finger up the slot, feeling for a wad of cotton. The cotton was there but when he removed it no money followed. He dialed the operator and got a busy signal. Tried again. Still busy. He bought another glass of beer at the bar and returned to the phone booth. It was occupied. He sat down nearby, staring at the man inside the booth, pointedly waiting. The man ignored him. Henry went outside to a public phone on the street, one of the new economical installations shielded from rain and wind by nothing but a little plastic hood. Yelping teenagers in eight-cylinder Camaros with four-barrel jets and overhead cams, gigantic trailer trucks hauling uranium ore to the mill, bearded bandits on snarling Kawasaki motorcycles—all raced by on the street, six feet from where he crouched with his head inside the tiny quasi phone booth designed evidently for midgets and Filipinos. After a while he obtained an operator's ear—one finger in his own—and explained his problem. The unrefunded two dollars and eighty-five cents. She needed to know both numbers again, the one called, the one called from. He asked her to hold on, dashed into the bar. The inside booth was still occupied. He tried to peer through the glass to read the number on the telephone. Could not be done. The man inside the booth scowled at Henry, revealing yellow fangs and molars full of lead. Henry backed off, ordered another beer, waited. Finally he got a second chance at the inside booth. He dialed the operator again and asked for the return of his two dollars and eighty-five cents. The operator asked for Henry's name and address.

Address? he said. I'm in Woody's Bar.

We'll have to mail you the money, she explained.

He asked her, in that case, to give him credit and he would simply repeat the call to Denver. Do you have a Mountain Bell credit card? No I do not have a Mountain Bell credit card, that's not what I meant, he explained, what I meant was that you give me credit for the money that this telephone—this goddamned telephone machine right here in Woody's Bar—stole from me about fifteen minutes ago. Sorry, sir, she explained, no credit calls without a credit card. Then all right, mail me the fucking goddamned money. It's a violation of federal law to use obscenities over the telephone, the operator said.

Listen, ma'am, Henry said, you take that two dollars and eighty-five cents and you go to the bank and get it changed for two hundred and eighty-five bright new copper pennies and you go home with them pennies and get a wooden mallet and you lie down on the floor and wrap your legs around your ears—are you listening to me, operator?

All he heard was a busy signal. The FBI would be flying into Moab within hours armed with arrest warrants and automatic shotguns. He dialed the operator, tied a bandana over his mouth and said that he wished to place a collect call. By and by the Mellon telephone began to ring. Presently he heard the drawling voice of Mother Mellon:

Ah yes . . . ?

Collect call from Robert Redford for Claire Mullins, the operator said, will you accept?

The name is Mellon. Not Mullins.

For Claire Mellon. Will you accept?

From whom, please?

From Robert Redford.

I'm afraid we don't know any Mr. Redford.

The actor, Henry burst in, Robert Redford the noted film actor. It's about Miss Mellon's audition. We have some good news for her. She—

Will you accept the call, please? the operator repeated.

No, said Mrs. Mellon. Decidedly not.

Henry brooded over his beer. He found a dime in his pocket and called Bliss Quickly. Later, near midnight, he drove the thirty miles of sand and stone, flushing nighthawks from the road, that led to his lonely hut among the erect and impotent phalli of the hoodoo desert.

He lit his Aladdin lamp and began a letter. "Dear darling Claire," he wrote, "If I cannot see you again I will surely die. . . ."

S U R E L Y D I E ? What a redundancy is death. He wrote that he would come to visit in early October, at the end of his working season at the park. She wrote back, after a time, that she was leaving for New England in early September. To a town called Northampton, Mass. To a school named Smith, entering as a junior. Why? Because of its proximity to Boston, she said, and the world of music. She wished Henry the best of everything (except herself) and hoped that he would continue to "drop her a line" now and then when the "mood took him." She planned to spend the following summer at Tanglewood. Good-bye. Claire.

He patrolled his back roads and walked his foot trails. He searched for lost little boys, helped fear-frozen rock climbers down from cliffs and shepherded fat bull snakes and faded pygmy rattlesnakes out of the garbage dump. He listened to his old battery-powered Hallicrafter radio late at night, receiving strange signals from Quebec, Ciudad Juárez, Radio Havana, Lubbock, Texas, and a police station in Ethel, Oregon. Where the town-limit signs read ENTERING ETHEL.

Well then, he considered, if she was going to be that way he'd make a dash for Denver on his next two days off. Only 350 miles from Moab—an easy seven-hour drive. If his pickup would run. Since it was down he'd take the Greyhound, catch the eastbound at 10:00 P.M., arrive in Denver at 8:00 A.M., walk to Claire's house, spend the day and evening with her, catch the 2:00 A.M. bus back to Junction, be home by suppertime. Simplicity enclosing *felicitas.* Embracing *claritas.* He hoped. He concluded, after further consideration, that his reentry into Denver had best be stealthy, unannounced. The surprise visit entailed severe risks but the more formal and courteous approach lent itself to a formal and courteous rejection. On one pretext or another she could make herself unavailable. The pattern was becoming plain, even to a fool as blinded by desire as Lightcap. As the moth is drawn to the candle he was determined to plunge into pain, to drown his anxiety, misery and uncertainty in despair. It seemed a reasonable, commonsensical solution.

Canvas satchel in hand, he boarded the bus. Old women with anxious eyes, grim faces, prim knees, filled the supervisory seats in front, assisting the driver in his duties. Henry stumbled to the rear, found adjoining vacant seats, staked his claim to both. He sat in the dark sipping from a square bottle of Jim Beam bourbon, eating peanuts from a sack.

The whiskey purled in his brain. The bus rolled softly eastward into the dark. He tried not to think of Claire by focusing his thoughts on Joy, on Jill, on Loralee, on Whatshername, on Candy, on Bliss. Useless.

He switched on the little overhead reading light, opened a book and began to read the Navajo Creation Myth, a guaranteed soporific.

The First World, Ni'hodilqil, was black as black wool. It had four corners and over these appeared four clouds. These four clouds contained within themselves the elements of the First World. They were a black cloud, a white cloud, a blue cloud and a red cloud. . . .

He dozed. He read. He read and dozed. He dreamed a dream that meandered on in various directions but mostly four and involved a man disguised as a badger, a badger disguised as a woman, a woman disguised as a man and an ear of corn on the cob, actually White Shell Girl who becomes the Moon and Yellow Corn Boy who becomes the Sun but the entire scheme is wrecked when Coyote-Who-Was-Formed-In-Water steals a blue turquoise charm that belongs to Water Buffalo's Babies which makes the Great Yei, Hasjelti, very angry. . . .

He was awakened by lights in the bus station at Grand Junction, Colorado, and the hiss and grunt of air brakes. He got off the bus to pee, entered the men's pissoir and read the wisdom on the wall:

Why dont Jesus walk on water anymore?
Because his feet leak.

(We need more Jews like Jesus.)

If all college girls was laid end to end—
I wouldn't be surprized.

(All Honkies must die.)

The blue-and-silver bus rolled eastward into night. Henry drank his bourbon, emptied the bottle and slept. Uneasily. In fits. Dreaming bad, lengthy and complex dreams that faded, when he woke, back into the addled cells from which they'd come. Buses roused his latent claustrophobia. But he was a poor boy, couldn't afford air flights or even Amtrak. He rode the bus and dreamed his suffocating dreams.

The red dawn found them grinding over Shrine Pass east of Vail, 11,050 feet above sea level. Blue snowfields on either side. Sick from the booze but too stubborn to puke it up, Henry steeled his stomach for grim gray grimy hours ahead. The bus rumbled down the grade, pistons braking against gravity, as they headed on for Dillon, Silver Plume, Lawson, Golden and Denver City. Henry sank into a queasy coma, one dead soldier upright between his thighs, and floated forth onto another lake of complicated nightmares.

He dreamed. He endured. He hoped. He groped toward consciousness out of the anesthesia of alcohol and discovered himself, Henry Lightcap, sitting on a stool in a steel stall with his pants down around his ankles. Canvas satchel on the cement deck. He read the writing on the inside of the stall door.

Here I sit all brokenhearted
Paid a nickel to shit and only farted

He washed his hangover face at the washbasin, shaved the blue stubble from his jaws, shampooed and combed his hair and put on once again his best and cleanest shirt. Feeling slightly better, roughly human, he found the bus station coffee shop and treated himself to a mug of steaming, translucent-black coffee and one stale but greasy doughnut.

Where are we? he asked the waitress.

God only knows, she said. More coffee?

Thanks.

You look awful, she added. She was a bigboned middleaged squareshouldered woman with plucked eyebrows and purple lips. A chin mole with bristles added the only decorative touch to her square and honest face. What's wrong with you?

I'm in love, Henry explained. That explains it; you look like I do. I'm in love with you. You are sick. What's your name? Read my tag; see?—June. What's yours? Henry. Well Henry, if I was you I'd go find a nice park bench and get some sleep. Looks that bad, huh? You'll get over it.

He left her a dollar tip and wandered outside into the gray and concrete boulevards of Denver. The brown air reeked with exhaust gases. Didn't really know where he was. Went back into the bus depot, found a phonebook and looked for a map of the city.

The clock on the wall said nine-thirty. He checked his satchel in a locker and headed north past the U.S. mint and the state capitol, then east along Colfax Avenue toward the city park, the museums, the opera house, the prep schools, the elm-shaded streets of her neighborhood.

What exactly would he do when he arrived? How would she receive this unexpected pleasure? And suppose—suppose she were not even at home?

He stepped up the pace.

Mountain clouds hung above the Mile-Hi City, casting transient shadows across the glassy façades of The Bank of Denver, The Federal Savings & Trust, The All-America Building, The Brown Palace, The Hilton Tower. A light rain began to fall but that was all right with Henry, it added drama to his pain and cooled the air.

He stopped for a few minutes in the park to recomb his wet hair—he wore no hat today—and to rebrush his teeth at a drinking fountain. He was feeling better. The brisk walk had restored his confidence. He glanced at his visage in the window of a parked automobile and it seemed presentable. Well, passable. The rain stopped. He marched north again, the last mile beyond the music hall, and came to the wall on the corner, the gate, the handsome square and bourgeois house. Lilacs and hollyhocks in bloom.

Now what, Lightcap?

He tried the gate. It was unlocked. He opened it and followed the curving flagstone walk to the portico, climbed two broad stone steps and found himself standing before the door. He hesitated. He listened. He heard music within, the duet of piano and violin, a phrase broken off and repeated and broken again, followed by sweet laughter, the tenor tones of a man's voice and more laughter. Unwelcome sounds to Henry's ear. One hand on the bronze knocker, he still hesitated. He heard the music resume, violin and piano in sibilant concord and he recognized the piece: filthy Mozart, the Sonata in F Major, Köchel 376. Parlor music.

Rain began to fall again.

Who was the scoundrel in there with her? A lover—or only a friend? A friend or only a teacher? Or both? All three? He waited, stiff with anxiety, heart chilled with fear. Rainwater trickled from his hair, down his face and neck. He realized more fully than before the depth of his folly in coming here uninvited, unannounced. He was a fool. He was a lunatic. A pathetic fool, a pitiable lunatic.

The music continued, halted, repeated itself, went on. Henry lowered the heavy knocker silently and stole away on tippytoe, down the walk, out the gate and around the corner before any eye detected him.

One block away he halted once more. In painful thought. He had to see her. That much was clear. He would not travel seven hundred miles by stinking Greyhound without even a glimpse of the girl he loved.

He returned to a point from which he could see the front of Claire's home, the wall, the gate. Perhaps the man inside would soon leave. There were a number of cars parked along the street, all new, enamel gleaming under the renewed descent of rain. Perhaps one of them belonged to Claire's visitor. No doubt he'd soon be departing.

Henry leaned against the trunk of an elm, turned up the collar of his shirt and lit a cigar, assuming a pose of casual and innocent introspection. An automobile passed, tires hissing on the wet asphalt. And then another. But no pedestrians, not one, appeared on the sidewalks. Henry began to feel conspicuous. He longed for the relative anonymity of hat and umbrella. He noticed curtains stirring in a front window of a nearby square three-storied house of brick, important-looking. He left his post under the leaky shelter of the tree and walked up the sidewalk past Claire's house, on the opposite side of the street. He walked two blocks, glancing back from time to time, then returned and resumed his place under the dripping tree. He waited.

After a while a police car came around the corner and stopped beside the tree. The two men in blue stared at Henry; he stared at them. Neither got out of the car. The driver beckoned Henry close with two significant twitches of a thick forefinger. He wore three chevrons on his sleeve.

Yessir?

Let's see some I.D. The policemen stared intently at Henry as he pulled out his wallet and fished his Utah driver's license—illustrated—from its once-clear now-grizzled plastic case. He gave it to the driver. The driver studied it. His partner watched Henry, a short-barreled riot gun held upright between his knees.

The rain poured gently but steadily on Henry's head.

What's your date of birth, Henry? the driver asked. He told them. Where do you live, Henry? Moab, Utah. Says here your address is P.O. Box 69, Moab, Utah; you live in a mailbox? No sir; I get my mail there. Where's your car, Henry? He explained. All right, you came by bus. The driver returned his license. What are you doing here? Henry hesitated. I'm waiting to see a friend. Waiting to see a friend. Why here? Kind of wet, wouldn't you say? She was gonna meet me here. She a little late? Again he hesitated. Henry Lightcap wore no wristwatch. Neither wristwatch nor underwear. I'm not sure, he said; I guess so. You guess so. Funny place to meet. Where's she live? Sir? Your lady friend; where's her house? Henry made a vague gesture up the street, pointing with thumb and chin. His hair and shirt were now soaked with rain. He shivered. The police sergeant opened his door, getting out. Turn around, he said to Henry. Sir? Turn your back to me; lean against the car; spread your legs. Henry did as ordered. The policeman searched him quickly, running his hands up and down Henry's body from armpits to boots. He removed the jackknife from Henry's pocket. You always carry a knife, Henry? Yes sir. Doesn't everybody? But that was the wrong remark. He felt steel cuffs clamped on his wrists. Get in the car. What? Get in the car. The driver opened the rear door. Henry crouched low and eased himself into the back seat. At least he was out of the rain. The driver slammed the door shut. The door lacked an inside handle, as did the opposite door. Henry found himself separated from the two men in front by a black mesh of heavy-duty steel. He could hardly see their faces.

Now Henry, the driver said, where's this lady friend live?

He hesitated again. Both of the cops looked like reasonable, intelligent men. Surely he could explain everything easily enough—but how?—maybe even get a free ride back to the bus station. Well, he said, she lives up the block. I think.

Up the block you think. The driver twisted in his seat, looking back at Henry. Both men watched him. Maybe I'd better explain your situation, Henry. There's been a dozen rapes and robberies in this part of town in the last six months. The driver paused.

Henry said nothing.

That mean anything to you, Henry? Henry said, I never heard of a woman getting raped in broad daylight. On a public street. I have, the driver said. He looked at Henry. I'd like to believe your story, Henry. But it's not a good one. Now show us where this friend lives or we're taking you to city hall. What's the charge? Oh we'll hold you for a while, put you in the lineup, see what the victims have to say. We'll think of something. Henry shivered. Guilt rose up to match the sick dread in his stomach. All right, the driver said, putting the car into drive and moving forward, I didn't believe you anyhow.

Straight ahead, Henry said. What? Straight ahead. She lives in that place on the corner. Right or left? On the right. The car stopped before the Mellon residence. Light rain pattered on the roof of the car, on the sidewalk, on the trees. This it, Henry? He looked down at his lap, his groin—source of his troubles—shook his wet, shaggy hair, tried to raise his hands. He groaned. What's that? Yes, he moaned. But for godsake . . . Both policemen got out of the car. The one with the shotgun opened the door by the sidewalk. Out of the car, he muttered. Move.

Henry bent low, crawled out, straightened up. He shuffled between the two policemen as they advanced through the open gate and up the flagstone walk toward the house—a gaunt soaked scarecrow between a pair of uniformed gladiators. As the three tramped up the steps of the porch he heard the music from inside the house—K. 376 still, andante movement—come to a sudden stop. A murmur of voices. Before the police sergeant could push the doorbell button the front door was opened from within. Opened wide.

Mrs. Mellon stood in the doorway. Behind her, near a baby grand piano, stood Claire with her violin and bow. At her side—chin on her shoulder— stood a fair young man of medium height (short) with pink cheeks and a blond mustache; he wore a blue blazer, a tie, a white shirt with button-down collar. His left arm lay about Claire's slender waist, his small white graceful hand resting lightly but protectively, with possessive assurance, on the warm curve of her hip. He smiled, affecting disdainful amusement but staring all the same. Claire looked pale, beautiful, alarmed, amazed.

Politely the sergeant tipped his black-visored cap to the lady of the house. He tightened his grip on Henry Lightcap's upper arm. Madame, he said, we found this—this fellow here—lurking under a tree down the street. He looked at Henry, then back at Mrs. Mellon. He claims he knows you. Care to identify him?

Mrs. Mellon looked at Henry, at the police sergeant, at the manacled prisoner and his keepers. A glitter appeared in her distinguished eyes. Her mouth formed a small satisfied smile, revealing in the chink between her lips the firm set of her whitened whetted central incisors, the points of her canines.

Claire took a deep breath.

THEY WERE MARRIED ten months later. The modest ceremony took place at Point Imperial on the north rim of the Grand Canyon, on a peninsula of limestone overlooking Marble Gorge, Saddle Mountain, Cape Solitude, the mouth of the Little Colorado River, the Vermilion Cliffs, the Echo Cliffs, Coconino County, the Navajo Reservation, the Painted Desert, Navajo Mountain, the San Francisco Peaks, one-sixth of Arizona and various other features of geological, historical, morphological and ethnographic interest. Eight thousand eight hundred and three feet above sea level. At evening, under the new moon.

Claire's idea.

Presiding was an Episcopalian priest flown all the way from Denver, along with Mrs. Mellon and friend and friends of the bride, in a chartered Learjet. A solemn comely bearded man, Father Cheswick spoke with a slight lisp, concluding his every other sentence with the phrase *et thetera* or alternately *and soo* [*sic*] *forth*. He liked cigars with his champagne.

He was Mrs. Mellon's idea.

The bride and groom were attended by two uniformed park rangers (one a female), three big ugly river guides from Lee's Ferry and six members of the North Rim fire-fighting crew wearing their yellow hard hats and orange fire-resistant shirts. (Two females.) A pumper unit mounted on a government Dodge three-quarter-ton four-by-four stood by, available for action in case, as the boys said, the nuptial embraces became overheated.

Music for the occasion was supplied by Slim Randles and The Dusty Chaps, an amateur jug band of cooks, dishwashers and mule wranglers from the North Rim Lodge. The band performed a honky-tonk version of Wagner's "Wedding March," a medley of tunes by Johnny Cash, Phil Ochs, Johnny Paycheck, Marty Robbins, Willie Nelson, Ernest Tubb, Kinky Friedman, Hank Williams, Bob Wills ("still the King") and Claude "Curly" Debussy (*Claire de Lune*).

Henry's idea.

The groom wore formal attire, a traditional gangster suit of blue serge with mighty padded shoulders, rented for the occasion from McCabe's Funeral Home, Kanab, Utah. Since the pants were six inches too short for his legs he tucked the cuffs into the top of his machine-tooled dude boots and looked fairly presentable.

The bride wore virgin white, a filmy diaphanous ankle-length multilayered froth of lace, gauze, vapor, satin and soo forth, with a coronet of silverleaf lupine, scarlet gilia and white campion at rest on the crown of her yellow hair. Like the groom (but as only he knew) she wore no undies. Excepting, in her case, the requested black lace garter high on the left thigh. She carried a bouquet of mountain wild flowers matching the coronet. When she tossed the bouquet to her maids an errant gust of wind carried it over the edge of the cliff. One of the river guides leaped after it, caught it in midair and disappeared. The band played on—Ernie Ford's "Tennessee Waltz"—without missing a beat. Mrs. Mellon's sister fainted. Father Cheswick looked concerned, hiked up his gown and pulled a sterling-silver flask from his hip pocket. The firefighters danced with the ladies from Denver. One of the rangers tossed a coil of purple Perlon line over the rimrock and hoisted up the gnarly, scratched but grinning river guide, the bride's bouquet still clutched in his bloody right hand.

The bride's mother smiled at Henry when they danced but the glint in her eyes was not the light of love. Nor of charity.

The sun went down. The music got louder. Violet-green swallows jetted through the air. The music got faster. The bride and groom slipped off through the dusk to Henry's pickup truck, fell into the cab and sank from view. Henry sat up a minute later with a moist nose and the torn garter clenched in his teeth. The bride rearranged her skirts, Henry stepped on the starter and nothing happened. Laughter burst from the nearby shrubbery. Henry rolled out cursing, waddled awkwardly to the front of his truck, uncinched the hood and looked inside. He reattached a battery cable, got back in the cab, started the engine, geared down and engaged clutch. Nothing happened. He gunned the motor to a furious roar—wheels spinning— but the truck did not move. He slid out, found the rear axle chained to a tree. More laughter. He unhooked the chain, returned to the wheel, shifted into low, raced the engine and popped the clutch. The rear wheels spun and fish-tailed in the dirt, blasting the nearby scrub oak with a spray of heavy shot. Somebody yelled. The wheels dug in, found hard ground, the truck leaped forward like a prod-stung bull and vanished into the timber, dragging a ten-foot tail of beer cans.

They spent their wedding night in a grove of aspens a quarter mile from Henry's fire lookout cabin. He had left his truck parked at the door. They made love immediately and then lay awake for a time, still connected, still one flesh, smiling up at the stars and listening to the uproar of gunfire, bongo drums, bugles, coyote howls and drunken song from the clearing around the cabin. Still *in situ* he felt himself swelling within her. She felt it too.

Henry—what're you doing? Who, me? No, him. That hain't me, Honey-dew, that's Gawd Hisself entering into you: all ten inches of sacred cock. Ten inches my foot, you blasphemer. It's all I got, but there's more to come; it's the thought that counts. It's the diameter that fulfills. You mean the circumference. Don't be a pedant; if you're the Holy Ghost I'm the Virgin Mary. Not now you're not. Oh Henry, Henry, oh my God Henry I love you. . . .

The leaves of the quaking aspens twinkled above them. A golden meteor soared eastward across the Pleiades. The new moon went down in the western sky and the sounds of the shivaree began to fade.

Nine thousand five hundred feet and ten inches above sea level.

THEY SPENT the remainder of that summer at the fire lookout on North Rim. The regulation ninety days of passion came and passed and even so he continued to marvel in her, to dote upon her, to adore each detail of her flesh and hair and mind and character. They quarreled about nothing, now and then, when the isolation of the place cast a pall of melancholy over her spirit but resolved each quarrel in a warm solution of sexual salts, weeping, laughter, plenty of wine and long walks through the woods.

Mornings she worked on her Mozart sonatas and Bach partitas, sawing away on her fiddle inside the board-and-batten shack, sitting on a rickety chair before her music stand, turning pages. While Henry in his open-aired lookout ninety feet above closed his book or put down his binoculars and listened, found himself leaking tears over the perfection of Mozart and struck into awe by the vast echoing unanswerable vision of the grand Bach chaconne.

In the afternoon Claire straddled her ten-speed Peugeot and bicycled fourteen miles in a couple of hours to her evening job at the lodge, where she worked as hostess in the restaurant. Henry would meet her at the end of her shift, spend half her tips on drinks at the bar with buddies from the fire crew and their girlfriends. Half tipsy then they loaded her bike in his pickup—their bike, their pickup—and motored easily, idly through the woods and past the open meadows where deer grazed in the moonlight and up the dirt lane under the aspens to their cabin and tower on the highest point of the entire Kaibab Plateau. The air would be chill by then but a fire was set in the stove: Henry lit the fire and by its light undressed her (tired poor working girl) inch by inch and rolled her on her belly and putting his large hairy hands to practical use massaged her neck and ears, her shoulders, her shoulder blades and back, the small of the back above the twin dimples at the base of her spine, her rounded, full and lightly suntanned rump, her thighs calves ankles feet toes— and then, and then he made the return journey up her legs but always hesitated, paused near the midpoint of his pilgrimage to bite each plump buttock once, not too gently, and to roll her over again or perhaps to simply slide upon her as she was, belly down, and spread her legs with his knees, take the nape of her neck in his teeth, grasp her breasts in each hand, whisper sweet vile proposals in her ear before inserting himself to perform his duly obligated lawfully approved formally licensed divinely consecrated conjugal duty. She murmured in reaction, half asleep, then less asleep began to whimper like a child, like a girl, like a roused and dangerous woman until she had squeezed from that curious inner-space probe of his the last full measure of devotion. After which, sprawled and tangled limb on limb, they slept and snored innocent as babes in the wood. This sort of thing went on and on for weeks, months, years, shocking the great horned owls of the forest, the star-nosed moles beneath the cabin floor, the giant fur-winged Luna moths that gathered outside the window screens.

On rainy days he came down from his tower. If the air was cold and she wanted to continue practice he built a fire for her. This often led to the usual collusion:

Come on. I can't. Come on; two more times; you can do it. Henry, I can't. We'll set a new world's record. Most multiple multiple-orgasm by WASP wench in lookout cabin in southwest USA since Frieda Von Richthofen Lawrence diddled Mabel Dodge Luhan in the men's room in the Taos Inn. I'm tired; you're disgusting. Think about what we're doing; feel that? I feel it. Then come again. I can't. You can.

She could. Afterward, in the rain, they wandered through the spruce and fir picking morels, puffballs, chanterelles, wild onions, wild currants and strawberries, lamb's quarter, pokeweed greens. She believed in a diet of fresh and raw vegetables. He preferred pigmeat, poached venison, potatoes, gravy and beer. They compromised by trying everything, culinary and sexual, that seemed mutually appealing.

Mrs. Lightcap had no desire to return to Smith College in September. One year in that place, she explained, was enough. Henry felt grateful. The prospect of eight months in a town named Northampton in a state of New England had filled him with claustrophobic angst, though he'd kept mostly silent about it.

Thoreau liked it there, she said. Thoreau was a creepy little pederast. That's a lie. He liked to take young boys on huckleberry parties; and I mean take. You have the lowest, filthiest mind; you're worse than any pederast; Thoreau was a flutist and a wilderness lover; he should be a hero of yours. He did have an elegant prose style. He still does. But his poems are mediocre even for a Harvard man. That's true; get out your flute, Henry. This one? That one.

He uncased his old beaten secondhand Haines. Claire placed on the mu-

sic stand some Bach gigues, gavottes and bourrées which she had transcribed
for him. He attempted the first.

Too many flats, he complained. I made it as simple as I could; anyhow the
notes are not your problem. What's my problem? You have a good tone; you
have clear phrasing, decent timbre, adequate fingering; but—. Yes? This is
Bach, not some Irish folk tune; not a cowboy song. What do you mean? I mean
that it has to be played with metrical precision; you're not counting, Henry;
you don't seem to have any sense of measure; how could you ever play with
other musicians? Well, I never tried; I'm a soloist. But this is J. S. Bach, soloist
or not. Well, I'm Henry H. Lightcap and I don't care who knows it. Sweet-
heart, we're aware of that. But you don't have to be so aggressive about it. It
suggests a certain quality about you which, well, is not your best.

Claire was smiling at him as she said it, her hand on his knee. He looked
away, out the open doorway of the cabin, and felt, for a moment, a sickly
sadness trickle through his nerves. He waited for his inward anger to subside
and said, I know what you mean.

Of course you do.

I've suffered from it all my life.

We all do. She watched him with her gray-blue eyes, her gaze level and
sympathetic, her lips parted in a tentative smile.

What the French call *ressentiment*, he said. Is there such a word? A kind
of sick resentment of anything—excellent. Beyond my reach. Superior. Incomprehensible. Like quadratic fucking equations. Fucking symbolic logic.
Like fucking Benedict Spinoza. Like—many things.

Oh Henry. . . .

But: I accept my limitations, he proclaimed. Proudly.

She smiled at that. By God you'd better.

And they collapsed together in a fit of laughter. To merge in heat.

Instead of New England they squandered the autumn in a tour of the
hidden Southwest. He showed her his secret places, his treasured canyons,
holy rivers, sacred mountains. Sleeping on a mattress in the bed of the pickup
truck, they camped for a week by a cold bright creek in the San Miguel Mountains eating brook trout for breakfast, Claire's stir-fried rice and vegetables
for supper, each other for lunch. When the sun was shining. When a second
motor vehicle came groaning up the dirt track and parked only half a mile
below, Henry loaded his backpack with tent, fly rod, grub, sleeping bag etc.—
"and soo forth," as she said—and led her by deer path five miles farther and
three thousand feet higher to a nameless small lake at timberline. He set up
the tent and caught a mess of native browns. They stayed there for five days

and on the fifth climbed the craggy peak above the lake, embraced in the wind at 14,211 feet above sea level, glissaded down a snowfield, inspected the ruins of an abandoned gold mine and returned to camp. Next morning they descended to the truck through the first blizzard of the mountain fall.

He took her next to the high desert, to the canyonlands of southern Utah and northern Arizona. Down in the canyons at the side of pools the leaves of the cottonwoods were beginning to change from acid-green to pale yellow. The shade beneath the trees had a green-gold tone, reflected by the water. The canyon walls appeared rosy red at dawn, buff brown at noon, pink and lavender and purple through the continuum of evening and twilight. He parked the truck under the trees by a waterfall with plunge pool big enough for swimming. They played in the water nude as fish and made love in the hot sun on a limestone ledge slick as marble. He pointed out the ancient pictographs and petroglyphs on the rock wall above; she found new ones that he had overlooked. They filled their pockets with raisins and venison jerky and hiked for five miles up the canyon, wading the water, and found more pictures on the canyon walls, a dwelling of mud and stone in an inaccessible alcove in the cliff and a natural arch sculptured by erosion through a sandstone fin. The fin was twenty feet wide, a hundred high. The moon of evening floated on the ellipsoid patch of sky inside the arch: like a blue eye with white iris and pupil mounted in the socket of a rose-colored skull. One mourning dove chanted in the distance.

Are there more of those in here?

Natural arches? This is the biggest.

This place should be a national park.

He put a finger to his lips and looked around. The walls have ears.

And eyes. She smiled. Are we being selfish?

You're damn right. Let them others find this place like we did. By looking for it. By dreaming of it.

They lingered in the canyons for two weeks, exploring pockets and corners in a maze of wonders. They slept under the stars, swam in the pools beneath waterfalls, climbed the range monoliths.

Henry, I'm frightened.

Why?

Because I'm so happy; I've never been so happy in my life; it's frightening.

He held her in his arms, stroked her flowing hair, caressed the supple rondure of her breasts, arms, hips. He said nothing. He understood her fear and had no answer for it.

They camped for three days and nights on a point of naked stone two thousand five hundred feet above the Colorado River. The place had no name on the maps. Henry broke a bottle of wine on the rock and christened it Cape Claire. They were eighty miles by burro path, jeep trail and dirt track from the nearest county highway—a gravel-surfaced road connecting a place called Pipe Spring (pop. 10) to a place called Wolf Hole (pop. 0). They watched five small pretty boats—dories—pass beneath them on the river, pitching and yawing through whitewater rapids, bound for the stagnant cesspool of Lake Mead sixty miles downstream. They saw bighorn sheep scrambling from ledge to ledge on the cliffs below, on the crags above. Golden eagles, red-tailed hawks, black vultures and raucous blue-black ravens circled in the air above and below. Lean stalks of agave grew by the side of sandy basins in the stone, seedpods rattling in the wind. A squall of rain passed through one night transforming each basin into a shallow tiger's eye of water. They refilled their water cans cup by cup. The sun emerged from a range of clouds, the wind blew and by evening the pools were dry. They walked in twilight on a path through a silent village of basaltic boulders set on pedestals of mudstone. A coiled and excited rattlesnake challenged their advance. Henry squatted on his heels, spoke to the snake, stroked the underside of its neck with his stick until the snake became quiet, then lifted it draped on the stick to the side of the trail and set it safely down. They walked on, climbed a ridge, circled back to camp and watched the red sun sink beneath a quilted ceiling of clouds, a grand excessive baroque display of color and fire that overspread the entire sky for an hour and lingered in the west for three hours more.

They worked their way off Cape Claire, driving the unreliable two-wheel-drive pickup down stony ravines and across sand-filled washes and onto the deep-rutted jeep trail that meandered in various directions around numerous obstacles but kept bearing north. Henry stopped frequently to get out his shovel and bevel off cutbanks, remove rocks and circle ahead on foot in search of the route when it disappeared on acres of bare hardpan. They found a shortcut through the Grand Wash Cliffs, camped under the Virgin Mountains and by noon of the second day reached a town named Mesquite and the paved highway that led to Las Vegas. By late afternoon they were lying together in a tub of hot soapy water in a room on the tenth floor of the Mint Hotel. They stayed there for two nights, saw Woody Allen at Caesars Palace, ate the bargain meals at the Stardust, admired the Las Vegas architecture, won seventy dollars at the blackjack tables in the Fremont Casino and left town quickly.

I don't like this, she said.

Why not?

We're too lucky.

Don't worry, said Henry. We deserve it.

They drove the pickup, refueled, retuned and repaired, across the basins and over the ranges of the Amargosa Desert, the Grapevine Mountains, Death Valley, the Panamint Range, Saline Valley, Eureka Valley, the Inyo Mountains and down into Lone Pine on the eastern slope of the Sierra Nevadas, left their signatures in the hikers' register on the summit of Mount Whitney (14,494 feet above sea level), drove south to Mojave, Santa Monica, Laguna Beach, Oceanside, dipped their feet and immersed their bodies together in the green waves and white surf of the western sea. Unable to afford a hotel room, they drove eastward to the crest of the Vallecito Mountains and made camp on a high good place from which they could see west to the Pacific, east to Arizona. They counted their money. Four dollars and two cents.

We're broke, she said, delighted by the novelty of the sensation.

You want to go back to Denver?

And live with Mother? You're kidding of course. No thanks. Anywhere but there. Let's go someplace different.

Different from what?

Different from Denver.

They drove east next day across the desert, past the Salton Sea, the Chocolate Mountains, the Sand Hills, across the Colorado through Yuma and deep into the Sonoran Desert, refueling at Gila Bend, Fan Belt Capital of southern Arizona, soon after dark. Claire disapproved, as Henry knew she would, but finally agreed out of necessity to stand guard while Henry dipped his siphon hose into the tank of a city car behind City Hall. They drove on to Tucson that night and camped in the saguaro forest west of the city. Tucson, they decided, would do for the winter. In the morning Claire found a job as a waitress at the Arizona Inn near the University; she placed an ad in the school paper offering tutorial instruction in music theory, history, piano, flute and violin. Henry stood in line for two hours at the State Department of Employment Security, downtown, made formal application for a position as professor of philosophy, park ranger, fire lookout or social worker, and filed a claim against Utah and the National Park Service for unemployment compensation. Such gall, such brass, such insolence—but was he not "entitled," by custom and by law? He was. But he knew what his old man would have said about such beggary and he dared not even imagine what his brother Will would think. The economic honeymoon was over.

To soothe his conscience and appease Claire, Henry took a part-time job (for a time) as *plongeur* or pearl diver in the kitchen of Mother Hooper's Café, a dark den for transients, winos, welfare recipients and other derelicts such as himself. Within two weeks he and Claire had accrued enough cash and credit to rent a three-room "studio" apartment in the student ghetto of the University. They took the mattress from the bed of the pickup, beat the dust out of it, laid it on their parlor floor. They bought four gallons of latex enamel and repainted the walls. They improvised bookcases, repaired a salvaged sofa, reglued a pair of chairs, equipped the kitchen with toaster and new table from the Goodwill store and bullied the landlord into fixing the plumbing. Claire rented an upright piano, had it tuned and trundled into the apartment. She picked volunteer snapdragons from the weedy yards in the neighborhood and set them in beer cans and jelly jars on top of the piano, in the kitchen, in the bath. When her students (some of them boys) began to appear, one by one, Henry would sneak off surly to the University library for study or to the bar downtown known as the Dirty Shame Saloon where he began to acquire a circle of cronies, possibly friends, with names like Lacey, Harrington, Richard "Rick" Arriaga and Daniel K. "Decay" Hooligan. The isolate honeymoon was over.

The basic honeymoon was over but Claire and Henry remained lovers nonetheless. He loved her for her brisk energy, her calm courage, her cheerful determination to make a functional marriage of this bizarre connection with an elderly academic bum and liberated libertine like Henry H. Lightcap. What was the point of him? He posed the question often enough himself:

What are you going to do with your life, Henry?

My life? *Do* with my life? Why should I *do* anything with my life? I live my life. Or—is it mine? Or am I merely the temporal instrument of my life? A reed in the wind, a seed passing through the bowels of a cactus wren, a swirl of dust rising from an alkaline playa in the heart of the Black Rock Desert, a ripple of motion across the surface of a pond, an ephemeral downward shift of sand on the slipface of a dune? Eh? Speak, O vocalissimus.

Claire never charged him with idleness. But there was a kind of wonder in her eyes sometimes when she asked him, How can you spend so much time reading books?

He smiled. I'd rather be on a horse. Then we'll get you a horse. We'll need a one-horse ranch to keep it on. We'll get you a ranch. Sure. A wedding gift from your mother, I suppose. Henry remembered the gleam of hatred in Mrs. Mellon's eyes when she'd embraced him, smiling, after the modest ceremony at Point Imperial.

My mother would do anything for us if I asked her; but I don't intend to ask her. Good, said Henry; I'm sure glad to hear that. But I will come into a trust fund when I'm twenty-five. We won't need it, he said. ("Come into"? he thought.) It's not much; about twenty thousand a year. (Henry's heart skipped a beat. That was twice what he'd ever earned in a single year.) But we could buy a piece of land somewhere, build a house on it. Make a home, raise a garden, keep a pair of horses if you wish.

And a pair of children, I suppose?

Yes.

All right. But I'm not living on your money. I'm a working man. I believe in working for my bread—six months a year. That's the way we're going to live. In honest poverty. Voluntary simplicity, like Thoreau said. The pederast? Yeah—him.

THEY WOULD SETTLE for the time being on Tucson, Arizona, a re-sort town for trust funders and rednecks both, with a symphony orchestra for ambitious violinists. In January Claire enrolled at the University, beginning her senior year as a student of higher learning. Henry complained when he discovered that she had borrowed money from her mother in order to pay the high tuition fees required of nonresidents.

Nonresident? he said; we live here.

We have to live here for a year to qualify as residents.

Lie.

I'd rather not, Henry; and you've still got Utah plates on that truck of yours.

Well, goddamnit I'm your husband; I pay the bills around here, not your mother.

Then you'd better get a job, earn some money.

All right, I'll earn some money. While she was at school he disassembled, cleaned and reassembled his revolver and his deer rifle and went off into the desert with D. K. Hooligan for target practice. Borrowing his friend's ear protectors, he fired five rounds out of six into a beer can at fifty feet with the .357 and seven out of seven at a hundred feet with the .30-.30. Satisfied, Hooligan hired him for a one-night job at a nameless dirt airstrip on the Papago Indian Reservation fifty miles southwest of Tucson. The plane came in at twilight from the south, circled twice, put down and taxied to a stop. The pilot did not shut off the motor. There was an exchange of light signals between the airplane and Hooligan. Hooligan put away his flashlight, unchained the huge wallet from the hip pocket of his jeans and walked to the side of the plane,

under the wing. Henry waited fifty feet away under the branches of a mesquite tree, rifle in his hands, revolver in his belt. He watched the door of the
plane open, heard a quiet exchange of words, saw a dozen squarish bundles in
white sacking tumble out, saw Hooligan pay and shake hands with the man
inside. The engine roared, the pilot released the brakes, the airplane rolled
then raced down the remainder of the strip, bouncing over bursage and panic
grass and took off, wings waggling, into the flamboyant Papago sunset.

Henry and D. K. loaded the odd-size bales of what looked and felt like
alfalfa into Hooligan's van and started off for Tucson.

Friends of yours? Henry asked.

We've been doing business for a while.

Why'd you need me?

Hooligan smiled his rich and satisfied smile. That's the kind of business it
is, he said. Friendly but not too friendly.

They knew I was there? Under the tree?

You bet. That's the first thing I told them. About my friend Dogmeat the
Green Beret. They could see you. They trust my judgment.

Three hours later they reached the Dirty Shame. Hooligan paid Henry
five hundred dollars in cash for the evening's work and bought them each a
drink. Arriaga and Lacey appeared and joined them for a second round.
Sometime after midnight Hooligan drove Henry to his apartment house.
Henry entered to find Claire sitting up in her nightgown, wide awake, waiting
for him. She said nothing as he stood the rifle in the corner, sat down beside
her on the rehabilitated sofa and slipped an arm around her bare shoulders.

I'm home, Honeydew. She said nothing. He felt his sheepish, guilty grin
slipping away. I've been working, he said. Earning money. Dinero. Moola.
Frogskins. She said nothing. He pulled a wad of bills from his pocket, placed
it in her palm and folded her fingers over it. Give that to your mother, he said.

She looked at the four century notes, the three or four twenties, the fives
and ones. She crushed the bills into a ball and put them in the big ceramic
ashtray on the apple-box coffee table before them. Two of Henry's cigar butts
rested in the ashtray, together with matchbooks labeled Pandora's Box and
the Dirty Shame.

Say something, he demanded.

She struck a match and applied the clear yellow flame to the crinkled pile
of paper money. The finely engraved, labor-ennobled, leathery-textured legal tender began to burn, slow but willing. Henry watched.

I risked my life for that money.

She made no immediate reply except to strike a second match and encourage the fire. She said, I know what Hooligan's business is. You don't have to tell me.

They watched the flames creep over the noble faces of Washington, Lincoln, Jackson, Franklin.

It's only marijuana, he pleaded. No proof yet it does anybody any harm. Good placebo anyhow. He pulled a plastic Baggie from his jacket. Brought a sample home for you. For you, Honeydew. You like the stuff don't you? Seems like I see you smoke it now and then.

She said nothing. They watched the flames continue their patient consumption of his earnings.

That's more than I get in four weeks of unemployment compensation, he complained. Finally she looked at him. Henry, are you really as stupid as you pretend? How stupid is that? You really don't understand what I'm angry about? I guess not. You don't like Hooligan? The stink of burning money passed his nose, floated on. Is that it? I don't care about Hooligan, I care about you. You mean—? Keep trying. You mean that if something happens to me, if I got killed so to speak, you'd never speak to me again?

She lifted her arms and hung her interlocked hands around his red skinny vulturine neck. From a distance of six inches she peered into his eyes: soft gray-blue the color of smoked sapphire peering into squinty bloodshot gooseberry green. Looking very serious, she touched his lips with her lips. She licked the lobe of his left ear with her tongue, veiling his face with the fall of her hair. Her pink-tipped breasts within the filmy stuff of her gown pressed upon his white chest.

She said, Take a shower Henry and brush your teeth and come to bed. I'll explain everything to you in terms that you can understand.

THROUGH THE WINTER he filed his applications. In March the offers began to arrive: seasonal ranger jobs at Arches, Isle Royale, Grand Canyon, Gila Wilderness, Glen Canyon; fire lookouts at North Rim, Glacier Park, Tonto National Forest. . . . Nixon still in office, the war yet smoldering on, prosperity burgeoning, Henry Lightcap the permanent part-time career anarchist enjoyed a wide choice of attractive low-paying untenured futureless upwardly immobile temporary jobs. The only kind he wanted. The only type he thought he needed.

In April he made his selection and on May Day (Law Day in the US, Workers' Day in the SU, Fertility Day in pagan Europe, Homecoming Day in Henry's heart) he started work as a five-month fire lookout on a mountaintop near Globe, Arizona, one hundred miles by road from Tucson. He might have preferred other places but by this choice he remained within easy driving distance of his young wife, who had three weeks of school remaining in May and would return to school in early September. They would sublet the apartment through the summer.

In mid-June they celebrated their first conjugal anniversary with caviar (red), champagne, wild flowers and commemorative love on the lookout's chair (mounted on insulators) inside the cabin of the fire lookout tower. Love at timberline again, seven thousand nine hundred ninety-two feet above sea level.

That same day, in the evening by a ceremonial fire on a rim of rock overlooking five separate mountain ranges, the canyons of the Salt River and a *gran finale* of a sunset beyond Four Peaks and the Superstitions, Claire informed Henry that she wanted a baby. That she wanted to become a mother. That she was out of b.c. pills and ready to begin ovulating most any time. Like right now.

Anatomy is destiny, agreed Henry, but what about your musical career? Lightning crackled nearby—the smell of ozone blended with his wife's Shalimar by Guerlain Inc., New York. His choice, not hers.

Fuck my musical career, she said, leaning toward him in the firelight. Her eyes shone like a tiger's eyes. No, blue-gray but fiery, like the eyes of an ocelot. Fuck me.

Goodness gracious. Such language from my child bride. Honeydew Mellon, I'm shocked, really.

Thunder rumbled through the woods.

Shut up and kiss me you fool. She sprawled upon him, flattening him to the stone. Her tongue probed his mouth, her knees clutched him by the rib cage. Defenseless, overwhelmed, he lay on his back with his pants down, his prick up and one hand hanging idly, helpless, over the edge of a fifty-foot drop-off straight down to a nest of timber rattlers sleeping in a bed of stiletto-bladed yuccas. Raindrops splashed on his face, dribbled through his hair, soaked the shirt on Claire's slender back and ran in rivulets down the sweet cleft perfection of her bottom, trickling from there onto his balls. The rain increased but failed to quench or even dampen the fire of their reciprocating lust. They came when they came—her phrase—like overlapping fumaroles spouting molten magma in the night. His image. Coiled together they lay in the falling rain, drenched, besotted, gasping for air, searching for their scattered wits.

We done it that time, he said.

We did it. I could feel it. Now we're really in the animal soup.

Henry pulled up his jeans as he struggled from beneath her relaxed weight. It's raining, he mentioned, tugging her to her feet. Hand in hand they ran for the lookout cabin. Ribbons of pink lightning skittered across the black sky—an insane scribbling, a blind demented fury. They laughed and slammed the door, stripped off their soaked clothes and tumbled into bed and slept for ten hours. Blue light flashed and vanished beyond the windowpanes. Thunder echoed thunderblast as the rain came down in advancing then retreating waves.

Henry dreamed of woodsmoke. He awoke at sunrise to see two pine snags flaring like torches a mile below. Naked as a jaybird he switched on the forest radio to report the fires while Claire, wearing nothing but her pink ruffled apron, made coffee, folded an omelet of eggs, peppers and tomatoes in the skillet and quartered two fat oranges into eight golden sections. Facing each other across the tiny foldout table they drank the coffee, ate the omelet, sucked on the oranges and strove but failed to contain their idiotic smiles. Henry stuck a section of orange over his gums and offered her his patent golden grin.

Henry, Henry. . . .

He removed the orange. I know, he said.

I can't bear it. I'm so happy I want to weep.

I know, he said. Me too—happy as a dead pig in the sunshine, like Grandma always said.

I think I'm going to cry.

Me too.

They wept for a while together then wandered off through a mist of fog and the tang of smoke to hunt for mushrooms.

IN AUGUST she announced that she was pregnant. I'm preggers, she said, the rabbit never lies.

That night on the rimrock? When it rained? That was the night. I hope it's twins, he said. Might as well have an instant family, get this thing going whole hog. How nicely you put it. He embraced and kissed her, letting his hands slip down to her haunches. How nice it is to put. You're so vulgar. Henry H. Lightcap here. Man of the people. Voice of the common man. *L'homme sensual,* as the Frogs say. That's not quite the way the French pronounce it. What can you expect from a Frog?

Mildly panicked, he worried about money. She reminded him that she would receive an income of her own in only a few more years. That was some comfort but small consolation to Henry: assuaged his fear but provoked his pride.

Your money is your money, he said. I'll support my family myself. Somehow. (Furthermore, he thought, there's something tainted about trust fund money.)

I see, she said. What's yours is mine but what's mine is mine?

That's right. (Would have to talk to her about that. That matter of unearned income. Someday.)

That's not right, that's a double standard. Well goddamnit you're a woman I'm a man. There's your double standard, built into biology. I've got a million years of mammalian tradition behind me. Some of us don't accept that kind of thinking anymore. I've read about it. I've read Beauvoir and Friedan too and that long-nosed goon-eyed harpy Virginia Woolf. Those lilies of the valley. A room of their own? They should each have a cell in a nunnery. On Lesbos Island.

You can be so cruel. There's a mean streak in you, Henry. That's one of the things I don't like about you. Only one? What else? Oh—the way you blow your nose on the ground then wipe your hand on a tree. Can't you use a handkerchief? Did you ever hear of Kleenex? What else? Come on, let's hear it. Peeing in the bathroom washbasin. You'd rather see me piss in the kitchen sink? Why can't you use the toilet like everybody else? Because the damn things are built for Puerto Ricans, that's why. If I piss in the toilet bowl I splash piss all over the wall. Try sitting down. I'm a man. An American. Only Hindus squat to piss, for christsake. Hindus and women. Anyhow I usually piss off the back porch, you know that. It's unnatural to piss indoors. Unsanitary.

I give up. Suppose the baby is born deformed or something? What are you talking about? You heard me; what should we do? Suppose it's a Mongoloid idiot? You mean Down's Syndrome? I mean Mongoloid idiot; what should we do?

She stared at him. Tears welled up in her eyes. Henry, please, don't even think such a thing.

Well. . . . Ashamed of himself, he tried to hug her to him. She turned away. Just thought . . . he said. But he wasn't thinking very well.

Visitors appeared from time to time. Claire's friends from the music department at the University—a violist, a cello player, another violinist. With Claire and her fiddle they played a Haydn quartet and a Mozart quartet among the noble columns of a grove of Ponderosa pines. Henry on duty in the fire lookout heard the music ascending past his tower and thought of Vienna, the Hapsburgs, elegant salons lit by a thousand candles, ladies in powdered wigs and hoopskirts, gentlemen in pigtails and satin knee britches, the silent stream of servants flowing from kitchen to salon and back, the greasy slaveys in the scullery, the ragged prisoners in the dungeons, chains on the wall, torches burning in the darkness of an inquisitorial chamber, the sweating ogre in the black leather hood . . .

Mozart. Papa Haydn. Them good old rococo times. Or as it should be spelled, he thought, R°o°C°o°C°oo.

Without torturers like Igor, explained Le Duc de Camembert (a soft dense mellow fellow) to Le Duc d'Angoisse-Frisson, there could be no gentlemen like us. *Ipsissima verba.* The very words.

But Henry had a sick imagination, obsessed with history. Aloft in his tower too long he'd been reading too much Gibbon, Mommsen, Acton, Toynbee, Becker, Wells, Braudel, Prescott, Beard, Wittfogel. . . . Torture, massacre, slavery, peonage and serfdom, rank and caste and hierarchy, the nightmare unfolding for five six seven thousand years or ever since the first Pharaoh hissed, uncoiled and rose like a hooded cobra from the slime of the Nile and our hydraulic tyranny began its self-perpetuating growth.

Sometimes he heard voices:

It is not enough to understand the world of man. The point is to change it. He looked around. Who said that?

Dr. Harrington arrived one day, accompanied by Lacey and Arriaga and their wives. There was a picnic on the rim at evening and a liberal flow of wine, beer, Pepsi-Cola. From white-haired Keaton Lacey, a gentleman bowman and gunner, Henry learned that one of their favorite Arizona game ranges would soon be closed to hunting.

How come?

Lacey explained: An outfit called Lovers of Fur Bearers has received a big bequest from some millionaire animal sentimentalist in California. They bought out the cow ranch at the mouth of Turkey Creek Canyon. That means they control access to about ten-by-ten miles of state land and federal land. Sixty-four thousand acres. They're gonna make it what they call a wildlife preserve. Closed to hunting.

That'll make a lot of people very unhappy.

It makes me unhappy.

Those critter freaks are going to need a gamekeeper.

They sure are. About a dozen gamekeepers. Well-armed gamekeepers. Drunk and ignorant suicidal gamekeepers.

Sounds like work for you, Lacey. You and Hooligan.

We're not that drunk and ignorant.

Henry drove into town on his next day off and applied for the position himself. He would soon be a family man, needing steady employment. He was interviewed by Mr. Joseph S. Harlow, III, stockbroker by trade, who occupied an office suite on the top floor of the Pioneer Building in downtown Tucson, only two blocks in fact from the green spittoons, rancid air, creaky floorboards and eroded slate pool tables of the Dirty Shame Saloon. But what an abysm yawned between.

Mr. Harlow, gray-haired and square-headed, peered at Henry over spectacles lowered to the tip of his nose. Feet on desk, he clipped the tip from a Macanudo, passed a lighter to Henry, brushed copies of *Forbes* magazine, the *Wall Street Journal*, *Audubon* magazine and the *Sierra Club Bulletin* to the side. Henry lit his cigar—a huge fat gentleman's smoke of a quality to which he was not, actually, fully accustomed.

Any background in law enforcement, Mr. Lightcap?

Henry mentioned his year and a half with the Military Police in Italy, his six months with the Border Patrol in Big Bend, Texas, his seven or eight intermittent years as a park ranger in Utah, Arizona, Montana, Florida.

Six months with the Border Patrol?

Yessir.

Why only six months?

I didn't really like the work.

You're a liberal, I suppose?

No sir, I'm a bigot. It was shooting those damn Mex cows with the hoof-and-mouth disease that got me down. Can't stand the noise a hollow-point bullet makes when it hits a living body.

A brief pause.

Married? Yessir; twice. Divorced? Yep; once. Children? None on the streets; one in the oven.

Pause. Lightcap and Harlow puffed on their great rich turdlike cigars, blowing ragged clouds of smoke at the ceiling. Portofino fog.

Are you a Harvard man, Mr. Lightcap?

Me?

You're wearing a Harvard tie.

I am? Henry looked down and lifted the crimson pennon, like the parboiled tongue of a cow, that dangled from his collar. He gazed at the thing in wonder. A gift from my mother-in-law, he explained. The Snag. No sir, as a matter of fact I went to school in New Mexico.

Familiar with horses?

Yes. But not too familiar.

Good. We understand each other. Most of the Turkey Creek preserve can be patrolled by jeep but some will require a horse. Extremely rugged terrain. You'd have eight or nine horses in your care, about forty miles of fencing to keep up, three windmills, two alfalfa fields and a small citrus orchard to look after. From time to time you'd be expected to give the grand dames of our organization a tour of the premises—and they'd be very disappointed, I might add, if our caretaker failed to produce a few live deer, javelina, coatimundi, a bobcat or two. Keep that in mind. But of course the difficult part of the job involves public relations with the local citizenry. Have you ever confronted a group of drunken pig hunters, Mr. Lightcap, on the opening day of javelina season?

No sir.

Demanding access over private property to public lands?

No.

How do you think you would handle such a situation?

Henry paused for thought. Thought seemed appropriate here. Inwardly he decided, I'd have Lacey with his steel crossbow and Hooligan with a light machine gun enfilading from the shrubbery. Aloud he said, I'd treat them with tact and delicacy, sir, but politely forbid access.

Suppose they offered violence?

I would honor the offer.

A pause. Harlow considered that remark, savoring its facetious ambiguity, then said, This could be dangerous work, Mr. Lightcap, at least for the first few years or until our legal rights are respected.

Yessir. Well, it sounds like interesting work to me. I'm ready to try something different.

You sure?

You only live once.

True; a comforting thought. A pause. Now as to emolument, Mr. Lightcap, we could offer something in the neighborhood of, say, twelve thousand per annum?

Henry looked thoughtfully at his cigar.

Plus expenses, of course: fuel for vehicles and horses, fencing and equipment repair. Living quarters provided, including utility bills. Not a bad deal. The organization has a group medical-insurance plan and a pension plan. I'm sure our wildlife caretaker would be included in both.

What kind of pension? A widow's pension?

Disability, retirement or death. Whichever comes first.

I'd need a little extra help during hunting season.

Certainly. That would come under annual operating expenses.

Henry paused for reflection while Harlow continued his study of Henry's physiognomy. I'll take the job, Henry said.

Mr. Harlow lowered his feet from the desk and rose gracefully from his chair. He extended his right hand. Good-bye, Mr. Lightcap. We're not taking employment applications yet actually, not formally I mean, but if you will leave your name and address with my secretary out front . . .

Yessir. They shook. Henry departed, satisfied. He felt he had made his point.

He was correct. In early September came the letter on official Lovers of Fur Bearers stationery offering Henry H. Lightcap, Esq., the position of "wildlife warden" at the newly established Emily Ives Bancroft Sanctuary for Fur-Bearing Quadrupeds. Prompt reply requested. Signed, Caroline Currier Mills, Executive Director, Washington, D.C. Among the trustees listed on the letterhead was Joseph S. Harlow, III, Tucson, Arizona.

What about fur-bearing bipeds? asked Claire. Such as Mother.

Good point. As a matter of fact the javelina is not a fur-bearing beast. Hairy yes, piglike yes, but not furry.

Like yourself?

Yeah—like me.

The Wooden Shoe
Conspiracy

THERE WAS this bum on the beach.
Fiercely bearded, short, squat, malevolent, his motor vehicle loaded with dangerous weapons: this bum. Did nothing; said nothing; stared.

They ignored him.

Smith's assistant boatman did not appear. Never did appear. Smith rigged his boat alone, chewing on jerky. He sent his girl friend to Page with the truck to pick up the passengers arriving that morning by air.

The bum watched. (As soon as the work was completed he would probably ask for a job.)

Flight 96 was late, as usual. Finally it emerged from a cloudbank, growled overhead, banked and turned and landed into the wind on the strictly limited Page runway—limited at one end by a high-tension power line and at the other end by a three-hundred-foot cliff. The aircraft itself was a bimotored jet-prop job with an antiquarian look; it might have been built in 1929 (the year of the crash) and seemed to have been repainted several times since, in the manner of a used car touched up for sale on the corner lot. (Square Deal Andy's. Top Dollar Johnny's.) Somebody had painted it recently with one thick coat of yellow, which failed, however, to quite conceal the underlying

From *The Monkey Wrench Gang* (1975)

coat of green. Little round glass ports lined the sides of the craft, through which the white faces of passengers could be seen, peering out, crossing themselves, their lips moving.

The plane turned from the runway and lumbered onto the apron of the strip. The engines smoked and grumbled and backfired but provided enough power to bring the plane almost to the loading zone. There the engines died and the plane stopped. The airport ticket agent, flight traffic controller, manager and baggage handler removed his ear protectors and climbed down from the open-air control tower, buttoning his fly.

Black fumes hovered about the plane's starboard engine. From the interior came little ticking noises; a hatch was opened and lowered by hand crank, transforming itself into a gangway. The stewardess appeared in the opening.

Flight 96 discharged two passengers.

First to alight was a woman. She was young, handsome, with an arrogant air; her dark shining hair hung below her waist. She wore this and that, not much, including a short skirt which revealed tanned and excellent legs.

The cowboys, Indians, Mormon missionaries, Government officials and other undesirables lounging about the terminal stared with hungry eyes. The city of Page, Arizona, pop. 1,400, includes 800 men and sometimes three or four good-looking women.

Behind the young woman came the man, of middle age, though his piebald beard and steel-rimmed spectacles may have made him look older than he really was. His nose, irregular, very large, cheerily refulgent, shone like a polished tomato under the bright white light of the desert sun. A stogie in his teeth. Well dressed, he looked like a professor. Blinking, he put on a straw hat, which helped, and came tramping up to the terminal door beside the woman. He towered over the girl at his side. Nevertheless everybody present, including the women, stared at the girl.

No doubt about it. Under a wide-brimmed straw hat, wearing huge black opaque sunglasses, she looked like Garbo. The old Garbo. Young Garbo.

Smith's girl friend greeted them. The big man took her hand, which vanished within the clasp of his enormous paw. But his grasp was precise, gentle and firm. The surgeon.

"Right," he said. "I'm Dr. Sarvis. This is Bonnie." His voice seemed strangely soft, low, melancholy, issuing from so grand (or gross) an organism.

"Miss Abbzug?"

"Miz Abbzug."

"Call her Bonnie."

Into the truck, duffel bags and sleeping bags in back. They whipped out

of Page past the thirteen churches of Jesus Row, through the official government slums and the construction workers' trailer-house slums and out of town
into the traditional pastoral slums of Navajoland. Sick horses loitered along
the highway looking for something to eat: newspapers, Kleenex, beer cans,
anything more or less degradable. The doctor talked with Seldom's driver;
Ms. Abbzug remained aloof and mostly silent.

"What utterly ghastly country," she said once. "Who lives here?"

"The Indians," Doc said.

"It's too good for them."

Down through Dynamite Notch to Bitter Springs to Marble Canyon and
under the paranoid gargoyled battlements of the Jurassic Age to Lee's Ferry,
into the hot-muck green-willow smell of the river. The hot sun roared down
through a sky blue as the Virgin's cloak, emphasizing with its extravagant light
the harsh perfection of the cliffs, the triumphant river, the preparations for a
great voyage.

A second round of introductions.

"Dr. Sarvis, Miz Abbzug, Seldom Seen Smith. . . ."

"Pleased to meet you, sir; you too, ma'am. This here's George Hayduke.
Behind the bush. He's gonna be number-two nigger this trip. Say something,
George."

The bum behind the beard growled something unintelligible. He
crunched an empty beer can in his hand, lobbed the wreckage toward a
nearby garbage can, missed. Hayduke was now wearing ragged shorts and a
leather hat. His eyes were red. He smelled of sweat, salt, mud, stale beer. Dr.
Sarvis, erect and dignified, his beard smartly trimmed, regarded Hayduke
with reservations. It was people like Hayduke who gave beards a bad name.

Smith, looking at them all with his happy grin, seemed pleased with his
crew and passengers. Especially with Miz Abbzug, at whom he tried hard not
to stare. But she was something, she was something. Smith felt, down below,
belowdecks, that faint but unmistakable itching and twitching of scrotal hair
which is the sure praeludium to love. Venereal as a valentine, it could have no
other meaning.

About that time the remainder of the passenger list arrived by car: two
secretaries from San Diego, old friends of Smith, repeaters, who had been
with him on many river trips before. The party was complete. After a lunch of
tinned snacks, cheese, crackers, beer and soda pop, they got under way. Still
no regular assistant boatman; Hayduke had himself a job.

Sullen and silent, he coiled the bow line in nautical trim, gave the boat a
shove from shore and rolled on board. The boat floated into the current of the

river. Three ten-man rubber rafts lashed snug together side by side, a triple rig, it made a ponderous and awkward-looking craft but just right for rocks and rapids. The passengers sat in the middle; Hayduke and Smith, as oarsmen, stood or sat on each side. Smith's truck driver waved good-bye from shore, looking wistful. They would not see her again for fourteen days.

The wooden oars creaked in the oarlocks; the vessel advanced with the current, which would carry it along at an average of four to five miles an hour through most of the canyon, much faster in the rapids. Not as in a rowboat but facing forward, like gondoliers, pushing (not pulling) on the oars, Hayduke and Smith confronted the gleaming river, the sound of fast water around the first bend. Smith stuck a stick of jerky in his teeth.

Back-lit by the afternoon sun, the rolling waters shone like hammered metal, like bronze lamé, each facet reflecting mirror-fashion the blaze in the sky. While glowing dumbly in the east, above the red canyon walls, the new moon hung in the wine-dark firmament like a pale antiphonal response to the glory of the sun. New moon in the afternoon, fanatic sun ahead. A bird whistled in the willows.

Down the river!

Hayduke knew nothing about river-running. Smith knew he knew nothing. It didn't matter too much, so long as the passengers didn't find out right away. What did matter to Smith was Hayduke's broad and powerful back, his gorilla arms, the short strong legs. The kid would learn all he had to learn quick enough.

They approached the riffles of the Paria, under the bluff where the park rangers lived. Tourists watched them from the new metallic campground on the hill. Smith stood up to get a better view of the rocks and rough water immediately ahead. Nothing much, a minor rapid, Grade 1 on the boatman's scale. The green river curled around a few fangs of limestone, the sleek smooth waters purling foam. A toneless roar, what acousticians call "white noise," vibrated on the air.

As prearranged, Hayduke and Smith turned the boat ninety degrees and bore sideways (this foolish craft was wider than long) onto the glassy tongue of the little rapid. They slipped through with barely a splash. Through the tail of the turmoil they rode into the confluence, where the Paria (in flood) mixed its gray greasy bentonite waters with the clear green of the dammed Colorado. From twelve mph their speed slowed to four or five again.

Hayduke relaxed, grinning. Wiped the water from his beard and eyebrows. Why, hell's fuck, he thought, that's nothing. Why shit I'm just a natural riverman.

They passed beneath Marble Canyon Bridge. From above looking down the height had not seemed so great; there was no standard for scale. But from the river looking up they realized the meaning of a vertical four hundred feet: about thirty-five skyscraper stories from here to there. The automobile creeping across the bridge looked like a toy; the tourists standing about on the observation point were insect size.

The bridge moved away behind them, vanished beyond the turning of the canyon walls. They were now well into Marble Gorge, also known as Marble Canyon, sixty miles of river three thousand feet below the level of the land, leading into the Grand Canyon at the mouth of the Little Colorado River.

Seldom Seen Smith as usual was fondling memories. He remembered the real Colorado, before damnation, when the river flowed unchained and unchanneled in the joyous floods of May and June, swollen with snow melt. Boulders crunching and clacking and grumbling, tumbling along on the river's bedrock bed, the noise like that of grinding molars in a giant jaw. That was a river.

Still, even so, not all was lost. The beaded light of afternoon slanted down beyond the canyon walls, whiskey-gold on rock and tree, a silent benison from the flawless sky, free from your friendly solar system. Cut off, then reappearing, the pale elided wafer of the new moon followed after. A good spirit, a faery queen, watching over them.

Again the white roar. Another rapids coming. Smith gave the order to fasten life jackets. They turned another corner. The noise swelled alarmingly, and down the canyon where all now stared they saw rocks like teeth rising through a white rim of foam. The river apparently went underground at that point; from boat level nothing of it could be seen beyond the rapids.

"Badger Crick Rapids," Smith announced. Again he stood up. Grade 3, nothing serious. All the same he wanted a good look before diving in. He stood and read the river as others might read the symbols on a score, the blips on a radarscope, or signs of coming weather in cloud formations far away. He looked for the fat swell that meant hidden fang of stone, the choppy stretch of wavelets signifying rocks and shallow water, the shadow on the river that told of a gravel bar six inches under the surface, the hook and snag of submerged logs that could gash the bottom of his rubber boats. He followed with his eye the flecks of foam gliding steadily down the mainstream, the almost invisible ripples and eddies on the river's flanks.

Smith read the river, the ladies reading him. He was not aware of how comic and heroic he looked, the Colorado man, long and lean and brown as the river used to be, leaning forward on his oar, squinting into the sun, the strong and uncorrupted teeth shining in the customary grin, the macho bulge at the fly of his ancient Levi's, the big ears out and alert. Rapids closing in.

"Everybody down," Smith orders. "Grab rope."

In a frantic clamor of tumbled water, the mass of the river crashes upon the rubble of rock fanning out from the mouth of a side canyon—Badger. The deep and toneless vibration all around, a mist of spray floating on the air, little rainbows suspended in the sunlight.

Again they swing the craft about. Smith heaves mightily on his oar, taking the bow, and steers the boat straight onto the tongue of the rapids, the oil-smooth surge of the main current pouring like a torrent into the heart of the uproar. No need to cheat on this, a minor rapid; he'll give his customers a thrill, their money's worth, what they paid for.

A wave eight feet high looms above Smith, crouched in the bow. The wave stands there, waiting, does not move. (On the river, unlike the sea, the water moves; the waves remain in place.) The front end of the boat climbs the wave, pushed up by momentum and the weight behind. Smith hangs on to the lines. The tripartite boat almost folds back upon itself, then bends over the wave and slides down into the trough beyond, the middle and third parts following in like fashion. A wet and shining boulder stands dead ahead, directly in their course. The boat pauses before it. A ton of water, recoiling from the rock, crashes into the boat. Everyone is instantly soaked. The women scream with delight; even Doc Sarvis laughs. Smith hauls on his oar; the boat rolls off the boulder and careens like a roller coaster over the waves in the tail of the rapids, then slows in the steadier water below. Smith looks back. He has lost an oarsman. Where George Hayduke should have been the unmanned oar swings loosely in its lock.

There he comes. Hayduke in his orange life jacket bobs down the billows, grinning with ferocious determination, knees up under his chin, the fetal pose, using his feet and legs as shock absorbers, caroming off the rock. Instinctive and correct response. Has lost his hat. Makes no sound. . . .

In the calmer water below the rapid they dragged him back aboard.

"Where you been?" Smith said.

Grinning, sputtering, Hayduke shook his head, popped the water from his ears and managed to look both fierce and sheepish. "Fucking river," he muttered.

"You got to grab a line," Smith said.

"I was holding onto the fucking oar. Jammed it on a rock and it hit me in the stomach." Nervously he pawed his tangled mass of soaked hair. His hat, an old leather sombrero from Sonora, was floating on the waves, about to go down for the third time. They retrieved it with an oar.

The river bore them calmly on, through the plateau, into the Precambrian mantle of the earth, toward the lowlands, the delta and the Sea of Cortez, seven hundred miles away.

"Soap Crick Rapids next," Smith said. And sure enough, they heard again the tumult of river and stone in conflict. Around the next bend.

"This is ridiculous," Abbzug said privately to Doc. They sat hunched hard together with a wet poncho spread over their laps and legs. She was beaming with pleasure. Water dripped from the brim of her exaggerated hat. The doctor's stogie burned bravely in the damp.

"Absolutely ridiculous," he said. "How do you like our boatmen?"

"Weird; the tall one looks like Ichabod Ignatz; the short one looks like a bandit out of some old Mack Sennett movie."

"Or Charon and Cerberus," Doc said. "But try not to laugh; our lives rest in their uncertain hands." And they laughed again.

All together now they plunged into another maelstrom, Grade 4 on the river runner's chart. More gnashing river, heaving waves, the clash of elementals, the pure and brainless fury of tons of irresistible water crashing down upon tons of immovable limestone. They felt the shock, they heard the roar, saw foam and spray and rainbows floating on the mist as they rode through chaos into the clear. The adrenaline of adventure, without the time for dread, buoyed them high on the waves.

This was the forty-fifth trip down the Grand for Smith, and so far as he could measure, its pleasure was not staled by repetition. But then no two river trips were ever quite alike. The river, the canyon, the desert world was always changing, from moment to moment, from miracle to miracle, within the firm reality of mother earth. River, rock, sun, blood, hunger, wings, joy—this is the real, Smith would have said, if he'd wanted to. If he felt like it. All the rest is androgynous theosophy. All the rest is transcendental transvestite transactional scientology or whatever the fad of the day, the vogue of the week. As Doc would've said, if Smith had asked him. Ask the hawk. Ask the hungry lion lunging at the starving doe. They know.

Thus reasoneth Smith. Only a small businessman, to be sure. Never even went to college.

In the grand stillness between rapids, which was half the river and most of the time, Smith and Hayduke rested on their oars and let the song of a canyon wren—a clear glissando of semiquavers—mingle with the drip of waterdrops, the gurgle of eddies, the honk of herons, the rustle of lizards in the dust on shore. Between rapids, not silence but music and stillness. While the canyon walls rose slowly higher, 1,000, 1,500, 2,000 feet, the river descending, and the shadows grew longer and the sun shy.

A chill from the depths crept over them.

"Time to make camp, folks," Smith announced, sculling for shore. Hayduke pitched in. Close ahead, on the right bank, lay a slope of sand, fringed by thickets of coppery willow and stands of tamarisk with lavender plumes nodding in the breeze. Again they heard the call of a canyon wren, a little bird with a big mouth. But musical, musical. And the far-off roar of still another rapids, that sound like the continuous applause of an immense and tireless multitude. The grunt and breath of two men laboring, oars scraping. The quiet talk of the first-class passengers.

"Dig the scene, Doc."

"No technical jargon, please. This is a holy place."

"Yeah but where's the Coke machine?"

"Please, I'm meditating."

The bow grated on gravel. Hayduke, general swamper, coiled line in hand, splashed through ankle-deep water and tethered the boat to a stout clump of willows. All came ashore. Hayduke and Seldom passed each passenger his/her river bag, the rubberized dunnage, the little ammo boxes containing personal items. The passengers wandered off, Doc and Bonnie in one direction, the two women from San Diego in another.

Smith paused for a moment to watch the retreating figure of Ms. Abbzug.

"Now, ain't she something?" he said. "Ain't she *really* something?" He closed one eye, as if sighting down a rifle barrel. "Now that little girl is a real honey. Finger-lickin' good."

"Cunt is cunt," said George Hayduke, philosopher, not bothering to look. "Do we unload all this stuff now?"

"Most of it. Lemme show you."

They wrestled with the heavy baggage, the big ammo boxes full of food, the ice chest, the wooden box holding Seldom's cooking pots, frypans, Dutch oven, grills, other hardware, and lugged it all onto the beach. Smith outlined an area on the sand as his kitchen where he set up the cookstove, his folding table, his pantry, the bar, the black olives and fried baby clams. He chipped off little chunks of ice for all the begging cups that would soon appear and poured a spot of rum for Hayduke and himself. The passengers were still back in the bushes, changing into dry clothing, fortifying themselves in private for the cool of the evening.

"Here's to you, boatman," Smith said.

"*Hoa binh,*" said Hayduke.

Smith built a fire of charcoal, peeled the butcher paper from the standard first-night entree—huge floppy steaks—and stacked them near the grill. Hayduke prepared the salad and, as he did so, chased the rum with his tenth can of beer since lunch.

"That stuff'll give you kidney stones," Smith said.

"Bullshit."

"Kidney stones. I oughta know."

"I been drinking beer all my life."

"How old are you?"

"Twenty-five."

"Kidney stones," Smith said. "In about ten more years."

"Bullshit."

The passengers, dry and refurbished, came straggling in one at a time, the doctor first. He placed his tin cup on the bar, installed one miniature iceberg and poured himself a double shot from his bottle of Wild Turkey.

"It is a beauteous evening, calm and free," he announced.

"That's true," Smith said.

"The holy time is quiet as a nun."

"You said a mouthful, Doctor."

"Call me Doc."

"Okay, Doc."

"Cheers."

"Same to you, Doc."

There was some further discussion of the ambience. Then of other matters. The girl came up, Abbzug, wearing long pants and a shaggy sweater. She had shed the big hat but even in twilight still wore the sunglasses. She gave a touch of tone to Marble Gorge.

Meanwhile the doctor was saying, "The reason there are so many people on the river these days is because there are too many people everywhere else."

Bonnie shivered, slipping into the crook of his left arm. "Why don't we build a fire?" she said.

"The wilderness once offered men a plausible way of life," the doctor said. "Now it functions as a psychiatric refuge. Soon there will be no wilderness." He sipped at his bourbon and ice. "Soon there will be no place to go. Then the madness becomes universal." Another thought. "And the universe goes mad."

"We will," Smith said to Abbzug. "After supper."

"Call me Bonnie."

"Miss Bonnie."

"Miz Bonnie," she corrected him.

"Jesus fucking Christ," muttered Hayduke nearby, overhearing, and he snapped the cap from another can of Coors.

Abbzug cast a cold eye on Hayduke's face, or what could be seen of it behind the black bangs and the bushy beard. An oaf, she thought. All hairiness is bestial, Arthur Schopenhauer thought. Hayduke caught her look, scowled. She turned back to the others.

"We are caught," continued the good doctor, "in the iron treads of a technological juggernaut. A mindless machine. With a breeder reactor for a heart."

"You said a mouthful, Doc," says Seldom Seen Smith. He started on the steaks, laying them tenderly on the grill, above the glowing coals.

"A planetary industrialism"—the doctor ranted on—"growing like a cancer. Growth for the sake of growth. Power for the sake of power. I think I'll have another bit of ice here." (*Clank!*) "Have a touch of this, Captain Smith, it'll gladden your heart, gild your liver and flower like a rose down in the compost of your bowels."

"Don't mind if I do, Doc." But Smith wanted to know how a *machine* could "grow." Doc explained; it wasn't easy.

Smith's two repeaters from San Diego emerged from the bushes, smiling; they had unrolled his sleeping bag between their own. One young woman carried a bottle. Something about a river trip always seems to promote the consumption of potable drugs. Except for Abbzug, who sucked from time to time on a little hand-rolled Zig-Zag cigarette pinched between her fastidious fingers. There was the smell of some kind of burning hemp in the air around her head. (Give a girl enough rope and she'll smoke it.) The odor reminded Hayduke of dark days and darker nights. Muttering, he set the table, buffet-style, with the salad, the sourdough bread, corn on the cob, a stack of paper plates. Smith turned the steaks. Doc explained the world.

Hog-nosed bats flickered through the evening making radar noises, gulping bugs. Downriver the rapids waited, gnashing their teeth in a steady sullen uproar. High on the canyon rim a rock slipped or was dislodged by something, gave up its purchase anyway, and tumbled down from parapet to parapet, lost in the embrace of gravity, into the alchemy of change, one fragment in the universal flux, and crashed like a bomb into the river. Doc paused in mid-monologue; all listened for a moment to the dying reverberations.

"Grab a plate," said Smith to his customers, "and load up." There was no hesitation; he served the steaks. Last in line and disdaining a plate, Hayduke held out his G.I. canteen cup. Smith draped a giant steak over the cup, covering not only the cup but Hayduke's hand, wrist and forearm.

"Eat," said Smith.

"Sweet holy motherfuck," said his boatman, reverently.

Smith kindled a campfire, now that his passengers and help were feeding, with driftwood from the beach. Then he heaped a plate for himself.

All eyes turned toward the fire as the darkness of the canyon gathered around them. Little blue and green flames licked and lapped at the river wood—sculptured chunks of yellow pine from the high country a hundred miles away, juniper, pinyon pine, cottonwood, well-polished sticks of redbud, hackberry and ash. Following the sparks upward they saw the stars turning on in staggered sequence—emeralds, sapphires, rubies, diamonds and opals scattered about the sky in a puzzling, random distribution. Far beyond those galloping galaxies, or perhaps all too present to be seen, lurked God. The gaseous vertebrate.

Supper finished, Smith brought out his musical instruments and played for the assembled company. He played his harmonica—what the vulgar call a "mouth organ"—his Jew's harp, or what the B'nai B'rith calls a "mouth harp," and his kazoo, which last, however, added little to anyone's musical enrichment.

Smith and the doctor passed around the firewater. Abbzug, who did not as a rule drink booze, opened her medicine pouch, removed a Tampax tube, took out some weed and rolled a second little brown cigarette twisted shut at one end. She lit up and passed it around, but no one cared to smoke with her except a reluctant Hayduke and his memories.

"The pot revolution is over?" she said.

"All over," Doc said. "Marijuana was never more than an active placebo anyway."

"What nonsense."

"An oral pacifier for colicky adolescents."

"What utter rubbish."

The conversation lagged. The two young women from San Diego (a suburb of Tijuana) sang a song called "Dead Skunk in the Middle of the Road."

The entertainment palled. Fatigue like gravitation pulled at limbs and eyelids. As they had come so they departed, first Abbzug, then the two women from San Diego. The ladies first. Not because they were the weaker sex— they were not—but simply because they had more sense. Men on an outing feel obliged to stay up drinking to the vile and bilious end, jabbering, mumbling and maundering through the blear, to end up finally on hands and knees, puking on innocent sand, befouling God's sweet earth. The manly tradition.

The three men hunched closer to the shrinking fire. The cold night crawled up their backs. They passed Smith's bottle round and around. Then Doc's bottle. Smith, Hayduke, Sarvis. The captain, the bum and the leech. Three wizards on a dead limb. A crafty intimacy crept upon them.

"You know, gentlemen," the doctor said. "You know what I think we ought to do. . . ."

Hayduke had been complaining about the new power lines he'd seen the day before on the desert. Smith had been moaning about the dam again, that dam which had plugged up Glen Canyon, the heart of his river, the river of his heart.

"You know what we ought to do," the doctor said. "We ought to blow that dam to shitaree." (A bit of Hayduke's foul tongue had loosened his own.)

"How?" said Hayduke.

"That ain't legal," Smith said.

"You prayed for an earthquake, you said."

"Yeah, but there ain't no law agin that."

"You were praying with malicious intent."

"That's true. I pray that way all the time."

"Bent on mischief and the destruction of government property."

"That's right, Doc."

"That's a felony."

"It ain't just a misdemeanor?"

"It's a felony."

"How?" said Hayduke.

"How what?"

"How do we blow up the dam?"

"Which dam?"

"Any dam."

"Now you're talking," Smith said. "But Glen Canyon Dam first. I claim that one first."

"I don't know," the doctor said. "You're the demolitions expert."

"I can take out a bridge for you," Hayduke said, "if you get me enough dynamite. But I don't know about Glen Canyon Dam. We'd need an atom bomb for that one."

"I been thinking about that dam for a long time," Smith said. "And I got a plan. We get three jumbo-size houseboats and some dolphins—"

"Hold it!" Doc said, holding up a big paw. A moment of silence. He looked around, into the darkness beyond the firelight. "Who knows what ears those shadows have."

They looked. The flames of their little campfire cast a hesitant illumination upon the bush, the boat half grounded on the sandy beach, the rocks and pebbles, the pulse of the river. The women, all asleep, could not be seen.

"There ain't nobody here but us bombers," Smith said.

"Who can be sure? The State may have its sensors anywhere."

"Naw," Hayduke said. "They're not bugging the canyons. Not yet anyhow. But who says we have to start with dams? There's plenty of other work to do."

"Good work," the doctor said. "Good, wholesome, constructive work."

"I hate that dam," Smith said. "That dam flooded the most beautiful canyon in the world."

"We know," Hayduke said. "We feel the same way you do. But let's think about easier things first. I'd like to knock down some of them power lines they're stringing across the desert. And those new tin bridges up by Hite. And the goddamned road-building they're doing all over the canyon country. We could put in a good year just taking the fucking goddamned bulldozers apart."

"Hear, hear," the doctor said. "And don't forget the billboards. And the strip mines. And the pipelines. And the new railroad from Black Mesa to Page. And the coal-burning power plants. And the copper smelters. And the uranium mines. And the nuclear power plants. And the computer centers. And the land and cattle companies. And the wildlife poisoners. And the people who throw beer cans along the highways."

"I throw beer cans along the fucking highways," Hayduke said. "Why the fuck shouldn't I throw fucking beer cans along the fucking highways?"

"Now, now. Don't be so defensive."

"Hell," Smith said, "I do it too. Any road I wasn't consulted about that I don't like, I litter. It's my religion."

"Right," Hayduke said. "Litter the shit out of them."

"Well now," the doctor said. "I hadn't thought about that. Stockpile the stuff along the highways. Throw it out the window. Well . . . why not?"

"Doc," said Hayduke, "it's liberation."

The night. The stars. The river. Dr. Sarvis told his comrades about a great Englishman named Ned. Ned Ludd. They called him a lunatic but he saw the enemy clearly. Saw what was coming and acted directly. And about the wooden shoes, *les sabots*. The spanner in the works. Monkey business. The rebellion of the meek. Little old ladies in oaken clogs.

"Do we know what we're doing and why?"

"No."

"Do we care?"

"We'll work it all out as we go along. Let our practice form our doctrine, thus assuring precise theoretical coherence."

The river in its measureless sublimity rolled softly by, whispering of time. Which heals, they say, all. But does it? The stars looked kindly down. A lie. A wind in the willows suggested sleep. And nightmares. Smith pushed more drift pine into the fire, and a scorpion, dormant in a crack deep in the wood, was horribly awakened, too late. No one noticed the mute agony. Deep in the solemn canyon, under the fiery stars, peace reigned generally.

"We need a guide," the doctor said.

"I know the country," Smith said.

"We need a professional killer."

"That's me," Hayduke said. "Murder's my specialty."

"Every man has his weakness." Pause. "Mine," added Doc, "is Baskin-Robbins girls."

"Hold on here," Smith said, "I ain't going along with that kind of talk."

"Not people, Captain," the doctor said. "We're talking about bulldozers. Power shovels. Draglines. Earthmovers."

"Machines," said Hayduke.

A pause in the planning, again.

"Are you certain this canyon is not bugged?" the doctor asked. "I have the feeling that others are listening in to every word we say."

"I know that feeling," Hayduke said, "but that's not what I'm thinking about right now. I'm thinking—"

"What are you thinking about?"

"I'm thinking: Why the fuck should we trust *each other?* I never even met you two guys before today."

Silence. The three men stared into the fire. The oversize surgeon. The elongated riverman. The brute from the Green Berets. A sigh. They looked at each other. And one thought: What the hell. And one thought: They look honest to me. And one thought: Men are not the enemy. Nor women either. Nor little children.

Not in sequence but in unison, as one, they smiled. At each other. The bottle made its penultimate round.

"What the hell," Smith said, "we're only talkin'."

The Raid at Comb Wash

THEIR PREPARATIONS were thorough.

First, at Captain Smith's suggestion, they cached supplies at various points all over their projected field of operations: the canyon country, southeast Utah and northern Arizona. The stores consisted of (1) food: tinned goods, dried meats, fruits, beans, powdered milk, sealed drinking water; (2) field equipment: medical kits, tarps and ponchos, fire starters, topographical maps, moleskin and Rip-Stop, sleeping bags, canteens, hunting and fishing equipment, cooking gear, rope, tape, nylon cord; and (3) the basic ingredients: monkey wrenches, wrecking bars, heavy-duty wirecutters, bolt cutters, trenching tools, siphon hoses, sugars and syrups, oil and petrol, steel wedges, blasting caps, detonating cord, safety fuse, cap crimpers, fuse lighters and adequate quantities of Du Pont Straight and Du Pont Red Cross Extra. Most of the work was carried out by Smith and Hayduke. Sometimes they were assisted by the doctor and Ms. Abbzug, flying up from Albuquerque. Hayduke objected, for a while, to the presence of the girl.

"No fucking girls," he hollered. "This is man's work."

"Don't talk like a pig," said Bonnie.

"Here now, here now," the doctor said. "Peace."

From *The Monkey Wrench Gang* (1975)

"I thought we were gonna keep the cell down to three men," Hayduke insisted. "No girls."

"I'm no girl," Bonnie said. "I'm a grown-up woman. I'm twenty-eight and a half years old."

Seldom Seen Smith stood somewhat aside, smiling, rubbing the blond furze on his long jaw.

"We agreed on only three people," Hayduke said.

"I know," the doctor said, "and I'm sorry. But I want Bonnie with us. Whither I goest Bonnie goeth. Or vice versa. I don't function very well without her."

"What kind of a man are you?"

"Dependent."

Hayduke turned to Smith. "What do you say?"

"Well," he said, "you know, I kinda like this little girl. I think it's kinda nice to have her around. I say let's keep her with us."

"Then she has to take the blood oath."

"I'm not a child," said Bonnie, "and I refuse to take any blood oaths or play any little-boy games. You'll just have to trust me. If you don't I'll turn you all in to the Bureau of Land Management."

"She's got us by the balls," Smith said.

"And no vulgarity either," she said.

"Testicles," he said.

"Grab 'em by the testicles, and their hearts and minds will follow," the doctor said.

"I don't like it," Hayduke said.

"Tough," Bonnie said. "You're outvoted three to one."

"I don't like it."

"Peace," the doctor said. "I assure you she'll be very useful."

The doctor had the last word. After all, it was he who would be financing the campaign. He was the angel. Avenging angel. Hayduke knew it. And the expense was great. Ninety dollars for a decent sleeping bag. Forty dollars for a good pair of boots. Even the price of pinto beans had gone up to 89 cents a pound. By far the biggest expense, however, was not supplies but simply transportation over the immense, rugged and intricate expanses of the Southwest, with gasoline selling at 49 to 55 cents per gallon and a new truck tire (six-ply heavy duty) at least $55. Plus the air fare for the doctor and his Bonnie—$42.45 each, one way, Albuquerque to Page.

Many of these expenditures could be itemized as business expenses, tax deductible, by Smith (Back of Beyond Expeditions), but even so the initial outlay was heavy. The good doctor provided the cash, which Smith seldom had available, and wrote most of the checks. Explosives, of course, were tax write-offs; Doc would list them on his IRS return as ranch improvement costs—for the little 225-acre tax shelter he owned out in the Manzano Mountains east of Albuquerque—and as assessment work on a cluster of mining claims he also held, in the same area.

"Gloves!" Hayduke demanded. "Gloves! No fucking monkey business without gloves!"

So Doc bought everyone in the crew three pair each of top-quality buckskin gloves.

"Sno-Seal!" (For boots.)

He bought Sno-Seal.

"Sidearms!"

"No."

"Guns!"

"No."

"Peanut butter!" said Bonnie.

"Guns *and* peanut butter!" Hayduke roared.

"Peanut butter, yes. Guns, no."

"We gotta defend our fucking selves."

"No guns." Doc could be stubborn.

"Them fuckers'll be shooting at us!"

"No violence."

"We gotta shoot back."

"No bloodshed." The doctor stood fast.

Again Hayduke was outvoted, again by a vote of three to one. So for the time being he kept his own weapons concealed, as best he could, and carried only the revolver hidden in the inner pocket of his pack.

Doc bought six cases of Deaf Smith organic peanut butter, an unblanched, unhydrogenated product manufactured from sun-dried peanuts grown on composted soil without benefit of herbicides, pesticides or county agents. Seldom Seen Smith (no relation) and Hayduke distributed the peanut butter strategically about the Colorado Plateau, a jar here, a jar there, all the way from Onion Creek to Pakoon Spring, from Pucker Pass to Tin Cup Mesa, from Tavaputs, Utah, to Moenkopi, Arizona. Rich brown peanut butter.

Once, early in the campaign, filling their fuel tanks at a gas station, Doc was about to pay with his credit card. Hayduke pulled him aside. No credit cards, he said.

No credit cards?

No fucking credit cards; you want to leave a fucking documented trail one mile wide with your fucking signature on it everywhere we go?

I see, said Doc. Of course. Pay cash, let the credit go. Nor heed the rumble of a distant drum.

Nor did they actually steal, buy or use explosives, at first. Hayduke urged their use immediately, energetically and massively, but the other three opposed him. The doctor was afraid of dynamite; it suggested anarchy, and anarchy is not the answer. Abbzug pointed out that any type of fireworks was illegal in all the Southwestern states; she had also heard that blasting caps could cause cervical cancer. The doctor reminded Hayduke that the use of explosives for illegal (however constructive) purposes was a felony, as well as being a Federal offense where bridges and highways were concerned, whereas simply pouring a little Karo syrup into the fuel tank and sand or emery powder into the oil intake of a dump truck was merely a harmless misdemeanor, hardly more than a Hallowe'en prank.

It became a question of subtle, sophisticated harassment techniques versus blatant and outrageous industrial sabotage. Hayduke favored the blatant, the outrageous. The others the other. Outvoted as usual, Hayduke fumed but consoled himself with the reflection that things would get thicker as operations proceeded. For every action a bigger reaction. From one damn thing to another worse. After all, he was a veteran of Vietnam. He knew how the system worked. Time, lapsing and collapsing from day to day, advanced on his side.

Each cache of provisions was made with scrupulous care. All edible, potable or otherwise perishable or destructible items were placed in metal footlockers. Tools were sharpened, oiled, sheathed or cased and wrapped in canvas. Everything was buried, if possible, or well covered with rocks and brush. The sites were camouflaged and tracks swept away with broom or bough. No cache was considered satisfactory until it passed inspection by both Hayduke and Smith, senior military advisers to the—the Foxpack? Sixpack? Wilderness Avengers? Wooden Shoe Mob? They couldn't even agree on a name for themselves. Peanut Butter Cabal? Raiders of the Purple Sage? Young Americans for Freedom? Woman's Christian Temperance Union? Couldn't agree. Who's in charge here? We're all in charge here, Bonnie says. Nobody's in charge here, says Doc. Lousy way to run a fucking revolution, Hayduke complained; he suffered from a faint authoritarian streak, ex-Sgt. Geo. Wash. Hayduke.

"Peace, please, *pax vobiscum*," Doc said. But his own excitement was growing too. Look what happened, for example, at the fifty-million-dollar new University Medical Center, in one of the new Bauhaus million-dollar classroom buildings. The building smelled of raw cement. The windows, long and narrow and few, looked like gunports in a pillbox. The air-conditioning system was of the very latest design. When Dr. Sarvis entered the classroom where he was to give a lecture one day—"Industrial Pollution & Respiratory Illness"—he found the room overheated, the air stale. The students seemed sleepier than usual, but unconcerned.

Need some air in here, the doctor grumbled. A student shrugged. The rest were nodding—not in agreement but in slumber. Doc went to the nearest window and tried to open it. But how? There didn't seem to be any sort of hinge, sash, latch, catch, crank or handle. How do you open this window? he asked the nearest student. Don't know, sir, the student said. Another said, You can't open it; this's an air-conditioned building. Suppose we need air? the doctor asked, calm and reasonable. You're not supposed to open the windows in an air-conditioned building, the student said. It screws up the system. I see, Doc said; but we need fresh air. (Outside, below, in the sunshine, little birds were singing in the forsythia, fornicating in the hydrangea.) What do we do? he asked. I guess you could complain to the Administration, another student said, a remark always good for a laugh. I see, said Dr. Sarvis. Still calm and reasonable, he walked to the steel-framed desk by the blackboard, picked up the steel-legged chair waiting behind the desk and, holding it by seat and back, punched out the window glass. All of it. Thoroughly. The students watched in quiet approval and when he was finished gave him a sitting ovation. Doc brushed his hands. We'll skip rollcall today, he said.

ONE FINE DAY in early June, bearing west from Blanding, Utah, on their way to cache more goods, the gang paused at the summit of Comb Ridge for a look at the world below. They were riding four abreast in the wide cab of Seldom's 4×4 pickup truck. It was lunchtime. He pulled off the dusty road— Utah State Road 95—and turned south on a jeep track that followed close to the rim. Comb Ridge is a great monocline, rising gradually on the east side, dropping off at an angle close to ninety degrees on the west side. The drop-off from the rim is about five hundred feet straight down, with another three hundred feet or more of steeply sloping talus below the cliff. Like many other canyons, mesas and monoclines in southeast Utah, Comb Ridge forms a serious barrier to east-west land travel. Or it used to. God meant it to.

Smith pulled the truck up onto a shelf of slickrock within twenty feet of the rim and stopped. Everybody got out, gratefully, and walked close to the edge. The sun stood high in the clouds; the air was still and warm. Flowers grew from cracks in the rock—globe mallow, crownbeard, gilia, rock cress— and flowering shrubs—cliff-rose, Apache plume, chamisa, others. Doc was delighted.

"Look," he said, "*Arabis pulchra. Fallugia paradoxa. Cowania mexicana,* by God."

"What's this?" Bonnie said, pointing to little purplish things in the shade of a pinyon pine.

"*Pedicularis centranthera.*"

"Yeah, okay, but what is it?"

"What is it?" Doc paused. "What it is, no man knows, but men call it . . . wood betony."

"Don't be a wise-ass."

"Also known as lousewort. A child came to me saying, 'What is the louse-wort?' And I said, 'Perhaps it is the handkerchief of the Lord.' "

"Nobody loves a wise-ass."

"I know," he admitted.

Smith and Hayduke stood on the brink of five hundred feet of naked gravity. That yawning abyss which calls men to sleep. But they were looking not down at death but southward at life, or at least at a turmoil of dust and activity. Whine of motors, snort and growl of distant diesels.

"The new road," Smith explained.

"Uh huh." Hayduke raised his field glasses and studied the scene, some three miles off. "Big operation," he mumbled. "Euclids, D-Nines, haulers, scrapers, loaders, backhoes, drills, tankers. What a beautiful fucking layout."

Doc and Bonnie came up, flowers in their hair. Far off south in the dust, sunlight flashed on glass, on bright steel.

"What's going on down there?" Doc said.

"That's the new road they're working on," Smith said.

"What's wrong with the old road?"

"The old road is too old," Smith explained. "It crawls up and down hills and goes in and out of draws and works around the head of canyons and it ain't paved and it generally takes too long to get anywhere. This new road will save folks ten minutes from Blanding to Natural Bridges."

"It's a county road?" Doc asked.

"It's built for the benefit of certain companies that operate in this county, but it's not a county road, it's a state road. It's to help out the poor fellas that own the uranium mines and the truck fleets and the marinas on Lake Powell, that's what it's for. They gotta eat too."

"I see," said Doc. "Let me have a look, George."

Hayduke passed the field glasses to the doctor, who took a long look, puffing on his Marsh-Wheeling.

"Busy busy busy," he said. He returned the glasses to Hayduke. "Men, we have work to do tonight."

"Me too," Bonnie said.

"You too."

One thin scream came floating down, like a feather, from the silver-clouded sky. Hawk. Redtail, solitaire, one hawk passing far above the red reef, above the waves of Triassic sandstone, with a live snake clutched in its talons. The snake wriggled, casually, as it was borne away to a different world. Lunchtime.

After a little something themselves the gang got back in Smith's truck and drove two miles closer, over the rock and through the brush, in low range and four-wheel drive, to a high point overlooking the project more directly. Smith parked the truck in the shade of the largest pinyon pine available, which was not big enough to effectively conceal it.

Netting, Hayduke thought; we need camouflage netting. He made a note in his notebook.

Now the three men and the girl worked their way to the rim again, to the edge of the big drop-off. Out of habit Hayduke led the way, crawling forward on hands and knees, then on his belly the last few yards to their observation point. Were such precautions necessary? Probably not, so early in their game; the Enemy, after all, was not aware yet that Hayduke & Co. existed. The Enemy, in fact, still fondly imagined that he enjoyed the favor of the American public, with no exceptions.

Incorrect. They lay on their stomachs on the warm sandstone, under the soft and pearly sky, and peered down seven hundred vertical feet and half a mile by line of sight to where the iron dinosaurs romped and roared in their pit of sand. There was love in neither head nor heart of Abbzug, Hayduke, Smith and Sarvis. No sympathy. But considerable involuntary admiration for all that power, all that controlled and directed superhuman force.

Their vantage point gave them a view of the heart, not the whole, of the project. The surveying crews, far ahead of the big machines, had finished weeks earlier, but evidence of their work remained: the Day-Glo ribbon, shocking pink, that waved from the boughs of juniper trees, the beribboned stakes planted in the earth marking center line and shoulder of the coming road, the steel pins hammered into the ground as reference points.

What Hayduke and friends could and did see were several of the many phases of a road-building project that follow the survey. To the far west, on the rise beyond Comb Wash, they saw bulldozers clearing the right-of-way. In forested areas the clearing job would require a crew of loggers with chain saws, but here in southeast Utah, on the plateau, the little pinyon pines and junipers offered no resistance to the bulldozers. The crawler-tractors pushed them all over with nonchalant ease and shoved them aside, smashed and bleeding, into heaps of brush, where they would be left to die and decompose. No one knows precisely how sentient is a pinyon pine, for example, or to what degree such woody organisms can feel pain or fear, and in any case the road builders had more important things to worry about, but this much is clearly established as scientific fact: a living tree, once uprooted, takes many days to wholly die.

Behind the first wave of bulldozers came a second, blading off the soil and ripping up loose stone down to the bedrock. Since this was a cut-and-fill operation it was necessary to blast away the bedrock down to the grade level specified by the highway engineers. Watching from their comfortable grandstand bleachers, the four onlookers saw drill rigs crawl on self-propelled tracks to the blasting site, followed by tractors towing air compressors. Locked in position and linked to the compressors, the drill steel bit into the rock with screaming teconite bits, star-shaped and carbide-tipped. Powdered stone floated on the air as the engines roared. Resonant vibrations shuddered through the bone structure of the earth. More mute suffering. The drill rigs moved on over the hill to the next site.

The demolition team arrived. Charges were lowered into the bore holes, gently tamped and stemmed, and wired to an electrical circuit. The watchers on the rim heard the chief blaster's warning whistle, saw the crew move off to a safe distance, saw the spout of smoke and heard the thunder as the blaster fired his shot. More bulldozers, loaders and giant trucks moved in to shovel up and haul away the debris.

Down in the center of the wash below the ridge the scrapers, the earth-movers and the dump trucks with eighty-ton beds unloaded their loads, building up the fill as the machines beyond were deepening the cut. Cut and fill, cut and fill, all afternoon the work went on. The object in mind was a modern high-speed highway for the convenience of the trucking industry, with grades no greater than 8 percent. That was the immediate object. The ideal lay still farther on. The engineer's dream is a model of perfect sphericity, the planet

Earth with all irregularities removed, highways merely painted on a surface smooth as glass. Of course the engineers still have a long way to go but they are patient tireless little fellows; they keep hustling on, like termites in a termitorium. It's steady work, and their only natural enemies, they believe, are mechanical breakdown or "down time" for the equipment, and labor troubles, and bad weather, and sometimes faulty preparation by the geologists and surveyors.

THE ONE ENEMY the contractor would not and did not think of was the band of four idealists stretched out on their stomachs on a rock under the desert sky.

Down below the metal monsters roared, bouncing on rubber through the cut in the ridge, dumping their loads and thundering up the hill for more. The green beasts of Bucyrus, the yellow brutes of Caterpillar, snorting like dragons, puffing black smoke into the yellow dust.

The sun slipped three degrees westward, beyond the clouds, beyond the silver sky. The watchers on the ridge munched on jerky, sipped from their canteens. The heat began to slacken off. There was talk of supper, but no one had much appetite. There was talk of getting ready for the evening program. The iron machines still rolled in the wash below, but it seemed to be getting close to quitting time.

"The main thing we have to watch for," Hayduke said, "is a night watchman. They just might keep some fucker out here at night. Maybe with a dog. Then we'll have problems."

"There won't be any watchman," Smith said. "Not all night, anyhow."

"What makes you so sure?"

"It's the way they do things around here; we're out in the country. Nobody lives out here. It's fifteen miles from Blanding. This here project is three miles off the old road, which hardly nobody drives at night anyhow. They don't expect any trouble."

"Maybe some of them are camping out here," Hayduke said.

"Naw," Smith said. "They don't do that kind of thing either. These boys work like dogs all day long; they wanta get back to town in the evening. They like their civilized comforts. They ain't campers. These here construction workers don't think nothing of driving fifty miles to work every morning. They're all crazy as bedbugs. I worked in these outfits myself."

Doc and Hayduke, armed with the field glasses, kept watch. Smith and Bonnie crawled down from the ridge, keeping out of sight, until they were below the skyline. Then they walked to the truck, set up the campstove and began preparing a meal for the crew. The doctor and Hayduke, poor cooks, made good dishwashers. All four were qualified eaters, but only Bonnie and Smith cared enough about food to cook it with decency.

Smith was right; the construction workers departed all together long before sundown. Leaving their equipment lined up along the right-of-way, nose to tail, like a herd of iron elephants, or simply *in situ*, where quitting time found them, the operators straggled back in small groups to their transport vehicles. Far above, Doc and Hayduke could hear their voices, the laughter, the rattle of lunch buckets. The carryalls and pickups driven by men at the eastern end of the job came down through the big notch to meet the equipment operators. The men climbed in; the trucks turned and ground uphill through the dust, into the notch again and out of sight. For some time there was the fading sound of motors, a cloud of dust rising above the pinyon and juniper; then that too was gone. A tanker truck appeared, full of diesel fuel, groaning down the grade toward the machines, and proceeded from one to the next, the driver and his helper filling the fuel tanks of each, topping them off. Finished, the tanker turned and followed the others back through the evening toward the distant glow of town, somewhere beyond the eastward bulge of the plateau.

Now the stillness was complete. The watchers on the rim, eating their suppers from tin plates, heard the croon of a mourning dove far down the wash. They heard the hoot of an owl, the cries of little birds retiring to sleep in the dusty cottonwoods. The great golden light of the setting sun streamed across the sky, glowing upon the clouds and the mountains. Almost all the country within their view was roadless, uninhabited, a wilderness. They meant to keep it that way. They sure meant to try. *Keep it like it was.*

The sun went down.

Tactics, materials, tools, gear.

Hayduke was reading off his checklist. "Gloves! Everybody got his gloves? Put 'em on now. Anybody goes fucking around down there without gloves I'll chop his hand off."

"You haven't washed the dishes yet," Bonnie said.

"Hard hat! Everybody got his hard hat?" He looked around at the crew. "You—put that thing on your head."

"It doesn't fit," she said.

"Make it fit. Somebody show her how to adjust the headband. Jesus Christ." Looking back at his list. "Bolt cutters!" Hayduke brandished his own, a twenty-four-inch pair of cross-levered steel jaws for cutting bolts, rods, wire, most anything up to half an inch in diameter. The rest of the party were equipped with fencing pliers, good enough for most purposes.

"Now, you lookouts," he went on, addressing Bonnie and Doc. "Do you know your signals?"

"One short and a long for warning, take cover," Doc said, holding up his metal whistle. "One short and two longs for all clear, resume operations. Three longs for distress, come help. Four longs for . . . what are four longs for?"

"Four longs mean work completed, am returning to camp," Bonnie said. "And one long means acknowledgment, message received."

"Don't much like them tin whistles," Smith said. "We need something more natural. More eco-logical. Owl hoots, maybe. Anybody hears them tin whistles will know there's two-legged animals slinkin' around. Lemme show you how to hoot like a owl."

Training time. Hands cupped and close, one little opening between thumbs, shape the lips, blow. Blow from the belly, down deep; the call will float through canyons, across mountainsides, all the way down in the valley. Hayduke showed Dr. Sarvis; Smith showed Abbzug, personally, holding her hands in the necessary way, blowing into them, letting her blow into his. She picked it up quickly, the doctor not so fast. They rehearsed the signals. For a while the twilight seemed full of great horned owls, talking. Finally they were ready. Hayduke returned to his checklist.

"Okay, gloves, hats, wire cutters, signals, Now: Karo syrup, four quarts each. Matches. Flashlights—be careful with those: keep the light close to your work, don't swing it around, shut it off when you're moving. Maybe we should work out light signals? Naw, later. Water. Jerky. Hammer, screwdriver, cold chisel—okay, I got them. What else?"

"We're all set," Smith said. "Let's get a move on."

They shouldered their packs. Hayduke's pack, with most of the hardware in it, weighed twice as much as anyone else's. He didn't care. Seldom Seen Smith led the way through the sundown gloom. The others followed in single file, Hayduke at the rear. There was no trail, no path. Smith picked the most economic route among the scrubby trees, around the bayonet leaves of the yucca and the very hairy prickly pear, across the little sandy washes below the crest of the ridge. As much as possible he led them on the rock, leaving no tracks.

They were headed south by the stars, south by the evening breeze, toward a rising Scorpio sprawled out fourteen galactic worlds wide across the southern sky. Owls hooted from the pygmy forest. The saboteurs hooted back.

Smith circumvented an anthill, a huge symmetric arcologium of sand surrounded by a circular area denuded of any vestige of vegetation. The dome home of the harvester ants. Smith went around and so did Bonnie but Doc stumbled straight into it, stirring up the formicary. The big red ants swarmed out looking for trouble; one of them bit Doc on the calf. He stopped, turned and dismantled the anthill with a series of vigorous kicks.

"Thus I refute R. Buckminster Fuller," he growled. "Thus do I refute Paolo Soleri, B. F. Skinner and the late Walter Gropius."

"How late was he?" Smith asked.

"Doc hates ants," Bonnie explained. "And they hate him."

"The anthill," said Doc, "is sign, symbol and symptom of what we are about out here, stumbling through the gloaming like so many stumblebums. I mean it is the model in microcosm of what we must find a way to oppose and halt. The anthill, like the Fullerian foam fungus, is the mark of social disease. Anthills abound where overgrazing prevails. The plastic dome follows the plague of runaway industrialism, prefigures technological tyranny and reveals the true quality of our lives, which sinks in inverse ratio to the growth of the Gross National Product. End of mini-lecture by Dr. Sarvis."

"Good," Bonnie said.

"Amen," said Smith.

The evening gave way to night, a dense violet solution of starlight and darkness mixed with energy, each rock and shrub and tree and scarp outlined by an aura of silent radiation. Smith led the conspirators along the contour of the terrain until they came to the brink of something, an edge, a verge, beyond which stood nothing tangible. This was not the rim of the monocline, however, but the edge of the big man-made cut *through* the monocline. Below in the gloom those with sufficient night vision could see the broad new roadway and the dark forms of machines, two hundred feet down.

Smith and friends proceeded along this new drop-off until they reached a point where it was possible to scramble down to the crushed rock and heavy dust of the roadbed. Looking northeast, toward Blanding, they saw this pale raw freeway leading straight across the desert, through the scrub forest and out of sight in the darkness. No lights were visible, only the faint glow of the town fifteen miles away. In the opposite direction the roadbed curved down between the walls of the cut, sinking out of view toward the wash. They walked into the cut.

The first thing they encountered, on the shoulder of the roadbed, were survey stakes. Hayduke pulled them up and tossed them into the brush.

"Always pull up survey stakes," he said. "Anywhere you find them. Always. That's the first goddamned general order in the monkey wrench business. Always pull up survey stakes."

They walked deeper into the cut to where it was possible, looking down and west, to make out though dimly the bottom of Comb Wash, the fill area, the scattered earth-moving equipment. Here they stopped for further consultation.

"We want our first lookout here," Hayduke said.

"Doc or Bonnie?"

"I want to wreck something," Bonnie said. "I don't want to sit here in the dark making owl noises."

"I'll stay here," Doc said.

Once more they rehearsed signals. All in order. Doc made himself comfortable on the operator's seat of a giant compactor machine. He toyed with the controls. "Stiff," he said, "but it's transportation."

"Why don't we start with this fucker right here?" Hayduke said, meaning Doc's machine. "Just for the practice."

Why not? Packs were opened, tools and flashlights brought out. While Doc stood watch above them his three comrades entertained themselves cutting up the wiring, fuel lines, control link rods and hydraulic hoses of the machine, a beautiful new 27-ton tandem-drummed yellow Hyster C-450A, Caterpillar 330 HP diesel engine, sheepsfoot rollers, manufacturer's suggested retail price only $29,500 FOB Saginaw, Michigan. One of the best. A dreamboat.

They worked happily. Hard hats clinked and clanked against the steel. Lines and rods snapped apart with the rich *spang!* and solid *clunk!* of metal severed under tension. Doc lit another stogie. Smith wiped a drop of oil from his eyelid. The sharp smell of hydraulic fluid floated on the air, mixing uneasily with the aroma of Doc's smoke. Running oil pattered on the dust. There was another sound, far away, as of a motor. They paused. Doc stared into the dark. Nothing. The noise faded.

"All's clear," he said. "Carry on, lads."

When everything was cut which they could reach and cut, Hayduke pulled the dipstick from the engine block—to check the oil? not exactly—and poured a handful of fine sand into the crankcase. Too slow. He unscrewed the oil-filler cap, took chisel and hammer and punched a hole through the oil strainer and poured in more sand. Smith removed the fuel-tank cap and emptied four quart bottles of sweet Karo syrup into the fuel tank. Injected into the cylinders, that sugar would form a solid coat of carbon on cylinder walls and piston rings. The engine should seize up like a block of iron, when they got it running. If they could get it running.

What else? Abbzug, Smith and Hayduke stood back a little and stared at the quiet hulk of the machine. All were impressed by what they had done. The murder of a machine. Deicide. All of them, even Hayduke, a little awed by the enormity of their crime. By the sacrilege of it.

"Let's slash the seat," said Bonnie.

"That's vandalism," Doc said. "I'm against vandalism. Slashing seats is petty-bourgeois."

"So okay, okay," Bonnie said. "Let's get on to the next item."

"Then we'll all meet back here?" Doc said.

"It's the only way back up on the ridge," Smith said.

"But if there's any shit," Hayduke said, "don't wait for us. We'll meet at the truck."

"I couldn't find my way back there if my life depended on it," Doc said. "Not in the dark."

Smith scratched his long jaw. "Well, Doc," he said, "if there's any kind of trouble maybe you better just hightail it up on the bank there, above the road, and wait for us. Don't forget the hoot owl. We'll find you that way."

They left him there in the dark, perched on the seat of the maimed and poisoned compactor. The one red eye of his cigar watched them depart. The plan was for Bonnie to stand watch at the far west end of the project, alone, while Hayduke and Smith worked on the equipment down in the wash. She murmured against them.

"You ain't afraid of the dark, are you?" Smith asked.

"Of course I'm afraid of the dark."

"You afraid to be alone?"

"Of course I'm afraid to be alone."

"You mean you don't want to be lookout?"

"I'll be lookout."

"No place for women," Hayduke muttered.

"You shut up," she said. "Am I complaining? I'll be lookout. So shut up before I take your jaw off."

The dark seemed warm, comfortable, secure to Hayduke. He liked it. The Enemy, if he appeared, would come loudly announced with roar of engines, blaze of flares, an Operation Rolling Thunder of shells and bombs, just as in Vietnam. So Hayduke assumed. For the night and the wilderness belong to *us*. This is Indian country. Our country. Or so he assumed.

Downhill, maybe a mile, in one great switchback, the roadway descended through the gap to the built-up fill across the floor of Comb Wash. They soon reached the first group of machines—the earthmovers, the big trucks, the landscape architects.

Bonnie was about to go on by herself. Smith took her arm for a moment. "You stay close, honey," he told her, "only concentrate on looking and listening; let me and George do the hard work. Take the hard hat off so you can hear better. Okay?"

"Well," she agreed, "for the moment." But she wanted a bigger share of the action later. He agreed. Share and share alike. He showed her where to find the steps that led to the open cab of an eighty-five-ton Euclid mountain mover. She sat up there, like a lookout in a crow's nest, while he and Hayduke went to work.

Busywork. Cutting and snipping, snapping and wrenching. They crawled all over a Caterpillar D-9A, world's greatest bulldozer, the idol of all highwaymen. Put so much sand in the crankcase that Hayduke couldn't get the dipstick reinserted all the way. He trimmed it short with the rod-and-bolt cutter. Made it fit. Sand in the oil intake. He climbed into the cab, tried to turn the fuel-tank cap. Wouldn't turn. Taking hammer and chisel he broke it loose, unscrewed it, poured four quarts of good high-energy Karo into the diesel fuel. Replaced the cap. Sat in the driver's seat and played for a minute with the switches and levers.

"You know what would be fun?" he said to Smith, who was down below hacking through a hydraulic hose.

"What's that, George?"

"Get this fucker started, take it up to the top of the ridge and run it over the rim."

"That there'd take us near half the night, George."

"Sure would be fun."

"We can't get it started anyhow."

"Why not?"

"There ain't no rotor arm in the magneto. I looked. They usually take out the rotor arm when they leave these beasts out on the road."

"Yeah?" Hayduke takes notebook and pencil from his shirt pocket, turns on his flashlight, makes notation: *Rotor arms.* "You know something else that would be fun?"

Smith, busy nullifying all physical bond between cylinder heads and fuel injection lines, says, "What?"

"We could knock a pin out of each tread. Then when the thing moved it would run right off its own fucking tracks. That would really piss them."

"George, this here tractor ain't gonna move at all for a spell. It ain't a-goin' *nowheres*."

"For a spell."

"That's what I said."

"That's the trouble."

Hayduke climbed down from the cab and came close to Smith, there in the black light of the stars, doing his humble chores, the pinpoint of his flashlight beam fixed on a set screw in an engine block the weight of three Volkswagen buses. The yellow Caterpillar, enormous in the dark, looms over the two men with the indifference of a god, submitting without a twitch of its enameled skin to their malicious ministrations. The down payment on this piece of equipment comes to around $30,000. What were the men worth? In any rational chemico-psycho-physical analysis? In a nation of two hundred and ten million (210,000,000) bodies? Getting cheaper by the day, as mass production lowers the unit cost?

"That's the trouble," he said again. "All this wire cutting is only going to slow them down, not stop them. Godfuckingdammit, Seldom, we're wasting our time."

"What's the matter, George?"

"We're wasting our time."

"What do you mean?"

"I mean we ought to really blast this motherfucker. This one and all the others. I mean set them on fire. Burn them up."

"That there's arson."

"For chrissake, what's the difference? You think what we're doing now is much nicer? You know damn well if old Morrison-Knudsen was out here now with his goons he'd be happy to see us all shot dead."

"They ain't gonna be too happy about this, you're right there. They ain't gonna understand us too good."

"They'll understand us. They'll hate our fucking guts."

"They won't understand why we're doin' this, George. That's what I mean. I mean we're gonna be misunderstood."

"No, we're not gonna be misunderstood. We're gonna be hated."

"Maybe we should explain."

"Maybe we should do it right. None of this petty fucking around."

Smith was silent.

"Let's *destroy* this fucker."

"I don't know," Smith said.

"I mean roast it in its own grease. I just happen to have a little siphon hose here in my pack. Like I just happen to have some matches. I mean we just siphon some of that fuel out of the tank and we just sort of slosh it around over the engine and cab and then we just sort of toss a match at it. Let God do the rest."

"Yeah, I guess He would," Smith agreed. "If God meant this here bulldozer to live He wouldn't of filled its tank with diesel fuel. Now would He of? But George, what about Doc?"

"What about him? Since when is he the boss?"

"He's the one bankrolling this here operation. We need him."

"We need his money."

"Well, all right, put it this way: I like old Doc. And I like that little old lady of his too. And I think all four of us got to stick together. And I think we can't do anything that all four of us ain't agreed to do beforehand. Think about it that way, George."

"Is that the end of the sermon?"

"That's the end of the sermon."

Now Hayduke was silent for a while. They worked. Hayduke thought. After a minute he said, "You know something, Seldom? I guess you're right."

"I thought I was wrong once," Seldom said, "but I found out later I was mistaken."

They finished with the D-9A. The siphon hose and the matches remained inside Hayduke's pack. For the time being. Having done all they could to sand, jam, gum, mutilate and humiliate the first bulldozer, they went on to the next, the girl with them. Smith put his arm around her.

"Miss Bonnie," he says, "how do you like the night shift?"

"Too peaceful. When's my turn to wreck something?"

"We need you to look out."

"I'm bored."

"Don't you worry about that none, honey. We're gonna have enough excitement pretty soon to last you and me for the rest of our lives. If we live that long. How you think old Doc is doing back there all by his lonesome?"

"He's all right. He lives inside his head most of the time anyway."

Another giant machine looms out of the darkness before them. A hauler; they chop it up. Then the next. Bonnie watches from her post in the cab of a nearby earthmover. Next! The men go on.

"If only we could start up the motors on these sombitches," Hayduke said. "We could drain the oil out, let the motors run and walk away. They'd take care of themselves and we'd be finished a lot faster."

"That'd do it," Smith allowed. "Drain the oil and let the engines run.

They'd seize up tighter'n a bull's asshole by fly time. They never would get
them buggers prised open."

"We could give each one a try anyhow." And acting on his words, Hayduke climbed to the controls of a big bulldozer. "How do you start this
mother?"

"I'll show you if we find one ready to go."

"How about a hot wire? Maybe we could start it that way. Bypass the
ignition."

"Not a caterpillar tractor. This ain't no car, George, you know. This is
a D-Eight. This here's heavy-duty industrial equipment; this ain't the old
Farmall back home."

"Well, I'm ready for driving lessons anytime."

Hayduke climbed down from the operator's seat. They worked on the
patient, sifting handfuls of fine Triassic sand into the crankcase, cutting up
the wiring, the fuel lines, the hydraulic hoses to fore and aft attachments,
dumping Karo into the fuel tanks. Why Karo instead of plain sugar? Smith
wanted to know. Pours better, Hayduke explained; mixes easier with the diesel, doesn't jam up in strainers. You sure about that? No.

Hayduke crawled under the bulldozer to find the drain plug in the oil
pan. He found it, through an opening in the armored skid plate, but needed a
big wrench to crack it loose. They tried the toolbox in the cab. Locked. Hayduke broke the lock with his cold chisel and hammer. Inside they found a few
simple and massive instruments: an iron spanner three feet long; a variety of
giant end wrenches; a sledgehammer; a wooden-handled monkey wrench;
nuts, bolts, friction tape, wire.

Hayduke took the spanner, which looked like the right size, and crawled
again underneath the tractor. He struggled for a while with the plug, finally
broke it loose and let out the oil. The great machine began to bleed; its life-
blood drained out with pulsing throbs, onto the dust and sand. When it was all
gone he replaced the plug. Why? Force of habit—thought he was changing
the oil in his jeep.

Hayduke surfaced, smeared with dust, grease, oil, rubbing a bruised
knuckle. "Shit," he said, "I don't know."

"What's the matter?"

"Are we doing this job right? That's what I don't know. Now the operator
gets on this thing in the morning, tries to start it up, nothing happens. So the
first thing he sees is all the wiring cut, all the fuel lines cut. So putting sand in
the crankcase, draining the oil, isn't going to do any good till they get the
motor to run. But when they fix all the wiring and lines they're gonna be

checking other things too. Like the oil level, naturally. Then they find the sand. Then they see somebody's drained the oil. I'm thinking if we really want to do this monkey wrench business right, maybe we should hide our work. I mean keep it simple and sophisticated."

"Well, George, you was the one wanted to set these things on fire about a minute ago."

"Yeah. Now I'm thinking the other way."

"Well, it's too late. We already showed our hand here. We might as well go on like we started."

"Now think about it a minute, Seldom. They'll all get here about the same time tomorrow morning. Everybody starts up the engine on his piece of equipment, or tries to. Some'll discover right away that we cut up the wiring. I mean on the machines we already cut. But look, on the others, if we let the wiring alone, let the fuel lines alone, so they can start the engines, then the sand and the Karo will really do some good. I mean they'll have a chance to do the work we want them to do: ruin the engines. What do you think about that?"

They leaned side by side against the steel track of the Cat, gazing at each other through the soft starlight.

"I kind of wish we had figured all this out before," Smith said. "We ain't got all night."

"Why don't we have all night?"

"Because I reckon we ought to be fifty miles away from here come morning. That's why."

"Not me," Hayduke said. "I'm going to hang around and watch what happens. I want that personal fucking satisfaction."

A hoot owl hooted from the earthmover up ahead. "What's going on back there?" Bonnie called. "You think this is a picnic or something?"

"Okay," Smith said, "let's keep it kinda simple. Let's put these here cutters away for a while and just work on the oil and fuel systems. God knows we got plenty of sand here. About ten thousand square miles of it." Agreed.

They went on, quickly and methodically now, from machine to machine, pouring sand into each crankcase and down every opening which led to moving parts. When they had used up all their Karo syrup, they dumped sand into the fuel tanks, as an extra measure.

All the way, into the night, Hayduke, Smith, they worked their way to the end of the line. Now one, now the other, would relieve Bonnie at the lookout post so that she too could participate fully in field operations. Teamwork, that's what made America great: teamwork and initiative, that's what made America what it is today. They worked over the Cats, they operated on the earthmovers, they gave the treatment to the Schramm air compressors the Hyster compactors the Massey crawler-loaders the Joy Ram track drills the Dart D-600 wheel loaders not overlooking one lone John Deere 690-A excavator backhoe, and that was about all for the night; that was about enough; old Morrison-Knudsen had plenty of equipment all right but somebody was due for headaches in the morning when the sun came up and engines were fired up and all those little particles of sand, corrosive as powdered emery, began to wreak earth's vengeance on the cylinder walls of the despoilers of the desert.

When they reached the terminus of the cut-and-fill site, high on the folded earth across the wash from Comb Ridge, and had thoroughly sandpacked the last piece of road-building equipment, they sat down on a juniper log to rest. Seldom Seen, reckoning by the stars, estimated the time at 2:00 A.M. Hayduke guessed it was only 11:30. He wanted to go on, following the surveyors, and remove all the stakes, pins and flagging that he knew was waiting out there, in the dark, in the semi-virgin wilds beyond. But Abbzug had a better idea; instead of destroying the survey crew's signs, she suggested, why not relocate them all in such a manner as to lead the right-of-way in a grand loop back to the starting point? Or lead it to the brink of, say, Muley Point, where the contractors would confront a twelve-hundred-foot vertical dropoff down to the goosenecks of the San Juan River.

"Don't give them any ideas," Hayduke said. "They'd just want to build another goddamned bridge."

"Them survey markings go on west for twenty miles," Smith said. He was against both plans.

"So what do we do?" says Bonnie.

"I'd like to crawl into the sack," Smith said. "Get some sleep."

"I like that idea myself."

"But the night is young," Hayduke said.

"George," says Smith, "we can't do everything in one night. We got to get Doc and get back to the truck and haul ass. We don't want to be around here in the morning."

"They can't prove a thing."

"That's what Pretty-Boy Floyd said. That's what Baby-Face Nelson said and John Dillinger and Butch Cassidy and that other fella, what's his name—?"

"Jesus," Hayduke growls.

"Yeah, Jesus Christ. That's what they all said and look what happened to them. Nailed."

"This is our first big night," Hayduke said. "We ought to do as much work as we can. We're not likely to get more easy operations like this. Next time they'll have locks on everything. Maybe booby traps. And watchmen with guns, shortwave radios, dogs."

Poor Hayduke: won all his arguments but lost his immortal soul. He had to yield.

They marched back the way they'd come, past the quiet, spayed, medicated machinery. Those doomed dinosaurs of iron, waiting patiently through the remainder of the night for buggering morning's rosy-fingered denouement. The agony of cylinder rings, jammed by a swollen piston, may be like other modes of sodomy a crime against nature in the eyes of *deus ex machina*; who can say?

A hoot owl called from what seemed far away, east in the pitch-black shadows of the dynamite notch. One short and a long, then a pause, one short and a long repeated. Warning cry.

"Doc's on the job," Smith said. "That there's Doc a-talkin' to us."

The men and the girl stood still in the dark, listening hard, trying to see. The warning call was repeated, twice more. The lonesome hoot owl, speaking.

Listening. Nervous crickets chirred in the dry grass under the cottonwoods. A few doves stirred in the boughs.

They heard, faint but growing, the mutter of a motor. Then they saw, beyond the notch, the swing of headlight beams. A vehicle appeared, two blazing eyes, grinding down the grade in low gear.

"Okay," says Hayduke, "off the roadway. Watch out for a spotlight. And if there's any shit we scatter."

Understood. Caught in the middle of the big fill, there was nowhere to go but over the side. They slid down the loose rock to the jumble of boulders at the bottom. There, nursing abrasions, they took cover.

The truck came down the roadway, moved slowly by, went as far as it could and stopped among the machines huddled at the far end of the fill. There it paused for five minutes, engine still, lights turned off. The man inside the truck, sitting with windows open, sipped coffee from a thermos jug and listened to the night. He switched on his left-hand spotlight and played the beam over the roadbed and the machinery. So far as he could see, all was well. He started the engine, turned back the way he had come, passed the listeners fifty feet below, drove on up the grade through the notch and disappeared.

Hayduke slipped his revolver back into his rucksack, blew his nose through his fingers and scrambled up the talus to the top of the roadway. Smith and Abbzug emerged from the dark.

"Next time dogs," says Hayduke. "Then gunners in helicopters. Then the napalm. Then the B-52s."

They walked through the dark, up the long grade into the eastern cut. Listening for the bearded goggled great bald owl to sound.

"I don't think it's quite like that," Smith was saying. "They're people too, like us. We got to remember that, George. If we forget we'll get just like them and then where are we?"

"They're not like us," Hayduke said. "They're different. They come from the moon. They'll spend a million dollars to burn one gook to death."

"Well, I got a brother-in-law in the U.S. Air Force. And he's a sergeant. I took a general's family down the river once. Them folks are more or less human, George, just like us."

"Did you meet the general?"

"No, but his wife, she was sweet as country pie."

Hayduke silent, smiling grimly in the dark. The heavy pack on his back, overloaded with water and weapons and hardware, felt good, solid, real, meant business. He felt potent as a pistol, dangerous as dynamite, tough and mean and hard and full of love for his fellowman. And for his fellow woman, too, e.g., Abbzug there, goddamn her, in her goddamned tight jeans and that shaggy baggy sweater which failed nevertheless to quite fully conceal the rhythmic swing, back and forth, of her unconstrained fucking mammaries. Christ, he thought, I need work. Work!

They found Doc sitting on a rock at the edge of the cutbank, smoking the apparently inextinguishable and interminable stogie. "Well?" he says.

"Well now," Smith says, "I'd say I reckon we done our best."

"The war has begun," says Hayduke.

The stars looked down. Preliminary premonitions of the old moon already modifying the eastern reaches. There was no wind, no sound but the vast transpiration, thinned to a whisper by distance, of the mountain forest, of sagebrush and juniper and pinyon pine spread out over a hundred miles of semi-arid plateau. The world hesitated, waiting for something. At the rising of the moon.

Death Valley Junk

FRIDAY AFTERNOON, at 1611 hours, Terry and I jumped out of the airplane. Death Valley, like a dream, revolved below us in a web of alkali and phosphorescent chemicals. Years ago.

Unwrapping the small packet of tinfoil, Terry gave me a single capsule containing a bluish powder in a base of white cornstarch. "Three hundred and fifty micrograms," he said, grinning. He removed one for himself. We broke the capsules open for quicker action and gulped them down with a slug of beer. Except for the beer, our stomachs were empty.

Smoking some California weed, we drove far out on the valley floor, ten miles beyond the end of the pavement, deep into the desert. We found a spot we liked and built a fire of arrowwood and mesquite. We sat down on the sand to wait. Terry leafed through a newspaper—the *LA Times*. I did nothing, feeling nervous, irritable, uncomfortable. The setting sun seemed very hot, the light a painful glare. Nothing was happening.

Except for this cold grip, this icy hand on the back of my neck. Nobody there, of course; I felt to make sure, reaching back with an arm that seemed fourteen feet long. That first sensation passed, but as the sun went down behind Telescope Peak and the Panamints, I began to feel surprisingly cold.

From *Abbey's Road* (1979)

Clumsily, groggily—each movement seemed to require special attention—I dragged myself closer to the fire. I noticed then an extreme sensitivity in my sense of touch. Sitting on the ground, my rear end felt like a cluster of ice-cold needles. My bones squeaked as if made of glass.

Our bones are constructed of calcium, I told myself. They could turn to powder at any moment. This experiment, I decided, is not necessary. I swear I'll never touch another drop. Never drop another touch.

Terry sat on the opposite side of the fire, cross-legged, grinning like an idiot Buddha, staring at nothing I could see. But he was aware of my discomfort. Maybe that's why he was grinning. He was an old hand at this business, a master of the occult arts, lysergic acid, meditation.

The flies annoyed me; they buzzed around my face as if I were already dead. Nor did I much care for the praying mantis or whatever crawling up my backbone.

Something stirred in my hair.

I raised a slow-moving hand to my head, touched my hair. A huge, glittering butterfly shimmered off into the brush. *Butterfly,* I thought, startled but silent.

"What butterfly?" Terry said.

"There was a butterfly on my head."

"No. There wasn't any butterfly."

Why you liar, I thought.

Lightly, I touched my left eyelid. I don't know why; maybe it itched a bit. Suddenly there was a flash of golden lightning through the radiant pink and silent emptiness of Death Valley. A flash of lightning under a cloudless sky. I waited for the sound of thunder. Waited and waited, and after a while, forgot about it. I was having other problems.

I kept shifting my position on the cool sand, trying to get comfortable. But it's hard to get comfortable when you're sitting on a glass ass and your joints clank at every move with a metallic snapping noise like the bending of a beer can.

The solemn slowness of the time. I never knew a sundown so lingering. The fire burned steadily but did not consume the wood. I never saw such clear, such leisurely, such passionate flames.

The ground is breathing.

Let's pretend we don't notice that. Let's read this here newspaper lying on the sand. I could read all right, though the print tended to swim before my eyes and the words to leak out and run down the margins of the page. After a minute—thirty minutes?—I gave it up. Nothing could have seemed more trivial, less interesting, than the "news."

The ground *is* breathing.

The ground, the sandy desert earth between my legs, was palpitating slowly up and down, up and down, like the lungs of a sleeping animal.

Well, all right. I can accept that. And the writhing dance of the mesquite trees, I'll accept that too, though I don't like it, though plainly there is not the faintest breath of a breeze moving through the hot evening air.

The mountains across the valley, glowing in the sunset light, looked glorious, vividly palpable and tangible—as indeed they are—but don't always appear. Called the Funeral Range, as a matter of fact. The Fun-for-All Mountains. They, too, were breathing. And they no longer looked like mountains; they looked like raw lungs, a mile-high mass of pink lungs, alive and well, breathing at me for chrissake.

My sense of time and duration fell apart. There was no duration. I was trapped in limbo between two worlds—a place too queasy and queer to be the waking world, too bright and definite and three-dimensional to be the world of dreams. I didn't know where I was, except that I didn't much like it. Jelled in this static medium, where nothing happened but the clatter of my tin joints when I essayed to move, I felt paralyzed. An infantile paralysis.

I played old songs on my harmonica. "Red River Valley." "Down in the Valley." "Lonesome Valley." The secondary theme from the third movement of Beethoven's Fourteenth String Quartet. Oh, I've never heard such sweet and poignant tunes, such vibrant tones. I wanted to weep for the tragic beauty, the lovely sorrow of our lonely, floating, lonesome world. And I did.

Looking down at my legs I was amused to see how absurdly long, misshapen and remote they appeared. The legs of a deformed giant, seen from the shelter of a two-holed cave, far away.

The stars began to move.

They moved in a kind of viscous dance, as if caught in a web. As if trapped and tangled in a quivering spiderweb with moony spokes of light radiating from the hidden center. I felt sorry for the stars. God is the Great Night Spider.

Cassiopeia was a silver blue firefly snared alive in the quilted folds of the cobweb sky. The stars were points of light shining through pinholes in that rumpled mass. (Oh ho, I thought, so the ancients were right all along. Thales, Anaximander, Anaxagoras, those boys.)

I didn't like this jellyfish world. Worth visiting once, maybe, but I don't want to live here. An intellectual nausea rose in my soul. When do we get out of here? How do we get out of here? Panic gripped me for a moment. It passed.

Taking great care, I got to my feet and cautiously walked away from the fire, the bones in my pelvis grinding on one another like splintered glass. My body was a foreign object, a gigantic robot; I was the tiny pilot behind the eyesockets high in the bridge of the skull.

I noted the extravagant, excessive clarity of everything about me and within me, as if I were wandering through a grade B 3-D movie. What am I doing here?

What I meant to do, feeling my way around in the Valley of Death, was take an ordinary bourgeois piss. But when I started taking that weird thing out of the fly of my jeans—shall I describe that? that way it kept unreeling, like a firehose?—I discovered I couldn't. Because I knew, knew with absolute conviction, that if I urinated I would be urinating blood. So I stuffed it back inside, carefully, which took about an hour.

Terry still sat by the fire, motionless, the beatific grin on his saintly, silly, obnoxious face, enjoying his metaphysical picnic. His brains turning soft as Camembert in the acid bath. Well, he had the proper set, the correct predisposition. The power of faith. Miracles come to those who need them. I envied and hated him.

"Look at that swine," I said loudly, addressing the Great Spider in the Sky. "Look at him sitting there grinning at me like a diabolical Fu Manchu, like a sinister Svengali son of a bitch." The firelight gleamed on his prescription spectacles; all I could see of his nearsighted eyes were two opaque, mirrorlike disks. His balding dome. His groovy mustache.

"Say something," I roared. No reply. I roared again.

Nothing moved him. He merely sat there staring at me, smiling.

I knew by now that nothing more was going to happen. The peak had passed. Whatever might happen to others, it was not going to happen in me. And I didn't care; I was happy, pleased with what I considered my power and strength. By God, no lousy little 350 mikes of LSD was going to blow *my* brains to the moon. My sense of self was too strong to be dissolved in mere chemicals.

Once I decided I had whipped the acid god, I was able to take pleasure in this miserable, strictured mode of intoxication. The mesquite flames rising serene from their bed of incandescent coals seemed more than beautiful. They were enchanted flames, magical, holy, mystical. The writhing trees, the palpitating mountains of fresh liver and raw lung, the breathing earth, the stars struggling in the cobweb sky, all struck me now as no longer strange and fearful but simply as the way things are—amusing, charming, delightful.

But there was no sense of joy or exultation in the floating opera of my nervous system. Sometime late in the dead shank of the night, with our firewood gone and the fire down to a few smoldering rubies—but oh the intensity of those glowing coals; they watched me like radiant red eyes—we put our beer-can bones and crystal limbs in gear and shambled toward my old pickup truck. Terry drifted onto the passenger's side of the seat. Out of habit I slammed his door shut behind him—that door was always hard to latch— then turned back to the remains of the fire to get something I'd forgotten: a shoe, a sausage, I forget what, maybe a shovel.

"Ed!" he screamed, "don't go!"

I stopped, returned, hugged him to me, did my best to comfort him for several minutes. Several hours? He was in a bad state, trembling, sweating, terrified. The slamming door, my turning away, had shattered his bliss.

We rattled home to Furnace Creek. Although I had driven the acid clean out of my head and felt—up there—clear and triumphant as a winning warrior, my bones and flesh remained hypersensitive for hours. On the dirt road each pebble, each grain of sand beneath the wheels, set my teeth on edge. All the same it was good to know I was free from the glassy paralysis and coming home, coming back to earth. Nothing had ever seemed better. I had escaped, or so I thought, that dreadful web in which the stars are trapped, that galactic spider out yonder in the dark attic of space.

Later though, for weeks following my abortive flight, I suffered from a shade of disappointment and loss. Some ancient way remembered but not found. The trail not taken. For me at least, it now seemed clear—there was not going to be any magic shortcut into wisdom, understanding, peace. There would be no easy way.

Meeting the Bear

I N T H E E V E N I N G I descend from my tower and go for a walk in the woods.

What tower? What woods? Hard, brutal questions, which I decline to answer. The specificity demanded I regard as an invasion of privacy. But I shall offer a few clues (out of homage to Nabokov) for the entertainment of any readers who may still be with me. Think of Montaigne. Yeats. Rapunzel. Childe Roland. Of Stephen Dedalus and "stately, plump Buck Mulligan." Of a warm, secret place for the gestation of ideas—not so much an ivory as an ovary tower. It matters little if the ideas fail to emerge.

Like the American Legion and the American Medical Association, I am pleased to report that my mind has not been violated by an original thought since the end of World War II. If it ever ended. Though a sucker for philosophy all of my life I am not a thinker but—a toucher. A *feeler,* groping his way with the white cane of the senses through the hairy jungle of life. I believe in nothing that I cannot touch, kiss, embrace—whether a woman, a child, a rock, a tree, a bear, a shaggy dog. The rest is hearsay. If God is not present in this young prickly pear jabbing its spines into my shin, then God will have to get by without my help. I'm sorry but that's the way I feel. The message in the bottle is not for me.

From *Down the River* (1982)

As for the woods, let us say that they lie in a slovenly manner across a disorderly range of middle-aged mountains somewhere between Sombrero Butte on the east, Noisy Mountain to the south, Malicious Gap on the west and several small rivers—a bit farther off—to the north and northwest, namely, those the Spanish called Fool Creek, Little Red, the River of Souls and the River of Dolors. (Not dollars.) These are honest hints, fairly offered. Anyone familiar with the geography of the American West can work it out.

What do I do up in that tower all day? Nothing. Or nearly nothing. Or to phrase it positively, I participate in the nothingness of Being, as Heidegger would say. Somebody has to do it. No easy task, which is why they pay me $4.25 an hour. And who are They? Another riddle. They live in the castle, that's all I know. The paychecks come in the mail, regularly but always two weeks late. The signature is illegible, the code numbers indecipherable. A strange business and for a long time, when I thought about it, it troubled me. Then I stopped thinking about it and it troubled me no more. A form of grace, I suppose, this money—like manna—from Heaven. But it works, it's legal tender, it pays for the bacon, the beans, the beer, the turnips and onions.

I've been mostly alone in this place since the year I was born, and there are times when I think the solitude may have affected my mental stability in a possibly unhealthy way. That's why I descend each evening, rain or shine, for a walk in the woods. My dog Ellie barks with delight as I come, clanging like a jailer, down the fifty-two steel steps of the tower. I open a gate in the fence. We plunge off the brow of the mountain, down the trail into the twilight forest. The Dark Forest. Perhaps I'm a Ranger of some kind. Was I not a student of Dark Forestry, long ago, in that medieval school? Was it Heidelberg? Wittenberg? Edinburgh? In some former life? Pale phantom memories float like clouds across the eroded topography of a sick and disordered mind.

Bear scat lies steaming on the trail. Reality. Fresh reality, warm to the touch, full of berry seeds. The mess resembles red caviar. Almost whimpering in the ecstasy of her excitement, Ellie dives into the brush. I call her back. Reluctantly, or maybe not so reluctantly, she returns. Part Labrador, part German shepherd, two years old, she whines, growls, shivers all over as she strives for speech, trying to tell me something of urgent importance. I pause to stroke and quiet her. I know, I tell her, I know, I know. . . .

We go on, downward into the gloom. The setting sun flickers through the treetops, through the oak and fir and yellow pine. We pass beneath the vultures' roost, where they gather each evening, and I am startled as always when the stillness is shattered by the sudden violent beating of ponderous wings.

Once aloft they circle in silence until we've passed on. They never learn. But neither do I.

From a certain distance, from just beyond the zone of cautious silence that always surrounds a human walking through nature, comes the call of the hermit thrush. A silvery music, a flute song, simple and sweet and piercing to the heart. A twilight music, painful in its beauty. If there is a Heaven, an ideal realm beyond space and time, it must contain the hermit thrush. Otherwise, what good is it? And there must be trees too, of course. And mountains. And a sun that sets each evening and rises each morning. And winding through the woods, a trail with pine needles, stones, oak leaves, fresh bear shit. Naturally.

A mirror image of the earth we know, is that the best that I can imagine? This little planetary world, with its torture, cruelty, insult, degradation, greed, stupidity, spiraling without significance other than itself toward some black hole in the singularity of Einstein's universe? The mind strains toward an understanding, toward some idea of ultimate, absolute perfection—or of absolute horror. Either will do. But can no more grasp it, can no more define and communicate this thing than can Ellie my dog make explicit her emotions to me.

Forget it. We diverge onto an older, dimmer path, one that leads slightly uphill toward a small brown stagnant pond I know. When we get there I sit down on a log, keeping Ellie at my feet, and wait, watch, listen.

A cloud of gnats, like the molecules of a gas confined within an invisible retort, dances in place at one side of the pond. A few dragonflies, some red, some blue—four-winged, ornate, glittering, Victorian creatures—skim above the water. Water striders walk upon it, making the most delicate of ripples. My dog loves to slosh into the water, pursue those insouciant insects, snap them up and gulp them down. But this time I restrain her, waiting for something more interesting. For what? I don't know, yet.

The sun goes down. The song of the hermit thrush becomes distant, hesitant, fading into evening.

The twilight condenses. But the new moon will light our way out of here. Or I can always feel my way. It's straight uphill back to the lookout tower. Cannot get lost. Far off, an owl hoots, once, twice, echoed by another at an equally vague location. Then all becomes quiet. We wait.

The dog stiffens with tension beneath my hand. I can feel even before I hear it the soft snarl beginning deep in her throat. I press down, hushing her alarm.

Out of the silence, surprisingly close, upwind, comes the noise of a heavy, shambling body forcing its way with arrogant or perhaps only carefree indifference through the scrub oak, thorny locust, jumbled and decaying logs. I hear sniffing and snorting sounds, the unmistakable, unintelligible mutter of another oafish hermit talking to himself. But I can see nothing, nobody. The sounds come closer, stop. Still as a bump on the log, I hold Ellie down (though she makes no effort to rise) and stare into the dark beyond the pond.

The bear is staring at me. It is a mature male, a huge and powerful black bear, golden-brown despite its breed, and it stands—*looms*—above the oak brush on the other side of the water. The bear peers directly at where I sit but cannot really see me, cannot quite perceive and identify what I am. The close-set red eyes squint with effort, the ears twitch, the nostrils flex in the upturned black muzzle, trying to smell me out. We are so close to one another that if I wanted to I could count the flies circling around the bear's massive head. I can smell him. I can smell that odor, rich rank tangy as skunk, of wild and living beast.

I can't speak for the bear, but for myself I can say that I feel no trace of fear. It never occurs to me to feel fear. Instead I am overcome by the usual naïve presumption that this bear, like any other stranger, will like me, be pleased to meet me, want to know me better. This same enchanted innocence has borne me in and out of a hundred Saturday night cowboy bars without a scuffle and once carried me for a season safely through the streets of Bedford-Stuyvesant in Brooklyn during a previous incarnation as a public-welfare caseworker. As with a day of rock climbing, the fear comes afterward during sleep, in those hectic dreams that wake you at four o'clock in the morning.

And, so, I begin to rise, extending my hand in greeting. Now at last the bear perceives me, giving a start as he catches the scent of man the enemy. The bear shakes his head, somersaults backward and crashes away through the tangle, disappearing into our history.

That's all that happens. Nothing more. Ellie stops trembling. I let her chase the water striders for a while (back home on the farm we called them water skippers). The new moon floats like a slice of lemon on the wine-dark sky. Its light comes down in columns through the dark trees.

After a time I get up, grope along the path to the main trail, Ellie cruising in wide circles around me, and trudge uphill toward my tower on the mountain's summit. The vultures, well settled in their roost, let us pass this time without reaction.

What does it mean? Where will it all end? The questions now seem trivial, meaningless. For the present, why should we care? We have seen the bear and are content.

Aravaipa Canyon

SOUTHEAST OF PHOENIX and northeast of Tucson, in the Pinal Mountains, is a short deep gorge called Aravaipa Canyon. It is among the few places in Arizona with a permanent stream of water and in popular estimation one of the most beautiful. I am giving away no secrets here: Aravaipa Canyon has long been well known to hikers, campers, horsemen and hunters from the nearby cities. The federal Bureau of Land Management (BLM), charged with administration of the canyon, recently decreed it an official Primitive Area, thus guaranteeing its fame. Demand for enjoyment of the canyon is so great that the BLM has been obliged to institute a rationing program: no one camps here without a permit and only a limited number of such permits are issued.

Two friends and I took a walk into Aravaipa Canyon a few days ago. We walked because there is no road. There is hardly even a foot trail. Twelve miles long from end to end, the canyon is mostly occupied by the little river which gives it its name, and by stream banks piled with slabs of fallen rock from the cliffs above, the whole overgrown with cactus, trees and riparian desert shrubbery.

Aravaipa is an Apache name (some say Pima, some say Papago) and the

From *Down the River* (1982)

commonly accepted meaning is "laughing waters." The name fits. The stream is brisk, clear, about a foot deep at normal flow levels, churning its way around boulders, rippling over gravelbars, plunging into pools with bright and noisy vivacity. Schools of loach minnow, roundtail chub, spike dace and Gila mudsuckers—rare and endemic species—slip and slither past your ankles as you wade into the current. The water is too warm to support trout or other varieties of what are called game fish; the fish here live out their lives undisturbed by anything more than horses' hooves and the sneaker-shod feet of hikers. (**PLEASE DO NOT MOLEST THE FISH.**)

The Apaches who gave the name to this water and this canyon are not around anymore. Most of that particular band—unarmed old men, women, children—huddled in a cave near the mouth of Aravaipa Canyon, were exterminated in the 1880s by a death squad of American pioneers, aided by Mexican and Papagos, from the nearby city of Tucson. The reason for this vigilante action is obscure (suspicion of murder and cattle stealing) but the results were clear. No more Apaches in Aravaipa Canyon. During pauses in the gunfire, as the pioneers reloaded their rifles, the surviving Indians could have heard the sound of laughing waters. One hundred and twenty-five were killed, the remainder relocated in the White Mountain Reservation to the northeast. Since then those people have given us no back talk at all.

Trudging upstream and over rocky little beaches, we are no more troubled by ancient history than are the mudsuckers in the pools. We prefer to enjoy the scenery. The stone walls stand up on both sides, twelve hundred feet high in the heart of the canyon. The rock is of volcanic origin, rosy-colored andesites and buff, golden, consolidated tuff. Cleavages and fractures across the face of the walls form perfect stairways and sometimes sloping ramps, slick as sidewalks. On the beaches lie obsidian boulders streaked with veins of quartzite and pegmatite.

The walls bristle with spiky rock gardens of formidable desert vegetation. Most prominent is the giant saguaro cactus, growing five to fifty feet tall out of crevices in the stone you might think could barely lodge a flower. The barrel cactus, with its pink fish-hook thorns, thrives here on the sunny side; and clusters of hedgehog cactus, and prickly pear with names like clockface and cows-tongue, have wedged roots into the rock. Since most of the wall is vertical, parallel to gravity, these plants grow first outward then upward, forming right-angled bends near the base. It looks difficult but they do it. They like it here.

Also present are tangles of buckhorn, staghorn, chainfruit and teddybear cholla; the teddybear cholla is a cactus so thick with spines it glistens under the sun as if covered with fur. From more comfortable niches in the rock grow plants like the sotol, a thing with sawtooth leaves and a flower stalk ten feet tall. The agave, a type of lily, is even bigger, and its leaves are long, rigid, pointed like bayonets. Near the summit of the cliffs, where the moisture is insufficient to support cactus, we see gray-green streaks of lichen clinging to the stone like a mold.

The prospect at streamside is conventionally sylvan, restful to desert-weary eyes. Great cottonwoods and sycamores shade the creek's stony shores; when we're not wading in water we're wading through a crashing autumn debris of green-gold cottonwood and dusty-red sycamore leaves. Other trees flourish here—willow, salt cedar, alder, desert hackberry and a kind of wild walnut. Cracked with stones, the nuts yield a sweet but frugal meat. At the water's edge is a nearly continuous growth of peppery-flavored watercress. The stagnant pools are full of algae; and small pale frogs, treefrogs and leopard frogs leap from the bank at our approach and dive into the water; they swim for the deeps with kicking legs, quick breaststrokes.

We pass shadowy, intriguing side canyons with names like Painted Cave (ancient pictographs), Iceberg (where the sun seldom shines) and Virgus (named in honor of himself by an early settler in the area). At midday we enter a further side canyon, one called Horsecamp, and linger here for a lunch of bread, cheese and water. We contemplate what appears to be a bottomless pool.

The water in this pool has a dark clarity, like smoked glass, transparent but obscure. We see a waterlogged branch six feet down resting on a ledge but cannot see to the bottom. The water feels intensely cold to hand and foot; a few tadpoles have attached themselves to the stony rim of the pool just beneath the surface of the water. They are sluggish, barely animate. One water-bug, the kind called boatman, propels itself with limp oars down toward darkness when I extend my hand toward it.

Above the pool is a thirty-foot bluff of sheer, vesiculated, fine-grained, monolithic gray rock with a glossy chute carved down its face. Flash floods, pouring down that chute with driving force, must have drilled this basin in the rock below. The process would require a generous allowance of time—ten thousand, twenty thousand years—give or take a few thousand. Only a trickle of water from a ring of seeps enters the pool now, on this hot still blazing day in December. Feels like 80°F; a month from now it may be freezing; in June 110°. In the silence I hear the rasping chant of locusts—that universal lament for mortality and time—here in this canyon where winter seldom comes.

The black and bottomless pool gleams in the shining rock—a sinister paradox, to a fanciful mind. To any man of natural piety this pool, this place, this silence, would suggest reverence, even fear. But I'm an apostate Presbyterian from a long-ago Pennsylvania: I shuck my clothes, jump in and touch bottom only ten feet down. Bedrock bottom, as I'd expected, and if any Grendels dwell in this inky pool they're not inclined to reveal themselves today.

We return to the Aravaipa. Halfway back to camp and the canyon entrance we pause to inspect a sycamore that seems to be embracing a boulder. The trunk of the tree has grown around the rock. Feeling the tree for better understanding, I hear a clatter of loose stones, look up, and see six, seven, eight bighorn sheep perched on the rimrock a hundred feet above us. Three rams, five ewes. They are browsing at the local salad bar—brittlebush, desert holly, bursage and jojoba—aware of us but not alarmed. We watch them for a long time as they move casually along the rim and up a talus slope beyond, eating as they go, halting now and then to stare back at the humans staring up at them.

Once, years before, I had glimpsed a mountain lion in this canyon, following me through the twilight. It was the only mountain lion I had ever seen, so far, in the wild. I stopped, the big cat stopped, we peered at each other through the gloom. Mutual curiosity: I felt more wonder than fear. After a minute, or perhaps it was five minutes, I made a move to turn. The lion leaped up into the rocks and melted away.

We see no mountain lions this evening. Nor any of the local deer, either Sonoran whitetail or the desert mule deer, although the little heart-shaped tracks of the former are apparent in the sand. Javelina, or peccary, too, reside in this area; piglike animals with tusks, oversized heads and tapering bodies, they roam the slopes and gulches in family bands (like the Apaches), living on roots, tubers, the innards of barrel cactus, on grubs, insects and carrion. Omnivorous, like us, and equally playful, if not so dangerous. Any desert canyon with permanent water, like Aravaipa, will be as full of life as it is beautiful.

We stumble homeward over the stones and through the anklebone-chilling water. The winter day seems alarmingly short; it is.

We reach the mouth of the canyon and the old trail uphill to the roadhead in time to see the first stars come out. Barely in time. Nightfall is quick in this arid climate and the air feels already cold. But we have earned enough memories, stored enough mental-emotional images in our heads, from one brief day in Aravaipa Canyon, to enrich the urban days to come. As Thoreau found a universe in the woods around Concord, any person whose senses are alive can make a world of any natural place, however limited it might seem, on this subtle planet of ours.

"The world is big but it is comprehensible," says R. Buckminster Fuller. But it seems to me that the world is not nearly big enough and that any portion of its surface, left unpaved and alive, is infinitely rich in details and relationships, in wonder, beauty, mystery, comprehensible only in part. The very existence of existence is itself suggestive of the unknown—not a problem but a mystery.

We will never get to the end of it, never plumb the bottom of it, never know the whole of even so small and trivial and useless and precious a place as Aravaipa. Therein lies our redemption.

IV

Postlude

WHEN TOM MCGUANE wrote in response to galleys of *Abbey's Road*: "Abbey's the original fly in the ointment. Give him money and prizes. Don't let anything happen to him," McGuane didn't really expect Ed to win a major prize from the Academy of Arts and Letters, which he did in 1986. Nor did McGuane and other supporters such as Larry McMurtry, Irving Howe, Wallace Stegner and Wendell Berry expect him to refuse the prize, with these words: "It's too late. Besides, prizes are for little boys." Arrogance? Was Cactus Ed just too prickly for his own good? Abbey believed awards and prizes, "like the air, the sun, like the earth," as he had written, "belong to everyone—and no one."

By 1980 Ed Abbey had become a literary divine, like it or not. It was the essays rather than the fiction that had enshrined him, so reported Grace Lichtenstein in the *New York Times*. Yet it would be unwise to be dismissive of his fiction or to position Abbey's "fat masterpiece," as he called *The Fool's Progress*, alongside the broadly comic *The Monkey Wrench Gang*, its sequel, *Hayduke Lives!*, which was hastily completed only weeks before his death, or *Good News*, his attack on the military-industrial state—with especial relevance to an MX missile site once proposed for Arizona (after Ed died his friends buried him in an unmarked grave on military land in the desert where he could keep an eye on air force jets screaming overhead; another version places the burial closer to Tucson on land where all four giant cacti grow naturally).

Exuberant, overwrought, oversexed, his fictional alter ego was Abbey's favorite; readers who want to get closer to his fictive persona can do no better than *The Fool's Progress.* John Baker of *Publishers Weekly* put it this way in the book's first review: "An epic exploration of Abbey's passionate loves and hatreds set forth in a wild, picaresque novel that reads at times like a combination of Thomas Wolfe and Jack Kerouac. . . . Seizes hold of the imagination, as absurdly moving as anything you have read in years."

But the birth wasn't easy. Before the novel was put under contract—after I had read several partial drafts—I asked Ed to consider how it should be edited. He knew what I had in mind, but was unresponsive. My only hope was to bribe him. The following clause was added to the contract: "A bonus of Fifteen-thousand Dollars ($15,000.00) against earnings will be paid if the final manuscript conforms to Publisher's editorial request, as outlined in the letter of May 22, 1985 (copy attached)."

Ed wrote me on August 23, 1985: "Sacco and Vanzetti executed on this date in 1927, the year of my birth. Jack Macrae is next." The novel, then called *The Confessions of Henry Lightcap,* was well advanced, Ed reported. He had just returned from the high plateaus of Utah and Colorado "refreshed and ready to return to work. . . . What I hope is to get another 300 pages or so on your desk by Christmas—the final 300–400 page section by May Day 1986. Then we'll begin the hard work of editing, revising and—if necessary—reshaping the whole." Abbey had taken a year's leave from his teaching job at the University of Arizona in order to work full-time on the novel. "Now or never! Mt. Olympus or bust!" he added in a postscript.

When *The Fool's Progress* arrived in the summer of 1987 it was 901 pages. In November an academic acquaintance of Ed's named Donn Rawlings, Ph.D., cautioned Abbey in a detailed critique not to make major cuts: "Give your readers a chance to learn how to read this novel. Don't let those eastern editors get their scissors on this one—they may not understand where the frontiers of American fiction really are." Despite Dr. Rawlings's advice the published book came in at under five hundred pages; Ed wrote me a gracious note in appreciation of the editing, which I hasten to add was in large measure his, not mine. One worry of the academic reader was that other readers would make a too-simple equation between the persona of Abbey and the fictional Henry Lightcap. He wanted Ed to tell readers that "some fictive selection and distancing is going on," to help readers "to look at the redneck Henry more objectively, as a free-standing creation, however much he may overlap the known biography and views of the essay-persona Abbey."

Ed wouldn't have sent me Rawlings's letter unless he agreed with its overall assessment. His one demurrer was Rawlings's suggestion that the "Archie Bunkerisms" be cut. (Ed responded to this criticism by writing in the margins of the academic's letter: "I'm not going to toady to chickenshit liberalism anymore; fuck it. I've already been called fascist, racist, élitist as well as communist, terrorist, misanthrope, bleeding-heart, etc. so often it doesn't bother me anymore. To hell with all those petty, taboo-ridden dogmatic minds.") Abbey was heartened by the letter's attention to the novel's rhythm and its "big, baggy richness." As he was with *Publishers Weekly*'s Baker and *Time* magazine's John Skow, who said *The Fool's Progress* "is skilled enough to pull sympathetic readers into his own mood of regret, not just for long-gone youth and foolishness, but for small-town, big-sky Western life as it was before shopping malls and industrial parks ate the best of it." Other critics disagreed. Rawlings and many other astute Abbey fans admired the novel's pacing, the shifts of person and tense, the excesses and the "marvelous humor." Even though Rawlings made my job more difficult I knew he was right when he wrote Ed, "The complacent critical cranks will go on cranking without ever allowing themselves to see what is there."

When I sent Don Congdon Ed's bonus check for $15,000, author and agent said they had forgotten about the "edit clause." After Ed's death, Clarke Abbey, his widow, acting on one of his last requests, asked Avon Books, the paperback reprinter of *The Fool's Progress*, to restore one of my cuts, which they did. Thus the high folio of the hardback edition is 484 , the paperback 513.

Included as the final piece in this anthology is a copy of Ed's "Postlude," as he edited it.

J.M.

A Colorado River
Journal

B RIGHT-EYED AND BUSHY-TAILED, we assemble at Lee's
Ferry, Arizona, on the banks of the brand-new cold green Colorado
River. Green because of microplankton. Cold because this water is issuing
from the bottom of a dam twelve miles upstream—that Glen Canyon Dam.
The temperature of the water here is 47°F. (I place a six-pack of Michelob in
the water for quick chilling.) And brand-new? This river is not the Colorado
we knew and loved. The real Colorado died in 1964 when the engineers of the
Bureau of Reclamation closed the gates at Glen Canyon Dam, changing the
Colorado from a wild and free river into the domesticated, well-regulated
conveyor belt for baloney boats that it is today. Probably no man-made arti-
fact in all of human history has been hated so much, by so many, for so long as
Glen Canyon Dam.

There's John Blaustein himself, loading his little wooden boat, a dory
called *Peace River*. He looks anxious. Can't blame him. He has many problems on his mind—cameras, the passengers, the rapids.

His boss, one Martin Litton, who owns and manages Grand Canyon Dories, is hanging around nearby. Nine years ago I was the ranger here at Lee's
Ferry. I used to squeeze Martin's life jackets, testing them for safety.

From *The Hidden Canyon: A River Journey* (1977)

"Look here, Martin," I say, giving one of his flimsy boats a kick in the slats, "you don't really expect us to float down the river and run the rapids in a thing like this. What's it made of, plywood? One rap on a rock and it'll crack like an egg." Talking of old times and new problems, he ignores my facetious fears.

I turn my attention to the boatmen and to my fellow passengers on this suicidal journey down the river of no return.

There are seven dories, bright and gaily painted craft, each named after some natural feature destroyed or maimed by the works of man: the *Peace River* (dammed in Canada); *Tapestry Wall*, *Moqui Steps*, *Music Temple* (lovely places in Glen Canyon now sunk beneath the stagnant waters of Lake Powell National Sewage Lagoon); the *Vale of Rhondda* (a ravaged coalfield in Wales); and the *Columbia* and the *Celilo Falls* (drowned by the Dalles Dam on the Columbia River). The boats are about seventeen feet long from stem to transom, seven feet wide at the beam. Closed hatches at bow, midships and stern make them virtually unsinkable, we are told. An obvious lie. I don't believe it for a moment. "Virtually unsinkable." "Virtually" indeed. What sinister ambiguities are contained in that sly equivocation? Why not say "virtually floatable"? How about "virtually sunk," "virtually drowned" or "virtually dead"? Yeah, *virtually*; I can see through this transparent scheme. It's a conspiracy to get us down there among those awful wavelets in the Paria Riffle. Asphyxiation.

And the boatmen, they look even worse than the boats. Seven little wooden boats and seven furtive, grinning boatmen with fourteen hairy, crooked legs. They look like overgrown gnomes. I feel like Snow White, stumbling into the wrong fairy tale. A Disneyfied nightmare. Time to back out of this deal. I knew there was something queer about the whole setup, this supposedly free ride on the new Grand Canyon subway. Be wiser to hike it, maybe, stepping from boat to boat all the way to Lake Mead, our destination, 277 miles downstream.

I'm looking for a way to creep off unnoticed when my escape is interdicted by the approach of two of my twenty or so fellow passengers. Some fellows. One is a dark brown exotic wench in a tiger-skin bikini; she has the eyes and hair of Salome. The other is a tall slim trim sloop of a girl with flaxen hair, and elegant sateen thighs emerging from the skimpiest pair of Levi's cutoffs I have ever seen. I pause. I hesitate. I reconsider.

Following my bowsprit back to the beach, I join the crowd around Wally Rist, the head boatman, who is demonstrating—on the exotic Salome—the proper way to fasten a life jacket.

Minutes later, all too soon, without adequate spiritual preparation, we are launched forth on the mad and complex waters of the frigid river. John Blaustein, photographer and boatman, has cajoled me into his dory, making certain I do not escape at the last moment.

We pass through the Paria Riffle without upset, much to everyone's relief, as John strains at the oars. Nine years earlier, when I was ranger here, I took my girl friends for rides down these riffles, whacking the waves with a Park Service motorboat. How many propellers did I screw up that summer, pivoting off rocks and driving blindly into unobserved gravel bars? Three or four. (Too much beer, too little bikini.)

A nice little runoff comes in from the Paria River, staining the Colorado a healthy hue of brown. Anything, any color—Day-Glo purple, chartreuse, shocking pink—is better than the unnatural translucent green, like Gatorade, of our river as it comes strained through the penstocks of that Glen Canyon Dam.

We pass the little beach where, years before, I used to lie on the sand and watch my favorite birds: turkey vultures, shrikes, ruby-throated hummingbirds, rosy-bottomed skinnydippers. Above, on a windswept sunbaked stony bench under the mighty Vermilion Cliffs, is the new Park Service all-metal campground, packed with Winnebagos, house trailers, pickup-campers, trail bikes, jeeps, motorboats and the other paraphernalia necessary to a holiday in the wilds. Four miles downriver from Lee's Ferry we glide beneath the Navajo Bridge, 467 feet above, which spans the opening to Marble Gorge. As the canyon walls rise on either side of us, a new rock formation appears: the Coconino sandstone.

This is Marble Gorge, entrance to the Grand Canyon. Entering here over a century ago, Major John Wesley Powell wrote as follows in his diary:

> August 5, 1869—With some feeling of anxiety we enter a new canyon this morning. We have learned to observe closely the texture of the rock. In softer strata we have a quiet river, in harder we find rapids and falls. Below us are the limestones and hard sandstones which we found in Cataract Canyon. This bodes toil and danger.

Toil and danger. Don't care for the sound of those words. Danger is bad enough; toil is reprehensible. Hope these savage-looking boatmen know what they're doing. They certainly don't look like they know what they're doing. Of course I've been down here before. Used to drive the Park Service motorboat as far as Mile 8, Badger Creek Rapid, and twice went all the way down the canyon on a big motor-driven pontoon boat.

The Kaibab limestone formation rises on either side of us, forming walls that cut off most of the sky. We float through a monstrous defile a thousand feet deep; two thousand feet deep? How deep is the river? one of the passengers asks John. How high are the walls? How fast is the current? The traditional questions. He answers patiently. What's that big blue heronlike bird down there that flies like a pterodactyl? Heron.

John tells us that the Canyon is nearly all rock. How much can you say about rock? It's red here, gray there, it's hard, it's badly eroded, it's a mess. The geologists can't even make up their minds how the Canyon was formed. They once thought it was an entrenched meander, the ancient silt-bearing river grinding down into its bed as the plateau gradually rose beneath it. Now some think it's the result of two rivers, one capturing the other in the vicinity of the present Little Colorado. Old-time geologists spoke of a monster cataclysm. One thing is certain: the Grand Canyon is unique.

Now from up ahead comes the deep toneless vibration of the first major rapid, Badger Creek. The sound resembles that of an approaching freight train on a steel trestle. On the standard scale of 1 to 10 this rapid is rated 4–6. Of intermediate difficulty. Staring, we see the river come to an edge and apparently vanish. Curling waves leap, from time to time, above that edge. Wally Rist, in the leading boat, stands up for a good look, sits down, turns his boat and, facing forward, slides over the glassy rim of water. His boat disappears. He disappears. Two more boats follow. They disappear. Our turn.

"Buckle up," commands John.

We fasten our life jackets. John stands up in the center of the boat, taking his look. Pooled behind the wall of boulders that forms the rapid, the river slows, moving with sluggish ease toward the drop. The roar grows louder. I think of Pittsburgh, the old Forbes Field, seventh game of the 1961 World Series, bottom of the ninth, Yankees leading 8 to 7, two men out, one man on, and the roar that greeted Lou Mazerowski's pennant-winning homer.

Wake up. Daydreaming. John has seated himself, the bow of the dory is sliding down the oily tongue of the rapid, holes and boils and haystack waves exploding all around us. John makes a perfect run straight down the middle. One icy wave reaches up and slaps me in the chest, drenches my belly. *Cold!* The shock of it. But we are through, easy, riding the choppy tailwaves of the rapid. John catches the bottom of the eddy on the right and with a few deft strokes brings our boat to the beach at the mouth of Badger Creek. The other boats join us. Boatmen and passengers clamber ashore. Here we'll make camp for our first night on the river. True, we haven't gone far, but then, we didn't get started till noon.

Setting up camp for the night is a routine chore for the boatmen. All food supplies for the eighteen days, and personal belongings, are neatly packed into the watertight compartments below the decks of the boats. The large cans of food are packed first, their weight on the bottom of the boat adding stability for the rapids. Next go large waterproof containers with things like bread, eggs and flour, and army surplus rubber bags for clothing and sleeping gear. Cameras and small personal gear are carried in surplus ammunition cans.

Most of the passengers line up behind the boats to retrieve their rubber bags and immediately disperse up the beach to find a flat spot in the sand on which to set up their camps. There is an ample supply of semiprivate nooks and crannies among the tamarisk trees, so I see no reason to rush, and decide instead to have a cold beer.

One of the boatmen, the one they call Sharky, a fiercely bearded lad with burning blue eyes, is in charge of toilet facilities. In the old days passengers and crew simply dispersed to the bushes, women upstream, men downstream. Now that the Canyon is so popular, however, with some fifteen thousand souls per summer riding through, it has become necessary for sanitary and aesthetic reasons to make use of portable chemical toilets. Sharky is our porta-potty porter. He removes the unit from his boat and sets it up among the shady tamarisk far from the beach, in a spot with a pleasant view of the river and canyon walls. He is the kind who thinks of such things. Later, some of the passengers will wander around half the night hunting for it.

The boatmen set up the "stove"—a metal box, filled with dry driftwood and covered with a steel grate. The cooks begin at once preparing supper. Our cooks are two able and handsome young women named Jane and Kenly. Both are competent oarswomen as well, and can substitute for the boatmen if necessary.

Drinking water is taken right from the river, and chemically purified. If the water is extra muddy, lime and alum are added to settle it.

After dinner—pork chops, applesauce, salad, soup, peaches, coffee, tea, etc., the "etc." in my case being a mug of Ron Rico 151—we are subjected to a lecture by Head Boatman Wally. Now that they've taken our money and gotten us down here beyond reach of civilization, he talks about the realities of Grand Canyon life: how to use the portable unit (no simple matter); about cactus, scorpions, centipedes and "buzzworms" (rattlesnakes); about loose rocks and broken bones, quicksand, whirlpools and asphyxiation, the remoteness of medical aid. Wally instructs us on what to do if a boat tips over, as it sometimes does; tells us the hazards of diving into the river and swimming in the current.

We pay scant attention to all that rot and soon afterward Sharky digs out his recorder, his ukelele and his kazoo and announces a porta-potty porter's party. Bottles appear. Darkness settles in, decorum decays. Salome dances in the sand.

One more nip on the Ron Rico and two more songs and then I slink away. I unroll my sleeping bag, but the air is so warm I hardly need to crawl into it. By dawn I will. Two shooting stars trace lingering parabolas of blue fire across the sky. From below rises the sound of rowdy, unseemly music. Crickets chirp. The steady, rhythmic rumble of the river pouring over the rocks is somehow soothing. I soon drop off to sleep.

A COOL MORNING, overcast sky.

More birds for Renée's list: brown-headed cowbird, western tanager, black-necked stilts, violet-green swallows, black-throated swifts. The swifts like to skim close to the waves in the rapids, attracted, it would seem, by the turbulent air. According to Rich Turner, one of our boatmen, they sometimes hit the waves and drown.

River rising but not high enough. Boatmen nervous about running the serious rapids with insufficient water. Those rocks, those granite fangs foaming with froth in the charging stream. Bad dreams.

We push onto a river the color of bronze, shimmering like hammered metal under the desert sun. Through Unkar—made it! Then 75 Mile Rapid (4–7). Still alive. We pull ashore above Hance Rapid (7–8) for study and consultation.

Hance is always a problem for the dorymen, especially in low water. Just too many goddamned rocks sticking up, or even worse, half-hidden near the surface. No clear route through. A zigzag course. Huge waves, treacherous boils, churning holes that can eat a boat alive. A kind of slalom for oarsmen, with the penalty for a mistake a possible smashed boat. The big advantage of rubber boats is that they can usually be bounced off the well-polished boulders in the rapids without suffering damage. Usually. But rigid crafts like dories or kayaks may split, puncture, crack like an eggshell. Therefore their safe passage through a big rapid—through any rapid—requires more maneuvering on the part of the boatman. More skill? Let's play it safe and say . . . more *care*. A little more . . . *love*.

The boatmen stand on high points beside the rapid, study the obstacles, consult among themselves. We, the passengers, are herded downriver along the shore by Kenly and Jane, the cooks, and assembled below the rapid. The boatmen are going through this one without us. The boats will be lighter and will draw less water, making them more maneuverable. None of the passengers seem to object to this arrangement. Most of them are busy loading their cameras.

The boatmen run it without us, one by one, not easily but safely. We rejoin our boats. The river carries us swiftly into the Granite Gorge. Like a tunnel of love, there are no shores or beaches in here. The burnished and river-sculptured rocks rise sheer from the water's edge, cutting off all view of the higher cliffs, all of the outer and upper world but a winding column of blue sky. We glide along as in a gigantic millstream. As usual, Powell described the scene as well as anyone ever will:

> The gorge is black and narrow below, red and gray and flaring above,
> with crags and angular projections on the walls. . . . Down in these
> grand gloomy depths we glide, ever listening, ever watching.

Grand, we'd agree, but not really gloomy. *Glowing* is the word. The afternoon sun is hidden by the narrow walls but indirect light, reflected and refracted by the water, by the pink granitic sills and dikes in the polished cliffs, by the blue lenses of the atmosphere, streams upon us from many angles, all radiant. However, unlike Powell and his men, we are fresh, well fed, well supplied, secure in our bulging life jackets, confident in our dories, too ignorant (except the boatmen) for fear.

Two miles below Hance we crash through the well-named Sockdolager Rapid (5–7), and two and a half miles later into and through Grapevine Rapid (6–7), both so named by Major Powell. Litton's buoyant boats ride high on the waves but not high enough to escape the recoil of the descending 52° waters. Screams of delight, shock, astonishment ring through the canyon as we ride this undulating roller coaster. Unlike the sea, here on the river the water moves, the waves remain in place, waiting for us. Soaked and chilled, we bail out the boats and watch mysterious glenlike tributary canyons pass by on either side. Asbestos Canyon (remains of an old mine up there), Vishnu Creek, Lonetree Canyon, Clear Creek, Zoroaster Canyon, Cremation Creek (what happened there? no one in our party knows) and others. In the early afternoon we pull all seven boats ashore at Phantom Ranch.

Phantom Ranch, combination ranger station and tourist hostel, is the only outpost of civilization within the Canyon. From here broad and well-maintained foot and mule trails lead to both the North and South Rims. Also a telephone line. And a waterline, built at taxpayers' expense, for the motels on the South Rim. There is even a clearing for helicopters. The two foot-bridges above the river are the only Colorado River crossings from Navajo Bridge to Hoover Dam.

Here we pause for an hour. Some of the passengers are departing us at this point, having contracted for only the first part of the voyage. Their places are taken by others who have hiked the trail down from South Rim. Loaded and ready. One by one the boats shove off, deeper into the inner gorge.

This time my wife and I sit in the bow of the leading dory. Our oarsman is young Rich Turner—musician, philosopher, ornithologist, schoolteacher, rock climber, high diver, veteran oarsman, one of Litton's most experienced hands. Two other passengers are on board: Jane the cook and a newcomer, fifteen-year-old Jenny, a girl from Henderson, Kentucky. Active, athletic Jenny has never been on a river trip of any kind before. As we drift down the river, Rich plying the oars at a leisurely pace, she asks us if we don't get bored sometimes with this effortless mode of travel. Sure we do, but none of us will admit it. We tell her about the birds and the interesting geological formations; the pleasant afternoons in the cool shade, with the sun setting on the high canyon walls; the contrast of the quiet beauty of the side canyons and grottoes with the violent crashing roar of the rapids at the mouth of each side canyon.

Rich suggests that we buckle life jackets. Horn Creek Rapid (7–9) coming up, he reminds us. He says something about The Great Wave. For Jenny's benefit he reviews routine upset procedures: take deep breath when entering rapids; hang on; if boat turns over, get out from under and grab lifeline strung along gunwales; stay on upstream side of boat to avoid being trapped between boat and a hard place; climb up onto bottom of boat as soon as possible; grasp flip line and assist boatman in righting boat; bail out water; relax and enjoy the view.

"What was that about a great wave?" Renée asks.

"I didn't say 'a' great wave," says Rich. "I said '*The* Great Wave.'"

More boatman's hype—short for hyperbole? Dorymen love to melodramatize the peril of the rapids. Makes their idyllic jobs seem important, gives the gullible passenger the illusion that he's getting his money's worth.

Comes the now familiar growing roar of uproarious waters. Not far ahead the river plays its usual conjuring trick, seeming to pour over the edge of the known world and disappear down into some kind of grumbling abyss. Above the watery rim I can see hints of a rainbow in the mist, backlit by the westering sun. We've seen it before.

What I've forgotten is that Horn, unlike the longer rapids above and below, makes its descent abruptly, in one dive, through a constricted channel where the river is squeezed into sudden acceleration. Rich stands up for a last look but sits down quickly. The boat slides down the glassy tongue of the current. Into a yawning mouth. I take a deep breath—involuntarily. "Hang on!" Rich shouts.

The dory plunges down into the watery hole, then up the slope of the standing wave. Water topples upon us, filling the boat in an instant. The force of the river carries us through the first wave and into a second, deeper hole. "One more!" Rich yells, his oars stroking empty air. We dive into a second wave, taller than the first; it hangs there above my head, a rippling, translucent, liquid wall. Our sluggish boat plows through it.

"And one more!" cries Rich. One more indeed. The dory drops into the deepest hole yet. I think I can almost see bedrock bottom. The third wave towers above us. Far above. The Great Wave. Heavily our water-loaded boat, askew, climbs up its face. Never makes it. As the wave hits us from the portside our dory turns over with the grave, solemn, inevitable certainty of disaster. No one says a word as we go under.

Below the surface all is silent and dark. Part of the current, I do not even feel a sense of motion. But before there is really time to think or feel much about anything, the life jacket brings me to the top. The dory, upside down, is only a stroke away. I grab the lifeline. Renée is hanging on beside me. And Rich and Jenny near the stern, Jane on the other side. The wrong side.

The river carries us swiftly toward the sheer canyon wall below the rapid, on the left. Jane still seems a bit dazed like the rest of us, unaware of her danger. Rich pulls himself onto the flat bottom of the boat and drags her up with him. The boat crunches into the rock. Sound of splintering plywood. The weight of the current forces down the upstream side of the boat, pushing me and Renée underwater again. Down in the darkness I let go of the boat's lifeline and kick away.

After what seems an unnecessarily long time I rise to the surface, gasping for air. A wave splashes in my face. Good God I'm drowning, I think, choking on a windpipe full of muddy water. Instinctively I swim toward shore and find myself caught in a big eddy, pulled in a circle by the swirling current. Where's Renée? I see the boat go sailing past, upside down, three people crawling on it, none of them my wife. The eddy carries me close to the wall and I make a futile effort to find a handhold on the glossy, polished stone. I give up and let the eddy carry me down again, toward a tumble of broken rock fallen from the wall. I succeed in getting onto the rocks and stand up, free of the hungry river at last. Renée? I hear her calling me. Ah, there she is, below me on an adjoining shelf of rock. Reunited, we stand on our island in the stream and watch Rich, Jane, Jenny and the capsized dory float away, getting smaller and smaller. We've forgotten for the moment that there are six other dories still up the river. We are relaxing into a foolish despair, feeling abandoned, when good old John Blaustein—none other!—comes charging through The Great Wave, spots us, rows close enough for rescue. With six soaked passengers aboard, he rows hard after Rich and catches him. Rich is having trouble righting his boat. Not enough weight. John and I assist, pulling on the flip lines, and the boat comes over right side up again. Transfer of bodies, the restoration of our original order.

Rich rows, Renée and Jane and I bail. We open the hatches—not quite watertight after all—and bail them out too. Resting at last, we finally become aware of how chilled we are, through and through. Nobody timed it but we must have been immersed in that frigid water for a considerable spell. Even the sun seems slow in bringing warmth back to our bones.

That evening in camp, as Rich patches up his injured dory with glue and yards of duct tape, it dawns on me why the boatmen sometimes refer to the major rapids as Christian Falls. Why? Because they make a believer out of you.

IN THE MORNING the river is low. John looks grim. I check the rock. High and dry, and the river dropping slowly.

Breakfast is finished. We load the dories. Some of the boatmen are concerned that their boats are too light, since most of the food is gone. They place large rocks in the bottom of the hatches for ballast. The extra weight down low may help at Mile 179.

August 13, 1869—What falls there are, we know not; what rocks beset the channel, we know not; what walls rise over the river, we know not. . . . The men talk as cheerfully as ever; jests are bandied about freely this morning; but to me the cheer is somber and the jests are ghastly.

Write on, good Major Powell. How prescient you were. I know exactly how you felt. I can read your every emotion on the face of John Blaustein.

We push off. Sunlight sparkles on the laughing wavelets of the master stream. Little birds twitter in the tamarisk.

It looks like a good day to die. All days are good but this one looks better than most.

As Sharky pulls us into the current, lashing about lustily with the oars, I glance back at the beach we are now departing. Only once. A black shadow lies across the unwet rugosities of oracle rock.

The highest sheer walls in the Canyon rear above our heads. Two thousand feet straight up. With terraces and further higher walls beyond. Toroweap Overlook rises at Mile 176, three thousand feet above the river. The suicide's nemesis. We float beneath it.

When I worked at Grand Canyon, a young English major from Yale, unlucky in love, drove his car all the way from New Haven, Connecticut, to jump from Toroweap Overlook. Would have more class, he thought, than the banal routine off Golden Gate Bridge. Arriving here, he took one good look down into our awful chasm ("Gaze not too long into the abyss/Lest the abyss gaze into thee"—F. Nietzsche), walked back to his car (1970 Chevrolet Impala Supersport), attached a vacuum cleaner hose to the tailpipe, ran the other end of the hose into the car, started the motor and gassed himself to death. While gassing he wrote a note explaining his procedure; also a final poem on life, death and the bitterness of youth that all the critics agreed was not very good. It begins:

> I came to Toroweap today
> To look, to laugh, to leap away
> From all these cares of mortal clay;
> I looked—and found a better way. . . .

You see the fatal flaws. Inept alliteration. Heavy-handed rhyme scheme. Iambic tetrameter—wrong foot for elegies. ("Foot like a hand.") Cliché filter not functioning. Sorry lad, you'll have to do better than that. *C minus*.

The river slides seaward in its stony groove. Will never make it. Mohave Desert–type vegetation now—mesquite, ocotillo, catclaw acacia, barrel cactus, clock-face and cow's-tongue prickly pear adore as best they can the talus slopes below the cliffs. Names, names, the naming of the names. What's this? What's that? they ask me, pointing to this bush, that bush. I give my standard reply: What it *is*, ma'am, no one knows; but men call it—creosote bush. *Larrea tridentata*. What's in a name?

We stop for lunch at Mile 177, not far above *that riffle,* from which point we can see the first remnants of the lava flows.

August 25, 1869—What a conflict of water and fire there must have been here! Just imagine a river of molten rock running down into a river of melted snow. What a seething and boiling of the waters; what clouds of steam rolled into the heavens!

Looking solemn, head boatman Rist gives his final harangue of the trip. "Listen!" he begins.

We listen. Don't hear a damn thing. Sigh of the river maybe, swooning round the next bend. Cicada keening in the dry grass. Faint scream of the sun, ninety-three million miles above. Nothing significant.

"You don't hear it but it's there," he says. "Lava Falls (ten plus)." Mile 179. "It's always there. Every time we come down this river, there it is. Drops thirty-seven feet in two hundred yards. The greatest rapid in North America. So we're gonna need help from you people. Anybody who's hoping to see a disaster, please stay out of sight. All passengers will walk around this one except volunteers. Yes, we'll need—"

Hands are rising.

"Not yet," Wally says. "We want everybody to see it first. Anybody who thinks he or she wants to ride through Lava has to get down there and walk below it and look up through the waves. Then you decide if you really want to do it. We want people who can handle the oars, who can help right the boat if it flips and who can climb around on wet boulders if necessary. Nobody has to do it but I'll tell you this much: when you're out there in the middle of Lava, it's nice to hear another heart beating besides your own. *But nobody has to do it.* Nobody has to prove anything—to himself or us. OK? From everybody else, we ask maximum moral support, as before, only more so. After Lava we'll have a party. Any questions?"

Commander Wally's briefing. Tapestry Wally. You'd think we were in a U-boat about to enter a combat zone. Walter Rist—there is something Teutonic about that chap. The straight blond hair. The Nordic nostrils. The sardonic grin. That iron cross, like an amulet, pinned to his life jacket. Yeah, I see through your crude ruse. Nobody has to do it, eh? Not even looking at me he says that. Pretending to talk to everybody but me. Clever, very clever. But you've tipped your hand, Rist. I can read you like the writing on the wall, Wally. No thanks. I glance furtively up and down the river, trapped but not yet panicked. Where is that place? That Separation Canyon? That EXIT from this Hall of Horrors?

Salami on rye, potato salad, peanut butter and Ry-Krisp for lunch. Not half bad. It's all bad. The condemned man revealed no emotion as he ate his lunch. Ironic laughter in the background. No place to hide. All boats shove off, loaded, onto the shining Colorado. Once more into your britches, friends.

At Mile 178 a great black basaltic rock appears, standing silent in the middle of the river. Vulcan's Anvil, they call it. It looks like a forty-foot tombstone. Staring at it, we hear this weird whimpering noise from midships. Sharky singing his Martian funeral song. Wordless, it rises and falls in hemidemisemitones of unearthly misery. The dirge of the damned.

A muttering sound ahead, beyond the next bend. Wordless voices grumbling in subterranean echo chambers. All boats put ashore on the right bank. Wally leads us, passengers and crew, up a path through the tamarisk jungle and onto a slide of volcanic boulders big as bungalows, high above the river. Lava Falls bellows in the sunlight. He stops. We stop. He waves us on. "Volunteers will assemble here," he shouts, above the tumult from below. "*After* you've looked it over."

We go on, all but the boatmen, who remain clustered around Wally, commencing their customary hopeless confabulations. The sad smiles, the weary head-shakings. Same old hype. I smile too, slinking away.

Chuckling, I join the sensible passengers, who gather in a safe shady place near the foot of the uproar. Breathing easily now, I watch these people ready their cameras. Comfortable, we consider the dancing falls, the caldron of colliding superwaves, the lava rocks like iron-blue bicuspids protruding from the foam—here, there, most everywhere, a fiendish distribution of dory-rending fangs. I study the channel on the far left: nothing but teeth. The "slot" in the middle: gone. Hah, I think, they're going to have to run it on the right. Right up against this basalt boxcar I'm relaxing on. Well, serves them right for making such a big deal out of what's advertised as a tax-deductible business trip.

Time passes. Can't see the boatmen from here. I look back up at the "volunteers'" assembly point. Sure enough, a few suckers have showed up, seven or eight of them. And that tall girl in the big hat—my wife? It is my wife. Good Lord, what's she doing there? You can't take my wife. My suture to the future. Who's going to care for me in my dotage, succor my senility? Impossible. They wouldn't dare.

Not all the boatmen are in hiding. John Blaustein crouches on a rock nearby, staring up at the rapids, his battery of cameras dangling from his neck. Like me, he's doing what we're supposed to do: *observe.*

A red, white and yellow dory appears on the tongue upstream. The Tapestry Wall. There's Captain Wally standing on his seat, one hand shielding his eyes. He looks pretty, all right, I'll grant you that, heroic as hell. Two passengers with him, sunk deep in their seats, white knuckles clenched on the gunwales. Wally lowers himself into the cockpit, takes a firm grip on the oars. Here they come. They disappear. They emerge, streaming with water. Dive and disappear again. Dark forms barely visible through the foam. The boat rears up into sunlight. Wally has crabbed an oar, lost an oarlock. He's in trouble. He's struggling with something. They vanish again, under the waves, to reappear not twenty feet from where I sit, bearing hard upon this immovable barrier. The dory yaws to port, Wally is standing up, he's only got one oar, looks like he's trying to climb right out of the boat onto my rock. I'm about to offer a futile hand when I realize he's climbing the high side, preventing the boat from capsizing. Cushioned by a roil of water, the boat and its three occupants rush past me, only inches from the iron rock. Who's that lady in the stern, smiling bravely, waving one little brown paw at me? That's no lady, that's my life! Renée. The violent current bears them away, out of sight.

Jesus . . .

One made it. Six more to go. We have to sit and watch this? Too late now, here comes Dane Mensik at the control console of the *Vale of Rhondda*. A passenger in the bow. He makes a perfect run, bow first through the holes, over the big waves, and clears Death Rock by a safe and sane three feet. And after him Mike "Miltie" Davis in the *Music Temple*. Likewise, a perfect run.

Three safely past, four to go. Now come in quick succession Sharky Cornell ("You saw it first in the *Columbia*, folks"), Mike "Scorpion" Markovich in the big *Moqui Steps* (his good right hand no longer numb) and Rich Turner in the patched-up *Celilo Falls*. With a light payload of ballast—one passenger each—they make it right side up, one way or the other way, through the sound and the fury of Mile 179.

Thank God . . .

Only one to go. Poor old John Blaustein in the (ill-named) *Peace River*. I glance up at the volunteers' assembly point. The slave block. One little girl stands there clutching her life jacket, hopefully waiting. No, it can't be. Yes it is, it's Jenny, the kid who changed our luck at Horn Creek. The innocent Jonah. Now I really feel sorry for John. Not only are the scales of probability weighing against him—for if six made it through, the seventh is doomed for certain—but he and he alone has to ride with that sweet little jinx we picked up at Phantom Ranch. Tough luck, John. Kismet, you know. Bad karma. (But better him than me.)

Where is John by the way?

I feel a firm hand on my shoulder. "Let's go," he says.

Well, of course I knew it would turn out like this all along. I never had a chance.

We trudge up the rocks, pick up Jenny, trudge through the jungle and down to the lonely boat, hyperventilating all the way. Buckle up. John gives stern instructions, which I don't hear. Push off. Me and little Jenny in the bow. The sun glares at us over the oily water, blazing in our eyes. John points the boat the wrong way, right down the tongue into the heart of the madness. The moment of total commitment. This is absurd. We dive head first into the absurdity . . .

Twenty seconds and it's all over. Twenty seconds of total truth and then we're cruising through the tail of the rapid, busy with the bailers, joining the procession of dories before us. Nothing to it. Like I always say, running the big rapids is like sex: half the fun is in the anticipation. Two-thirds of the thrill is in the approach. The remainder is only ecstasy—or darkness.

ON THE BEACH. The moon is shining bright. The boatmen, armed with heavy grog, are having a private "debriefing" session downstream some- where. Lewd silhouettes prance before our fire. Salome dances. The Abbeys dance. Inhibitions fall like dandruff. Our four French passengers are finally speaking with our two Austrian passengers. (Dieter and his daughter—ah, there's a story.) The others—a twenty-three-year-old schoolteacher; a news- paper publisher, his wife and three kids; a stockbroker; a retired lawyer; a dental hygienist; a physician—go over the exciting events of the day. No one seems to be able to agree on what happened exactly during those twenty sec- onds in Lava Falls. No matter; we made it alive. That's what counts.

Dinner is served, vaguely. The seven merry boatmen stagger up from the lower beach, smiling and content. The sense of exhilaration and victory lasts all through the night, waning only with the sunrise.

From Good News

IT MAY HAVE BEEN, *as the man on the Tower would say, a failure of courage. Or to use his preferred cliché, a failure of nerve. It may never have happened at all. There was indeed, in those fading years of the doomed century, a sense of overwhelming illusion in the minds of men and women. The cities became unreal. Not so much unbearable as unreal. To the millions crowded within them—for it seemed they could not live elsewhere, in a landscape owned by corporations and dominated by gigantic machines—the ever-growing cities assumed the shape of nightmare. Not a nightmare of horror but a nightmare of dreariness, a routine and customary tedium. Reality became personal, individual, limited to the walls of a room in the center of an enormous hive. The blue eye that glowed from the center of the wall opened only into deeper realms of loneliness. Friends clung together, then were torn apart. Men and women feared one another and searched for safety in isolation. Families withered, scattered across a continent, attached by the thinnest strands of brief, tenuous, one-dimensional and unreliable communication. To leave the illusory safety of the room was only to find oneself in a corridor without windows leading out into the corridor of the streets, where the walls were of glass and steel, the floor of concrete and asphalt, and the ceiling a dense umber haze through which a pale sun, ever more feeble, shone rays without warmth and little light. At night the layer of smoke and fog and industrial gases cut off all view of the stars, reflecting the vast illuminations of the cities, which extended for hundreds of miles in all directions. The streets were jammed with clamorous machines, crowded with endless hordes of silent humans, most of them wearing air-filtering masks; one saw only the eyes of others, and all eyes were wary, alert with fear or blank, withdrawn into the inner space of abstraction. A terrible restlessness infected every movement, every gesture.*

The disintegration was personal and, at the same time, international. The fear that paralyzed the emotions of men and women in their lonely rooms also poisoned the reaction of nations to one another. As each solitary human sought to preserve his own integrity, so each nation strove to ensure its survival at the expense of all others. The fragile webs of a planetary economy frayed apart in an ever-intensifying struggle for the resources to support a worldwide industrial system. One breakdown in a small Mideastern nation led to massive dislocations, anger and panic in great nations thousands of miles away. War became continuous, limited in scale but never ceasing, breaking out in a new locality as it subsided into chaos and civil war in another. Nuclear weapons were used, as they had been used once before by the first nation to develop them, not on the grand and universal scale envisioned by the most fearful, but in local and regional strife, a practical application of means always available, for ends deemed reasonable by military and diplomatic minds. The unthinkable had always been thinkable. In the effort to compensate for losses abroad, each industrial nation attempted to supply its needs by exploiting to the limit—and then beyond—its own resources of land and forest, water and metals and minerals. The fuel needs of the machine were considered paramount, but the effort to keep the machine operating led to destruction of basic resources needed for the production of food. Agriculture itself had long before been mechanized, industrialized, assimilated into the corporate empire, the farmland submerged beneath the growing cities or mined and stripped to produce the power needed to keep the cities functioning, the machines in motion, agribusiness alive. The immediate result, as certain cities vanished, was the economic strangulation of others. Religious fanaticism joined with nationalism and secular ideologies to destroy and sometimes to self-destroy the sources of power on which the overindustrialized nations depended. Invisible poisons spread through the atmosphere, borne by the winds from the guilty to the innocent. But all were innocent, all were guilty.

The majority of nations had lost the ability to be self-sufficient, even to satisfy the elementary needs of their people for food. Now every nation was losing this ability. The cities could not feed themselves; they were largely abandoned as urban millions spread into the countryside in search of food. Those who suffered least were those accustomed to poverty and hunger; those who suffered most were the inhabitants of the rich nations. And in the richest nation of them all the harshest changes came to the few but precarious, monstrous cities that had once appeared, briefly, in that nation's arid West; in those desert lands where, as the cautious had foreseen, "cities were not meant to be." Most of the people had disappeared, fleeing to the greener regions from which, as everyone knew, their packaged food came. But even in the most desolate and devastated of the remote cities a few men and women survived, clinging to the ruins, trying to rebuild the simple farming and pastoral economy that had been destroyed by the triumph of the city, trying to re-create a small society of friends in a community of mutual aid and shared ownership of land. For a few years they were left in peace, forgotten by a world that seemed, for all they could tell, to have forgotten itself—and then the gates of the citadel were opened and certain men came forth with aspirations far more grand than those of farmers and herdsmen and hunters. The oldest civil war of all, that between the city and the country, was resumed.

TWO MEN SIT on a rock halfway up the slope of a desert mountain. Sundown: The air is still, caught in the pause between the heat of day, the cool of evening. Doves call in twilight, testing the tentative peace. Downslope from the men a rattlesnake slides from its dark den, scales hissing over stone; the yellow eyes glow with hunger—death in its glance.

The men are roasting the remains of a small mammal—too small for goat, too large for rabbit—on a bed of mesquite coals. Their horses stumble nearby, hobbled, browsing on thorny acacia, prickly pear, bursage. The feed is scanty here and the horses look ganted and weary; like the men they have come a long way.

One man pokes at the fire with a stick and turns the meat over. "How do you want it, boss?"

The other man, staring at something far in the west, does not immediately reply. His gaze is fixed on the fires of a burning city, where towers of dark glass stand in smoke and dust against the yellow sky of sunset. "What's that?" he says. "What'd you say?"

Patiently the first man says, "Rare, medium or well done?"

"What was it?"

"Part Airedale, maybe. Part coyote. Maybe a few other things."

"Oh God, Sam, I don't care. Any way you like it."

The one addressed as Sam shrugs his bare shoulders and draws a big knife from his belt. "I'll have mine rare, boss. This here warrior is hungry." He lifts the roast dog from the embers with the point of the knife, lays it on the rock, slices off a thin steak, puts the rest back on the fire. Lifting the meat to his jaws he looks again at his companion. "You got to eat, boss. Keep up your strength. You're going to need it."

From nearby comes the clash of steel on stone. The second man says, "Those horses need it. Look at them poor devils."

"I know, boss. We'll take them down in the canyon after dark. Safer then." Sam chews on his supper, grunting with pleasure. He is a short, heavy, shirtless fellow; his brown skin, smooth and nearly hairless, shines with an oily gleam; the hair on his head is blue-black, rich and coarse, bound in a club at the nape of the neck. Neither the body nor his face—a round, full, saddle-colored face, wily, wise, humorous—offers much clue to his age. He could be thirty, he could be fifty-five. He could be a shaman, a wizard, a witch doctor, altering his age from time to time to suit the circumstances.

The second man is hard to see, hard to make out. In the twilight of evening he might be a ghost. But he is clearly old, well advanced in his mortality—the sunburned beak of nose projects above a narrow, pointed, cadaverous jaw that bristles, like cactus, with stiff frosty stubble. Under the shadow of his broad-brimmed hat the eyes, set deep and wide in cavernous sockets, look out on the world with asymmetric intensity: one eye clear, bright, lifeless, the other old and dark and tired but alive, all the same, with a melancholy passion. The left eye is glass but the other—his shooting eye—is living plasm, wired to the circuits of the mind and soul.

"Eat, boss." Sam proffers at knifepoint a chunk of burned flesh. "This dog is good dog. This dog died for our sins. If we do not eat him his death becomes meaningless."

"Ain't really hungry, Sam."

"You think too much, boss. Thinking is good but you must not think too much. You are very thin—turn sideways I can hardly see you. Look at me."

"No." The old man stares at the sunset, the burning city, the phantoms of memory. "And you don't need to call me 'boss' anymore."

"What shall I call you?"

"You know my name. We're partners now. You come as far as you had to."

"Look at me."

"No."

"Look at me, Jack Burns. Look at my hands."

"Oh Christ . . ." Reluctantly the old man turns toward the Indian. "No more of your goddamn tricks, Sam. I ain't in the mood."

"Watch. See this knife?" Sam waves the greasy, glittering blade back and forth, slowly, with the weaving motion of a snake at bay. "Now watch closely, boss." The blade glitters, flashes; there is a hissing noise, a sudden rasping vibration, and where the knife had been, a rattlesnake appears, its body draped over Sam's shoulder, tail a whirring blur, the spade-shaped head gliding forward over Sam's half-open right hand, toward Burns.

The old man lurches to his feet. "Goddamnit Sam, don't *do* that. Jesus *Christ . . .*"

"Don't be afraid." Sam strokes the snake with his left hand, murmurs a few words in a Tewa dialect. The buzzing stops, the serpent peers at Burns with half-lidded eyes, black tongue out and sensing the air. "This is our friend, boss. Someday this snake will save our lives. Touch him."

"What?"

"Touch him. Stroke his head."

"Come on, Sam. I know a rattlesnake when I see one. I know I'm crazy but I ain't that crazy."

"Are you sure?" Smiling, Sam speaks in Tewa to the snake. Then to Burns: "Hold your hand toward him, flat up."

"He won't strike?"

"He will not strike."

Fascinated, Burns puts his left hand slowly forward. "You sure, Sam?" The good eye on the snake, the other eye on nothing. "You know what you're a-doin'?"

"Don't be afraid. This is our friend."

Smiling a little in spite of himself, mesmerized, the old man pushes his hand slowly, hesitantly forward, to within three inches, two inches, one inch of the dark and heavy head. The black tongue flicks across his open palm. He sees and feels the head come to rest there. Gently he closes his hand about it; he is holding the leatherbound haft of Sam's big knife, the blade still in Sam's fingers. "No. No. Damn it, Sam . . ."

The Indian smiles. "Take it, boss. Cut the meat."

Burns sighs, relaxing, and sits down once more, cautiously, on the rock beside his companion. "Sam, you got to stop doing this. You're gonna give me a heart attack yet." He stares at the knife in his hand. Firelight shines on the glossy steel.

"You have a strong heart, boss. No ordinary rattlesnake will ever stop your heart."

"That was no goddamn ordinary rattlesnake."

"What was it then?"

Burns stares at the solid and substantial weapon in his hand, seeing, feeling, knowing its dogmatic reality. "I don't know. Do you know?"

"I was born into the Sun clan." Sam watches the fire, holding out his strong, open hands, spreading the clever fingers. "I was initiated into the One Horn Society when I was twelve. I learned many secret things."

"Where was that?"

"Down in the kiva. Many secret things. For ten years, before I went away . . ." He pauses. "Before I went away I was leader of the flute ceremony. The shaman taught me himself. Before he died. And then . . ."

A coyote begins to bark, far off, out in the desert. Answered at once by a second, in a different quarter. And a third. The barking passes, by slow degrees of modulation, into a quavering howl. The horses stop and lift their heavy heads to stare, through the dark, at something men cannot see.

"Well," says the old man, still studying Sam's knife, "then what?"

"Eat your supper."

Burns leans forward with the knife, picks up the meat. "You can tell me, Sam. What the hell, we're partners." He carves a hunk off the blackened roast of dog. "How'd you do it?"

"Holy secret, boss. You tell me something."

"Call me 'Jack,' damnit."

"You tell me something, Jack."

"Yeah?"

The Indian points toward the smoldering city, the scatter of fires and lights spread across ten miles of the horizon. "How do you think we're going to find him? In that dying mess? All those frightened people? You don't even know what he looks like now."

"I know his name." Burns chews slowly and grudgingly, with little appetite, on the unsalted meat. "I'll know him when I see him."

"You think so? You last saw him twenty years ago. How old was he then?"

"Rrrmmm . . ." The lean jaws make a clicking sound as the old man eats; he readjusts his loose bridgework. "How old was he? Hah . . ." Staring at the embers of the fire, Burns smiles. He draws an ancient wallet from his hip pocket, opens to a picture under cracked celluloid. Smiling, he contemplates the faded image of a solemn, towheaded, handsome boy of ten or twelve. "Good-lookin' devil . . . just like his daddy. We'll know him when we see him, Sam. No doubt about that."

"How do you know he's even there? In the city?"

Smile fading, the old man puts away the picture. "You touch on a tender spot, partner. We don't know. All I know is he was there four years ago when I got that last letter. The last letter anybody got, I reckon. If he ain't there anymore then I don't know where to look. We'll ride on to California. I'll find the little bastard somewheres."

"How do you know California is still there? How do you know he'll know you? Or want to?"

"All right, Sam . . ." Burns frowns at his big, powerful, interlocked hands. "You sure know where the fear is, all right. Don't you, you son-of-a-bitch. I don't know."

"Who wrote that last letter?"

The old man does not answer.

"Did the boy ever write to you himself?"

Burns makes no answer. He drops the half-burned, half-raw slab of meat back on the coals. Places a wad of tobacco in his cheek. After further pause, he says, "We better find some feed for them horses."

Sam places a hand on the old man's forearm. Then on his shoulder. "Jack," he says, "I'm not trying to be cruel. Too much hope—false hope—is cruel. Hope is the cruelest thing that Greek lady let out of the box."

"Sam, I know that. But I don't like to think about it."

The twilight condenses around them, thickening to night. A few stars appear, forming incomplete constellations—Scorpio, Cassiopeia, the Bear. The new moon, a sickle of silver, hangs low in the west. The lights of the distant city seem as dim as the dying coals of their campfire. Small bats dart through the gloaming.

"And that city," the Indian says. "That city . . . some strange things going on there."

"Always was. We'll find the boy and get the hell out."

"No politics."

"Politics?" The old man rises, resets the heavy gunbelt on his hip, tugs down his hat brim. "What do we know about politics? We're tourists. We don't even talk the same language. What do we care about politics, us igno-rant aborigines?" He spits on the fire. "You coming or you gonna sit here all night?"

Sam sheaths his knife, wraps the remainder of the roast dog in a greasy rag and gets up. He stuffs the bundle into a saddlebag, hoists his saddle to his shoulder and grins at Burns. "Grab your saddle."

"Who's the boss around here? Ain't we coming back?"

"Somebody might have seen the fire."

The old man grunts in assent. He kicks dirt over the hot ashes, covering them, and follows the Indian down through the brush to the horses, which make little effort to get away. Giant saguaro cactus stand from the rocky slope nearby, lifting thorny arms, like supplicant humans, toward the stars. Sam the shaman bridles a docile pinto; Jack Burns saddles his mare, a gray-skinned, rack-ribbed, broom-tailed, towering specter of a horse seventeen hands high. Despite hunger and fatigue and long association the mare tosses her head high when he slips the bridle on; her big feet clang like frying pans as she sashays aside. "Rosie," he growls, hanging on to her neck, "Rosie, Rosie, you brainless hammerhead, stand still or I'll chew your goddamn ear off. . . ."

They ride down through starlight toward the shadowy cleft of a canyon, down to where the sycamores grow, and the hackberry, and the elephantine cottonwood—in the desert, the tree of life. A sound of spring-green trembling leaves. The smell of still water. The horses snort with anxious anticipation.

"You're so smart, Sam, why don't you conjure up a bale of alfalfa and a bucket of grain for these poor beasts?"

"What do you think I am, a witch doctor? A wizard? A miracle worker? I'm a magician, boss, a professional; I don't deal in the supernatural. Horses are wiser than you humans—they believe in what they can smell. Nothing else."

"Yeah? Is that so?" Burns ponders on this for a while. "Well, let me tell you something, Sam. I know bullshit when I smell it."

"A man knows what he can know."

"Yeah? God, there's nothing worse than a smart Indian. And that reminds me of something else. If you're really a goddamn Indian why the hell don't you talk like a goddamn Indian?"

"You're a bigot, white man."

"I'm no bigot, I hate *everybody*. Talk like an Indian."

"How? I don't know how. I'm a spoiled Indian. Harvard ruined me."

Burns ruminates, chewing his cud. "*My* daddy always said the only good Indian is a dead Indian."

"Mine would've said the only good Indian is a bad Indian. But he was a troublemaker. He was shot dead at Pine Ridge, South Dakota. By good Indians. His last words were, and I quote, 'Let me go, my friends, you have hurt me enough.' "

"Sam, you don't play fair. I'll say no more."

They ride on in silence, down over the rocks and into the trees. At first they cannot find the water; they give rein to the horses; the horses find it immediately, upcanyon, among the boulders, where the musk of startled javelinas floats on the air. The men fill their canteens and let the horses drink.

"If we could get one of them wild pigs," the old man says, "we wouldn't have to eat your mongrel dog."

"Bigotry again. There's more and better meat on a dog. Next best thing to a horse."

Burns looks at the horses. "Sure ain't much meat on ours. We better let them feed for a while, if there's much more here than up on the hill. Did I see filaree under those sycamores?"

They lead the horses back to the grove of trees and turn them loose, hobbled again, with trailing reins. The men squat against the comfortable bole of the biggest sycamore, deep in darkness, and listen with pleasure to the shuffling feet, the work of powerful jaws ripping up the sweet dry grass. Neither man is sleepy; they had slept earlier, during the heat of the afternoon. They will ride still farther tonight.

"That ole charger of mine," says Burns, "she ain't doing too bad. She'll make it yet." He ejects a stream of tobacco juice through the gap in his front teeth and onto the ground between his boots. "Since that raid she's the only horse I got left with enough sense and enough strength for a long march. She ain't much but she'll do."

Sam lights his little clay pipe. "I've seen uglier horses. Not many."

"Now Sam . . ." Thinking, the old man says, "We'll liberate a few on the way home. Should be lots of strays around the city."

"Is your son a rider?"

"Last time I seen him he was on a goddamn bicycle. But he's my son." That should be sufficient; but the old man adds, "Any son of mine can't ride will be shot, personally." Smiling in the dark, Burns looks at his partner. "You think I'm getting old, Sam? Old and creaky and cranky? Maybe a little touched in the head?"

"Yes."

"You're right. That's why we need him."

"We'll find him, boss."

"Jack! The name is Jack, for Chrissake."

"We'll find him, Jack. For your sake."

The horses stop suddenly, lifting their heads, nostrils flexing. From miles away, upwind on the barely moving air, off in the mountains dark against the stars, comes the sound of a high, faint, inhuman wail. They listen. The sound is not repeated. The horses wait, then lower their heads.

Jack Burns spits on the ground. "I ever tell you about my honeymoon, Sam?"

"Which one?"

"The first. That first premature honeymoon. Took this here city girl out camping in the woods. When it got dark we bedded down under the pines and then I told her about some of the things that creep around out there in the night. Trying to make her hang on tight, you see." The old man stares at the horses, smiling at his thoughts.

"Well? What happened?"

Burns's face wrinkles with a leathery, deeper grin. "She fell asleep. I was awake all night; every time a pine cone dropped I damn near jumped out of my skin."

The Indian nods in agreement. "Yes. We create our own fears. And at four o'clock in the morning we create the worst fear of all. The fear of living."

The horses shuffle about in the starlight. The old man says, "I look at it this way, Sam. If the worst thing that can happen to a man is death—then there ain't nothing that's worth fearing."

"Yes again. If that is the worst."

Leaning against the tree and against each other, they doze off. From far away, dim and distant, the wail sounds again, borne on the gentle wind, a cry of anguish or of ecstasy deeper than despair, wilder than joy. The men stir at the sound but do not awaken. The horses, after another pause, continue feeding. Bright stars burn, clusters of blue, red, green fires in random constellation turning on the wheel of space. In silence.

Hours later, well past midnight, roused by an inner clock, Jack Burns opens his eyes. He nudges his companion. They rise and grope through the dark of the trees toward the noise of their horses, catch them and mount. They follow a path through the rocks, downcanyon, and come to a clear and definite trail. They follow the trail for a mile, two miles, and reach an old road, stony, deeply gullied, overgrown with brush and cactus. They ride the road, single file through the obstructions, over a ridge and into the next valley and come to a fence with open gate.

"Smoke," mutters Sam; "I smell smoke."

They go through the gateway, ride on for another mile, passing two abandoned, weed-grown automobiles on the way. Ancient and gigantic cottonwood trees loom ahead, their leaves making a constant rustling noise as of running water. Beyond the trees they find the ruins of a burned-out ranch-house, a leveled barn; fiery coals wink among the ashes; smoke twists up from the charred, fallen timbers. The men look at the ruins and then at one another, through the fading starlight, and say nothing.

A gust of predawn wind flows down from the mountains. The tail vane of an unlocked windmill turns with the wind; steel grates on rusted steel. The sound is like that of a human groan. The Indian and Burns look toward the corral a hundred yards away and the tall tower—a skeleton of metal—standing within it. There they see, dangling on a rope, black in silhouette against the eastern sky, the first of the hanged men.

Desert Images

O F ALL NATURAL FORMS the sand dunes are the most elegant—so simple, severe, bare. Nature in the nude. Nothing can mar for
long their physical integrity. Broken down by foot traffic or machines, the
sand is re-formed by the winds into fresh new dunes, formally perfect, advancing with the winds across the desert, where nothing but a mountain range
can halt their progress.

Sand—unlike dust—is not airborne at great altitudes. Students of the
matter have learned that even the strongest winds can seldom lift sand more
than a foot or two above the ground. Where the ground is hard and fairly flat,
however, the wind steady, the supply of sand sufficient, this lifting power is
enough to form dunes.

A dune begins with any obstacle on the surface—a stone, a shrub, a log,
anything heavy enough to resist being moved by the wind. This obstacle forms
a *wind shadow* on its leeward side, resulting in eddies in the current of the air,
exactly as a rock in a stream causes an eddy in the water. Within the eddy the
wind moves with less force and velocity than the airstreams on either side,
creating what geologists call *the surface of discontinuity*. Here the wind tends
to drop part of its load of sand. The sand particles, which should be visualized

From *Beyond the Wall: Essays from the Outside* (1984)

as hopping or bouncing along the surface before the wind (not flying through the air), begin to accumulate, the pile grows higher, becoming itself a barrier to the wind, creating a greater eddy in the air currents and capturing still more sand. The formation of a dune is under way.

Viewed in cross section, sand dunes display a characteristic profile. On the windward side the angle of ascent is low and gradual—twenty to twenty-five degrees from the horizontal. On the leeward side the slope is much steeper, usually about thirty-four degrees—the angle of repose of sand and most other loose materials. The steep side of the dune is called the *slip face* because of the slides that take place as sand is driven up the windward side and deposited on and just over the crest. When the deposit on the crest becomes greater than can be supported by the sand beneath, the extra sand slumps down the slip face. As the process is repeated through the years, the whole dune advances with the direction of the prevailing wind, until some obstacle like a mountain intervenes. At this point the dunes, prevented from advancing, pile higher. At Death Valley and in Great Sand Dunes National Monument in Colorado the highest dunes reach five hundred feet. The only higher sand dunes are in Iran, where they attain a world's record of seven hundred feet.

Seen from the bird's point of view, most of these desert sand dunes have a crescent shape, like the new moon. The horns of the crescent point downwind, with the slip face on the inside of the curve. This type of dune is called a *barchan*—a Russian term. (A sea of sand, as in Mexico's Gran Desierto near the mouth of the Colorado River, is called an *erg*, a Hamitic word.) Dunes sometimes take other forms. There are transverse dunes, ridges of sand lying at a right angle to the course of the wind, and longitudinal dunes, which lie parallel to the wind. And there are parabolic dunes—barchans in reverse. Why dunes assume these different shapes is a question not yet resolved by those who have studied the problem.

How fast does a sand dune move? About twenty-five feet, sometimes up to fifty feet, in a year. Eventually the dunes achieve a point where they can advance no farther, climb no higher. When this happens, they resume the equally ancient process of consolidating themselves into sandstone. Into rock. We are talking here of a leisurely natural process, of millions of years. Sand and rock may observe a cosmic timetable, may follow some kind of pulse of their own, but if so this lies beyond human comprehension.

In our traditional conception of the desert we imagine it consisting entirely of billowing seas of sand, with here and there a palm tree, a gaunt saguaro cactus, the skull of a cow emerging from the sandy waves. Not so.

Most of the Great American Desert is made up of bare rock, rugged cliffs, mesas, canyons, mountains, separated from one another by broad flat basins covered with sunbaked mud and alkali, supporting a sparse and measured growth of sagebrush or creosote or saltbush, depending on location and elevation. In the American desert sand dunes are rather rare, relative to the size of the area of which they are a part. Death Valley; the San Luis Valley in Colorado; Monument Valley in Arizona and Utah; the White Sands of New Mexico; the sand dunes near Yuma, Arizona, and in the Mojave Desert of Southern California; a few places in Nevada—that sums it up. But like many things that are rare, a field of dunes makes up in beauty what it lacks in vast expanse.

A simple but always varied beauty. Shades of color that change from hour to hour—bright golden in morning and afternoon, a pallid tan beneath the noon sun, platinum by moonlight, blue-sheened under snow, metallic silver when rimed with hoarfrost, glowing like heated iron at sunrise and sunset, lavender by twilight. With forms and volumes and masses inconstant as wind but always shapely. Dunes like nude bodies. Dunes like standing waves. Dunes like arcs and sickles, scythe blades and waning moons. Virgin dunes untracked by machines, untouched by human feet. Dunes firm and solid after rain, ribbed with ripple marks from the wind. Dunes surrounding ephemeral pools of water that glitter golden as tiger's eye in the light of dawn. The clear-cut cornice of a dune, seen from below, carving out of the intense blue of the sky a brazen, brassy arc of monumental particulars. Yes—and the dunes that flow around and upon a dying mesquite tree in the Mojave, suffocating a stand of junipers and yellow pine in some lovely piece of back-country Utah. Sand and beauty. Sand and death. Sand and renewal.

It is time for a walk on the dunes. There may not be many years left. I leave the road and walk out on the dunes, following the delicate footprints of a fox. Past the arrowweed on the salt flats, past the little bosks of mesquite in the foothills of the dunes, up the windward side along the crest where the sand is so firm my feet leave only a faint impression. On the sand are other tracks even more delicate than those of the fox—the imprints of mice, beetles, lizards, birds.

I trail my fox into the lifeless heart of Death Valley, wondering where he might be bound. The morning sun rises higher above the purple Grapevine Mountains on the east, illuminates with a rosy glow the Panamint Mountains on the west. The tracks go high, then descend, then climb still higher on the next and greater dune. In general, with all its wandering, the fox seems to be bearing toward the highest dune of them all, four hundred feet above the valley floor. That fox should be hungry; a fox in the wild lives mostly on the keen edge of starvation. Yet his course is leading him farther and farther from any likely source of food. The fox's prey live below, among the clumps of vegetation between the dunes; the tracks of rodents and lizards become scarce, then nonexistent, as we climb higher.

Maybe this fox is crazy. Or rabid. Or old and looking for a place to die. Or a sightseer like me. Why the summit of the sands? Yet that is where the trail finally leads me. To the high point of the highest dune. And there, as I can plainly read on the open page of the sand, the fox paused for a while, turning in one place, before plunging over the cornice and down, in great leaps, through the soft, unstable sand of the slip face, disappearing into the brush on the flats below.

What brought that fox up here? I don't know. A light wind is blowing now and all tracks, including my own, are beginning to soften, blur, fade out in a serried pattern of ripples in the sand. I lie belly down on the cornice of the dune, looking over the edge. Fine grains of sand, backlit by the sun, shining like particles of light, are swirling in the air. I can hear them tinkling and chiming as they fall on the sand below. Like crystals of quartz; like tiny fragments of broken glass. There is no other sound in this desert world.

I roll over on my back and gaze up at the cloudless, perfect, inhuman, unsheltering sky. The inevitable vulture soars there, a thousand feet above me. Black wings against the blue. I think I know that bird. He looks familiar. I think he's the one that's been following me, everywhere I go in the desert, for about thirty-five years. Looking after me. I follow the fox. The vulture follows me.

"I LOVE ALL THINGS that flow," said James Joyce. "If there is magic on this earth it lies in water," Loren Eiseley said. And nowhere is water so beautiful as in the desert, for nowhere else is it so scarce. By definition. Water, like a human being or a tree or a bird or a song, gains value by rarity, singularity, isolation. In a humid climate, water is common. In the desert each drop is precious.

Way down in a corner of Arizona, near the Mexican border, is a tiny spring called Sweet Water. This spring is the only permanent, reliable, natural source of water between Quitobaquito on the east and the Tinajas Altas ("High Tanks") on the west—a distance of sixty miles by road. That road, surfaced in sand alternating with long stretches of blue-black lava rock, was called the Vulture's Road. Long since abandoned, bypassed by paved highways far to the

north and south, the Vulture's Road can still be followed here and there, the
route identifiable by dim tracks across the stone, by cast-off wagon-wheel rims
and antique Ford mufflers dissolving in rust and by the mounds of stones and
iron crosses that mark the burial sites of those who never made it. No one with
any brains ever traveled that road in summer. In winter the low desert can be
comfortable, even exhilarating, if you're properly equipped for survival; but in
summer it is intolerable. The shimmer of heat waves, hanging like a scrim
across the horizon, is enough in itself to confuse the senses, puzzle the mind.
The mountains float like ships on the waves of superheated air, drifting away
from one another, then returning, merging, inverting themselves, assuming
shapes out of fantasy. The madness of mirage.

Some of those passing on that road must have wondered, as they endured
the heat and the thirst, what lay within the folds of a certain small mountain
range to the north. A typical desert range: blue hills prickly with cactus, agave,
spiny shrubs and stinging nettles, mostly bare of any vegetation at all, scaled
and plated with loose rock, the high ridges notched with points like a dragon's
backbone. What a few men knew was that there was water in there—the
spring of Sweet Water. Not that the knowledge would have done the travelers
much good. The spring is far from the road, difficult to reach; the effort required to get there might have taken more lives than the little trickle of water
could have saved. In the desert it is usually more important to ration bodily
energy than water itself; sweat may be as costly as blood.

One morning in March I drove my government truck into the area,
through the cactus forest to the end of the dim track, then walked the last few
miles. I had plenty of water with me and within me; I was being paid to patrol
these parts, investigate worked-out gold mines, check game trails, inspect
animal droppings, test the water of hidden tanks and secret springs.

There is no man-made trail, only a deer path, a bighorn-sheep path, a lion
run, leading to the spring. The stones are loose and tricky, the drop-offs vertical, the brush and cactus thick, resistant, hostile. One proceeds with care. A
broken leg could be a serious mistake, especially when alone. Accidents are
forbidden. But the birds like it here: I was serenaded on my way by the sharp
whistles of a thrasher—that signal so humanlike that the first few times you
hear it you always stop and look around, expecting to see a boy or another
man. Or a woman, now that women have liberated themselves from certain
genteel constraints. ("Whistling girls and crowing hens," my grandmother
used to say, "both shall come to no good ends.")

Other birds are also present. I heard a cactus wren, its voice like the chat-
ter of a rusty adding machine. And the sweet brief tunes of cardinal, pyrrhu-

loxia, phainopepla—the last a shy and furtive little bird, hard to get to know.

I reached a saddle in the mountains without finding the spring, though the convergence of tracks left by many small feet suggested that I was getting close. Plus the variety of scat on the trail: not only bighorn sheep and deer but also coyote, rabbit, kit fox and the messy little clots of dung of the javelina, the wild pig or peccary of the southwestern deserts.

Once on the other side of the saddle and around a few more overhangs of rotten volcanic rock and through a tunnel in the thorny mesquite and catclaw acacia, where I crawled on hands and knees to save the shirt from being torn off my back, I found the spring. It was easy to spot: a clump of leafless but conspicuously coppery willows, a dwarf cottonwood barely beginning to leaf out with the soft green of a new growing season. The little trees made only a patch of deciduous life in the midst of many square miles of blue stone and olive-drab desert growth, but that single tiny patch was sufficient to indicate the presence of the desert's sweetest miracle—surface water. Or at the least, water very close to the surface. About fifty yards short of the spring and a little above it, downwind from the prevailing westerlies, I came upon a blind of saguaro ribs. I squatted down in the lattice shade of the thing armed with binoculars, notebook, a canteen of water, a hunk of longhorn cheese, a box of raisins, and I waited.

The sun went down. I put on my coat as the temperature dropped ten, fifteen, twenty degrees within twenty minutes. Binoculars ready, I watched the water hole—the only water hole within twenty miles. The bird songs faded away. Crickets began to rub their fore wings together down by the spring. The lavender dusk, in a precipitation of colors too subtle to name, spread across the desert hills, through the sky, across Sonora to the south, across the fifty miles of landscape within my range of sight. The sickle of moon grew brighter.

Most desert animals do not require water daily. The deer, the bighorn sheep, the javelina are believed to go two or three days at a time without a drink, getting by, that is, on what they've stored in their tissues. Early March, also, is not the best of times for finding wildlife at a water hole; cool days, natural tanks full of winter rains, fresh plant growth make needs less pressing. Midsummer—July, August, September—that's the best time. It was quite possible, therefore, that I would see nothing.

I waited. The air grew chillier, the moon slipped lower, the night came on. One more hour, I resolved, and then I give up; then it's back up the trail by moonlight and down the other side, back to the truck, a beer, something hot to eat, before laying out my bedroll on the desert floor.

I heard the clash of stone far down in the brush-filled ravine below the spring. I raised the field glasses and studied the area but could see nothing in motion. I waited, changing position again to ease my aching limbs. Again I heard the slight, faint, far-off click of something hard on stone. An animal was approaching, and as I watched, concentrating on the mesquite and acacia thickets, I saw first one then a second sleek, gracile, dun-colored form appear, climbing on delicate hoofs up the path toward the spring. Followed by a third, a fourth, a fifth, all in single file. And then two more. And still more, at least a dozen in all, quiet as shadows, pale and obscure as the twilight, bodies barely distinguishable from the dark background of stone and brush.

For a moment I thought they were small deer. But all young bucks! With black spikes. And then I recognized them as desert pronghorn, a species almost extinct in the United States, though once quite numerous in southern Arizona. These had probably come up from Mexico, sliding under the fence like illegal immigrants. I was glad to see them. They gathered about the spring, jostling one another until the basic order of precedence was reestablished, then drank, two or three at a time while the others waited and watched. I could hear the gurgling of water passing rapidly down those parched throats, the sighs and grunts of satisfaction. There is something in the feeding and drinking of large animals that gives, to the human onlooker, a sensation of deep pleasure. Mammalian empathy, perhaps.

Finally the pronghorns had enough. A long time, as it seemed to me, for of course I had to wait until the last had drunk its fill before I could stir; I didn't want to scare away from a much needed watering the lowest pronghorn in the pecking order. Not until all turned and started back the way they'd come did I stand up. At once, with a clatter of stones and armored feet, they took off. A dozen white rump patches flashed in the moonlight, vanishing two seconds later into the gloom below—soon gone beyond earshot as well as sight. I walked down and inspected the spring. A ring of dampness showed that the pronghorns had lowered the water level eight inches. I felt the muddy residue, then cupped my hands under the trickle that flowed from the algae-covered rock and drank.

Satisfied I followed the path back to the saddle of the mountain, through the moonlit tangle of cactus and brush, over the rocks, back to my headquarters for the night.

LIFE IS GAUNT and spare in the desert; that's what old time desert rats like best about it. They feel they cannot breathe properly without at least a cubic mile of unshared space about them. Let another man or woman appear on their horizon and they begin to feel the urge to decamp, move on, climb to the pass, investigate that purple range of barren hills beyond the gleaming salt flats, find out what's going on up in there, among those shadowy valleys, those ragged battlements of broken-down rock. Where, as they should know damn well, they'll find nothing but the same scatter of dried-out brittlebush, the same fireplugs of barrel cactus with spines like fishhooks, the same herd of feral burros gaping at them from the ridgeline, the same dun-colored rattler coiled beneath a limestone shelf, waiting its chance to strike. Don't tread on me.

Desert plant life is much the same—private. Even the commonest shrub, like the creosote bush, keeps its distance from the next. Each sets alone inside an ample circle of open ground. Botanists say that the roots of the plant secrete a poison, a growth inhibitor, that prevents new, seedling creosote from getting a start within that charmed circle of solitariness.

So it is with the flowers of the desert, though not without some exceptions. In certain years, not frequent, when the winter drizzles have fallen at the right times in the correct amounts, and when the weather achieves exactly the proper balance in March and April between heat and cold, sunlight and cloud cover, you may be lucky enough to see whole desert valleys and hills covered, "carpeted" as they say, with a solid blaze of flowering Mexican poppy, or globe mallow, or mimulus or coreopsis. These are splendid and rare occasions, attracting flower freaks, photographers and desert flora fanciers from half the cities of the nation, odd people who think nothing of grabbing a jet plane and flying two thousand miles to see the flare-up of sudden orange when the *Calochortus kennedyi* takes over some Mojave valley down in California's wastelands. That or the Mexican poppies. Or the brittlebush itself, an otherwise humble and obscure knee-high shrub, which can perform wonders: nothing is more striking than to see the grim black cinder cones in the Pinacate Lava Fields take on suddenly—almost overnight—a rash of yellow, when twenty thousand brittlebushes break out in simultaneous golden bloom. Ridiculous. And sublime.

But these are, as said, the exceptions. Generally the flowers of the desert reveal themselves in solitary splendor. A primrose lurking on a sand dune. A single paloverde flaring by an arid watercourse. One woolly clump of *Baileya multiradiata* gracing the edge of the asphalt, shivering in the breeze from forty-ton freight trucks. The great *Agave palmeri,* or century plant, blooms only once in its entire existence ("the garland briefer than a girl's"), but in that supreme assertion of love and continuity it more than justifies the sacrifice required. For a decade or so the century plant grows, emerging slowly from the rock; the heavy spine-tipped blades that function as leaves wax fat, with an interlocking bulge in the center resembling an artichoke. Here the food and energy are stored. One spring a signal is given—we don't know what or why. The bulge unfolds, like a slow-motion explosion, and a shaft rises from the center, growing rapidly, reaching a height of ten or twelve feet within a week. This is the flower stalk, efflorescing as it rises with a series of alternate flower-bearing stems from midpoint to the top. The yellowish, heavy blooms wait there, upright on the towering stalk, for a week, two weeks, are pollinated by bats and insects, then begin to fade. As they fade the plant dies slowly, by degrees, from stem to root, though the strong, rigid shaft, supported by the base, may stand erect for a year after death. The death does not matter; the seeds have been sown.

The desert offers a second outburst of flowering in September and October, after the customary summer rains. This is the time of the globe mallow, or pink-eye poppy as it's also known, and rabbit brush, a stinking shrub with a showy display of yellow bloom, and the sunflowers—acres and acres of waist-high mule-ear (so named for the shape of the leaves) *Helianthus annuus,* visible from miles away.

Down in dank and shady places grows a shady customer—moonflower, angel's-trumpet, the sacred *Datura meteloides.* A large gross ivory-colored thing, set amid dark and shiny green leaves, the whole plant, flowers, stem, leaves, roots, is rich in scopolamine, a potent alkaloid much prized by witch doctors. The correct dosage is said to be spiritually rewarding, but the problem is that a microgram too much may lead to convulsions, paralysis and death—also rewarding, perhaps, but usually considered premature.

I try to think of a favorite among my arid-country flowers. But I love them all. How could we be true to one without being false to all the others? Just the same I think I'll praise a few more individuals here, single them out from among the crowd.

The cliffrose, for example. A flowering shrub, *Cowania mexicana,* a true member of the rose family, the cliffrose can be found in many parts of the mesa country and high desert from Colorado to California. The shrub may grow from four to twelve feet high. Twisted and gnarled like a juniper, it is relatively inconspicuous most of the year. But in April and May it blooms, putting out a thick, showy cluster of pale yellow or cream-colored flowers with the fragrance of orange blossoms. On a breezy day in spring you can smell the faint, delicate but heart-intoxicating sweetness for miles. The cliffrose is a bold plant, flourishing in the most improbable places, clinging to the cliff's edge, overhanging the rim of a plateau, gracing the pockets of sand far out among the slickrock domes. Deer, bighorn sheep, domestic sheep and cattle all browse on the leaves of this plant in the winter, when little else is available.

Or how about the wild morning glory, *Evolvulus arizonicus*? Another beauty. A hardy annual that blooms from April to October. The flowers are small, scarcely half an inch in diameter, but of so clear and striking an azure blue, especially in contrast to the tiny leaves and scraggly stems of the plant itself, that they assert themselves—against the sun-bleached background of sand and rock—with eye-catching vigor.

Several varieties of lupine grow in the desert. In Arizona the violet-purple *Lupinus sparsiflorus*, in western Texas the blue-purple *L. havardii*, in southwest California the royal-purple *L. odoratus.* Bushy members of the pea family, the lupines generally grow from two to three feet tall in clusters along roadways, trails and the edges of valley bottoms, wherever the runoff from rains tends to be a little heavier. Sometimes they grow in pure stands, turning the burnt umber and dun brown of the desert into a wind-shimmering lake of blue-pink-purple radiance. The lupine is not good for anything bankable; hungry livestock eat them, get sick and die (alkaloids). All they have to offer us is their own rare beauty.

One more. A secret flower, a hidden special, little known, seldom publicized: the desert prince's plume, *Stanleya pinnata*, a man-high plant that blooms from May to July in some of the hottest, dreariest, most godforsaken and otherwise life-forsaken places in the Southwest. In dried-out mud flats along arid watercourses; on the shale and gravel talus slopes under a Moenkopi-formation rock bluff; around the alkaline edges of some desperate mudhole way out in the clay hills, the badlands, the Painted Desert. The flowers stand up in golden spikes, racemes of bright yellow blazing against the red cliffs and blue sky.

In those secret canyon glens where the hanging gardens grow, nourished on water percolating through the sandstone, you'll find yellow columbine. Certainly as beautiful a flower as anything on earth, though not so large and spectacular as the blue columbine of the mountains. Many others live here too, delicate as angel's breath, and tough. They've got to be tough, surviving in those precarious perches on a perpendicular slickrock wall.

And then you walk out in the badlands and see a single Indian paintbrush lifting its cup of salmon-colored, petallike bracts toward the sky. The paintbrush too is beautiful, with the special and extraordinary beauty of wild and lonely things. Every desert flower shares that quality. Anything that lives where it would seem that nothing could live, enduring extremes of heat and cold, sunlight and storm, parching aridity and sudden cloudbursts, among burnt rock and shifting sands, any such creature—beast, bird or flower—testifies to the grandeur and heroism inherent in all forms of life. Including the human. Even in us.

EVERYWHERE YOU GO in the southwestern deserts you come across drawings on the rocks, on the canyon walls. Some are inscribed into the rock—*petroglyphs*. Some are painted on the rock—*pictographs*. All of them, pictographs and petroglyphs alike, present an odd and so-far-untranslated language. If it is a language.

Not that the pictures are always hard to understand. Most consist of recognizable figures: deer, bighorn sheep, antelope, sometimes a mastodon (extinct no more than ten thousand years in North America), serpents, centipedes, rain clouds, the sun, dancing humans, warriors with shields and lances, even men on horseback—representations that cannot be more than four hundred years old, when the Spaniards introduced the horse to North America.

Some of the pictures, however, are disturbingly strange. We see semi-human figures with huge blank eyes, horned heads. Ghostly shapes resembling men, but without feet or legs, float on the air. Humanlike forms with helmets and goggles wave tentacles at us. What can they be? Gods? Goddesses? Cosmonauts from the Betelgeuse neighborhood? Here's a fighter with shield painted red, white and blue—the all-American man. And still other forms appear, completely nonrepresentational, totally abstract symbols of . . . of what? Nobody knows. The American Indians of today, if they know, aren't telling. Probably they are as mystified by them as we are. In any case the culture of the modern Native Americans has little connection with the culture of the vanished rock artists. The continuity was broken long ago.

But still we ask, what does the rock art mean? Unlike the story of the cliff ruins, fairly coherent to archaeologists, we know little of the significance of this ancient work. Perhaps it was only doodling of a sort. A bunch of Stone Age deer hunters sit in camp day after day with nothing to do (the game is gone), telling lies, chipping arrowheads, straightening arrow shafts with their doughnutlike straightener stones. One of them, wanting to record his lies for posterity, begins to chisel the image of a six-point buck on the overhanging cliff wall. I killed that animal, he boasts, with my bare hands.

Another liar takes up the challenge. I killed six bighorn rams, he claims, in this very canyon, only fourteen years ago. And he tallies the total on the soft sandstone with a hard-edged chunk of agate or basalt or flint.

These shallow scratchings may have been the beginning. Inevitably the power of art took over. Most hunter-warriors were artists. They had to be. They made their own weapons. A weapon, to be useful, has to be well made. A well-made weapon or any well-made tool, when crafted by hand, becomes a work of art.

Perhaps the rock art was created by specialists. By shamans and wizards, evoking sympathetic magic to aid the hunt. Portraying a deer slain by an arrow, the medicine man would believe that his wishes would serve as efficient cause in producing the desired result. Imitative magic: life imitates art. Thus the pictographs and petroglyphs may have had a religious denotation, hunting being central to any hunter's religion.

The art served as a record. As practical magic. And as communication between wanderers. Water around the next bend, a certain zigzag sign might mean. We killed eleven bighorn here, only two hundred years ago, says a second. *We were here, say the hunters. We were here, say the artists.*

What about the spectral forms—the ghosts, ghouls, gods? Supernatural beings are fished from dreams. From the caves of Altamira to the base of Ayers Rock in central Australia, all original, aboriginal people have believed in the power of dreams. In the Dream Time, say the wise old men of the outback, we made our beginning; from the Dream Time we come; into the Dream Time, after death, we shall return. The dream is the real; waking life is only a dream within a greater dream.

These are speculations. Only a few anthropologists, like New Mexico's Dr. Polly Schaafsma, have given the Indian rock art serious attention. Most have observed the drawings, recorded them, but made no further study. At this time there is no method known by which the pictographs and petroglyphs can be dated accurately; dendrochronology (tree rings) and the carbon-14 technique cannot be applied here. Nor can the art be correlated with other archaeological data—cliff dwellings, burial sites, the various styles of pottery-, basket- and toolmaking. In the absence of verifiable scientific information, the interpretation of rock art has been left by default to popular fancy: thus the early and premature labeling of this art as a form of "writing" or "hieroglyphs." Not surprising. The first reaction of anyone seeing these strange pictures for the first time is the naturally human: what do they *mean*?

Perhaps meaning is not of primary importance here. What is important is the recognition of art, wherever we may discover it, in whatever form. These canyon paintings and canyon inscriptions are valuable for their own sake, as work of elegance, freshness, originality (in the original sense of the word), economy of line, precision of point, integrity of materials. They are beautiful. And all of them are hundreds of years old—some may be much, much older.

The artist Paul Klee, whose surreal work resembles some of this desert rock art, wrote in his *Diaries 1898–1918*: "There are two mountains on which the weather is bright and clear, the mountain of the animals and the mountain of the gods. But between lies the shadowy valley of men." How's that for meaning?

On many walls in the desert we find the figure of the humpbacked flute player, Kokopelli (a Hopi name). A wanderer, for sure, and a man of strange powers, Kokopelli may have been the Pied Piper who led the cliff dwellers out of the canyons, out of their fear and down to the high, open country to the south, where the people could live more like humans and less like bats. Maybe he was a nomadic witch doctor, a healer of bodies and curer of feverishly imaginative savage souls. Nobody knows. The memory of the actual Kokopelli, if he was an actual person, has been lost. Only the outline of Kokopelli, his image chiseled into rock, has survived. Too bad. Many of us would like very much to hear the music that he played on that flute of his.

The American desert was discovered by an unknown people. They tried its deepest secrets. Now they have vanished, extinct as the tapir and the coryphodon. But the undeciphered message that they left us remains, written on the walls. A message preserved not in mere words and numbers but in the durable images of line on stone. *We were here.*

Language, in the mind of a poet, seeks to transcend itself, "to grasp the thing that has no name." It seems reasonable to suppose that the unknown people who left this record of their passage felt the same impulse toward permanence, the same longing for communion with the world that we feel today. To ask for any more meaning may be as futile as to ask for a meaning in the desert itself. What does the desert mean? It means what it is. It is there, it will be there when we are gone. But for a while we living things—men, women, birds, that coyote howling far off on yonder stony ridge—we were a part of it all. That should be enough.

The Damnation of a
Canyon

T HERE WAS A TIME WHEN, in my search for essences, I concluded that the canyonland country has no heart. I was wrong. The canyonlands did have a heart, a living heart, and that heart was Glen Canyon and
the golden, flowing Colorado River.

In the summer of 1959 a friend and I made a float trip in little rubber rafts
down through the length of Glen Canyon, starting at Hite and getting off the
river near Gunsight Butte—The Crossing of the Fathers. In this voyage of
some 150 miles and ten days our only motive power, and all that we needed,
was the current of the Colorado River.

In the summer and fall of 1967 I worked as a seasonal park ranger at the
new Glen Canyon National Recreation Area. During my five-month tour of
duty I worked at the main marina and headquarters area called Wahweap, at
Bullfrog Basin toward the upper end of the reservoir and finally at Lee's Ferry
downriver from Glen Canyon Dam. In a number of powerboat tours I was
privileged to see almost all of our nation's newest, biggest and most impressive "recreational facility."

Having thus seen Glen Canyon both before and after what we may fairly
call its damnation, I feel that I am in a position to evaluate the transformation

From *Beyond the Wall: Essays from the Outside* (1984)

of the region caused by construction of the dam. I have had the unique opportunity to observe firsthand some of the differences between the environment of a free river and a power-plant reservoir.

One should admit at the outset to a certain bias. Indeed I am a "butterfly
chaser, googly eyed bleeding heart and wild conservative." I take a dim view
of dams; I find it hard to learn to love cement; I am poorly impressed by
concrete aggregates and statistics in the cubic tons. But in this weakness I am
not alone, for I belong to that ever-growing number of Americans, probably a
good majority now, who have become aware that a fully industrialized, thoroughly urbanized, elegantly computerized social system is not suitable for
human habitation. Great for machines, yes. But unfit for people.

Lake Powell, formed by Glen Canyon Dam, is not a lake. It is a reservoir,
with a constantly fluctuating water level—more like a bathtub that is never
drained than a true lake. As at Hoover (or Boulder) Dam, the sole practical
function of this impounded water is to drive the turbines that generate electricity in the powerhouse at the base of the dam. Recreational benefits were of
secondary importance in the minds of those who conceived and built this dam.
As a result the volume of water in the reservoir is continually being increased
or decreased according to the requirements of the Basin States Compact and
the power-grid system of which Glen Canyon Dam is a component.

The rising and falling water level entails various consequences. One of
the most obvious, well known to all who have seen Lake Mead, is the "bathtub
ring" left on the canyon walls after each drawdown of water, or what rangers
at Glen Canyon call the Bathtub Formation. This phenomenon is perhaps of
no more than aesthetic importance; yet it is sufficient to dispel any illusion
one might have, in contemplating the scene, that you are looking upon a natural lake.

Of much more significance is the fact that plant life, because of the unstable water line, cannot establish itself on the shores of the reservoir. When
the water is low, plant life dies of thirst; when high, it is drowned. Much of the
shoreline of the reservoir consists of near-perpendicular sandstone bluffs,
where very little flora ever did or ever could subsist, but the remainder includes bays, coves, sloping hills and the many side canyons, where the original
plant life has been drowned and new plant life cannot get a foothold. And of
course where there is little or no plant life there is little or no animal life.

The utter barrenness of the reservoir shoreline recalls by contrast the
aspect of things before the dam, when Glen Canyon formed the course of the
untamed Colorado. Then we had a wild and flowing river lined by boulder-

strewn shores, sandy beaches, thickets of tamarisk and willow and glades of cottonwoods.

The thickets teemed with songbirds: vireos, warblers, mockingbirds and thrushes. On the open beaches were killdeer, sandpipers, herons, ibises, egrets. Living in grottoes in the canyon walls were swallows, swifts, hawks, wrens and owls. Beaver were common if not abundant: not an evening would pass, in drifting down the river, that we did not see them or at least hear the whack of their flat tails on the water. Above the river shores were the great recessed alcoves where water seeped from the sandstone, nourishing the semitropical hanging gardens of orchid, ivy and columbine, with their associated swarms of insects and birdlife.

Up most of the side canyons, before damnation, there were springs, sometimes flowing streams, waterfalls and plunge pools—the kind of marvels you can now find only in such small-scale remnants of Glen Canyon as the Escalante area. In the rich flora of these laterals the larger mammals—mule deer, coyote, bobcat, ring-tailed cat, gray fox, kit fox, skunk, badger and others—found a home. When the river was dammed almost all of these things were lost. Crowded out—or drowned and buried under mud.

The difference between the present reservoir, with its silent sterile shores and debris-choked side canyons, and the original Glen Canyon, is the difference between death and life. Glen Canyon was alive. Lake Powell is a graveyard.

For those who may think I exaggerate the contrast between the former river canyon and the present man-made impoundment, I suggest a trip on Lake Powell followed immediately by another boat trip on the river below the dam. Take a boat from Lee's Ferry up the river to within sight of the dam, then shut off the motor and allow yourself the rare delight of a quiet, effortless drifting down the stream. In that twelve-mile stretch of living green, singing birds, flowing water and untarnished canyon walls—sights and sounds a million years older and infinitely lovelier than the roar of motorboats—you will rediscover a small and imperfect sampling of the kind of experience that was taken away from everybody when the oligarchs and politicians condemned our river for purposes of their own.

The effects of Glen Canyon Dam also extend downstream, causing changes in the character and ecology of Marble Gorge and Grand Canyon. Because the annual spring floods are now a thing of the past, the shores are becoming overgrown with brush, the rapids are getting worse where the river no longer has enough force to carry away the boulders washed down from the

lateral canyons, and the beaches are disappearing, losing sand that is not replaced.

Lake Powell, though not a lake, may well be as its defenders assert the
most beautiful reservoir in the world. Certainly it has a photogenic backdrop
of buttes and mesas projecting above the expansive surface of stagnant waters
where the speedboats, houseboats and cabin cruisers ply. But it is no longer a
wilderness. It is no longer a place of natural life. It is no longer Glen Canyon.

The defenders of the dam argue that the recreational benefits available
on the surface of the reservoir outweigh the loss of Indian ruins, historical
sites, wildlife and wilderness adventure. Relying on the familiar quantitative
logic of business and bureaucracy, they assert that whereas only a few thousand citizens ever ventured down the river through Glen Canyon, now millions can—or will—enjoy the motorized boating and hatchery fishing
available on the reservoir. They will also argue that the rising waters behind
the dam have made such places as Rainbow Bridge accessible by powerboat.
Formerly you could get there only by walking (six miles).

This argument appeals to the wheelchair ethos of the wealthy, upper-
middle-class American slob. If Rainbow Bridge is worth seeing at all, then by
God it should be easily, readily, immediately available to everybody with the
money to buy a big powerboat. Why should a trip to such a place be the privilege only of those who are willing to walk six miles? Or if Pikes Peak is worth
getting to, then why not build a highway to the top of it so that anyone can get
there? Anytime? Without effort? Or as my old man would say, "By Christ, one
man's just as good as another—if not a damn sight better."

Or as ex-Commissioner Floyd Dominy of the U.S. Bureau of Reclamation pointed out poetically in his handsomely engraved and illustrated bro-
chure *Lake Powell: Jewel of the Colorado* (produced by the U.S. Government
Printing Office at our expense): "There's something about a lake which brings
us a little closer to God." In this case, Lake Powell, about five hundred feet
closer. Eh, Floyd?

It is quite true that the flooding of Glen Canyon has opened up to the
motorboat explorer parts of side canyons that formerly could be reached only
by people able to walk. But the sum total of terrain visible to the eye and
touchable by hand and foot has been greatly diminished, not increased. Because of the dam the river is gone, the inner canyon is gone, the best parts of
the numerous side canyons are gone—all hidden beneath hundreds of feet
of polluted water, accumulating silt and mounting tons of trash. This portion of Glen Canyon—and who can estimate how many cubic miles were
lost?—*is no longer accessible to anybody.* (Except scuba divers.) And this, do

not forget, was the most valuable part of Glen Canyon, richest in scenery, archaeology, history, flora and fauna.

Not only has the heart of Glen Canyon been buried, but many of the side canyons above the fluctuating waterline are now rendered more difficult, not easier, to get into. This because the debris brought down into them by desert storms, no longer carried away by the river, must unavoidably build up in the area where flood meets reservoir. Narrow Canyon, for example, at the head of the impounded waters, is already beginning to silt up and to amass huge quantities of driftwood, some of it floating on the surface, some of it half afloat beneath the surface. Anyone who has tried to pilot a motorboat through a raft of half-sunken logs and bloated dead cows will have his own thoughts on the accessibility of these waters.

Hite Marina, at the mouth of Narrow Canyon, will probably have to be abandoned within twenty or thirty years. After that it will be the turn of Bullfrog Marina. And then Rainbow Bridge Marina. And eventually, inevitably, whether it takes ten centuries or only one, Wahweap. Lake Powell, like Lake Mead, is foredoomed sooner or later to become a solid mass of mud, and its dam a waterfall. Assuming, of course, that either one stands that long.

Second, the question of costs. It is often stated that the dam and its reservoir have opened up to the many what was formerly restricted to the few, implying in this case that what was once expensive has now been made cheap. Exactly the opposite is true.

Before the dam, a float trip down the river through Glen Canyon would cost you a minimum of seven days' time, well within anyone's vacation allotment, and a capital outlay of about forty dollars—the prevailing price of a two-man rubber boat with oars, available at any army-navy surplus store. A life jacket might be useful but not required, for there were no dangerous rapids in the 150 miles of Glen Canyon. As the name implies, this stretch of the river was in fact so easy and gentle that the trip could be and was made by all sorts of amateurs: by Boy Scouts, Camp Fire Girls, stenographers, schoolteachers, students, little old ladies in inner tubes. Guides, professional boatmen, giant pontoons, outboard motors, radios, rescue equipment were not needed. The Glen Canyon float trip was an adventure anyone could enjoy, on his own, for a cost less than that of spending two days and nights in a Page motel. Even food was there, in the water: the channel catfish were easier to catch and a lot better eating than the striped bass and rainbow trout dumped by the ton into the reservoir these days. And one other thing: at the end of the float trip you still owned your boat, usable for many more such casual and carefree expeditions.

What is the situation now? Float trips are no longer possible. The only way left for the exploration of the reservoir and what remains of Glen Canyon demands the use of a powerboat. Here you have three options: (1) buy your own boat and engine, the necessary auxiliary equipment, the fuel to keep it moving, the parts and repairs to keep it running, the permits and licenses required for legal operation, the trailer to transport it; (2) rent a boat; or (3) go on a commercial excursion boat, packed in with other sightseers, following a preplanned itinerary. This kind of play is only for the affluent.

The inescapable conclusion is that no matter how one attempts to calculate the cost in dollars and cents, a float trip down Glen Canyon was much cheaper than a powerboat tour of the reservoir. Being less expensive, as well as safer and easier, the float trip was an adventure open to far more people than will ever be able to afford motorboat excursions in the area now.

What about the "human impact" of motorized use of the Glen Canyon impoundment? We can visualize the floor of the reservoir gradually accumulating not only silt, mud, waterlogged trees and drowned cattle but also the usual debris that is left behind when the urban, industrial style of recreation is carried into the open country. There is also the problem of human wastes. The waters of the wild river were good to drink, but nobody in his senses would drink from Lake Powell. Eventually, as is already sometimes the case at Lake Mead, the stagnant waters will become too foul even for swimming. The trouble is that while some boats have what are called "self-contained" heads, the majority do not; most sewage is disposed of by simply pumping it into the water. It will take a while, but long before it becomes a solid mass of mud Lake Powell ("Jewel of the Colorado") will enjoy a passing fame as the biggest sewage lagoon in the American Southwest. Most tourists will never be able to afford a boat trip on this reservoir, but everybody within fifty miles will be able to smell it.

All of the foregoing would be nothing but a futile exercise in nostalgia (so much water over the dam) if I had nothing constructive and concrete to offer. But I do. As alternate methods of power generation are developed, such as solar, and as the nation establishes a way of life adapted to actual resources and basic needs, so that the demand for electrical power begins to diminish, we can shut down the Glen Canyon power plant, open the diversion tunnels and drain the reservoir.

This will no doubt expose a drear and hideous scene: immense mud flats and whole plateaus of sodden garbage strewn with dead trees, sunken boats, the skeletons of long-forgotten, decomposing water-skiers. But to those who find the prospect too appalling, I say give nature a little time. In five years, at

most in ten, the sun and wind and storms will cleanse and sterilize the repellent mess. The inevitable floods will soon remove all that does not belong
within the canyons. Fresh green willow, box elder and redbud will reappear;
and the ancient drowned cottonwoods (noble monuments to themselves) will
be replaced by young of their own kind. With the renewal of plant life will
come the insects, the birds, the lizards and snakes, the mammals. Within a
generation—thirty years—I predict the river and canyons will bear a decent
resemblance to their former selves. Within the lifetime of our children Glen
Canyon and the living river, heart of the canyonlands, will be restored to us.
The wilderness will again belong to God, the people and the wild things that
call it home.

Gather at the River

IN MEDIAS RES, Alaska, June 24, 1983—We watch the little Cessna roar down the gravel bar toward the river, going away. Leaving. At full throttle, into the wind, pilot and airplane are fully committed: they must take off or die. Once again the miracle takes place: the fragile craft lifts itself from the ground and rises into the air, noisy as a bumblebee, delicate as a butterfly. Function of the airfoil, pulled forward by a whirling screw. Despite quantum mechanics and Heisenberg's uncertainty principle, planes fly. If only by statistical probability, they continue to fly, most of the time. And I am delighted, one more time, by the daring of my species and the audacity of our flying machines. There is poetry and music in our technology, a beauty as touching as that of eagle, moss campion, raven or yonder limestone boulder shining under the Arctic sun.

The airplane diminishes downriver, banks and turns through a pass in the hills and is gone, out of sight, suddenly silent, ephemeral and lovely as a dream.

I notice now that we have been left behind. Two of us, myself and Dana Van Burgh III, a handsome, hearty young man who looks a bit like Paul McCartney or maybe one of Elvis Presley's possible sons by way of Linda or Stevie or Jesse, good sound symmetric genes interlocked in a Rubik's Cube of

From *Beyond the Wall: Essays from the Outside* (1984)

hereditary coefficiency. But we're treading on a cluster of taboos here—better back off. I'm not too sure about Elvis anyway.

But we have definitely been left behind. The Cessna is bound for an Eskimo village called Kaktovik ("fish seining place") about one hundred miles away on the most dismal, desperate, degraded rathole in the world—Barter Island. If all goes well the plane will return in two hours with more of our equipment and two or three more members of our party. Our expedition. Mark Jensen's Alaska River Expeditions, Inc., Haines, Alaska.

The river at our side, more crystalline than golden, is called the Kongakut, and the plan, if all goes right, is to float down this river in two rubber rafts to another straight gravel bar eighty miles downstream. There, ten days from now, the airplane will pick us up and ferry us back to Kaktovik and Barter Island. Something to look forward to. But the river is alive with Arctic char and grayling, first-rate primeval fishing waters, and in the valley and among the treeless mountains around us roam the caribou, the wolf, the Dall sheep (close cousin to the bighorn) and of course the hypothetical grizzly bear. Himself, *Ursus arctos horribilis.* So they say.

If I seem skeptical about the bear it is because, after several efforts, I have yet to see with my own eyes a grizzly in the wild. I spent a summer as a fire lookout in Glacier National Park in Montana, saw a few black bear but not one grizzly. Even hiking alone, after dark, through alder thickets on a mountain trail, failed to attract the GRIZ. I sweated up another mountain trail behind Douglas Peacock, himself half grizzly, to a secret place he calls the Grizzly Hilton, where he has filmed, encountered, *talked with* many grizzlies, but on that one special day we saw nothing but flies, mosquitoes and the devil's club, a mean ugly plant with hairy leaves, thorny stems, a fist of inedible yellow berries on its top. Ten days on the Tatshenshini River in the wilderness of the Yukon and southeastern Alaska again failed to produce an authentic grizzly bear. I even tried the Tucson Zoo one time, but the alleged grizzly (if such there be) refused to emerge from its den in the rear of the cage. I could see a single dark paw with ragged claws, a host of loitering flies—nothing more.

The grizzly bear is an inferential beast.

Of course I've seen the inferential evidence—the photographs and movies, the broad tracks in the sand, the deep claw marks on a spruce tree higher than I could reach, the fresh bear shit steaming like hot caviar on the trail. And I've heard and read the testimony of many others. What does it come to? Inference. If p then q. It could all be a practical joke, a hoax, even a conspiracy. Which is more likely? asked Mark Twain (I paraphrase): that the unicorn exists or that men tell lies?

The grizzly bear is a myth.

The high peaks of the Brooks Range stand behind us, to the south, barren of trees, dappled with snowfields and a few small glaciers. To the east is Canada, the border perhaps another fifty miles away. The nearest city in that direction would be Murmansk. Murmansk, Russia. The nearest city to the west is also Murmansk. The nearest city in any direction is Fairbanks, almost 400 miles to the southwest. (If you are willing to allow Fairbanks a place in the category "city." And why not? We are a generous people.) The nearest permanently inhabited or reinhabited town, after Kaktovik up there in the Beaufort Sea, is an Athapaskan Indian settlement called Arctic Village a couple of hundred miles away on the other side, the southern wetter side, of the Brooks Range. White folks, I am told, are not welcome in Arctic Village, especially after sundown. And when the sun goes down in Arctic Village it stays down, in winter, for three months.

After the Australian outback, this is the most remote spot on which I've managed to install myself on this particular planet, so far. But it seems benign here, at the moment: especially the river flowing nearby, its water clean enough to drink, directly, without boiling or purifying. Imagine the rare, almost-forgotten pleasure of dipping a cup into a river—not a stream but a river—and drinking the water at once, without hesitation, without fear. There are no beaver in the Brooks, no domestic cattle, no permanent humans and extremely few transient humans, and therefore no coliform bacteria. So far.

And the sun keeps shining, circling, shining, not so intensely as in the desert or at high elevations (we're only twenty-five hundred feet above sea level here), but more persistently. With a doughty, dogged persistence: that midsummer sun never will go down.

The breeze continues to blow from downriver, a chill wind off the ice pack ninety miles north, but welcome to us here and now because it keeps the mosquitoes busy. They cling to the brush and weeds when the wind blows, come forth for blood transfusions only when it stops. . . .

The wind stops. Instantly, like magic, the air becomes *filthy* with little black bodies, hypodermic beaks, the whine of a billion tiny flapping wings. Dana and I smear hands, necks, hair, faces with a repellent poison and set to work erecting the cook tent. The mosquitoes are annoying but tolerable; they're here for better reasons than we are. And Dana for better reasons than I: he is a professional boatman, wilderness guide, mountaineering instructor, ice climber. He is paid to be here.

We gather firewood. Timberline begins at sea level on the north side of the Brooks Range divide, but there is a scrubby growth of willow, shoulder high, along the crystal river, and little groves of small slender cottonwoods—like baby aspens—tucked in sheltered corners here and there. We garner driftwood, enough for a couple of days, from the gravel bar.

Dana stops, hearing a noise in the willow thicket downstream. A noise like a thump and thud of heavy feet. He faces that way, watching intently. The noise stops. I look the other way, upstream and to both sides, afraid of something *fierce* creeping upon us from behind.

"It ain't wilderness," says my friend Doug Peacock, "unless there's a critter out there that can kill you and eat you."

Two pump-action short-barreled shotguns lie on our duffle a hundred feet away, loaded with twelve-gauge slugs. The shotguns have two purposes: one, to frighten away an aggressive bear; two, to stop and kill a charging bear. There are no trees fit to climb on the whole North Slope. A grizzly can run thirty-five miles an hour, uphill or down, with equal facility.

Back at the Barter Island airstrip Dana had explained the shotguns in the following way to one of our passengers: "You fire the first shot in front of the GRIZ, into the ground, to scare him away. If he don't scare but keeps advancing, you wait until you can't stand it anymore, then shoot to kill. First a shot to knock him down, next a shot to finish him off."

The masculine pronoun is a mere convention. The female grizzlies are as unpredictable as the males. There is no sure way anyhow, short of an intimate body examination, for a human to identify the sexes. A female with cubs, of course, is far more dangerous than the male. The males are bigger.

I especially like Dana's phrase *until you can't stand it anymore.* Thoroughly subjective but admirably rational. How close is too close? According to Edward Hoagland in his *Notes from the Century Before,* a book about British Columbia, survivors of close encounters with the grizzly report that one of the bear's most objectionable features is its foul breath. Don't shoot until you can smell the *Ursus halitosis.* Autopsies reveal that many grizzlies suffer from stomach ulcers. Why? We don't know. Like us, the bear is omnivorous, will eat anything—even humans—that it can catch. Eats our baggage too. A lone hiker in Glacier National Park was destroyed and mostly consumed ("harvested") by a bear a few years ago. The victim was a recent convert to the Moral Majority and carried a Bible in his pack. The park rangers' investigation disclosed that the grizzly had eaten most of the Bible also.

The man had been forewarned, if he'd read his gospel. There is a passage in the Old Testament in which God sics a bear upon a pack of unruly children.

Some people do not approve of carrying firearms in grizzly country. Again I refer to Douglas Peacock, who has lived and worked on close terms with the great bear for twelve years: to carry a gun, he says, distorts the psychology of the situation, makes a man cocky, noisy, overconfident, careless, reducing the opportunity for frequent, close and friendly relations with the grizzly. Doug says that he has been threatened many times and charged several times by nervous GRIZZ. He stands his ground, keeps talking in soft and mollifying tones, keeps on running his movie camera. So far the attacking bear has always turned aside before completing the charge, or soon enough to avoid losing face. "They decide I'm the dominant bear on the ridge," Doug says, standing over his campfire, smoking himself up in order to diminish the human scent. So far. Once a bear attacked his camp while Doug was away, ate his sleeping bag—a provocative act of inquiry. His study of the grizzly, he admits, is a two-way, mutual investigation. He hopes to finish his movie soon.

Doug Peacock usually works alone, responsible for nobody's life but his own. Commercial outfitters like Mark Jensen, and professional wilderness guides like Dana Van Burgh, feeling responsible for the safety of their clients—who have come a long way at considerable financial expense to enjoy the mosquitoes, white-sock blackflies, GRIZZ, polar bears, Arctic wind chill, avalanches, wolves, swamps, drunken Eskimos on motorized tricycles, the ice and isolation and other varied pleasures of Alaska—always bring shotguns.

The noise we heard is not repeated. Dana and I surmise a lone caribou browsing on willow leaves. We finish our work. Erecting my own tent—an Oval Invention from North Face—out on the gravel bar close to the river, where the breeze is breezier and the mosquitoes scattered, I happen to glance up and see a file of caribou, ten, twelve, fifteen of them, moving rapidly down the open mountainside on the other side of the Kongakut valley. They appear to be heading for an acre field of overflow ice, the white *Aufeis,* as the Germans call it, which covers much of the bottomland a half mile to our north. I watch them for a while through my binoculars. Pale brown or yellowish in color, as big as elk, each animal carries an impressive rack of antlers (not horns) on its head, the cow and yearling as well as the bull. They look to me like storybook reindeer, exactly the kind that Santa Claus once harnessed to his sleigh. The caribou gather on the ice and linger there, perhaps to escape for a time the flying swarms of devils that infest the grass, flowers, shrubs, heather and bracken of the tundra-upholstered hillsides.

Heather, bracken—there is much about this open, spacious, treeless terrain that recalls Scotland, the Hebrides, the maritime provinces of eastern Canada. We are, after all, not far from the Beaufort Sea, the ice packs of the Arctic Ocean. White Thayer's gulls, winging back and forth across the river, reinforce the resemblance.

The Cessna returns, circles once, floats down upon the rough shingle of the gravel bar, bounces to another hair-raising stop in an aura of dust. Dana has hung his rainbow-colored paper carp on a pole, providing a wind sock, but when we made the first landing there was no such indicator available. "How," I had asked our pilot, young Gil Zemansky, Ph.D. (biology), "do you determine wind direction in a place like this?" Looking down as we circled the apparent landing spot—and *spot* is the right word—I could see nothing, not even a drift of dust, to suggest the proper approach.

"I go by the feel of the plane," Dr. Zemansky replied. This technique was formerly known as "flying by the seat of the pants." He added, "Sometimes you can see wind ripples on the water."

The airplane is opened from within, disgorging the pilot, our trip leader Mark Jensen, another half ton of baggage and a lawyer. A lawyer on the Kongakut River? Everybody has to be somewhere, said the philosopher Parmenides, explaining his theory of the plenum. Her name is Ginger Fletcher, and she comes from Salt Lake City, where she works as a public defender. She's that kind of lawyer, public spirited, and a smart, lively, good-looking young woman to boot. (I list her more conspicuous attributes in random order of importance.) When she opens a bottle of schnapps from her bag, later that day, we name her Ginger Schnapps.

Like so many professional outdoors people, Mark Jensen is one of those depressing youngish types (thirty-four years old) with the body of a trained athlete, hands like Vise-Grips, a keen mind bright with ideas and full of enthusiasm for any project that promises the rewards of difficulty. He owns in fee simple the usual array of primary skills—being a first-class boatman, fisherman, hunter, camp cook, mountain climber and so on and so forth. I'm sick of these *Übermenschen* and wish that Fran Leibowitz and Nora Ephron were here. My kind of folks. He has hair like Robert Redford, drinks Wild Turkey and bears front and center on his face a sort of Robert Mitchum high-bridged nose, which gives him in profile the classical heroic Homeric look. Life is not fair. But in compensation he addresses everyone as "mate" or "partner," which fools no one.

Mark glances with approval at the standing cook tent, the twig fire crackling on its sheet-iron firepan, and says to his hired subordinate, "Coffee ready, mate?" Jensen is an insatiable coffee drinker.

Dana Van Burgh III is not overawed. "You forgot to pack it in the first load, blue eyes. You'll have to wait."

Jensen smiles, opens a big Thermos jug and pours each of us a cupful of hot smoking coffee. Gil Zemansky gulps his quickly, we pivot his aircraft around by hand, nose into the wind, and off he roars in all-out effort, racket-ing over the stones and gravel at sixty to eighty mph toward the willow thicket, the boulders, the river, departing earth as before at the last plausible mo-ment. He has one more trip to make, three more passengers to bring us, be-fore his work is done and the day ends. But of course, I remind myself, it's late June in the Arctic Zone; this day will not end, not for us. For us that sun never will go down.

We carry the baggage off the landing strip, build up the fire, start a two-gallon pot of coffee, eat a snack before supper. Or is it lunch? Ginger puts up her tent back in the caribou-cropped willows. We watch more caribou trickle over the mountain to join their friends on the ice field. A golden eagle sails overhead, and the gulls come and go, hoping for someone to catch and gut a fish. But seeing the growing assembly of caribou downriver, Mark Jensen and the others uncase their cameras and sneak that way, hoping for close-up pho-tographs. I follow with binoculars.

I realize that I have described all of these people, including the pilot, as young. Compared to me they are. Everywhere I go these days I seem to find myself surrounded by younger and younger humans. If one keeps hanging about, as I do, then the temporal horizon expands, the pursuing generations extend toward infinity. But why should I care? Sagging into my late middle age, I have discovered one clear consolation for my stiffening back (I never could touch my toes anyway, and why should I want to?), my mildewed pan-creas, my missing gall bladder, my *panza de cerveza,* my cranky and arthritic Anglo-Saxon attitudes. And the consolation is this—that I am content with my limitations.

The achievement of middle age is itself an achievement.

Unsuspecting, the caribou come to meet us, a herd of twenty-five or so. Anxious and bug-harassed creatures, they usually keep on the move. I can hear the lens shutters snapping in the thicket as the beasts splash through shallow water, approaching to within fifty feet of where I sit on the gravel beach. They pass me, their big ungulate feet clicking, then spot Dana's paper fish fluttering on its staff. They stop, turn, go the other way, finely attuned to one another's movements, ideas and opinions as a school of minnows. (Like literary critics.) Watching them at close range, I can see the velvet on their antlers, the large glowing eyeballs, the supple muscles, the spring and tension in their step. Each animal moves within its personalized cloud of gnats, flies, mosquitoes—every insect probing for entrance into an eye, nostril, ear, mouth, vagina, rectum or wound. I do not envy the caribou. North of here on the calving grounds, as we shall learn, the bear and wolves are attacking the newborn caribou at this very hour. The natives hound them on snowmobiles (or "snow machines," as Alaskans say), shooting them down by the thousands with high-powered, scope-sighted rifles ("subsistence hunting"). Even the golden eagle, according to some Alaska State Fish and Game officials, will attack and kill a caribou calf. Nobody envies the caribou. But like fruit flies, rabbits, alley cats, street rats and the human race, caribou possess one great talent for survival—not intelligence or the power of reasoning, but fertility, a high rate of reproduction.

The herd crosses the river again below the willow thicket, giving the photographers another chance at close pictures, and jogs in unison up the west side of the valley, beyond our camp. We return to campfire and coffee. Mark assembles his fly rod and goes fishing for char, not with a fly but a lure, the Luhr Jensen (made in Norway) "Krokodile," triple-hooked but without barbs. Mark has filed off the barbs. Anything he catches not big enough to be worth cooking and eating he can release and return to the river with minimal injury. Physical injury, I mean—who knows what psychic trauma the fish suffers? Experience suggests that refished fish are meaner, tougher, wilier than what one might call virginal fish.

Myself, I gave up fishing decades ago. Not so much on moral grounds—although I can see the point of animal liberationists when they argue that there is something unjust in fishing or hunting primarily for *sport*—but on account of sloth. I lack the diligence and industry to stand in one place for hours, casting and recasting, reeling in and reeling out, endeavoring to outwit a simple creature with a one-digit I.Q. and one-twentieth my body weight. In the time one man spends trying to catch one fish I have ascended a small mountain, explored five miles of river valley or probed to its secret heart a winding desert canyon.

I don't even much like to eat fish. In the outback I am content with a diet of cereal and powdered milk for breakfast, a hunk of cheese or a stick of jerky for lunch, a can of pork and beans for supper.

But these are private prejudices. I am aware of the argument that hunting and fishing can lead a man into an intense, intimate engagement with the natural world unknown to the casual hiker. When the hunting or fishing is based on hunger, on need, I know that this is true. But sport, in the end, is only sport—*divertissement*. A diversion, that is, from the central game of life. Which is—what? Let's not go into that. Furthermore, I have yet to taste the flesh of the fresh-baked Arctic char.

Once more our aerial taxicab returns, unloading the balance of the 1983 Kongakut expedition: John Feeley, a schoolteacher from a little town called

Whittier in southern Alaska; a legal secretary named Maureen Bachman from
Anchorage; and Mike Bladyka, an anesthesiologist from Los Angeles. Good
people, happy to be here. Each of us but John has been on a river trip with
Mark Jensen before. Obeying the territorial, nesting instinct, each sets up his
tent first thing. Maureen moves in with Ginger. John uncases his rod and goes
fishing, Mike joins the crowd in the cook tent, out of the wind, to manufacture
the salad for our first wilderness dinner. I too do my part: I sit on my ammo
can and activate my word processor. It's a good one. User-friendly, cheap,
silent, no vibrations or radiation, no moving parts, no maintenance, no power
source needed, easily replaceable, fully portable—it consists of a notebook
and a ball-point pen from "Desert Trees, 9559 N. Camino del Plata, Tucson,
Ariz." The necessary software must be supplied by the operator, but as
friendly critics have pointed out, an author's head is full of that.

Mark fails to land a worthwhile fish. John also fails—in fact he loses half
his tackle to a rock or submerged log or sunken fuel drum. They'll both do
better in the days to follow. For dinner we get by on soup, salad, spaghetti and
sauce with meatballs. We drink no beer on this trip. When air freight costs
one dollar a pound, beer is not cost effective; we subsist on wine, whisky,
schnapps and best of all, the forty-degree-cold immaculately conceived waters of the Kongakut River.

Jensen passes on the meatballs. A semivegetarian, he refuses on nutri-
tional grounds to eat beef and pork, asserting that in the ten years since giving
up on what he calls "dead red" he has become a healthier, happier, more
wholesome human being. He could be right about that, but the rest of us
disregard his advice and eat the meatballs. Every time we eat a cow, I remind
him, we save the life of a moose, two caribou, four mule deer or eight char
squared. He ponders the dilemma. I twist the knife: "Whose side are you on,
Jensen? God's side, Saint Francis's side, John Muir's side or the side of those
rangeland lawn mowers we call beef cattle?"

"Beef is bad for you, partner," he insists. "Look at this stunted little runt
Dana here, twenty-five years old and still not six foot high. Never will grow to
man size."

Dana helps himself to a second helping of the entrée. "At least I'm not
anemic. I can tie my shoes without gasping for air."

The sun angles sidewise behind some western peaks. But there is no sunset, no evening. Not even a twilight. The bald unmediated light continues to
shine on the mountainsides east of the river. There are a couple of wrist-
watches in our group but no one refers to them. There seems no point to it.
We plan to camp here for a second "day," a second "night." With only eighty

miles of river to run and ten days to do it in, this should be a leisurely journey. We sit on the surplus ammunition cans, the sturdy Gott coolers, and talk and drink too much coffee and contemplate the golden midnight light in the land of the midnight sun. At last and reluctantly, one by one, we let the wind or the mosquitoes or fatigue—it's been a long day—worry us into our tents.

The light inside my translucent nylon dome is bright enough to read a book by. The mosquitoes gather outside the netting of my doorway, poking their Pinocchio noses through the interstices, sniffing at me like bloodhounds. A few have followed me inside. I hunt them down, one at a time, and pinch their little heads off. For such resolute, persistent, vicious, bloodthirsty animalcules, they are surprisingly fragile. As individuals. One slap on the snout and they crumple. Collectively they can drive a bull moose insane. I feel no remorse in extinguishing their miserable lives. I'm a coldhearted bleeding heart. Yet I know that even the mosquito has a function—you might say a purpose—in the great web of life. Their larvae help feed fingerlings, for example. Certain of their women help spread the parasitic protozoa that give us dengue, breakbone fever, yellow fever and malaria, for example, keeping in control the human population of places like Borneo, Angola, Italy and Mississippi. No organism can be condemned as totally useless.

Nevertheless, one does not wish them well. I would not kill them all, but I will certainly kill every one I can catch. Send them back where they came from.

We sleep. I dream that I hear robins, two hundred miles north of the Arctic Circle. Dreaming of Home, Pennsylvania.

JUNE 25— Today we climb a mountain. We follow a brook up a deep ravine, over the rocks and a deep-pile carpet of tundra, lupine, buttercups, forget-me-nots, campion, mountain avens, bayrose, eight-petal dryas, kinnikinnick, saxifrage ("stonebreakers"), woolly lousewort (a favorite of mine), Labrador tea, drunken bumblebees, piles of caribou droppings like chocolate-covered almonds, pictographic lichen on the limestone and many little yellow composites. What are these? asks Ginger. Don't know, says Mark. Water gurgles under the rocks. Call it a virus, says Dana; that's what doctors do when they don't know. Ain't that right, Doc? Doctor Mike smiles, chuffing along with me in the rear guard of the party. Aside from myself, he is the only person here over the age of thirty-five.

We scramble up a pile of scree and eat lunch on the summit, twenty-five hundred feet above the river, five thousand feet above sea level. Snowy peaks lift hoary heads (as John Muir would say) in most—not all—directions. We are in that part of the Brooks Range called the Romanzof Mountains, which recalls the former colonizers of the Alaskan territory. To the Russians Alaska must have seemed like merely a two-bit extension of Siberia. Extreme East Slobbovia. No wonder they parted with it so cheaply.

Americans think Alaska is big. The Mackenzie Territory of northwest Canada is bigger. Siberia is several times bigger than both combined. So much for surface extension. If the state of Utah, which consists mostly of mountains, plateaus, mesas, buttes, pinnacles, synclines, anticlines, folds, reefs, canyons and vertical canyon walls, were ironed out flat it would take up more room on a map than Texas. What does that prove? It's what is there, or here, now, that matters. So much for chauvinism. Most of the mountains around us, so far as we know, have never been climbed by anybody but the Dall sheep. The majority have not even been named, except for the most prominent, like Michelson (9,239 feet) and Chamberlin (9,131).

We return to camp by a different route, finding fresh bear sign on the way—torn-up sod, where the bear was rooting for marmots and ground squirrels; a well-trod bear trail; a messy pile of bear dung. Dana carries his shotgun slung on shoulder, but we stay alert as we march along. There is an animal out here that is bigger than we are. And *he* sings, as he rollicks along, "Yea, though I walk through the valley of the shadow of death I will fear no evil, for I am the evilest motherfucker in the valley."

We tramp through a mile of muskeg at the foot of the hills. Now we see what the rubber boots are for. Muskeg consists of tussocks of balled-up grass, each tussock the size of a human head, all rooted in a bog. The thoughtless locals down in Fairbanks call these unstable obstacles "nigger heads" but "Swede heads" would be more appropriate, for they are blond, straight haired and long-headed. It is difficult to walk in the soft muck between them, even more difficult to walk upon or over them. Some "desert" this is. True, the average annual rainfall and snowfall is only between eight and ten inches. But the permafrost, the nearly universal permafrost, that hidden layer of never-thawing impermeable ice, prevents water from sinking below the surface of the ground. The North Slope is our swampiest desert; Alaska, our biggest, boggiest, buggiest state. We lurch and stumble through the mire, and as we advance great shimmering hosts of mosquitoes rise eagerly from the weeds to greet us. Dripping in sweat and the greasy oil of insect repellent, we stagger on. Takes guts to live in Alaska, no doubt about it. I am favorably impressed, once again, by the pluck and hardihood of these people, both native and white. I wonder though, sometimes, about their native intelligence.

We reach camp, the fresh breeze, the welcome hard ground of the gravel beach, wade into the icy river for a drink, then a shampoo, a bath—ladies upstream, men downstream.

Shivering in the wind, I dry myself with my cleanest dirty shirt. Forgot to bring a towel. The wind is coming up the river, as usual, from the north and the frozen Arctic Sea; I can feel that chill malignancy penetrate the marrow of my bones. Hurriedly I dress, layering on a shirt, a hooded sweatshirt and a parka. When I feel warm the wind stops.

And *they* come out again. I wait. One slap on the arm kills nine. Forgot to bring cigars. I reach for the repellent.

We have a Mexican dinner for supper, preceded by a pitcher of margaritas. The margaritas we ice with snow carried down from the mountain in a daypack by Mike, a thoughtful and foresighted man. We drink to his health. Life is rough on the Last Frontier. Don't feel quite right myself, but it's only a matter of acclimatizing: when I left Tucson three days ago the temperature was 106 in the shade; at Salt Lake City, where we paused for a day and a night, it was 65 degrees and stormy; at Fairbanks (elevation 440 feet), where I stayed for two nights, the air was hot, humid, muggy, close to 90 degrees and hotter than that in my little cell at the El Sleazo Hotel on the banks of the Chena River; from Fairbanks by DC-3 to Barter Island, on the edge of the Arctic ice pack, we found ourselves in the heart of the wind-chill factory—even the Eskimos were wearing their parkas; and now on the river, where the wind comes and goes, the temperature seems to fluctuate from subfreezing to 80 and back again. But no one complains about the weather except me, and I do it inwardly only; can't let the others know that the most sissified rugged outdoorsman in the West is now squatting among them on his ammo can, huddled in thermal long johns, wool pants, wool shirt, flannel sweatshirt, wool ski cap and a flannel-lined hooded parka.

Before turning in for the sun-bright night I requisition a handful of aspirins from the expedition infirmary; Mark also doses me with ten thousand milligrams of vitamin C and other huge jellied capsules, spansules and suppositories, each about horse-size. "Can't get sick on us, mate," he says; "you know there's no germs north of the Arctic Circle."

"Of course not," I agree. "But one could always show up." Crawling into my geodesic tent, sliding into my antique, greasy, duct-tape–mended mummy bag, I say to myself, No germs, eh? Well, if I was a germ I wouldn't want to live here either.

The sun shines all night long.

JUNE 26— I awake by degrees to the sound of robins chirping in the cherry trees. Impossible. But when I emerge from my cocoon the first thing I see is a fat robin redbreast bouncing along on the gravel bar. How could such a small, harmless, innocent bird travel so far? Or, as Jensen says, how many FPM (wing flaps per minute) to cover three thousand miles?

Mark has caught an eighteen-inch char for breakfast; four to five pounds. He packs it with herbs and butter, wraps it in aluminum foil and bakes it on a grill over the low driftwood fire. The flesh is firm, sweet, pink, something like fresh salmon but better, not so oily, much like the Dolly Varden we used to eat, years ago, from that little lake—Akakola—below the Numa Ridge fire lookout in Glacier Park. The Dolly Varden, in fact, is a type of char.

Today we plan to set out on the Kongakut. We inflate, rig and load the two neoprene rafts, strike tents, police the site. Like all good professional outfitters, Mark Jensen practices no-trace camping. Everything noncombustible is hammered flat with a stone and packed out. The ashes from the fire, collected on the metal firepan, are dumped into the river, where they will end their chemic lives blended with the Arctic Ocean. Even our footprints—since we've made camp on the floodplain—will be obliterated by the next rise in the river.

None of these measures is yet required by official regulations, although we are in the heart of the Arctic National Wildlife Refuge, a federal preserve. Mark does it because he believes in it, because it's right and because we may be followed, someday, by others. And he takes the opportunity to grumble a bit about the Eskimos, Indians, trophy hunters and oil-company exploration crews, who have left so much of Alaska littered with empty fuel drums, toilet paper, Pampers, whisky bottles, broken-down Ski-doos, Pop-Tart wrappers, tangled fishing tackle, Cat-train tracks, the swash plates and lag hinges from dilapidated helicopters.

Pampers? Oh yes, the plastic diaper is quite popular now with the natives. Universally used. Whereas the Alaskan women formerly employed fingers and tongues to clean their babies, they now prefer the synthetic substitute, like most mothers everywhere else (though cotton is better for babies' bottoms). Old ways die easily—they tumble over themselves in a *rush* to die— when confronted by the frills of high-tech Western civilization. However, it does seem hypocritical of the natives to complain, as they eagerly embrace the worst of our culture, that we are destroying the best of theirs. They can't have it both ways. The role of victim can be pushed too far. There even may be a limit to the white-liberal-guilt neurosis.

Back off, mate. You're stepping on taboos again. I can hear the stir and crackling of tired old middle-class hackles rising all around me.

We launch forth onto troubled waters. Check the time by Maureen's quartz crystal wristwatch: 2:00 P.M., Fairbanks time. We have again failed to crack the noon barrier. But here where high noon lasts for hours, it does not matter.

We float downstream through the treeless hills, among the golden tundra mountains. It's something like boating through Colorado at thirteen thousand feet. We see golden plovers out on the flats, another golden eagle overhead. And the gulls. And the robins. And a raven.

"My favorite bird," says Mark. "Smart, talented, handsome—"

"Like you," says Ginger.

"Like me. When I—" He points to the high mountainside on our left. "Sheep."

A herd of Dall sheep are grazing up there, a dozen of them—ewes, lambs, rams with curling horns. Placid, motionless, they watch us—phantom beings out of nowhere—drifting through their world.

"When I come back," continues Mark, "I want to come back as a raven."

"Crawling with lice," Ginger points out. "Smelling like a dead fish."

"With a beak even bigger than the beak you've got now," says Maureen. "Proportionately speaking."

Smiling, Mark stands up between the oars to survey the channel ahead. Like most Alaskan rivers, the Kongakut is a shallow river, broad and braided, hard to read, forcing the boatman to search constantly for the one navigable channel among many false options. We'll portage twice before this voyage is done, and jockey the boats several times over submerged gravel bars. Following us in the second boat, Dana watches carefully. Only Mark has seen this river before.

All goes well today. In the evening we make camp on another bar, a pleasant site with limestone cliffs overlooking the river, a grove of little ten-foot cottonwoods on the other shore, a vista upriver of the valley we have come through and the splendid craggy snowy mountains beyond. The classic Alpine-Arctic scene—photogenic, fundamental, perfect.

Why are there almost no trees on the north slope of the Brooks? Because of the permafrost two feet below the surface, a substratum of rocklike ice, which prevents trees from sinking roots. Only close to the river, where the ground is warmer, can the dwarf willows and midget cottonwoods take hold.

Years ago I was employed briefly as a technical writer for the Western

Electric Company in New York City. The company had a contract with the
War Department to prepare training manuals for the workers building the
Arctic radar stations and air bases of the Distant Early Warning system. One
hundred of us sat at desks in one huge office ten floors above Hudson Street
in lower Manhattan. Fluorescent lights glared down upon our bent, white-
shirted backs. (All technical writers were required to wear white shirts. With
tie.) Since my security clearance had not yet come through, I was assigned the
menial task of editing the manual called *How to Dispose of Human Sewage in
Permafrost.* I told the boss I wanted to be sent to the Arctic in order to con-
duct first-hand field studies. He told me that my job was spelling, grammar
and punctuation, not shit research. I returned to my desk among the other
stuffed bent white shirts—we all faced in the same direction—and stared
moodily out the window for two weeks, watching the sun go down over Hoboken, New Jersey.

The boss came to me. "Abbey," he says, "do you really want to work for
Western Electric?" "No, sir," I said, "not really." "I thought not," he said;
"we're letting you go as of seventeen hundred hours today." I could have
kissed him—and knowing New York, I probably should have. "That's all right,
sir," I said, "I'm leaving right now, as of thirteen-thirty hours." And I did.
Spent the afternoon at the White Horse Tavern on Hudson Street, then with
cronies at Minsky's Burlesque in Newark. Reported to my wife, drunk and
happy, at twenty-two hundred hours with what was left of my first and final
Western Electric paycheck. Pointed the old Chevy pickup south and west at
twenty-three hundred hours headed for Arizona. Never did learn how to dispose of human sewage (is there any other kind?) in permafrost.

But I know now. As I discovered on Barter Island, they dump it into a
sewage lagoon two feet deep, chlorinate the water and drink it. And how do
they dispose of general garbage on the North Slope? They don't; they leave it
on the surface, where it becomes the highest and most scenic feature of the
landscape.

Beef stroganoff for supper. The Russian influence lingers on in nostalgia-
loving Alaska.

Loaded with aspirin and more of Jensen's horse medicine, I retire early to
my tent, still not feeling too good. Forgot to bring a towel, forgot the cigars,
forgot to bring a book. So I borrow a paperback from Maureen—something
called *Still Life with Woodpecker*? Yes, that appears to be the title. I glance at
the blurbs, the summary on the back cover. "You didn't bring anything for
grown-ups?" She has not. "Did anybody?" I ask the group.

Dana offers me a book called *The Dancing Wu Li Masters* by a Mr. Gary

Zukav. Another California-type book. "How about a Gideon's Bible? Or a dictionary?" Mark offers his ammo-can edition of Merriam-Webster's. "Already read that one," I say. I borrow the first two, churlish ungrateful bastard, and skulk off. The wind has died; a number of dancing Wu Li masters follow me into my tent. I slaughter them and bed down with Tom Robbins and Mr. Gary Zukav. *Ménage a trois . . . de poupée . . . entente . . .*

I was sick for the next two days.

JUNE 27— Morning, so to speak. Mark asks me how I'm feeling. "Great!" I say, lying through the skin of my eyeteeth.

"You sure?"

"For Chrissake, Jensen, I was sleeping in elk pastures when you were wearing Pampers in the sixth grade."

"We can stay here another day, you know. Lots of time."

"To hell with that. Down the river! Onward!"

Breakfast goes by in a blur. We load the boats, shove off, glide down the current between walls of turquoise-colored *Aufeis*. An ice gulch. Horned white sheep, like woolly maggots, crawl upon the distant hillsides. Clouds cover the sun; the Arctic wind comes sweeping up the river. Dana strains at the oars, sweating hard to keep up with Mark while I sit huddled in the bow swaddled in layers of Pendleton and polyester and self-pity. Dana tries to keep the conversational hacky-sack in the air, working manfully to maintain both civility and headway against the wind. "Let me know if you see a GRIZ," I growl, nodding off. He nods.

Hours pass, along with some gravel bars, a few willow thickets, more walls of ice. This is the kind of thing, I say to myself, that no one actually wants to do. And afterward you're not even glad you did it. Unlike the infantry, or suicide, or exploratory surgery. I become aware of danger ahead. Trouble: I look up hopefully.

Mark has beached his rubber raft on a most unlikely, rough and difficult spot. Emphatically he signals Dana to bring his boat alongside. "Ready for a fast landing," Dana says, pulling hard toward shore. I pick the coiled bowline from under my rubber boots. We grate onto the ice and gravel, I stagger out with the rope and hold the boat against the violent tug of the current. Dana jumps out, we heave the boat higher onto the gravel. There is nothing here to tie up to: all hands are summoned to drag both boats out of the river.

Mark talks quietly with Dana. Followed by John, they go off to investigate something ahead. All that I can see, from where we have landed, is the river funneling into a narrow channel between vertical walls of blue ice six to ten feet high. Fifty yards ahead the river swerves around a bend, going out of view within the icy walls. We have stopped at the last possible takeout point short of a full commitment to the ice canyon.

"What seems to be the trouble here?" I say, holding out my GI canteen cup. Ginger is pouring hot coffee from the Thermos jug. My hands shake with cold; I need both hands to hold my cup steady.

"Don't know," she says. "Mark said he doesn't like the looks of the river here."

"Looks like the same old Styx to me," Mike says from deep within his parka hood. I'm glad to see that he too is feeling the cold. Los Angeles. He and I, the only southwesterners in the party, are equally thin blooded.

Mark, Dana, John come back. Mark looks somber, an unusual expression for his habitually cheerful face. "We'll camp here, mates."

"Here? On the ice?"

He points to the left bank, beyond the ice. "Over there." We unload the boats and carry our gear and baggage to dry land, then come back for the boats. By then we've seen what the problem is. Not far beyond the bend the river goes *under* the ice, emerging a hundred feet beyond. If we had gone on in the boats we would have been trapped and drowned beneath the ice, or if flushed through, probably died of hypothermia before we found dry matches and sufficient wood to get a big fire going.

"I had this feeling," Mark says.

Most of the party get out cameras for pictures of the ice tunnel. I pitch my tent and creep inside. Aspirins and river water and sleep for me. I am awakened frequently through the long hours that follow by the roar of huge chunks of ice calving from the frozen walls, crashing into the river.

Warm weather again. By breakfast time, which by now has slipped to ten or eleven in the morning, the ice tunnel is reduced to a narrow ice bridge. Then the bridge collapses, sending a small tidal wave upstream over the gravel bar on which we've erected the cook tent and camp headquarters. But no damage is done and the river is again clear.

JUNE 28— I totter down the hill from my tent and join the jolly bunch around the breakfast fire. Mutely, sadly, I hold out my tin cup; someone pours coffee into it. "How's it going, partner?" our leader says.

"Great," I mumble, "great."

"You don't look good," he says. "In fact you look sick. Time for more horse capsules, mate."

I swallow the jellied suppositories and watch Ginger and Mike squabbling politely over Mark's last blueberry pancake. You take it, she says. Naw, you take it, Mike says. They remind me, in my fluish delirium, of my friend Kevin Briggs, another river rat, and of his parable of the last pork chop.

My friend Kevin is a stout, husky fellow with a vigorous appetite. Being a graduate student of philosophy and literature he is always hungry. One day he and five classmates were invited to lunch by their teacher, Ms. Doctor Professor H——. A kind, well-meaning but frugal woman, Professor H—— seated her six guests at the dining table in her home and set a platter holding exactly seven pork chops at the head of the table. Kevin, seated on her right, too hungry to waste time counting the pork chops, helped himself to two from the top and passed the platter on. Professor H—— meanwhile had gone back to her kitchen. She returned with the mashed potatoes and gravy just as the platter had nearly completed its round of the table. One pork chop remained. She sat down. The young man on her left, who had not yet served himself, looked at the last pork chop, then at his hostess. She looked at him. Both laughed, awkwardly. You take it, he said. Oh no, she said, you take it. I'm really not hungry, he said. I'm not either, really, she said. Kevin by this time had gobbled down everything on his plate; he reached across the table with his fork and stabbed the last pork chop. I'll eat it, he said. And he did.

Moral? He who hesitates is second? No, Kevin explained to me, not at all. Remember the words of our Lord and Savior: "To him that hath much, much shall be given. But verily, from him that hath little, that little shall be taken away." (Matthew, X:xii.)

Mark Jensen, looking at me, says, "We'll stay here a couple of days. Who wants to climb another mountain?"

I creep back to my tent. I read the borrowed books.

I cough, I blow my nose, I read and finish *Still Life with Woodpecker* and try to imagine what the typical Tom Robbins reader (and there are millions) must be like. Well, first of all, she would be about twelve years old. She? No, it. *It* is about twelve years old, a thoroughly homogenized androgyne of neuter sex. It lives in California or north-central New Mexico, also likes Rod McKuen, studies kundalini yoga, loves stuffed koala bears, thinks the *Whole Earth Catalog* is a book, believes Bob "Dylan" is a poet and Neil Diamond a musician, disdains politics as "too political" and . . . enough! The soul staggers, sinking deep into the swampy muskeg of pop Kultur. Put it this way: one spoonful of Tom Robbins's prose is enough to sicken the mind for hours. To read a Tom Robbins book from end to end is like chugalugging a quart of Aunt Jemima's pancake syrup. Or like—like the time a Supai Indian and I were stranded for two days at the head of Topocoba Trail at Grand Canyon waiting for a truck that arrived two days late. We had nothing with us to eat, absolutely nothing, but a straw basket full of overripe figs. We ate them.

We should have eaten the basket, fed the figs to the horses.

I crawl from my tent on hands and knees, vomit on a harmless cluster of forget-me-nots, state flower of Alaska (there are flowers everywhere on the tundra in the bright, jocund Arctic spring), crawl back in the tent and open *The Dancing Wu Li Masters*. The title is not encouraging but I am sure that I will find something nice to say about this book. I have never met a book yet that did not have *something* good about it.

Until now.

Hours later I am stirred from a deep stupor by Mark Jensen, bringing me with his own hands a bowl of hot celery soup and a plate containing chunks of fish with noodles and mashed potatoes. It looks good and I am hungry.

"How's it going, partner?"

"Fine, Mark, fine. Say, this is damn good fish. You catch another char?"

"That's turkey. Out of a can."

"Damn good. See any GRIZZ?"

"Had a glimpse of one going over the next ridge. Only for a minute. A true silvertip—we could see the fur shining on the shoulder hump. You should've been there, mate."

"I know. What else?"

"Lots of sheep. A wolf. A lone bull caribou."

"Sure sorry I missed that bear."

"We thought of you, mate. If I'd had a good rope with me I'd have lassoed the son of a bitch and led him back here. Better take some more of these pharmaceuticals."

JUNE 30— Another gay, sunny, brisk, breezy Arctic morning. We carry the boats to the river, since the river will not come to us, and proceed as before, downstream. My flu has entered its terminal phase, and I am ready to meet my Maker, eyeball to eyeball, way up here on top of the world, as we say in these parts.

The top of the world. But of course, the giddy, dizzying truth is that the words "top" and "bottom," from a planetary point of view, have no meaning.

From out here in deep space, where I am orbiting, there is no top, there is no bottom, no floor, no ceiling, to anything. We spin through an infinite void, following our curving path around the sun, which is as bewildered as we are. True, the infinite is incomprehensible—but the finite is absurd. Einstein claimed otherwise, I know, but Einstein was only a mortal like us. No ceiling, no floor, no walls. . . . We are 250 miles north of the Arctic Circle, and we flow as we go, like spindrift, like bits of Styrofoam, through the outliers of what Mark says is the northernmost mountain range in the world, i.e., on Earth. Will we ever get back to downtown Kaktovik?

I think of the Eskimos, holed up all day inside their $250,000 air-freighted prefab modular houses (paid for with oil royalties), watching "Mr. Rogers' Neighborhood" on their brand-new color TV sets. A few grinning kids race up and down the dirt street, among the melting snowbanks, on their Honda ATCs. What we call "road lice" back in the Southwest. (Girls love horses. Little boys love machines. Grown-up men and women like to walk.) The kids seem to have nothing else to do. A dead bowhead whale—rare species—lies rotting on the waterfront, partially dismembered. Slabs of whale blubber—muktuk—are stacked in the yard of each house, along with empty plywood crates, diesel spills, oil drums, Ski-doo parts, caribou antlers, musk-ox bones, wolf pelts, moose heads, worn-out rubber boots, tin cans and liquor bottles and loose papers and plastic potsherds. In each yard lies one howling arthritic Huskie dog, token souvenir of former days, short-chained to a stake, out of reach of the muktuk. The dogs are never released from the chain.

When I entered the village store to buy some good cheap mosquito-repellent cigars I found the shelves loaded with cartons and cases of Pepsi-Cola, candy bars, Holsum bread, sweet rolls, cigarettes, Oreo cookies, Cheezits, Coleman fuel, propane bottles, not much else. No cigars. The manager of the store is a white man. The village post office (ZIP code 99747) is operated by a young white woman. The teachers in the ten-million-dollar school are all whites. When something goes wrong with the village plumbing or electricity (the steady bellow of diesel generators, louder than wind, makes a constant background noise at Kaktovik and Barter Island), as happens frequently, private contractors—white men—are flown in from Fairbanks or Anchorage, at enormous expense, to repair the damage. This has nothing to do with race discrimination; the natives don't want the jobs.

And the wind blows day and night, forever, out of the north, from beyond the dead whale on the beach, from beyond the mangled ice floes, out of the infinite wastes of the most awesome sight in the North: that pale cold no-man's-land, that endless frozen desert of ice leading as far as eye can perceive out over the Beaufort Sea and into the Arctic Ocean. Toward the Pole.

What will happen to these people when the North Slope oil gives out? The Eskimos and other Alaskan natives still enjoy the hunt, as much or more than ever, and when they do go hunting, on their screaming packs of snow machines, they kill everything that moves. (The musk-ox, for example, had to be reintroduced from Canada into the Arctic Wildlife Refuge because the natives, equipped with white man's machines and armed with white man's weapons, had exterminated the local herds.) But this kind of hunting, whether of land animals or of seals, whales, fish, polar bear, is entirely dependent upon technology. Impossible to imagine, I was told, that the new generations would or could return to the traditional nomadic way, following the game in its seasonal migrations from Alaska to Canada and back, surviving in hide tents and sod huts under the snow as their ancestors—their still-living grandparents—had done. Unimaginable. They'll all move to the slums of Fairbanks, Anchorage and Seattle, join the public-welfare culture, before consenting to such romantic humiliation. Can't blame them; until the coming of the white man the natives spent half their lives on the edge of starvation. Famine was common. Now, despite alcoholism, violence, suicide, their population is growing—and fast.

But we are told—and sometimes by the natives themselves—that they were a stronger, happier people before. They certainly don't appear to be happy now.

What happens to these people when they migrate to the city? I think of "Two Street" (Second Avenue), Fairbanks, which resembles the center of Flagstaff or Gallup on a Saturday night. There is even a "Navajo Taco Stand" on one corner, selling genuine Athapaskan tacos (fry bread, shredded lettuce and hamburger), and the street is lined with grim little bars jam-packed with brawling Indians and Eskimos. Drunken aborigines lean on the walls outside, sit on the sidewalks, stumble toward the taxicab lineup to get a four-block ride home to some chain-saw shanty on the edge of town. Half conscious, they stare at you through eyes the complexion of strawberries, and try to bum a dollar. I saw one man *descamisado*, naked from the waist up, staggering down the street with one foot on the sidewalk and the other in the gutter; he looked confused.

Trying to look friendly I stepped into the doorway of a bar, thinking I needed a beer. One glance inside and I knew this was no place for an innocent white boy from the far south. The bar was lined wall-to-wall with dark, sullen, hostile faces, and in the middle of the floor two five-foot three-hundred-

pound Athapaskan women stood toe-to-toe socking the piss out of each other.
Just like down home: the Club 66 in Flag, the Eagle in Gallup or the Silver
Dollar in Bluff, on the edge of the Navajo reservation—the only bar in Utah
where you can hear squaw dance music on the jukebox. I withdrew. The
sights, the smells and the noise were making me homesick.

The bars in Alaska are legally open twenty-one hours a day. From 5:00
A.M. to 8:00 A.M. they are required by law to close. It is then, say the white
locals, that you'll see "the moles crawl out of their holes."

Resentment on one side, contempt on the other: the race war in Alaska
looks as promising as it does most everywhere else on our overpopulated,
much-abused, ever-percolating planet.

Les misanthropes must love it here.

Back, for godsake, *back*—to the decency and the sanity of the wild river.
If there is a civilized society left anywhere on Earth it exists among the caribou, the wolves, the eagles, the bighorn and the moose of the Kongakut.

We camp today at a broad open place that Mark has named Velvet Valley.
Under a spiny, purple, crenellated mountain that looks like Mordor, like the
Hall of the Mountain King, like Darth Vader's childhood playpen, like the
home of the Wicked Witch of the North, extends a lovely valley clothed in
golden tundra, a million bloody blooming flowers, the lambent glowing light
of the midnight sun. (I dislike that word *lambent*, but it must be employed.) A
soft, benevolent radiance, you might say, playing upon the emerald green, the
virgin swales of grass and moss and heather and Swede heads.

The Arctic wind blows merrily; it takes four of us to get the cook tent up,
our only communal shelter. Feeling a mite better now, I scrounge for firewood with the others, and soon we've got a good fire burning near the entrance to the tent, a big meal under way inside.

More time slippage. We'd eaten lunch at five in the afternoon, we're having dinner at eleven. Time, says Einstein, is a function of space. Or time, said
another philosopher, is but the mind of space. How true. And is everything
finally only relative? It is not. The light is fixed and absolute. Especially the
Arctic light. We'll eat dinner at eleven and have a midnight snack in Seward's
Icebox at four in the morning if we bloody well feel like it. Who's to stop us?

The sun shines all night long.

JULY 2— John and Mark catch a big char and a small grayling for breakfast. A
fine kettle of fish.

We go for a walk up the Velvet Valley, through the willows, through the muskeg, up onto the tundra, deep into the valley. Flowers everywhere, each flower concealing a knot of mosquitoes, but we're accustomed to the little shitheads by now; they don't bother us. We rub on the bug juice and let the insects dance and hover—patterns of organic energy made visible—in futile molecular orbits one inch from the skin. Like the flies in Australia the mosquitoes here become simply part of the atmosphere, the décor, the ambience. We ignore them.

A ram watches us from a high point of rock; his flock grazes above. Mark kneels by a mountain stream trying to photograph the crosshatched ripples of converging currents. Dana glasses the high ridges for bear, shotgun at his side. John is fishing back at the river. Mike, Maureen and Ginger are eating cheese and crackers and identifying the many flowers (with the help of a guidebook) that I have not mentioned. I sit on the grass scribbling these notes, with a clump of Siberian asters fluttering at my elbow.

This is what I am writing:

Alaska is not, as the state license plate asserts, "the Last Frontier." Alaska is the final big bite on the American table, where there is never quite enough to go around. "We're here for the megabucks," said a construction worker in the Bunkhouse at Kaktovik, "and nothing else." At the Bunkhouse the room and board costs $150 per day, on the monthly rate, but a cook can earn $10,000 a month. Others much more. Alaska is where a man feels free to destroy an entire valley by placer mining, as I could see from the air over Fairbanks, in order to extract one peanut-butter jar full of gold dust. Flying from Barter Island to the Kongakut, pilot Gil Zemansky showed me the vast spread of unspoiled coastal plain where Arco, Chevron and others plan oil and gas exploration in the near future, using D-7 bulldozers pulling sledges, thus invading the caribou calving grounds and tearing up the tundra and foothills of the Arctic Wildlife Refuge, last great genuine wilderness area left in the fifty United States. Under the heavy thumb of James Watt, the Fish and Wildlife Service apparently has no choice but to knuckle under to the demands of the oil industry. In southeast Alaska the industrial tree farmers who now run the U.S. Forest Service are allowing the logging companies to clearcut and decimate vast areas of the Tongass National Forest, home of our national bird, the bald eagle, and officially, ostensibly, the legal property of the American public—all of us. With Dracula placed in charge of the blood bank (as Congressman Morris Udall has said), Alaska, like the rest of our public domain, has been strapped down and laid open to the lust and greed of the international corporations. "Last Frontier"? Not exactly: Anchorage, Fairbanks and outposts like Barter Island, with their glass-and-aluminum office buildings, their airlift prefab fiberboard hovels for the natives and the workers, their compounds of elaborate and destructive machinery, exhibit merely the latest development in the planetary expansion of space-age sleaze—not a frontier but a high-technology slum. For Americans, Alaska is the last pork chop.

What then is a frontier? The frontier, in my view, is that forgotten country where men and women live with and by and for the land, in self-reliant communities of mutual aid, in a spirit of independence, magnanimity and trust. (As Henry Thoreau once said.) A few people, but not many—few of the natives and even less of the whites—still attempt to inhabit Alaska in such a manner. The majority, it appears, or at least the majority of the vocal and powerful, are here for the profits. For the megabucks.

JULY 3— Down the river, through the portal of the mountains into the foothills, approaching the coastal plain, we float northward in our little air-filled boats. Seeing that I have come back to life, the literary natives on shipboard badger me with bookish questions. I am happy to oblige.

What's the best book about Alaska? The best book about the North, I say, is *The Call of the Wild*. In the words of a critic, Jack London captures there the essence of the mythos of the wilderness. No, she says, I mean about Alaska? *Winter News*, I say, by John Haines—pure poetry; and by "pure" I mean poetry about ordinary things, about the great weather, about daily living experience, as opposed to technical poetry, which is concerned mainly with prosody, with technique (one of my favorite lectures). Don't lecture me, she says, I'm talking about prose—about books in prose. (I sense a trap about to snap.) What's the best prose book about Alaska? I pause for a moment, pretending to reflect, and say *Going to Extremes* by Joe McGinniss. A brilliant book. Mandatory for anyone who wants a sense of what contemporary life in Alaska is like. My opinion does not set well with the locals. No! they say, McGinniss writes only about the sensational. Alaska is a sensational place, I reply. He's a scandalmonger, they say. Alaska is a scandalous place, I say; McGinniss tells the truth. How much time have you spent in Alaska? they want to know. About four weeks, all told, I answer. They smile in scorn. Four weeks of observation, I explain, is better than a lifetime of daydreaming. What about *Coming into the Country*? someone asks. I had to admit that I had started on that book but never finished it. More questions. I say, since I left Cherry Tree down in Tennessee, this is the first time I've been warm. McPhee, I explain, is a first-rate reporter, but too mild, too nice, too cautious—no point of view. You like Robert Service? I love him. But, says my first inquisitor, I don't think you really love Alaska, do you? The most attractive feature of Alaska, I say, is its small, insignificant human population, thanks to the miserable climate. Thanks a lot, she says. I like the mountains, the glaciers, the wildlife and the roominess, I hasten to add—or I would if the bugs would stop crowding me. I think you are a geographical chauvinist, she says; a spatial bigot. Special? Spatial. Well, I confess, I'll admit I've lived too long in the Southwest; I should have saved that for last. Then what are you doing in Alaska? she says.

Me?

You.

Slumming, I explain.

Quiet, whispers Mark, resting on the oars. Look over there.

We look where he points. Three wolves are watching us from another bar beside the river, less than a hundred feet away. Three great gray shaggy wolves, backlit by the low sun, staring at us. Silently we drift closer. Gently, Mark pulls the boat onto the gravel, where it stops. Don't get out, Mark whispers. The wolves watch, the cameras come out, the wolves start to move away into the willow thicket and toward the open tundra. A whistle stops the last one as it climbs the bank. I stare at the wolf through my binoculars, the wolf stares at me; for one, still, frozen, sacred moment I see the wild green fire in its eyes. Then it shrugs, moves, vanishes.

We drift on, silently, down the clear gray waters. After a while my friend says to me, When's the last time you saw something like that in Arizona? In your whole crowded, polluted Southwest?

Me?

You.

Moi?

Vous.

Another pause. Never did, I say.

You ought to be ashamed of yourself.

I am.

You ought to take back everything you've said.

I take it all back. (*But,* I think, all the same . . .)

Now the river tangles itself into a dozen different channels, all shallow. The main channel runs straight into a jungle of willow. We unload the boats, portage them and our gear around the obstruction. As I'm lugging two ten-gallon ammo cans across the damp silt I see a pair of tracks coming toward me. Big feet with claw marks longer than my fingers. The feet are not so long as mine but they are twice as wide. Double wides, size 10-EEEE. I stop and look around through the silence and the emptiness.

Old Ephraim, where are you?

He does not appear.

We go on. We camp for the day and the daytime night at what Mark calls Buena Vista—a grand view upriver of the Portal, Wicked Witch Mountain, the hanging glaciers of the high peaks beyond. Charbroiled char for supper. A female char, and Mark has saved the pinkish mass of hard roe for possible use as bait. "Ever eat fish eggs?" I ask him.

"I ate caviar once," he says.

"Only once?"

"Once was enough."

I'm inclined to agree; once was enough for me too. Caviar is cold, salty, slimy stuff—tastes like fish eggs. As Shakespeare says, caviar is for the general; let him eat it.

John and I go for a long walk into the hills, over the spongy tundra, taking one of the shotguns with us. Peacock can face his bear with only a camera; I want firepower. As we walk uphill toward the sun we see the mosquitoes waiting for us, about two and a half billion of them hovering in place above the field, the little wings and bodies glowing in the sunlight. "It looks like a zone defense," John says. But they part before us, lackadaisical atoms unable to make up their pinpoint minds, yielding before our scent and our more concentrated nodules of organic energy, as Alan Watts would say.

John is a quiet fellow, likable, attractive despite his Yasser Arafat–type beard. He tells me a little about life in Whittier, Alaska. To get to his classroom in winter he walks from his bachelor apartment in a dormitory through an underground tunnel to the adjacent but separate school building. The wind outside, he says, would knock you down; when there is no wind the snow comes up to your armpits. Yet Whittier is in the far south of central Alaska—the balmy part. (You have to be balmy to live there.) When the one road out of town is closed he buckles on touring skis and glides five miles over the pass to the railway station for a ride to the heart of Anchorage. He likes his life in Whittier. (He says.) Likes his students, the bright and lively Indian kids. Doesn't mind the isolation—he's a reader of books. Is fond of snow, ice, wind, mountains, the soft summer—bugs and icicles both. "How long do you plan to stay there?" I ask him.

"Oh, another year, maybe two."

"Then where?"

"Oh . . . back to the other world."

JULY 4— Mark celebrates with four blasts of the shotgun, shattering the morning air. Thinking a GRIZ is raiding the camp, I go running back only to see Mark and the others drinking coffee around the fire. Mark is always drinking coffee, and he makes strong coffee, stout and vigorous, powerful enough to deconstipate a sand-impacted Egyptian. "Listen, mate," he says, explaining his secret formula, "you don't need near as much water to make coffee as some people think."

John stands by the river with his camera, photographing another dead fish. He lost most of his rod to the Kongakut days ago but didn't let that stop him; he attached his reel and a new line to his rod case and went on fishing. We've had char and grayling coming out our ears for a week. We're up to our asses in fish. But good—beats bacon and beans by a country mile. And I *like* bacon and beans.

Last stop on the river. We're encamped at the place known as Caribou Pass, near another straight gravel bar on which Gil Zemansky will land to pick us up for the last flight to Barter Island, where we then will catch, tomorrow we hope, the Air North DC-3 for the journey over the Brooks Range to Fairbanks and points south.

Caribou Pass—but where are the caribou? They're supposed to be massing out on the coast one hundred thousand strong. So far the biggest bunch we've seen was twenty-five head. But here is where they should pass, through these low hills, on their annual trip into the Yukon and south from there to the edge of the forest, where they spend—where they endure, somehow—the dark and six-month-long Yukon winter.

On the hill above us, a mile away, stands a white wall-tent and a little below it four small bivouac tents—Bear Camp. A squad of wildlife students from the University of Alaska is living up there, trapping (alive) and identifying the rodents in the tundra, watching for the caribou herds, the wolves, the GRIZZ. Mark has told them about my grizzly problem, and when a young, blond-haired, brown-skinned man named Mike Phillips comes rushing down the hillside I climb up the hill to meet him. "A male grizzly," he reports, "one mile east of Bear Camp." He rushes up the hill, I trudge after him. When I get there, on the high point, the bear has disappeared. "Down in that willow thicket along the creek," says Mike, pointing. We glass the area for an hour but the bear is gone. "Probably took off behind the ridge," Mike explains, "and ambled over the divide." Of course, I think, it would, knowing that I was coming.

"The grizzly bear," I explain to Mike, "is apocryphal, like the griffin, the centaur and the yeti."

"You wouldn't think so," he replies, "if you'd been with me two days ago." And he tells me about the scene at the caribou birthing grounds, the leisurely arrogant grizzlies he'd observed circling the great herd, chasing the cows and devouring some of the newborn young.

We watch for another hour, but the grizzly does not show. I return to the river. There I find my own party staring at a spectacle two miles away on the hillside west of the river. A big herd of caribou, two thousand, three thousand of them, a compact animal mass, is advancing steadily to the south. If they go up the side valley over there they'll be blocked by the mountains; if they come our way they'll have to pass within a quarter mile of where we stand, waiting and hoping.

But something, we can't see what, spooks the herd, and after milling in confusion for a few minutes they reach consensus and reverse direction, returning north the way they had come, jogging along at a smart pace. Within ten minutes the entire herd is out of sight. The caribou, like the grizzly bear, is unpredictable. They refuse to be guided by precedent or reason or common sense or the wishes of a delegation of tourists.

"When you have a steering committee of three thousand chairpersons," says Dr. Mike sadly, "you never know what is going to happen." He limps about on stocking feet—injured his right foot two days ago. "It's like Proposition Thirteen."

"You see the racks on those bulls?" says John. "And those Dall rams—a trophy hunter would go crazy here."

Yes he would. Fly in, set down, bag the biggest bull, the finest ram, hack off the head, leave the meat to waste *in situ*, fly out, go home, mount head on rumpus-room wall. Is there anything lower, I ask myself, than a trophy hunter? Think hard. Put your mind to it. But all I can think of is squid shit.

An albino mosquito sets down on my forearm. She walks nervously back and forth on my naked skin, searching for the ideal pore to probe for blood. I wait. She selects a spot she likes, the needle nose, like the drooping snout of a supersonic jet, comes down and enters. Slight prickling sensation. I hear a definite gurgling sound—but no, I must be imagining that. I am about to slap the little thing into eternity, into its next cycle on the meat wheel of life, when something stays my hand. Let this little one live, a voice says in my inner ear. Just once, be merciful. I hesitate. Another voice says, Don't let that Buddhist karma run over your Darwinian dogma: mash the brute. But still I hesitate, and as I do, the tiny albino withdraws her dildo, waggles her wings and floats off into the mob. God only knows what ghastly plague I may have loosed upon humanity and the caribou by letting that one go. But I feel sort of good about it.

We deflate and unrig the rafts, roll them up into snug bundles, stack boats, oars, rowing frames, ammo boxes, rubber bags, icebox, tents and other dunnage at the downwind end of the imaginary airstrip.

The Cessna comes, Gil Zemansky at the controls, and the ferry operation to Barter Island begins. Mark assigns me the third and final flight, giving me four extra hours on the shore of the Kongakut. Last chance. Last chance for what? I know what but dare not bait the gods by even thinking of it. Last chance for an understanding with the spirit of the Arctic, that's what.

We wait. The plane comes and goes again with most of the cargo and all passengers but Maureen, John and I. Two more hours.

John sleeps. Maureen is reading a book and watching the hills and meditating. I go for a walk beside the river, over the gravel bars and through the willow, heading north. The cold green waters rush past at my side, breaking over the rocks with a surflike turbulence, bound for the northern sea. A mile beyond the airstrip I am cut off by a headland. I stop and look back. The shining river races toward me. The velvet-covered hills rise on either side, the great jagged wall of the Brooks extends across the southern horizon—seven hundred miles of largely unknown mountains, reaching across Alaska from the Yukon to the Bering Sea. The end of the Rockies. The final American wilderness.

Where is he?

The willow leaves flash their silvery undersides in the wind, McCone poppies and the purple lupine and red bayrose and yellow composites dance on the hillsides. Wordsworth would enjoy the spectacle. I think. But he might not care much for what I'm waiting for. Expecting. Both shotguns lean on the last pile of duffle where John lies sleeping, out of sight, out of hearing. I am unarmed, ready, open. Let it come.

Two shrikes watch me from the willows. Three screaming gulls pursue a golden eagle high above the river, diving and pecking at its head, trying to turn it into a bald eagle. I long to see that eagle flip on its back in midair, snatch one of those gulls in its deadly talons and—*rip its head off!* But the eagle sails on in straight, steady airline toward the hills, and the gulls drop away, bored.

My bear does not come.

AS THE PLANE takes off Gil says, "I'm going to show you something." He banks and turns off course and enters a pass through the foothills west of the river. We fly a thousand feet above the lion-colored tundra. Little ponds and bogholes wink, sparkle, glitter in the light. We cross another ridge.

And there below, suddenly, the hills appear to be in motion, alive, as if the skin of the earth had begun to crawl over its rockbound bones. A broad river of caribou streams in waves west-southwesterly up the ridges and through the valleys, all its elements in rapid, parallel advance. It takes me a moment to realize that I am looking down on the greatest mass movement of untamed four-hooved animals I may ever see. It's like the stampede of the wildebeests on the Serengeti Plain.

"My God," I say. "How many?"

Gil banks and circles, looking down. "Hard to tell. It's only a part of the Porcupine River herd. Maybe forty, maybe fifty thousand."

John and Maureen are busy taking pictures. I'm too excited to get out my binoculars. "Any GRIZZ down there?"

Gil looks again. "Bound to be a few," he says. "But they blend in so well we'd never see them."

He circles one more time, giving us all a good look, then bears northwest for Barter Island and Kaktovik, over the last foothills and two thousand feet above the coastal plain. Well, I'm thinking, now I'm satisfied. Now I've seen it, the secret of the essence of the riddle of the Spirit of the Arctic—the flowering of life, of life wild, free and abundant, in the midst of the hardest, cruelest land on the northern half of Earth.

And then, as we approach the coast and the tiny island at its edge, the frozen sea appears again, the ocean of ice, the crescent rim of *whiteness* stretching on, and on, and on, unbroken, apparently unlimited, toward the hazy stillness of the polar climax—and beyond. What can I say of that? The vision chills both thought and emotion.

What can I say except confess that I have seen but little of the real North, and of that little understood less. The planet is bigger than we ever imagined. The world is colder, more ancient, more strange and more mysterious than we had dreamed. And we puny human creatures with our many tools and toys and fears and hopes make only one small leaf on the great efflorescing tree of life.

Too much. No equation however organic, no prose however royally purple, can bracket our world within the boundaries of mind.

So what. "Gil," I say. "Doctor Gil Zemansky."

"Yes?" he says.

"Buy us a beer in downtown Kaktovik."

"I'll buy two," says Gil. "One for you and one for me."

River Solitaire

A Daybook

A T SATURDAY NOON, on November third, a few days before the
last general election, I rowed a small skiff into the current of the Colorado River, near the town of Moab, Utah, and disappeared for ten days.

By choice. Since I lacked the power to make a somewhat disagreeable
world of public events disappear, I chose to disappear from that world myself.
This was easily arranged. Nobody goes down the river—not the turbid,
muddy, freezing snowmelt of the Colorado—in November. I was assured of
having the river to myself. I preferred this kind of solitude not out of selfishness but out of generosity; in my sullen mood I was doing my fellow humans
(such as they are) a favor by going away.

A friend from Moab saw me off. Another friend—Ken Sanders—would
meet me at the end of my solo journey, seventy miles downstream at a nowhere place known as Spanish Bottom. From there we planned to run the
rest of the river together, my little rowboat following his big pontoon raft
through Cataract Canyon, rejoining American culture (such as it is) at the
Hite Marina on Lake Powell.

In my boat I carried enough food for two weeks, a one-man tent, a sleeping bag, some warm clothes in a rubberized bag, five gallons of drinking water

From *One Life at a Time, Please* (1988)

and the many other little items needed for a week or more in the wilds—cigars, bourbon, the *Portable Tolstoy*, matches, Demerol tablets, pen, notebook, a .357 and a P-38.

We launched ourselves, my little boat and I, onto the flowing river. Here is what happened:

SATURDAY

We float beneath the bridge. From the shade I gain a splendid view of the Moab valley, a vale of greenery walled in by red sandstone cliffs. Beyond the cliffs rise the snow-crowned La Sal Mountains, only fifteen miles away by line of sight. Valley, cliffs, mountains—one of the world's most magnificent settings for a human community. Unfortunately the town of Moab (about five thousand people) was overrun by the uranium industry back in the 1950s and remains an eyesore, a commercial-industrial slum. But that junk will rot and fade from the scene, given time, as a thousand other ephemerid boomtowns have vanished from the landscape of the American West, leaving what *belongs* here: some farms, a few little ranches, the original Moab, the national parks and perhaps, someday, a small college and arts center.

I row past the uranium mill, which is at present shut down, silent, empty except for a cadre of supervisors, watchmen, maintenance men. Like most people in the Moab area, I hope it stays this way—silent. But the enormous twenty-acre slime pit of uranium wastes remains in place beside the mill, on the shore of the river, a constant threat to the health and well-being of every living thing downwind and downstream.

The river flows around a swampy bottomland and enters the Portal—a fifteen-hundred-foot-deep notch in the red-rock wall, the gateway to what, only three decades ago, was still terra incognita: the canyonlands, the Needles, the Maze, the Confluence, Monument Basin, the grabens, the Fins, the Henry Mountains, the deep, intricate, uninhabited marvels of the Glen and Escalante Canyons. Half of this grandeur now lies submerged (for the time being) under the stagnant waters of artificial Lake Powell. But much remains. More than enough to make a journey into this region, whether by foot or horse or boat, still a delight for anyone who loves the primitive, the deep time of ancient stone, the bedrock foundation of soil, grass, flesh, spirit, life.

A few great blue herons stalk the sandbars, and many ducks—pintail, mallard, cinnamon teal—drift on the water. The mudslides of beaver indent the banks. A few hawks soar overhead. In the jungles of tamarisk and willow on the riverbank I can hear the quiet chirping—not often—of little birds.

Black-throated sparrows? Towhees? Verdins? Not many around, this time of year, and the few that stay through autumn and winter are quiet birds.

I pass a trailerhouse and mine workings on the left bank; then a potash mill on the right bank, an enormous silent exotic structure of grotesque design, poisonous green in color, where a dozen men are employed in the monitoring of machines that pump liquefied potash from three thousand feet below. A few cars stand parked inside the high-security fence; a wisp of steam rises from a pipe; the hum of electrical motors seeps through the metal walls; but human beings themselves are nowhere in sight. The plant is like an installation from Mars or Saturn—vast, complicated, sinister, an alien presence. I row vigorously for a few minutes until the bend of the river takes me beyond sight and sound of the mill. Again I am surrounded by desert, by red-rock walls and towering cliffs, and feel as if I have escaped the surveillance of hostile and otherworldly eyes.

Sun going down behind the western rim. I row and float another mile, another, looking through the chilling twilight for a place to camp. The river is walled by mudbanks and jungles of tamarisk on either side, permitting no place to land. I am cold, tired, hungry, anxious to get out of my little rowboat before darkness sets in.

A ledge of rock slopes up from the water on the right. I bear for that, tether my skiff to a willow tree and make camp for the night. The sky is clear, the stars bright and steady. I do not bother to pitch the tent. I build a fire of twigs and grill two pork chops over the flames. A beautiful night, beginning early. I drink a cup of cocoa and slip into my old greasy sleeping bag, using a lifejacket for a pillow. I fall asleep to the sound of water gurgling past the ledge, the whisper of a breeze through the dry dead leaves of the willow.

SUNDAY

The November nights are long. I wake in the dark, check my antique pocketwatch by flashlight: five o'clock. I rise and build another little fire on the coals of the one before, make myself a mug of tea. Tea, an apple, a slice of bread with jam, is all the breakfast I require. I load my gear into the boat, untie the bowline, climb aboard and shove off into the current. Starlight glitters on the silent river, flowing smooth and heavy as oil toward the west. I stroke the water with my oars, guiding the boat onto the bubble line of foam that indicates the center of the current, then ship oars and let the boat turn idly on the stream, floating without effort through the morning stillness.

The east glows with color. The highest canyon walls, two thousand feet above the river, take on the radiance of dawn. The river flows in absolute silence between mudbanks crowded with more willow, tamarisk and cotton-wood. A mute but bitter struggle goes on there—the invading, exotic tama-risk striving to drive out the native willow.

Deer tracks on the mud and sandbars. Signs of raccoon, beaver, fox and coyote. And again the birds—heron, sandpiper, killdeer, chukar.

Late in the morning the sun clears the vertical walls, shining down on me and skiff and water and the narrow strip of plant life on either bank. At noon I pull to shore and walk for a mile up sandstone ledges into a cul-de-sac, the closed end of a box canyon. I eat my lunch of raisins and cheese beside a pool of liquid quicksand under a two-hundred-foot overhanging pour-off—a dry waterfall.

Back to the river, drawn by the powerful tug of the stream. I see a bunch of deer, five does, passing like shadows through the trees and brush on the left bank. Two of them emerge from the jungle and step out on a sandbar for a drink from the river. Oars at rest, I glide past within twenty feet of their alert eyes and ears. They see me as only another piece of floating driftwood. If I had my bow now, and one broadhead arrow, I'd be feasting on poached liver and short ribs for supper. Maybe.

I make camp at mile twenty-five, on a sand island in the middle of the river. A fine campsite, at first glance: clean brown sand, plenty of driftwood for a fire, a splendid view upriver of the red-rock cliffs, the golden clouds.

Three o'clock in the afternoon. With the sun going down by five, I am determined to cook my supper by daylight. There is nothing more unsatisfactory than cooking and eating in the dark. I explore the island, gather wood, build a fire on the damp sand near my boat and fix a supper of chicken and rice, with a miniature bottle of rum and one fat cigar from Safeway (Garcia y Vega) for dessert.

The sun goes down, the temperature drops ten, twenty, thirty degrees—within thirty minutes. Cold on this slender isle, the icy Rocky Mountain wa-ters rolling by on either side. The sky is clear, clusters of stars like blazing chandeliers hanging overhead. A chill wind blows in from the north. I pitch the little tent—may need all the insulation I can get tonight. I put on ther-mal underwear, crawl into my mummy bag and read Tolstoy by candlelight for as long as I can stay awake. "The hero of my tale," he writes, "is truth." How true.

The wind moans about the tentflaps. I blow out the candle around eight o'clock and pull the hood of the bag above my ears. A long and bitterly cold night—should have known better than to camp on a sandbar. I do know better—but did it anyhow. Who can resist the appeal of a little, lonesome, one-man island in the middle of a great river?

MONDAY

In the morning I find my tent stiff with frost. Ice tinkles in the water jug when I raise it to my lips. I build a twig fire in the twilight of dawn and boil a pot of water for coffee.

Two ravens flap across the river, silent, bound in a straight line toward business of importance. A V-formation of ducks flutters by overhead, headed downriver. As I load and launch my rowboat I hear the splash of beaver sliding down their mudbanks into the water. I pull into the stream through the shade of the cliffs, under an overcast sky. My breath vaporizes when I exhale. The one thing we do not need, I think, wishing I had the power not even to mention it in my mind, is a storm. I don't mind being cold; I can bear getting wet; but I loathe the two together.

Don't think about it. Keep going. Once we get to Spanish Bottom we'll set up camp in some rocky nook with a southern exposure and let the wind rave, the sleet come down, the snow blanket everything. If I'd been ready, I recall, I could have taken that deer: I've got the Ruger .357 Magnum in the big ammo can, bedded between two loaves of bread. Loaded? Oh yes.

Eleven A.M. Weather improving, at the moment. I drift downstream on water like oily glass, aided by a gentle breeze that blows, for once, not against but with the current. The sunshine is pallid but warm, the sun barely visible behind the scrim of haze. We are headed due south into the sun.

The river is low. I go with the current, seeking the deepest channel, following the line of foam, the outside of the bends, under the overhanging walls, where the current of the river goes. Watch for mud, sandbars, waterlogged snags: I'd hate to have to get out into this forty-degree water to drag the boat free from some obstacle.

I pass more side canyons—Lathrop, Buck, others without names. Should stop and explore but the mouths of each are choked with a slough of quicksand, a jungle of brush. You'd have to fight your way in there with a machete or else slog through muck up to your thighs. Or both.

The willows, mountain ash and cottonwoods wear their autumn colors—bright gold against the somber red of the Moenkopi mudstones, the dark brown Cutler sandstone. The tamarisk is a rusty orange. Stands of wild cane with snowy seed plumes lean with the breeze, then snap back to an upright stance.

There's a giant cottonwood log balanced on a rock, twenty feet above the present waterline, revealing an old high-water mark. Beyond the living things at the river's edge rise the walls of rock, nude red sculptured stone surmounted by gargoyles, beaked heads, godlike profiles from the ancient times. Now and then I catch a glimpse of the high plateaus beyond the middle ground: the high rimrock of Dead Horse Point, Hatch Point, Needles Overlook, Grandview Point, Island in the Sky, Junction Butte. Most of these are places inaccessible from the river, cut off by perpendicular walls, one above another, of rotten rock.

I tie up my boat at the mouth of Indian Creek, on the left, and follow a deer path along the ledges into the canyon. I inspect the small Anasazi ruins in a cave—mounds of dust, stone parapets mortared with mud, the smoke-blackened ceiling, the potsherds and tiny corncobs, the usual clots of bat guano back in the corners—and then go on, through the clean clear light, up the canyon along a trickling stream. I pass more golden cottonwoods, each one special, unique, like humans, each displaying its individuality with a distinctive *flourish* of limbs, branches, masses of gold and green-gold leaves. The tracks and droppings of bighorn sheep precede me on the trail.

The canyon boxes up; I come to a vertical slot in the stone through which a cascade of silvery water pours, crashing down on the terraces below. The soothing white noise of falling water fills the canyon. Here I pause for an hour of abundant nothingness.

Returning to my boat, I become aware of the silence closing in again. As always when I'm alone in a deep and solitary canyon, I become intensely aware of the stillness around me, of a need to be strictly attentive, fully alert, cautious and delicate with every step, as if I were under some kind of preternatural observation. *Something is watching you,* I think—though I don't for a moment allow the notion to take full possession of my mind. The feeling has nothing to do with fear; there is no fear in it but simply the belief, the intuition, the conviction, that I should proceed as quietly and respectfully as possible.

Back on the river and down to the mouth of Monument Creek. I explore this canyon too but don't get far: one mile from the river I come to another box, another overhanging spout with classic dripping spring far above my head. Returning to the river by a different route I jump a bunch of mule deer from their shady place underneath the alders. I hear a loud *thump!* as they go bounding—not running—toward the shore.

Early in the evening I select my third campsite, a clean open bench of stone on the left bank, eleven miles upstream from the confluence of the Colorado and Green Rivers.

Beef stew for supper. A near full moon rises through a notch in the walls around me, barely visible through a dense overcast. No stars in sight. The air is cold and still, feeling like rain, or maybe snow. I set up the tent, then go for a walk along an old trail switchbacking up a talus slope. Topping out on a saddle of level stone, I find myself looking down on the Colorado River flowing in opposite directions—westward on one hand, northeast on the other. I am standing on the neck of a big meander called the Loop.

I hear no sound but the coursing of the blood through my ears. A world of stillness without even the whisper of a wind. Nothing in motion but the gleaming river four hundred feet below, the faint advance of moonlight across dark battlements of stone. Stealthily, afraid to attract attention by making noise, I pick my way back down the trail to camp. The moon, encircled by a rust-colored corona, grows dimmer by the minute behind the cloud cover.

TUESDAY

Up at six. The dense cloud cover remains but there is not a breath of wind. Tea, bread and jam for breakfast. I load my boat and push onto the river an hour later. Fifteen miles to Spanish Bottom, foot trails to the outer world, and our rendezvous point. The threat of bad weather now seems trivial; I am delighted with this solitary journey and regret only that it seems to be going so fast. Too fast.

Solitary: but not lonely. I've been too busy to be lonely. Navigating the river, trying to avoid gravel bars, hiking side canyons, hunting for a campsite, making camp, reading Tolstoy—I've hardly had a chance to even feel alone. Floating and contemplating keeps me busy.

Well, enough dawdling, row this boat. Best to set up base camp before the storm actually arrives and the rains come down. Followed by hail. Topped off by snow. Going around the Loop, I row four miles to arrive at a point about a quarter mile from where I started. But that's the way the canyons go, serpentine. Except for crystals and stratigraphy, there are few straight lines in nature.

Strange birdcries in the distance. A heron honking? Coyote scat and deer sign in every canyon. Beaver slides on the mudbanks. Quiet little anonymous birds flitting about in the brush. And autumn color everywhere: bright orange of alder, gold of cottonwood, red of ivy and scrub oak, copper of willows, tawny brown of grasses and greasewood, pale yellow of mountain mahogany, the dark olive green of junipers and piñon pine on the rim above and along the water's edge the tamarisk thickets, red as rust.

I keep hoping for a glimpse of bighorn sheep—no show. But there's one little brown cricket in the boat with me, chirping now and then. Last of a dying breed this time of year. I'm glad the cricket's aboard: means good luck. Everybody knows that.

Close to noon the sky clears a bit and I catch a look at the sun drifting across a tiny patch of blue. We make a halt below the mouth of Salt Creek Canyon, tie up to a willow and climb out on a limestone ledge. Groping for a better hold I see a cluster of fossil crinoids beneath my hand: the span of ages between my fingertips.

I walk for several miles up Salt Creek, following the clear stream as it pours through slick grooves and chutes in the polished limestone of the creekbed. My boots clash through layers of fallen gold leaves when I pass beneath the cottonwood trees. I climb around a fifty-foot waterfall, scrambling up from ledge to ledge, and walk for another mile before my way is blocked by a high dropoff that I lack either motivation or skill to climb.

By midafternoon, in my boat again, I approach the confluence of the two great desert rivers. As always, I feel a strange excitement in my heart. I row through a blast of headwinds coming upstream, work around a final bend and there it is—greenish Colorado merging with the golden-hued Green. My friend Sanders will be coming down that latter river. Just for the hell of it, I row up the Green River as far as I can, hugging the bank, and slipping from eddy to eddy. Half a mile and I give it up, ferry across the stream and drift downriver with the main current.

The wind grows rapidly stronger. Three miles to Spanish Bottom. I row against the wind, against the alarming waves topped with whitecaps, and have to strain at the oars before I finally reach the little silty beach at the upper end of the Bottom. I make camp at evening among the boulders, fix my supper of beef soup and crackers washed down with spring water and a slug of Jim Beam's Choice.

Clouding up again. Reluctantly, but glad I've brought it, I erect the old Springbar tent in a grove of sheltering hackberry trees above the beach, then go for a walk through intermittent moonlight across the broad fields, half a mile wide and close to a mile long, of Spanish Bottom. Cottonwoods shiver in the wind and a herd of mule deer—I count seventeen—bound across my path, fifty yards ahead. Canyon walls a thousand feet high rise on all sides but there is one trail up out of here, leading to a maze of pinnacles known as the Doll's House, and beyond that to the Maze, Lizard Rock, the Golden Stairs, Flint Trail and the high plateau country of Land's End.

At the southern corner of Spanish Bottom I hear the roar of the first big rapid, the entrance to Cataract Canyon. STOP, says a signboard on the right bank, facing the river; HAZARDOUS RAPIDS 200 YARDS AHEAD. Quite so; that's the way we'll go when Sanders gets here, down the river through twenty miles of white water until we reach the stagnant waters of Lake Powell and the end of our journey.

I gaze for a long while on the turbulent waves of the rapid, silvery and phosphorescent in the moonlight, before returning to camp, my tent, the welcome warmth of my sleeping bag.

WEDNESDAY, THURSDAY, FRIDAY

For three days I wait. I spend one whole day in the tent, reading, while icy rain pours down outside, then the next two days climbing the trail to the hoodoo land of rock above, exploring a number of coves and grottos and box canyons between the Doll's House and the Confluence Overlook, descending at night. I find a new arch, unmarked on the topographic maps and unknown to the Park Service (as I later learned). I name it Deception Arch, its archness not apparent until you get within fifty yards of it.

Sanders is supposed to be here Thursday. Returning to camp by flashlight and moonlight, Thursday night, I am disappointed to discover that he has not arrived. For the first time in my solitary week on the river I feel a twinge of true loneliness, melancholy triggered by failed expectation.

A final day of explorations. High on the sandstone benches above the river I find a series of potholes full of rain water. The water is cold but not nearly so cold as the river. I fill my canteens then take a soapless bath, scrubbing myself with fine sand, drying my body in the wind and the glare of the sunlight. Cold, fierce, exhilarating sensations. Thirty, forty miles away, across the red wilderness of canyons and spires and needles and buttes, the thirteen-thousand-foot peaks of the La Sal Mountains gleam with power, covered with fresh snow.

Much later, after dark, I stand at the top of the trail and look down on Spanish Bottom, fifteen hundred feet below. I see no flicker of campfire at our appointed meeting place. Disappointed again, doubly disappointed, I pick my way down the rocky trail by flashlight and trudge across the long weedy flats to camp, hearing the sound of the wind in the trees, the distant surflike mutter of the rapids at the mouth of Cataract Canyon. I foresee another night with only Leo Tolstoy for company. Tolstoy is good company but he's dead; there comes a time when you long for something more—vivacious.

I enter the grove of hackberrys where I've pitched my tent. I hear voices and see, now and at last, the glow of a fire. Below, under the sandbanks, out of sight from above, stands Ken Sanders with his arm around his girlfriend Lynn, three T-bone steaks grilling on the flames and a case of Dos Equis waiting at their feet.

Glory be.

Free Speech

The Cowboy and His Cow

UNIVERSITY OF MONTANA, APRIL 1985

WHEN I FIRST CAME WEST in 1948, a student at the University of New Mexico, I was only twenty years old and just out of the Army. I thought, like most simple-minded Easterners, that a cowboy was a kind of mythic hero. I idolized those scrawny little red-nosed hired hands in their tight jeans, funny boots and comical hats.

Like other new arrivals in the West, I could imagine nothing more romantic than becoming a cowboy. Nothing more glorious than owning my own little genuine working cattle outfit. About the only thing better, I thought, was to be a big-league baseball player. I never dreamed that I'd eventually sink to writing books for a living. Unluckily for me—coming from an Appalachian hillbilly background and with a poor choice of parents—I didn't have much money. My father was a small-time logger. He ran a one-man sawmill and a submarginal side-hill farm. There wasn't any money in our family, no inheritance you could run ten thousand cattle on. I had no trust fund to back me up. No Hollywood movie deals to finance a land acquisition program. I lived on what in those days was called the GI Bill, which paid about $150 a month while I went to school. I made that last as long as I could—five or six years. I couldn't afford a horse. The best I could do in 1947 and '48 was buy a third-

From *One Life at a Time, Please* (1988)

hand Chevy sedan and roam the West, mostly the Southwest, on holidays and weekends.

I had a roommate at the University of New Mexico. I'll call him Mac. He came from a little town in southwest New Mexico where his father ran a feed store. Mackie was a fair bronc rider, eager to get into the cattle-growing business. And he had some money, enough to buy a little cinderblock house and about forty acres in the Sandia Mountains east of Albuquerque, near a town we called Landfill. Mackie fenced those forty acres, built a corral and kept a few horses there, including an occasional genuine bronco for fun and practice.

I don't remember exactly how Mackie and I became friends in the first place. I was majoring in classical philosophy. He was majoring in screw-worm management. But we got to know each other through the mutual pursuit of a pair of nearly inseparable Kappa Kappa Gamma girls. I lived with him in his little cinderblock house. Helped him meet the mortgage payments. Helped him meet the girls. We were both crude, shy, ugly, obnoxious—like most college boys.

[*Interjection: "Like you!"*]

My friend Mac also owned a 1947 black Lincoln convertible, the kind with the big grille in front, like a cowcatcher on a locomotive, chrome-plated. We used to race to classes in the morning, driving the twenty miles from his house to the campus in never more than fifteen minutes. Usually Mac was too hung over to drive, so I'd operate the car, clutching the wheel while Mac sat beside me waving his big .44, taking potshots at jackrabbits and road signs and billboards and beer bottles. Trying to wake up in time for his ten o'clock class in brand inspection.

I'm sorry to say that my friend Mac was a little bit gun-happy. Most of his forty acres was in tumbleweed. He fenced in about half an acre with chicken wire and stocked that little pasture with white rabbits. He used it as a target range. Not what you'd call sporting, I suppose, but we did eat the rabbits. Sometimes we even went deer hunting with handguns. Mackie with his revolver, and me with a chrome-plated Colt .45 automatic I had liberated from the US Army over in Italy. Surplus government property.

On one of our deer-hunting expeditions, I was sitting on a log in a big clearing in the woods, thinking about Plato and Aristotle and the Kappa Kappa Gamma girls. I didn't really care whether we got a deer that day or not. It was a couple of days before opening, anyway. The whole procedure was probably illegal as hell. Mac was out in the woods somewhere looking for deer around the clearing. I was sitting on the log, thinking, when I saw a chip of bark fly away from the log all by itself, about a foot from my left hand. Then I heard the blast of Mac's revolver—that big old .44 he'd probably liberated from his father. Then I heard him laugh.

"That's not very funny, Mackie," I said.

"Now don't whine and complain, Ed," he said. "You want to be a real hunter like me, you gotta learn to stay awake."

We never did get a deer with handguns. But that's when I had my first little doubts about Mackie, and about the cowboy type in general. But I still loved him. Worshipped him, in fact. I was caught in the grip of the Western myth. Anybody said a word to me against cowboys, I'd jump down his throat with my spurs on. Especially if Mac was standing nearby.

Sometimes I'd try to ride those broncs that he brought in, trying to prove that I could be a cowboy too. Trying to prove it more to myself than to him. I'd be on this crazy, crackpot horse going up, down, left, right and inside out. Hanging on to the saddle horn with both hands. While Mac sat on the corral fence, throwing beer bottles at us and laughing. Every time I got thrown off, Mac would say, "Now get right back on there, Ed. Quick, quick. Don't spoil 'im."

It took me a long time to realize I didn't have to do that kind of work. And it took me another thirty years to realize that there's something wrong at the heart of our most popular American myth—the cowboy and his cow.

[*Jeers.*]

You may have guessed by now that I'm thinking of criticizing the livestock industry. And you are correct. I've been thinking about cows and sheep for many years. Getting more and more disgusted with the whole business. Western cattlemen are nothing more than welfare parasites. They've been getting a free ride on the public lands for over a century, and I think it's time we phased it out. I'm in favor of putting the public-lands livestock grazers out of business.

First of all, we don't need the public-lands beef industry. Even beef lovers don't need it. According to most government reports (Bureau of Land Management, Forest Service), only about 2 percent of our beef, our red meat, comes from the public lands of the eleven Western states. By those eleven I mean Montana, Nevada, Utah, Colorado, New Mexico, Arizona, Idaho, Wyoming, Oregon, Washington and California. Most of our beef, aside from imports, comes from the Midwest and the East, especially the Southeast—Georgia, Alabama, Florida—and from other private lands across the nation. More beef cattle are raised in the state of Georgia than in the sagebrush empire of Nevada. And for a very good reason: back East, you can support a cow on maybe half an acre. Out here, it takes anywhere from twenty-five to fifty acres. In the red-rock country of Utah, the rule of thumb is one section—a square mile—per cow.

[*Shouts from rear of hall.*]

Since such a small percentage of cows are produced on public lands in the West, eliminating that part of the industry should not raise supermarket beef prices very much. Furthermore, we'd save money in the taxes we now pay for various subsidies to these public-lands cattlemen. Subsidies for things like "range improvement"—tree chaining, sagebrush clearing, mesquite poisoning, disease control, predator trapping, fencing, wells, stockponds, roads. Then there are the salaries of those who work for government agencies like the BLM and the Forest Service. You could probably also count in a big part of the salaries of the overpaid professors engaged in range-management research at the Western land-grant colleges.

Moreover, the cattle have done, and are doing, intolerable damage to our public lands—our national forests, state lands, BLM-administered lands, wildlife preserves, even some of our national parks and monuments. In Utah's Capital Reef National Park, for example, grazing is still allowed. In fact, it's recently been extended for another ten years, and Utah politicians are trying to make the arrangement permanent. They probably won't get away with it. But there we have at least one case where cattle are still tramping about in a national park, transforming soil and grass into dust and weeds.

[*Disturbance.*]

Overgrazing is much too weak a term. Most of the public lands in the West, and especially in the Southwest, are what you might call "cowburnt." Almost anywhere and everywhere you go in the American West you find hordes of these ugly, clumsy, stupid, bawling, stinking, fly-covered, shit-smeared, disease-spreading brutes. They are a pest and a plague. They pollute our springs and streams and rivers. They infest our canyons, valleys, meadows and forests. They graze off the native bluestem and grama and bunch grasses, leaving behind jungles of prickly pear. They trample down the native forbs and shrubs and cacti. They spread the exotic cheatgrass, the Russian thistle and the crested wheat grass. *Weeds.*

Even when the cattle are not physically present, you'll see the dung and the flies and the mud and the dust and the general destruction. If you don't see it, you'll smell it. The whole American West stinks of cattle. Along every flowing stream, around every seep and spring and water hole and well, you'll find acres and acres of what range-management specialists call "sacrifice areas"—another understatement. These are places denuded of forage, except for some cactus or a little tumbleweed or maybe a few mutilated trees like mesquite, juniper or hackberry.

I'm not going to bombard you with graphs and statistics, which don't make much of an impression on intelligent people anyway. Anyone who goes beyond the city limits of almost any Western town can see for himself that the land is overgrazed. There are too many cows and horses and sheep out there. Of course, cattlemen would never publicly confess to overgrazing, any more than Dracula would publicly confess to a fondness for blood. Cattlemen are interested parties. Many of them will not give reliable testimony. Some have too much at stake: their Cadillacs and their airplanes, their ranch resale profits and their capital gains. (I'm talking about the corporation ranchers, the land-and-cattle companies, the investment syndicates.) Others, those ranchers who have only a small base property, flood the public lands with their cows. About 8 percent of the federal land permittees have cattle that consume approximately 45 percent of the forage on the government rangelands.

Beef ranchers like to claim that their cows do not compete with deer. Deer are browsers, cows are grazers. That's true. But when a range is overgrazed, when the grass is gone (as it often is for seasons at a time), then cattle become browsers too, out of necessity. In the Southwest, cattle commonly feed on mesquite, cliff rose, cactus, acacia or any other shrub or tree they find biodegradable. To that extent, they compete with deer. And they tend to drive out other and better wildlife. Like elk, or bighorn sheep, or pronghorn antelope.

[*Sneers, jeers, laughter.*]

How much damage have cattle done to the Western rangelands? Large-scale beef ranching has been going on since the 1870s. There's plenty of documentation of the effects of this massive cattle grazing on the erosion of the land, the character of the land, the character of the vegetation. Streams and rivers that used to flow on the surface all year round are now intermittent, or underground, because of overgrazing and rapid runoff.

Our public lands have been overgrazed for a century. The BLM knows it; the Forest Service knows it. The Government Accounting Office knows it. And overgrazing means eventual ruin, just like stripmining or clear-cutting or the damming of rivers. Much of the Southwest already looks like Mexico or southern Italy or North Africa: a cowburnt wasteland. As we destroy our land, we destroy our agricultural economy and the basis of modern society. If we keep it up, we'll gradually degrade American life to the status of life in places like Mexico or southern Italy or Libya or Egypt.

In 1984 the Bureau of Land Management, which was required by Congress to report on its stewardship of our rangelands—the property of all Americans, remember—confessed that 31 percent of the land it administered was in "good condition," and 60 percent in "poor condition." And it reported that only 18 percent of the rangelands were improving, while 68 percent were "stable" and 14 percent were getting worse. If the BLM said that, we can safely assume that range conditions are actually much worse.

[*Shouts of "bullshit!"*]

What can we do about this situation? This is the fun part—this is the part I like. It's not easy to argue that we should do away with cattle ranching. The cowboy myth gets in the way. But I do have some solutions to overgrazing.

[*A yell: "Cowboys do it better!" Answered by another: "Ask any cow!" Coarse laughter.*]

I'd begin by reducing the number of cattle on public lands. Not that range managers would go along with it, of course. In their eyes, and in the eyes of the livestock associations they work for, cutting down on the number of cattle is the worst possible solution—an impossible solution. So they propose all kinds of gimmicks. Portable fencing and perpetual movement of cattle. More cross-fencing. More wells and ponds so that more land can be exploited. These proposals are basically a maneuver by the Forest Service and the BLM to appease their critics without offending their real bosses in the beef industry. But a drastic reduction in cattle numbers is the only true and honest solution.

I also suggest that we open a hunting season on range cattle. I realize that beef cattle will not make sporting prey at first. Like all domesticated animals (including most humans), beef cattle are slow, stupid and awkward. But the breed will improve if hunted regularly. And as the number of cattle is reduced, other and far more useful, beautiful and interesting animals will return to the rangelands and will increase.

Suppose, by some miracle of Hollywood or inheritance or good luck, I should acquire a respectable-sized working cattle outfit. What would I do with it? First, I'd get rid of the stinking, filthy cattle. Every single animal. Shoot them all, and stock the place with real animals, real game, real protein: elk, buffalo, pronghorn antelope, bighorn sheep, moose. And some purely decorative animals, like eagles. We need more eagles. And wolves. We need more wolves. Mountain lions and bears. Especially, of course, grizzly bears. Down in the desert, I would stock every water tank, every water hole, every stockpond, with alligators.

You may note that I have said little about coyotes or deer. Coyotes seem to be doing all right on their own. They're smarter than their enemies. I've never heard of a coyote as dumb as a sheepman. As for deer, especially mule deer, they, too, are surviving—maybe even thriving, as some game and fish departments claim, though nobody claims there are as many deer now as there were before the cattle industry was introduced in the West. In any case, compared to elk the deer is a second-rate game animal, nothing but a giant rodent—a rat with antlers.

[*Portions of audience begin to leave.*]

I've suggested that the beef industry's abuse of our Western lands is based on the old mythology of the cowboy as natural nobleman. I'd like to conclude this diatribe with a few remarks about this most cherished and fanciful of American fairy tales. In truth, the cowboy is only a hired hand. A farm boy in leather britches and a comical hat. A herdsman who gets on a horse to do part of his work. Some ranchers are also cowboys, but most are not. There is a difference. There are many ranchers out there who are big-time farmers of the public lands—our property. As such, they do not merit any special consideration or special privileges. There are only about 31,000 ranchers in the whole American West who use the public lands. That's less than the population of Missoula, Montana.

The rancher (with a few honorable exceptions) is a man who strings barbed wire all over the range; drills wells and bulldozes stockponds; drives off elk and antelope and bighorn sheep; poisons coyotes and prairie dogs; shoots eagles, bears and cougars on sight; supplants the native grasses with tumbleweed, snakeweed, povertyweed, cowshit, anthills, mud, dust and flies. And then leans back and grins at the TV cameras and talks about how much he loves the American West. Cowboys also are greatly overrated. Consider the nature of their work. Suppose you had to spend most of your working hours sitting on a horse, contemplating the hind end of a cow. How would that affect your imagination? Think what it does to the relatively simple mind of the average peasant boy, raised amid the bawling of calves and cows in the splatter of mud and the stink of shit.

[*Shouting. Laughter. Disturbance.*]

Do cowboys work hard? Sometimes. But most ranchers don't work very hard. They have a lot of leisure time for politics and bellyaching (which is why most state legislatures in the West are occupied and dominated by cattlemen). Anytime you go into a small Western town you'll find them at the nearest drugstore, sitting around all morning drinking coffee, talking about their tax breaks.

Is a cowboy's work socially useful? No. As I've already pointed out, subsidized Western range beef is a trivial item in the national beef economy. If all of our 31,000 Western public-land ranchers quit tomorrow, we'd never even notice. Any public school teacher does harder work, more difficult work, more dangerous work and far more valuable work than the cowboy or rancher. The same thing applies to registered nurses and nurses' aides, garbage collectors and traffic cops. Harder work, tougher work, more necessary work. We need those people in our complicated society. We do not need cowboys or ranchers. We've carried them on our backs long enough.

[*Disturbance in rear of hall.*]

"This Abbey," the cowboys and their lovers will say, "this Abbey is a wimp. A chicken-hearted sentimentalist with no feel for the hard realities of practical life." Especially critical of my attitude will be the Easterners and Midwesterners newly arrived here from their Upper West Side apartments, their rustic lodges in upper Michigan. Our nouveau Westerners with their toy ranches, their pickup trucks with the gun racks, their pointy-toed boots with the undershot heels, their gigantic hats. And, of course, their pet horses. The *instant rednecks.*

[*Shouts.*]

To those who might accuse me of wimpery and sentimentality, I'd like to say this in reply. I respect real men. I admire true manliness. But I despise arrogance and brutality and bullies. So let me close with some nice remarks about cowboys and cattle ranchers. They are a mixed lot, like the rest of us. As individuals, they range from the bad to the ordinary to the good. A rancher, after all, is only a farmer, cropping the public rangelands with his four-legged lawnmowers, stashing our grass into his bank account. A cowboy is a hired hand trying to make an honest living. Nothing special.

I have no quarrel with these people as fellow humans. All I want to do is get their cows off our property. Let those cowboys and ranchers find some harder way to make a living, like the rest of us have to do. There's no good reason why we should subsidize them forever. They've had their free ride. It's time they learned to support themselves.

In the meantime, I'm going to say good-bye to all you cowboys and cowgirls. I love the legend too—but keep your sacred cows and your dead horses out of my elk pastures.

[*Sitting ovation. Gunfire in parking lot.*]

Theory of Anarchy

T H E B I B L E S A Y S that the love of money is the root of all evil. But
what is the essential meaning of money? Money attracts because it gives
us the means to command the labor and service and finally the lives of others—human or otherwise. Money is power. I would expand the Biblical aph-
orism, therefore, in this fashion: the root of all evil is the love of power.

And power attracts the worst and corrupts the best among men. It is no
accident that police work, for example, appeals to those (if not only those)
with the bully's instinct. We know the type. Or put a captain's bars on a perfectly ordinary, decent man, give him a measure of arbitrary power over others and he tends to become—unless a man of unusual character—a martinet,
another petty despot. Power corrupts; and as Lord Acton pointed out, absolute power corrupts absolutely. The problem of democracy is the problem of
power—how to keep power decentralized, equally distributed, fairly shared.
Anarchism means maximum democracy: the maximum possible dispersal of
political power, economic power and force—military power. An anarchist society consists of a voluntary association of self-reliant, self-supporting, auton-
omous communities. The anarchist community would consist (as it did in

From *One Life at a Time, Please* (1988)

preagricultural and preindustrial times) of a voluntary association of free and independent families, self-reliant and self-supporting but bound by kinship ties and a tradition of mutual aid.

Anarchy is democracy taken seriously, as in Switzerland, where issues of national importance are decided by direct vote of all citizens. Where each citizen, after his period of military training, takes his weapon home with him, to keep for life. Anarchy is democracy taken all the way, in every major sector of social life. For example, political democracy will not survive in a society which permits a few to accumulate economic power over the many. Or in a society which delegates police power and military power to an elite corps of professionals. Sooner or later the professionals will take over. In my notion of an anarchist community every citizen—man or woman—would be armed, trained, capable when necessary of playing the part of policeman or soldier. A healthy community polices itself; a healthy society would do the same. Looters, thugs, criminals, may appear anywhere, anytime, but in nature such types are mutants, anomalies, a minority; the members of a truly democratic, anarchistic community would not require outside assistance in dealing with them. Some might call this vigilante justice; I call it democratic justice. Better to have all citizens participate in the suppression and punishment of crime—and share in the moral responsibility—than turn the nasty job over to some quasi-criminal type (or hero) in a uniform with a tin badge on his shirt. Yes, we need heroes. We need heroines. But they should serve only as inspiration and examples, not as leaders.

No doubt the people of today's Lebanon, for example, would settle gladly for an authoritarian government capable of suppressing the warring factions. But such an authoritarian government would provoke the return of the irrepressible human desire for freedom, leading in turn to rebellion, revolt and revolution. If Lebanon were not so badly overpopulated, the best solution there—as in South Africa—would be a partition of territory, a devolution into self-governing, independent regions and societies. This is the natural tendency of any population divided by religion, race or deep cultural differences, and it should not be restrained. The tendency runs counter, however, to the love of power, which is why centralized governments always attempt to crush separatist movements.

Government is a social machine whose function is coercion through monopoly of power. Any good Marxist understands this. Like a bulldozer, government serves the caprice of any man or group who succeeds in seizing the controls. The purpose of anarchism is to dismantle such institutions and to prevent their reconstruction. Ten thousand years of human history demonstrate that our freedoms cannot be entrusted to those ambitious few who are drawn to power; we must learn—again—to govern ourselves. Anarchism does not mean "no rule"; it means "no rulers." Difficult but not utopian, anarchy means and requires self-rule, self-discipline, probity, character.

At present, life in America is far better for the majority than in most (not all) other nations. But that fact does not excuse our failings. Judged by its resources, intentions and potential, the great American experiment appears to me as a failure. We have not become the society of independent freeholders that Jefferson envisioned; nor have we evolved into a true democracy— government *by* the people—as Lincoln imagined.

Instead we see the realization of the scheme devised by Madison and Hamilton: a strong centralized state which promotes and protects the accumulation of private wealth on the part of a few, while reducing the majority to the role of dependent employees of state and industry. We are a nation of helots ruled by an oligarchy of techno-military-industrial administrators.

Never before in history have slaves been so well fed, thoroughly medicated, lavishly entertained—but we are slaves nonetheless. Our debased popular culture—television, rock music, home video, processed food, mechanical recreation, wallboard architecture—is the culture of slaves. Furthermore the whole grandiose structure is self-destructive: by enshrining the profit motive (power) as our guiding ideal, we encourage the intensive and accelerating consumption of land, air, water—the natural world—on which the structure depends for its continued existence. A house built on greed will not long endure. Whether it's called capitalism or socialism makes little difference; both of these oligarchic, militaristic, expansionist, acquisitive, industrializing and technocratic systems are driven by the same motives; both are self-destroying. Even without the accident of a nuclear war, I predict that the military-industrial state will disappear from the surface of the earth within a century. That belief is the basis of my inherent optimism, the source of my hope for the coming restoration of a higher civilization: scattered human populations modest in number that live by fishing, hunting, food gathering, small-scale farming and ranching, that gather once a year in the ruins of abandoned cities for great festivals of moral, spiritual, artistic and intellectual renewal, a people for whom the wilderness is not a playground but their natural native home.

New dynasties will arise, new tyrants will appear—no doubt. But we must and we can resist such recurrent aberrations by keeping true to the earth and remaining loyal to our basic animal nature. Humans were free before the word *freedom* became necessary. Slavery is a cultural invention. Liberty is life: *eros* plus *anarchos* equals *bios*.

Long live democracy.

Two cheers for anarchy.

Eco-Defense

IF A STRANGER batters your door down with an axe, threatens your family and yourself with deadly weapons and proceeds to loot your home of whatever he wants, he is committing what is universally recognized—by law and in common morality—as a crime. In such a situation the householder has both the right and the obligation to defend himself, his family and his property by whatever means are necessary. This right and this obligation is universally recognized, justified and praised by all civilized human communities. Self-defense against attack is one of the basic laws not only of human society but of life itself, not only of human life but of all life.

The American wilderness, what little remains, is now undergoing exactly such an assault. With bulldozer, earth mover, chainsaw and dynamite the international timber, mining and beef industries are invading our public lands—property of all Americans—bashing their way into our forests, mountains and rangelands and looting them for everything they can get away with. This for the sake of short-term profits in the corporate sector and multimillion-dollar annual salaries for the three-piece-suited gangsters (MBA—Harvard, Yale, University of Tokyo et alia) who control and manage these bandit enterprises. Cheered on, naturally, by *Time*, *Newsweek* and the

From *One Life at a Time, Please* (1988)

Wall Street Journal, actively encouraged, inevitably, by those jellyfish government agencies that are supposed to *protect* the public lands, and as always aided and abetted in every way possible by the compliant politicians of our Western states, such as Babbitt, DeConcini, Goldwater, McCain, Hatch, Garn, Simms, Hansen, Andrus, Wallop, Domenici and Co. Inc.—who would sell the graves of their mothers if there's a quick buck in the deal, over or under the table, what do they care.

Representative government in the United States has broken down. Our legislators do not represent the public, the voters or even those who voted for them but rather the commercial-industrial interests that finance their political campaigns and control the organs of communication—the TV, the newspapers, the billboards, the radio. Politics is a game for the rich only. Representative government in the USA represents money, not people, and therefore has forfeited our allegiance and moral support. We owe it nothing but the taxation it extorts from us under threats of seizure of property, imprisonment or in some cases already, when resisted, a violent death by gunfire.

Such is the nature and structure of the industrial megamachine (in Lewis Mumford's term) which is now attacking the American wilderness. That wilderness is our ancestral home, the primordial homeland of all living creatures including the human, and the present final dwelling place of such noble beings as the grizzly bear, the mountain lion, the eagle and the condor, the moose and the elk and the pronghorn antelope, the redwood tree, the yellow pine, the bristlecone pine and yes, why not say it?—the streams, waterfalls, rivers, the very bedrock itself of our hills, canyons, deserts, mountains. For many of us, perhaps for most of us, the wilderness is more our home than the little stucco boxes, wallboard apartments, plywood trailer-houses and cinderblock condominiums in which the majority are now confined by the poverty of an overcrowded industrial culture.

And if the wilderness is our true home, and if it is threatened with invasion, pillage and destruction—as it certainly is—then we have the right to defend that home, as we would our private quarters, by whatever means are necessary. (An Englishman's home is his castle; the American's home is his favorite forest, river, fishing stream, her favorite mountain or desert canyon, his favorite swamp or woods or lake.) We have the right to resist and we have the obligation; not to defend that which we love would be dishonorable. The majority of the American people have demonstrated on every possible occasion that they support the ideal of wilderness preservation; even our politicians are forced by popular opinion to *pretend* to support the idea; as they have learned, a vote against wilderness is a vote against their own reelection. We are justified then in defending our homes—our private home and our public home—not only by common law and common morality but also by common belief. We are the majority; they—the powerful—are in the minority.

How best defend our homes? Well, that is a matter of the strategy, tactics and techniques which eco-defense is all about.

What is eco-defense? Eco-defense means fighting back. Eco-defense means sabotage. Eco-defense is risky but sporting; unauthorized but fun; illegal but ethically imperative. Next time you enter a public forest scheduled for chainsaw massacre by some timber corporation and its flunkies in the US Forest Service, carry a hammer and a few pounds of 60-penny nails in your creel, saddlebag, game bag, backpack or picnic basket. Spike those trees; you won't hurt them; they'll be grateful for the protection; and you may save the forest. Loggers hate nails. My Aunt Emma back in West Virginia has been enjoying this pleasant exercise for years. She swears by it. It's good for the trees, it's good for the woods and it's good for the human soul. Spread the word.

Immigration and
Liberal Taboos

IN THE AMERICAN SOUTHWEST, where I happen to live, only sixty miles north of the Mexican border, the subject of illegal aliens is a touchy one—almost untouchable. Even the terminology is dangerous: the old word *wetback* is now considered a racist insult by all good liberals; and the perfectly correct terms *illegal alien* and *illegal immigrant* can set off charges of xenophobia, elitism, fascism and the ever-popular genocide against anyone careless enough to use them. The only acceptable euphemism, it now appears, is something called *undocumented worker.* Thus the pregnant Mexican woman who appears, in the final stages of labor, at the doors of the emergency ward of an El Paso or San Diego hospital, demanding care for herself and the child she's about to deliver, becomes an "undocumented worker." The child becomes an automatic American citizen by virtue of its place of birth, eligible at once for all of the usual public welfare benefits. And with the child comes not only the mother but the child's family. And the mother's family. And the father's family. Can't break up families, can we? They come to stay and they stay to multiply.

What of it? say the documented liberals; ours is a rich and generous nation, we have room for all, let them come. And let them stay, say the conser-

From *One Life at a Time, Please* (1988)

vatives; a large, cheap, frightened, docile, surplus labor force is exactly what the economy needs. Put some fear into the unions: tighten discipline, spur productivity, whip up the competition for jobs. The conservatives love their cheap labor; the liberals love their cheap cause. (Neither group, you will notice, ever invites the immigrants to move into their *homes*. Not into *their* homes!) Both factions are supported by the cornucopia economists of the ever-expanding economy, who actually continue to believe that our basic resource is not land, air, water, but human bodies, more and more of them, the more the better in hive upon hive, world without end—ignoring the clear fact that those nations which most avidly practice this belief, such as Haiti, Puerto Rico, Mexico, to name only three, don't seem to be doing well. They look more like explosive slow-motion disasters, in fact, volcanic anthills, than functioning human societies. But that which our academic economists will not see and will not acknowledge is painfully obvious to *los latinos*: they stream north in ever-growing numbers.

Meanwhile, here at home in the land of endless plenty, we seem still unable to solve our traditional and nagging difficulties. After forty years of the most fantastic economic growth in the history of mankind, the United States remains burdened with mass unemployment, permanent poverty, an overloaded welfare system, violent crime, clogged courts, jam-packed prisons, commercial ("white-collar") crime, rotting cities and a poisoned environment, eroding farmlands and the disappearing family farm, all of the usual forms of racial, ethnic and sexual conflict (which immigration further intensifies), plus the ongoing destruction of what remains of our forests, fields, mountains, lakes, rivers and seashores, accompanied by the extermination of whole species of plants and animals. To name but a few of our little nagging difficulties.

This being so, it occurs to some of us that perhaps ever-continuing industrial and population growth is *not* the true road to human happiness, that simple gross quantitative increase of this kind creates only more pain, dislocation, confusion and misery. In which case it might be wise for us as American citizens to consider calling a halt to the mass influx of even more millions of hungry, ignorant, unskilled and culturally-morally-genetically impoverished people. At least until we have brought our own affairs into order. Especially when these uninvited millions bring with them an alien mode of life which—let us be honest about this—is not appealing to the majority of Americans. Why not? Because we prefer democratic government, for one thing; because we still hope for an open, spacious, uncrowded and beautiful—yes, beautiful!—society, for another. The alternative, in the squalor, cruelty and corruption of Latin America, is plain for all to see.

Yes, I know, if the American Indians had enforced such a policy none of us pale-faced honkies would be here. But the Indians were foolish, and divided, and failed to keep our WASP ancestors out. They've regretted it ever since.

To everything there is a season, to every wave a limit, to every range an optimum capacity. The United States has been fully settled, and more than full, for at least a century. We have nothing to gain, and everything to lose, by allowing the old boat to be swamped. How many of us, truthfully, would *prefer* to be submerged in the Caribbean-Latin version of civilization? (Howls of "Racism! Elitism! Xenophobia!" from the Marx brothers and the documented liberals.) Harsh words: but somebody has to say them. We cannot play "let's pretend" much longer, not in the present world.

Therefore—let us close our national borders to any further mass immigration, legal or illegal, from any source, as does every other nation on earth. The means are available, it's a simple technical-military problem. Even our Pentagon should be able to handle it. We've got an army somewhere on this planet, let's bring our soldiers home and station them where they can be of some actual and immediate benefit to the taxpayers who support them. That done, we can begin to concentrate attention on badly neglected internal affairs. *Our* internal affairs. Everyone would benefit, including the neighbors. Especially the neighbors.

Ah yes. But what *about* those hungry hundreds of millions, those anxious billions, yearning toward the United States from every dark and desperate corner of the world? Shall we simply ignore them? Reject them? Is such a course possible?

"Poverty," said Samuel Johnson, "is the great enemy of human happiness. It certainly destroys liberty, makes some virtues impracticable, and all virtues extremely difficult."

You can say that again, Sam.

Poverty, injustice, overbreeding, overpopulation, suffering, oppression, military rule, squalor, torture, terror, massacre: these ancient evils feed and breed on one another in synergistic symbiosis. To break the cycles of pain at least two new forces are required: social equity—and birth control. Population control. Our Hispanic neighbors are groping toward this discovery. If we truly wish to help them we must stop meddling in their domestic troubles and permit them to carry out the social, political and moral revolution which is both necessary and inevitable.

Or if we must meddle, as we have always done, let us meddle for a change in a constructive way. Stop every *campesino* at our southern border, give him a handgun, a good rifle and a case of ammunition, and send him home. He will know what to do with our gifts and good wishes. The people know who their enemies are.

A Writer's Credo

I T I S M Y B E L I E F that the writer, the freelance author, should be and must be a critic of the society in which he lives. It is easy enough, and always profitable, to rail away at national enemies beyond the sea, at foreign powers beyond our borders and at those within our borders who question the prevailing order. Easy. And it pays. Ask the official guardians of Soviet literary morality. But the moral duty of the free writer is to begin his work at home: to be a critic of his own community, his own country, his own government, his own culture. The more freedom the writer possesses the greater the moral obligation to play the role of critic. If the writer is unwilling to fill this part then the writer should abandon pretense and find another line of work: become a shoe repairman, a brain surgeon, a janitor, a cowboy, a nuclear physicist, a bus driver. Whereof one fears to speak thereof one must be silent. Far better silence than the written word used to shore up the wrong, the false, the ugly, the evil. When necessary the writer must be willing to undertake the dangerous, and often ridiculous, and sometimes martyrlike role of hero or heroine.

That's all that I ask of the author. To be a hero, appoint himself a moral leader, wanted or not. I believe that words count, that writing matters, that

From *One Life at a Time, Please* (1988)

poems, essays and novels—in the long run—make a difference. If they do
not, then in the words of my exemplar Aleksandr Solzhenitsyn, the writer's
work is of no more importance than the barking of village dogs at night. The
hack writer, the temporizer, the toady and the sycophant, the journalistic
courtier (and what is a courtier but a male courtesan?), all those in the word
trade who simply go with the flow, who never oppose the rich and powerful,
are no better in my view than Solzhenitsyn's village dogs. The dogs bark; the
caravan moves on.

Why do I lay this special responsibility of speaking out upon the freelance writer alone—notoriously a timid, reclusive, craven type? For several
reasons. First, because the independent writer, his income derived from his
readers and not from a newspaper chain or TV system or other industrial
employer, has the freedom to speak the truth together with access—great or
small—to some portion of the means of public communication. Freedom of
speech means little to most citizens because for most there is no way by which
they can reach more than a few of their fellow citizens. When TV, radio, newspapers, magazines are controlled by a few giant corporations, with editorial
policies largely determined by the power of advertisers, then free speech—if
not meaningless—becomes nearly powerless. In the United States we have
thousands of newspapers, TV and radio stations, magazines and newsletters,
but when nearly all say about the same thing on any issue almost all the time,
what becomes of the value of the First Amendment to our Constitution? The
guarantee of freedom of speech is one thing; the means and ability to exercise
that right is another. Herein lies the function and the duty of those foolish
enough to call themselves writers: to make full use of whatever means of free
communication are available. The writer with an audience has that privilege,
that power, that freedom—and therefore the moral responsibility to use it.
Not to preach to his audience or to lecture them—who needs another sermon? another lecture?—but to speak *for* them, to let himself be used as the
voice for those who share his view of earthly affairs, his emotions and discov-
eries, aspirations and hopes.

The writer, I'm saying, must be of use—must be useful to his people, to
his community. Otherwise, who needs him? or her? If literary art, like so
much of our poetry, music and painting, is merely decorative, merely play
and no more, then we can get by with wallpaper, polyurethane abstract
sculpture, Bloomingdale's catalog, *Vanity Fair*, rock music (music to hammer out fenders by) and Andy Warhol. If literature, on the other hand, is
to be more than Muzak, then it must be involved, responsible, committed
(O dread clichés!). The independent writer is in a privileged position; there-

fore he works under special obligations. To do otherwise is to dishonor our profession.

Am I saying that the writer should be—I hesitate before the horror of it—*political*? Yes sir, I am. Yes ma'am, I am saying exactly that. And what do I mean by "political"? We'll get into it.

By "political" I mean involvement, responsibility, commitment: the writer's duty to speak the truth—especially unpopular truth. Especially truth that offends the powerful, the rich, the well-established, the traditional, the mythic, the sentimental. To attack, when the time makes it necessary, the sacred cows of his society. And I mean all sacred cows: whether those of the public-lands beef industry or the sacred cows of militarism, nationalism, religion, capitalism, socialism, conservatism, liberalism. To name but a few of our prevailing ideologies.

For instance: Motherhood. I am not alone in recognizing that the time has arrived (in view of the ongoing overpopulation catastrophe) to subject the idealization of Motherhood to a certain degree of intellectual pressure. But also its countercorrelative, Feminist Maternity: since motherhood really is a full-time, difficult, highly skilled and essential human occupation (I speak from personal experience), women who do not wish to be mothers should not have babies. Or consider the interesting question of immigration, race and culture: if we who still form the majority in America really care to preserve our democratic traditions, derived in the most part from our European heritage and ancestry, then we must be willing to reevaluate the possible effect of differential breeding rates and mass immigration from Latin American, African and Asiatic countries upon those traditions. Touchy delicate explosive questions, I agree; even to mention them exposes the writer to abuse of the harshest kind. But the willingness to risk abuse for the sake of truth is one of the writer's obligatory chores.

He who sticks out his neck may get his head chopped off. Quite so. Nevertheless it remains the writer's moral duty to stick out the neck, whether he lives in a totalitarian state or in a relatively open society such as our own. Speak out: or take up a different trade.

Somebody has to do it. That somebody is the writer. If the independent author will not speak truth for us, who will? What will? Do we get truth from politicians? From the bureaucrats of big government? Or local government? Can we expect to hear truth from the U.S. Chamber of Commerce, the Teamsters Union or United Technologies? Do we get much truth from *Time* or *Newsweek* or CBS or ABC or NBC or the daily press? From the TV evangelists of bunkshooter religion? Do we even get much truth from science and scientists? Well, as to that, we get some but not enough: most scientists are specialized technicians, each wedged into his niche of study, few of them capable of looking at life as a whole. Most scientists—in the East as in the West—sold their souls to industry, commerce, government, war, long ago. And what's the difference, anyway, among those massive and interlocking institutions? They form a monolith. A monolith in the shape of a pyramid. Whether laboring to launch our pharaohs safely into eternity or our astronauts into space, the fellaheen of the world have achieved little progress in modern times. By modern times I mean of course the last five thousand years. That trivial blip on the video screen of human history.

Since we cannot expect much truth from our institutions, we must expect it from our writers. Tolstoy said: "The hero of my work, in all of his naked unadorned glory, is truth . . ." Thoreau said: "The one great rule of composition is to speak the truth." And that other troublemaker said, "Ye shall hear the truth and the truth shall make ye free."

Truth, truth, what is truth? The word drops easily from the mouth but what does it mean? I venture to assert that truth for one thing is the enemy of Power, as Power is the enemy of truth. The writer, like the ancient Hebraic prophets, must dare to speak truth to Power and the powerful, face to face if need be. Hemingway said it once and said it good, in respect to Power: "A writer is like a gypsy. He owes no allegiance to any government. If he is a good writer he will never like any government he lives under. His hand should be against it and its hand will always be against him." (From a letter to Ivan Kashkin, his Russian translator, in 1935.)

What is truth? I don't know and I'm sorry I raised the point. I mean to dodge it if I can, for the question leads at once into a bog of epistemological problems too deep for me—or as I might say otherwise, beyond the scope of this essay. I will state only what I believe, that truth, like honor, generosity, tolerance, decency, is something real, that truly exists, whether we can define it or not. Subjectively, truth is that statement of cases which accords with my own view of the world—insofar as I have one—and which corresponds to the actual shape, color, substance of things and events—insofar as we can share and agree upon our perception of such matters. What is reality? For the purposes of daily life, as well as for the composition of stories, poems and essays, I am willing to go by appearances. It appears to me, for example, that torture is wrong, a hideous wrong, and always wrong; that the death penalty—the cold-blooded infliction of death by instruments of the state—is an evil greater than murder; it seems to me, judging by appearances only, that it's wrong to allow children to die of malnutrition and equally wrong—worse than wrong, criminally stupid—to bring children into the world when you are not prepared to feed and care for them; it appears to me that the domination of many by a few, whatever the creed behind it, whatever the means, leads always to injustice and is therefore wrong, always wrong, leading to greater wrongs. I cite these banal, crude and simple examples only to demonstrate that there is a moral area in which the true can easily be distinguished from the false. I cheerfully agree that there are other areas where the distinction is more difficult to ascertain.

But the writer's duty, I am arguing, goes beyond the utterance and support of commonly agreed-upon truths. Any hack can spout truisms, clichés, tautologies and redundancies by the bookful. The task of the honest writer— the writer as potential hero—is to seek out, write down and publish forth those truths which are *not* self-evident, not universally agreed upon, not allowed to determine public feeling and official policy. We can see this clearly enough when we look abroad. Most of us admire Solzhenitsyn for his courage in bringing to light the full extent and horror of the Gulag Archipelago and for defying his own government's effort to suppress his work. There are many other writers in the Soviet empire, less well-known than Solzhenitsyn, who continue to write and publish, through underground channels, the truth about what goes on in their native lands. There are similar writers at work, I hope, though we may not know their names, against the cruel and corrupt governments of South Africa, Kenya, Poland, Cuba, Chile, Zaire, South and North Korea, Ethiopia, Brazil, Indonesia, Vietnam, Guatemala, El Salvador and many other nations around the globe.

Easy enough to point out and condemn the faults and crimes of other nations. There's something relaxing in such exercises. But what about the writer's job in our own country, the US of A? To even mention the word *hero* in connection with the writer's lot in America invites laughter. The freelance writer in this country enjoys so much freedom in his work, by contrast say with the dark plight of the writer in Central and Eastern Europe, that the American writer's chief concern is—and should be—to avoid making a fool of himself. The typical American writer has knowledge of very little but opinions on everything. Leaping to conclusions is his favorite calisthenic, snap judgments an intellectual reflex. The literary interview is a popular device through which the supercilious author provides facetious answers to superficial questions from skeptical reporters for the momentary entertainment of the bored and indifferent. In general the serious writer should avoid interviews and the serious reader should avoid reading them.

Nevertheless, I reassert with only slight modification my beginning announcement: the *American* writer, precisely because of his freedom, his unique position, his audience, his many and ample rewards, has the moral obligation to act as a critic of his own society, his own nation, his own civilization. Or abandon his pretensions.

Have I said or even hinted that social criticism is the writer's only duty? Or his primary duty? I have not. But it is, I repeat, one of his duties. And what should the critic criticize? What do we privileged Americans have to complain about?

But first: We have many critics of the critics, especially loud and dominant in this regressive, guilty and servile decade. George Will, for example; William Buckley, for another; Tom Wolfe, for a third—and rising above mere columnar journalism, such distinguished literary gentlemen as Saul Bellow, John Updike and the late John Gardner. To name but some. There are dozens of them. Hundreds. Their argument, compacted, amounts to this: communism has proved so gross an evil, the Soviet Union so dangerous an enemy, that by contrast America and its Allies appear as continents of light, exploding with human happiness. Therefore it is the writer's simple duty to condemn the former, praise the latter. Furthermore we exist in a state of ideological war with the powers of totalitarianism—the "present danger"—which makes it not merely heretical but treasonous to question our own government's policies, to doubt the glory of planetary capitalism, to object to the religion of endless economic growth or to wonder about the ultimate purpose, value and consequences of our techno-military-industrial empire. Those who persist in raising doubts and questions are attacked by defenders of order as the "adversary culture."

Very well: let us be adversaries. If the writer should be, among other things, a critic of his society, what does the American writer, in this best of possible American worlds, have to complain about? Why the constant whining and carping by these literary pests who live in the richest, freest, happiest, *big* nation on earth? Who enjoy in addition the curious distinction of being paid, honored, even sometimes read, by inhabitants of the very nation-state which they seek, in their peculiar way, to sabotage, undermine, halt in its tracks, turn around?

Here I must speak for myself, acknowledging at the same time that none of the opinions I presently hold on matters of state are in the least bit novel, original or uncontroversial. Since they are, for the most part, banalities—but true banalities—I shall simply list them, not defend them.

1. The Soviet Union and the United States, while by no means morally equivalent, are basically similar in structure and purpose. Both societies are dedicated to nationalism, militarism, industrialism, technology, science, organized sport and above all, to the religion of growth—of endless expansion in numbers, wealth, power, time and space. In the SU, government controls industry; in the US, industry controls government; but each of the two great superstates is ruled in fact by an entrenched oligarchy—in the SU by the Communist Party; in the US by the power of concentrated wealth. (According to the Federal Reserve Board report of 1984, some 2 percent of US families control 40 percent of all assets.) We call our system a "representative democracy" but in fact our representatives, with honorable exceptions here and there, represent not the voters but those who finance their election campaigns. In the Soviet Union the egalitarian ideal of theoretical communism was betrayed from the beginning; in the United States the Jeffersonian vision of a decentralized society of independent agrarian freeholders was dead by the end of the nineteenth century while democracy, defined in Lincoln's words as "government *by* the people," has never even been tried.

2. Our century, the twentieth, has been a century of horrors. The century not only of Stalin's Gulag but of Hitler's concentration camps, where six million Jews, three million Russians, two million Poles and half a million Gypsies were methodically put to death. But America has done its bit; last nation on earth to abolish chattel slavery (and it required a civil war to accomplish that) we were the first to drop the nuclear bomb on our fellow humans, the Japanese—*after* their government had begun suing for peace. Then followed the thirty-year ordeal of Indochina (1945–1975), a great industrial undertaking whereby more millions of corpses were produced, an effort entirely financed and largely carried out by the American government. Our slaughters do not yet equal in magnitude those of Stalin and Hitler—but we tried, we are trying and we're not finished yet. Meanwhile the threat of nuclear annihilation, succeeded by the nuclear winter, hangs over the entire planet, with the devices of destruction continually being developed, refined and stockpiled on both sides. On several sides.

3. Old stuff. Consider a new idea, one that still seems absurd, even ridiculous, to most of the human population: I mean something called animal rights. The rights, that is, of the other animals (and plants) that share this still lovely, gracious and bountiful world with us. I refer to the deliberate torture of monkeys, dogs, rats, rabbits and other animals in the laboratories of what is called science, often for no purpose but the satisfaction of curiosity, the gen-

eration of unreadable monographs and the development of commercial products such as cosmetics, patent medicines and perfumes. I refer to the gruesome half-lives led by hundreds of millions of factory poultry, pigs, dairy cows and feedlot cattle in our mass-production industrialized agriculture.

Perhaps my hero Solzhenitsyn would scorn my saying so but I am tempted to believe that the systematic cruelty inflicted upon animals trapped in our food and research apparatus is comparable—for who can measure the aggregates of pain, the sum of suffering?—to the agony that contemporary despotisms have exacted from human beings caught in their archipelagos of tyranny. Not merely comparable but analogous. Not merely analogous but causally connected. Contempt for animal life leads to contempt for human life.

4. I could easily go on all night, all week, with this bill of indictment. But shall note one crime more and call a halt. I mean the destruction, through industrialism, scientific technology and multiplying human numbers, of the habitat of life. We are befouling and destroying our own home, we are committing a slow but accelerating race suicide and life murder—planetary biocide. Now *there* is a mighty theme for a mighty book but a challenge to which no modern novelist or poet has yet responded: Where is our Melville, our Milton, our Thomas Mann when we need him most?

Individuals do not live in isolation, nor do lovers, nor do families: any honest fiction or poetry which claims to deal with the lives of human beings must take into account the social context of those lives, directly or by implication. It's not a matter of restricting the writer to one mode of art—as in, say, the naturalism of Zola or the ponderous social realism of Dreiser—but rather of getting straight the connections between the fate of the author's fictional characters and the nature of the society which largely determines that fate. There is more truth in the sometimes airy fantasies of Kurt Vonnegut than in the tedious naturalism of John Updike's Rabbit Angstrom novels. Vonnegut writes as a critic of society; Updike in passive acceptance. As a result, assuming both do well what they set out to do, Vonnegut's work is more provocative, suggestive, meaningful—more interesting.

What I have said so far is much too crude, rough, plain, simple, even simple-minded to satisfy those who care about the arts of fiction, poetry and essay. I recognize as well the banality of my basic argument, its old-fashioned overpolitical ring. Here I make the qualifications and reservations.

The author's primary task and the only thing that justifies his miserable existence is the writing of readable books worth reading: to have something interesting to say and to say it well. The writer's first job is to write, not aspire to a position of moral leadership. Quite so. Nevertheless—in and through the work, somehow, the writer must play his morally obligatory role as social critic, as spiritual guidon, as intellectual leader.

I present this plain and simple argument not to defend but to define an old and honorable tradition in American letters, one still alive despite temporary muffling by this gross, slimy, gluttonous slum of a decade, this Age of Reaganism and Servility. The majority of American writers today have chosen passive nonresistance to things as they are, producing sloughs of poetry about their personal angst and anomie, cascades of short stories and rivers of novels obsessed with the nuances of domestic relationships—suburban hanky-panky—chic boutique shopping-mall literary soap opera. When they do speak out on matters of controversy they attack not the evils of our time but fellow writers who may still insist on complaining. Updike, for example, in a recent review of Edmund Wilson's work, attacks Wilson for condemning the uses to which our federal government puts the money it extracts from American citizens. Wilson, in his grave for many years now, cannot respond to Updike's attack. But Wilson's words will live, I predict, long after Updike's fussy, prissy, precious novels have sunk into the oblivion they so richly deserve.

Edmund Wilson was the best of modern American literary critics. But good literary critics are plentiful, common as lichens on an academic wall; Wilson became a great American *writer* because he was more than a critic of books, he was a critic of the state, of society, of organized religion, of modern civilization. It is the grandeur of Wilson's vision that makes him a scandal to our literary courtiers queuing in the Rose Garden for their turn to kiss the First Lady's foot.

Here is Wilson in *Patriotic Gore* (1962), one of his best books. Try to imagine any prominent American author of the 1980s writing such words:

> We Americans, whose public officials keep telling us we live in the "Free World," . . . are expected to pay staggering taxes of which . . . 70 percent goes not only for nuclear weapons capable of depopulating whole countries but also for bacteriological and biological ones which make it possible for us to poison the enemy with every abominable disease from pneumonia and encephalitis to anthrax, cholera, diphtheria and typhoid. . . . If we refuse to contribute to these researches we can be fined and clapped into jail. . . . We are, furthermore, like the Russians, being spied upon by an extensive secret police, whose salaries we are required to pay, as we pay also the sal-

aries of another corps of secret agents infiltrating foreign countries. And while all this expenditure is going on for the purpose of sustaining the United States as a more and more unpopular world power, as few funds as possible are supplied to educate and civilize the Americans themselves, who at worst live a life of gang warfare . . . in the buried slum streets of cities outside of which they can imagine no other world . . . while others find little spur to ambition when they emerge from four years in college to face two years in the armed services in preparation for further large-scale wars for which few feel the slightest enthusiasm.

Before Vietnam: imagine what Edmund Wilson would say were he alive today.

Wilson was never totally alone in his role as social critic. I have named Kurt Vonnegut, humanist and humorist in the Mark Twain tradition, whose work as a whole is alive with moral purpose. Remember the conclusion to his novel *Deadeye Dick*: "You want to know something? We are still living in the Dark Ages. The Dark Ages—they haven't ended yet."

There are others in the guard of honor, contemporary American authors whose books serve well as living in-print examples of what I am trying to say: Robert Coover, *The Public Burning*—a three-ring circus of a novel inspired by the trial and execution of the Rosenbergs; William Gaddis, *JR*—a maddening, hilarious, damning description of blind greed disguised as free enterprise; Thomas Pynchon, *Gravity's Rainbow*—a vast lament for humanity trapped in the engine room of our runaway technology; DeLillo, *Ratner's Star*—a satire on astrophysics, particle physics and contemporary mathe-metaphysics. And Joseph Heller's *Something Happened*, the toughest analysis yet of the corporate mentality and the effect of such a mindset upon human life.

These are massive, complex, ambitious novels, elaborate efforts at taking a fix on the modern techno-industrial-military world. Difficult books, none were or ever will be very popular—but they prove that a concern with contemporary society combined with conscientious scrutiny through fiction results in works of high literary art, maximal not minimal. (The skies deluge us with cautious minimalists.) Their authors, if not heroes in the sense that Solzhenitsyn is a hero, were certainly heroic in the expenditure of effort, study and thought that went into the making of such books. They serve my point: the writer worthy of his calling must be more than an entertainer: he must be a seer, a prophet, the defender of life, freedom, openness and always—*always!*—a critic of society.

"Resist much, obey little," said Walt Whitman. What contemporary American poet writes words like those? Whitman also wrote, in the preface to the 1855 edition of *Leaves of Grass*:

This is what you shall do. Love the earth and the sun and the animals. Despise riches. Give alms to everyone that asks. Stand up for the stupid and crazy. Devote your income and labor to others, hate tyrants, have patience and indulgence toward the people, take off your hat to nothing known or unknown, or to any man or any number of men, go freely with powerful uneducated persons and the young and with the mothers of families. . . . Re-examine all you have been told at school or church or in any book and dismiss whatever insults your own soul. . . .

Radical talk in 1855; subversive and "naive" today.

Think of Mark Twain and *Huckleberry Finn*. Somewhere near the end of that greatest (so far) of American novels young Huck confronts a moral crisis: shall he or shall he not help return the runaway slave, Jim, to Jim's rightful owner? Huck knows, based on everything he has been taught by church and state, that he is committing an awful sin in helping Jim escape. Burdened by his acculturated conscience, he writes a message to Jim's owner, Miss Watson, giving away Jim's location. But hesitates in sending the message. Trying to decide what to do, Huck stares at the piece of paper that will betray his comrade Jim but save his own official soul:

It was a close place [thinks Huck]. I took it up and held it in my hand. I was a-trembling, because I'd got to decide forever betwixt two things, and I knowed it. I studied a minute, sort of holding my breath, and then says to myself:

"Alright then, I'll *go* to hell"—and tore it up. It was awful thoughts and awful words but they was said. And I let them stay said and never thought no more about reforming. I shoved the whole thing out of my head; and said I would take up wickedness again, which was in my line, being brung up to it, and the other warn't. And for a starter I would go to work and steal Jim out of slavery again; and if I could think up anything worse I would do that too; because as long as I was in, and in for good, I might as well go the whole hog. . . .

Exactly. Like Huckleberry Finn, the American writer must make the choice, sooner or later, between serving the powerful few or the disorganized many, the institutions of domination or the spontaneous, instinctive, natural drive for human liberation. The choice is not so easy as my loaded phrases make it seem: to serve the powerful leads to financial rewards, public approval and official honors, your picture on the cover of *Time* and *Newsweek* (or *Pravda* and *Izvestia*) and the eventual invitation to a White House (or Kremlin) dinner; to oppose the powerful creates difficulties, subjects you to abuse and scorn, leads often—as in the interesting case of Noam Chomsky, for example—to what we call the silent treatment in the literary press: your books are not reviewed; your views and reviews no longer appear in the *New York Times* or the *New York Review of Books*.

What is the author's proper role? How should the writer view his art? Speaking for myself now, perhaps only for myself, this is what I believe. This is what I tell the young. Call it one writer's credo:

Ignore the literary critics. Ignore the commercial hustlers. Disregard those best-selling paperbacks with embossed covers in the supermarkets and the supermarket bookstores. Waste no time applying for gifts and grants— when we want money from the rich we'll take it by force.

A literary career should be not a career but a passion. A life. Fueled in equal parts by anger and love. How feel one without the other? Each implies the other. A writer without passion is like a body without a soul. Or what would be even more grotesque, like a soul without a body.

There is a middle way between subserving the mass market and pandering to our Jamesian *castrati literati*. You do not have to write endless disquisitions about computer science professors seeking God while pursuing faculty wives. You do not have to write about male mutilation, lesbians in bearskins, Toyota dealers or self-hating intellectuals longing for hierarchy to work and live happily as a writer in America, God bless her such as she is.

You do not need to be analyzed, psychoanalyzed, Rolfed, e-s-t-ed, altered, gelded, neutered, spayed, fixed, acupunctured, Zenned, Yogied, New Aged, astrocharted, computerized, megatrended, androgynized, evangelized, converted or even, last and least, to be reborn. One life at a time, please.

What *is* both necessary and sufficient—for honest literary work—is to have faith in the evidence of your senses and in your common sense. To be true to your innate sense of justice. To be loyal to your family, your clan, your friends and—if you're lucky enough to have one—your community. (Let the nation-state go hang itself.) Among the Americans, read Walt Whitman, Mark Twain, Henry Thoreau, Theodore Dreiser, Jack London, B. Traven, Thomas Wolfe, John Steinbeck, Nelson Algren and Dr. William Carlos Williams. For example. Emulate them until you find others emulating you. And then go on.

Why write? How justify this mad itch for scribbling? Speaking for myself, I write to entertain my friends and to exasperate our enemies. I write to record the truth of our time as best as I can see it. To investigate the comedy and tragedy of human relationships. To oppose, resist and sabotage the contemporary drift toward a global technocratic police state, whatever its ideological coloration. I write to oppose injustice, to defy power and to speak for the voiceless.

I write to make a difference. "It is always a writer's duty," said Samuel Johnson, "to make the world better." I write to give pleasure and promote aesthetic bliss. To honor life and to praise the divine beauty of the natural world. I write for the joy and exultation of writing itself. To tell my story.

~~Epilogue~~

Postlude

Roaring   top down,
~~thrashing~~ westward at evening, red sun of Texas burning
in their eyes. Smoke of El Paso--a city on fire ~~with hate~~
--smeared across a yellow sky. Barbed wire. ~~fences~~ Windrows
of dead tumbleweed piled on the fence. Scrub cattle with
splintered horns, fly-covered hides, broken hooves range
through the rocky desert, ~~browsing for~~ munching on cactus, on the
dried seedpods
~~shoots~~ of thorny mesquite. Newspapers yellow with lies,
bleached by the sun, flap like startled fowl with ragged wings
across the asphalt road. Welcome to the West.

Welcome to the West! he shouts in the wind, grinning his
vulpine grin, teeth hanging out, and hugs her tighter to his
side, his gaunt ribs, his beating swelling joyous heart.
By Gawd we're gonna get there, Ellie, we're a-gonna make it
yet, I tell you, there's no way they ~~sons~~ can stop us now.

The child gazes ahead in wonder, her dark eyes shining
in ~~mingled~~ fear and excitement, ~~her~~ long black hair ~~streaming~~
~~on the~~ whipped wildly by the stream of air pouring in mad
invisible vortices over the windshield, around their shoulders,
                                through
across and ~~between~~ the baggage--suitcases, duffelbags,

                    bedrolls,
stuffed bears, books, boxes, sacks full of ~~stuffed~~ food--
jammed in a fury of haste within the well and upon the back
seat of the open, boat-shaped, rollicking automobile.

Self-propelled. The open boat on the desert sea. A fat
faded near-antique almost-classic but rumpled-looking
motorcar, of ~~considerable value~~ dubious value, doubtful make,
uncertain age but clearly a piece of iron. Detroit iron.
                              mud
~~The fenders~~ A fringe of ~~mud~~ hangs from the fenders.
                          portside
Hubcaps missing. One savage ~~arm~~ sideswipe scar from headlight
to tailfin reveals the cancer of rust beneath the veneer
~~of bleached out color~~ of baked-on bleached-out once ~~mustard hued~~
                        A repaint job.
~~anxious~~   purple-hued enamel. The niggerized convertible.
The rednecked dreamboat. Choice of any country boy with
            limber
big feet, a ~~long~~ cock, a lank frame too long in the torso.

~~No grimness submit behit time and again, at the blue~~

~~highway tapering behind, into the darkening east~~
                          the girl
He lifts his eyes from ~~his daughter~~ to the road to the
rearview mirror and its image: blueblack highway tapering
off into the eastern dark. An empty highway, at the moment:
no red glare or blinking blue of police, no menacing array
of tractor-trailer rig, nothing nobody following whatsoever.
At the moment. But the wicked flee ~~anyhow~~ pursued or not.

Once we get there, he goes on, speaking hoarsely but
loudly above the rush of wind, we'll hide this junkyard
wreck under the willows down by the crick for a year or so,
give it some rest, let them pistons get some rest, we'll
      the
ride horses into town, you and me, yessir and we'll eat good
too I tell you.

Where do you mean, Daddy? What horses?

Most anywhere, honey, anywhere. Anywhere west of the Rio
Grandee. There's ~~Tuskegoruswale~~ Cherry Creek under Aztec Mountain.
There's Bisbee, good old hippie ~~town~~ town, we're welcome there.
Maybe Mexican Hat up in Utah. Over there under the cottonwoods
along that old Green River south of Ruby Ranch. Honey, I
know a hundred places. ~~Big Time~~ Lone Pine in the Owens
Valley. Cr why not Big Pine or by Gawd Independence? There's
Arcata on the coast. And just a little ways beyond lays that big
island down below. Brisbane's a good city. You might like
Alice Springs. Or what the hell, go all the way to 80-Mile
                 the Kimberly Mountains,
Beach, the Black Swan River, watch the sun go down over the
                       bleeding
bloody Indian Ocean toward Africa where it all began. Look
in my eyes, Ellie, tell me--

He checks the road once more, lets up on the gas pedal,
leans toward her, smiling, and stares straight into her big
solemn ~~dark~~ hazel-brown eyes with his small red squinty ~~open~~
iron-flecked happy eyes and says,

What do you see, Ellie?

She ~~anxious~~ looks hard, concentrating, thinking.

Hey? What do you see?

Dad? Well...you're crazy as a bedbug.

Yeah yeah, sure, but what else, what else? He glances at
the highway again, no traffic in sight, nothing ahead but the firey
glow
~~glow~~ of the city, the glare of the descending sun, the smoke,
~~dust~~ and returns his gaze to his daughter. What do you see,
~~honey? Look me in the eyes ball to ball and tell me what~~

sweetheart? Look me in the eyeballs ball to ball and tell
me what you see.

I see a crazy cuckoo Daddy.

What else?

Her nose is sunburnt, starting to peel, her lips chapped,
but she cracks a tiny smile. A growing smile, matching his.
I see...lights. Little lights jumping around.

Dancing. He checks the road again, the car slowing,
wheels grating on the tincans and gravel of the shoulder,
and looks again into the girl's eyes. What color?

She laughs. Red.

Right. And what does red mean?

She laughs again. Same as always: full speed ahead.

Right, he yells, you got it. He pulls her small body
~~tightly against~~ firmly to his side, ~~stepsdown hard on the~~
~~gas pedal, and then not though~~ steers back onto the asphalt,
~~grumbling like~~ presses the pedal to the floor.
The motor grumbles like a lion, ~~eighthearted engine~~
hesitating,
⌃ old, tired, ~~but eight-hearted, hesitates thenroars, driving~~
~~onward~~ then catches, fires and roars, eight-hearted
in its block of iron, driving onward.

A Few Words in Memory of
Edward Abbey

The old oak wears new leaves.
It stands for many lives.
Within its veil of green
A singer sings unseen.
Again the living come
To light, and are at home.
And Edward Abbey's gone.
I pass a cairn of stone
Two arm-lengths long and wide
Piled on the steep hillside
By plowmen years ago.
Now oaks and hickories grow
Where the steel coulter passed.
Where human striving ceased
The Sabbath of the trees
Returns and stands and is.
The leaves shake in the wind.
I think of that dead friend
Here where he never came
Except by thought and name;
I praise the joyous rage
That justified his page.
He would have liked this place
Where spring returns with solace
Of bloom in a dark time,
Larkspur and columbine.
The flute song of the thrush
Sounds of the underbrush.

—Wendell Berry

A Selected Bibliography of Works by Edward Abbey

Abbey's Road. New York: E.P. Dutton, 1979.

Appalachian Wilderness: The Great Smoky Mountains. Illustrated by Eliot Porter. New York: E.P. Dutton, 1970.

Beyond the Wall: Essays from the Outside. New York: Henry Holt, 1984.

Black Sun. New York: Simon & Schuster, 1971. Reprint. New York: Avon Books, 1982.

The Brave Cowboy. New York: Dodd, Mead, 1956. Reprint. New York: Avon Books, 1982.

Confessions of a Barbarian: Selections from the Journals of Edward Abbey, 1951–1989, edited by David Petersen. Boston and New York: Little, Brown, 1994.

Desert Solitaire: A Season in the Wilderness. New York: McGraw-Hill, 1968. Reprint. New York: Touchstone Books, 1969.

Down the River. New York: E.P. Dutton, 1982.

The Fool's Progress: An Honest Novel. New York: Henry Holt, 1988. Reprint. New York: Avon Books, 1990.

Good News: A Novel. New York: E.P. Dutton, 1980.

Hayduke Lives! New York: Little, Brown, 1990.

The Hidden Canyon: A River Journey. Illustrated by John Blaustein. New York: Penguin Books, 1977.

The Journey Home: Some Words in Defense of the American West. Illustrated by Jim Stiles. New York: E.P. Dutton, 1977.

The Monkey Wrench Gang. Philadelphia: J.B. Lippincott, 1975. Reprint. New York: Avon Books, 1976.

One Life at a Time, Please. New York: Henry Holt, 1988.

Slickrock: The Canyon Country of Southeast Utah. Illustrated by Philip Hyde. San Francisco: Sierra Club, 1971.

Slumgullion Stew: An Edward Abbey Reader. Illustrated by the author. New York: E.P. Dutton, 1984. Reprinted as *The Best of Edward Abbey.* San Francisco: Sierra Club, 1986.

Acknowledgments

GRATEFUL ACKNOWLEDGMENT is made to the following for permission to use selections by Edward Abbey: The Estate of Edward Abbey, by Don Congdon Associates, Inc.: "Drunk in the Afternoon"; *Black Sun*, copyright © 1971 by Edward Abbey; *The Brave Cowboy*, copyright © 1956 by Edward Abbey; *Desert Solitaire*, copyright © 1968 by Edward Abbey. HarperCollins Publishers: *The Monkey Wrench Gang*, copyright © 1975 by Edward Abbey. Henry Holt and Company: *Beyond the Wall*, copyright © 1971, 1976, 1977, 1979, 1984 by Edward Abbey; *The Fool's Progress*, copyright © 1988 by Edward Abbey; *One Life at a Time, Please*, copyright © 1978, 1983, 1984, 1985, 1986, 1988 by Edward Abbey. Penguin Books USA: *Abbey's Road*, copyright © 1972, 1975, 1976, 1977, 1978, 1979 by Edward Abbey, used by permission of Dutton Signet, a division of Penguin Books USA Inc.; *Appalachian Wilderness*, copyright © 1970 by E.P. Dutton, Inc., used by permission of Dutton Signet, a division of Penguin Books USA Inc.; *Down the River*, copyright © 1982 by Edward Abbey, used by permission of Dutton Signet, a division of Penguin Books USA Inc.; *Good News*, copyright © 1980 by Edward Abbey, used by permission of Dutton Signet, a division of Penguin Books USA Inc.; *The Hidden Canyon*, copyright © 1977 by The Viking Press, Inc., used by permission of Viking Penguin, a division of Penguin Books USA, Inc.; *The Journey Home*, copy-